D1275740

MAN & BEAST
REVISITED

Edited by Michael H. Robinson and Lionel Tiger

Smithsonian Institution Press • Washington and London

Library of Congress Cataloging-in-Publication Data
Man and beast revisited / Michael H. Robinson and Lionel Tiger, editors.
p. cm.
Papers and proceedings of a Smithsonian symposium.
Includes bibliographical references.
ISBN 0-87474-746-5.—ISBN 0-87474-775-9 (pbk.)
1. Human-animal relationships—Congresses. 2. Animals—Social aspects—Congresses.
I. Robinson, Michael H. II. Tiger, Lionel, 1937–0000. III. Smithsonian Institution.
QL85.M28 1990
591.51–dc20 90-9953

British Library Cataloguing in Publication Data is available.

Manufactured in the United States of America

95 94 93 92 91 5 4 3 2

♾ The paper used in this publication meets the minimum requirements of the American National Standard for Permanence of Paper for Printed Library Materials Z39.48-1984.

Editor: Catherine F. McKenzie
Production Editor: Jennifer Lorenzo

Contents

A Personal Note
Thomas A. Sebeok ix
Acknowledgments
Michael H. Robinson xv
Introduction
Lionel Tiger and Michael H. Robinson xvii

1. The Cosmic Setting for Man and Beast
Evolution from the Big Bang to the Brontosaurus
Irwin I. Shapiro 3

2. The Evolution of Man and Beast
Darwin Triumphant: Darwinism as a Universal Truth
Richard Dawkins 23

Untying the Knot: Evolution of Early Human Behavior
Richard Potts 41
Biochemical Insights into Our Ancestry
Sherwood L. Washburn 61

3. **Social Behavior**
Sociobiology and the Test of Time
Edward O. Wilson 77
Aggression: Then and Now
Robin Fox 81
Monogamy, Adultery, and Divorce in Cross-Species Perspective
Helen Fisher 95
Mammalian Social Organizations and the Case of *Alouatta*
John F. Eisenberg 127
Tactics of Primate Immaturity
Phyllis Dolhinow 139
Sexual Selection and Social Behavior
Mary Jane West-Eberhard 159

4. **Communication, Consciousness, and Intelligence**
Deceit and Self-Deception: The Relationship between Communication and Consciousness
Robert Trivers 175
Structures of Animal Communication
Martin H. Moynihan 193
Consciousness and the Ecology of Meaning: New Findings and Old Philosophies
John Hurrell Crook 203
The Brain as a Supercomputer
Richard M. Restak 225

5. **The Man and Beast Interface: Networking with Animals**
Man and Beast Interface: An Overview of Our Interrelationships
Leo K. Bustad 233

Animal Companions: More Companion Than Animal
Aaron Honori Katcher and Alan M. Beck 265
The Human-Animal Interface: Chasm or Continuum?
Andrew N. Rowan 279
One Man and the Beasts: An Autobiographical Approach
Michael H. Robinson 291

6. Have Man and the Beasts a Future?
Man's Future Needs the Beasts
Norman Myers 319
Human Nature and the Psycho-Industrial Complex
Lionel Tiger 331
Climate Change: Causes and Effects
Stephen H. Schneider 341

Notes on the Contributors 367
Author Index 375
Subject Index 383

A Personal Note

Thomas A. Sebeok

In May of 1969, I was invited to attend as an auditor and sporadic discussant the Third Annual Smithsonian International Symposium, the contributions to which appeared 2 years later embodied in a sizable book under the suggestive title, *Man and Beast: Comparative Social Behavior.* Our host was S. Dillon Ripley, then the Smithsonian's secretary and, of course, an ornithologist of great distinction. He wrote a sensitive and richly suggestive preface for the volume, justly characterizing it as "a feast of reason." He called for "a new morality" of which our biosphere is to be a focus, with "Nature is my friend" as our rallying cry.

Dr. Ripley later asked me back to the Smithsonian as regents fellow for 1983–84, an appointment which he thereafter courteously extended, with the title of research associate, until 1987. On my arrival at the Smithsonian in the fall of 1983, I paid the secretary a prompt courtesy call and asked him what he wanted me to do during my residency. He seemed genuinely perplexed and, with eyebrows and intonation rising, asked, "Do?"

I explained that I meant "do" beyond my normal routine, which entailed research and writing on a project of my choice. In other words, because I was so honored and delighted at the prospect of working for a year or so without interruption in the marvelously stimulating environment of the Smithsonian, I wondered, Was there any service I could perform during my stay there that might be directly useful to the Institution? We then reminisced about the *Man and Beast* symposium and together came up with the idea of a possible reprise, albeit with appropriate variations.

For me, the period of my residency was to be one of blissful peace and productivity. For the Smithsonian it turned out to be a year of turmoil and the onset of many changes. To begin with, my friend Charles Blitzer, with whom I looked forward to many discussions about the topic I was researching, had left his position as the Smithsonian's assistant secretary for history and art shortly before my arrival to assume the directorship of the National Humanities Center. I myself had been a fellow there in 1980–81, under the directorship of William Bennett, who, in turn, had just moved to Washington to become the chairman of the National Endowment for the Humanities (and later secretary of education). Some months afterward, I learned of the pending retirement of Dr. Ripley himself.

Aspects of my post involved not merely being luxuriously ensconced for the year in the rich environment of the National Museum of Natural History, then on the verge of its diamond jubilee, that fabulous building where I was given a handsome study. (This was situated amidst the Echinodermata and, as I recall, a Phanerozoic sequence of rocks. It overlooked the Castle across the Mall, with the Washington Monument towering chastely to my right, the Capitol dome gold-gleaming to my left.) My appointment entailed, in addition, formal links with two other related research establishments: the Woodrow Wilson Center for International Studies (then headed by James Billington, now the Librarian of Congress, himself succeeded this year by Charles Blitzer), lodged within the Castle itself, and the National Zoological Park. As it happened, the NZP, too, was then in the midst of an intensive search for a successor to its recently retired director, T. H. Reed. Reed was, the following year, replaced by Michael H. Robinson, coeditor of the present volume. Robinson had come from the Smithsonian Tropical Research Institute in Panama. In December 1983, I had paid a visit there in the course of which I met several scholars who eventually joined the participants in the meeting reported in this volume.

Soon after my initial conversation with Dr. Ripley, I went to call on another old friend, Wilton S. Dillon, longtime director of the Office of Smithsonian Symposia and Seminars, who was also coeditor of the original *Man and Beast* and author of its prolog. In that prolog, Dillon summarized the four basic, intertwined questions that informed the 1969 symposium and were answered only provisionally by the speakers:

What are the physiological and behavioral mechanisms underlying social behavior?

Is man unique?

Are creatures similar?

Can man endure?

Stimulated by my talk with Dr. Ripley, as well as Dillon's original interrogatory and the work I was engaged in at the Smithsonian, I recommended to Dillon that the problem area framed by his questions be reconsidered in a second symposium, but with a cast of a different complexion, a mix of contributors who had best been able to profit from data accumulated in the interim.

My own researches at the Smithsonian involved a congeries of problems related to animal behavior, and fell into two principal areas. I was actually at work writing a long exploratory study on the prefigurements of art. This was based on a simple hypothesis: historians and anthropologists have generally assumed that all of the arts originated in our species or, at any rate, within our hominid genus. The difficulty with this conventional view is to account for why the arts, nonverbal no less than verbal, should have uniquely emerged in the evolution of mankind, that is, to explain not merely the historical origins of each but also their current utility: what are the multiple functions of art in our lives?

Since I could find no rational consensus on these and related issues, I tentatively posed an alternative question: what if art (more particularly, the nonverbal arts) began actually to evolve among ancestral animal species? Accordingly, I undertook to sift the existing biological literature for empirical observations about such phenomena in four domains: dance, music, pictorial arts, and architecture. The apparently positive results of this investigation were later published in one of my books and are also slated to appear soon, separately, in a much elaborated form.

The animal origins of the nonverbal arts are, I continue to argue, to be traced to the biological need of all animals for constructing taxonomies of and within the species-specific models of their phenomenological world—in short, a universal propensity of all life forms to generate signification by stipulating redundancies in the course of classifying items of their environment. These results are in good conformity with, on the one hand, the theoretical biologist Jakob von Uexküll's very sophisticated neo-Kantian *Umweltlehre;* and, on the other, a key esthetic concept famously propounded by the English poet Gerard Manley Hopkins, which he called *parallelism.*

While in Washington, I also continued to collect further materials relating to a longtime preoccupation of mine with animal communication, paying special attention to interspecific information transmission, and the rich panoply of modes of dyadic coupling between animals and members of our own species in particular. This research resulted in a paper entitled "What Is an Animal," excerpts from which I presented at the symposium (but published, in its full form, elsewhere).

In studying the varieties of commerce between man and animals, it is easy to become disoriented. Although these topics were frequently alluded to in our symposium, it should be noted that many animal behaviorists continue to habitually confound three radically different concepts: communication (*all* animals, of course, communicate); language (a genus-specific universal adaptation of all species in *Homo*); and speech (a species-specific "exaptation," in the terminology of Stephen Jay Gould and Elisabeth Vrba, solely in *Homo sapiens*). Only a handful of investigators, cheerfully abetted by the media, still continue to insist that some of their apes had indeed learned the rudiments of language, but such claims are now regarded with deep scepticism among their fellow scholars, at least pending publication of far more extensive and replicable data and much more rigorous testing of learning than heretofore.

Another problem area which was much discussed chimed in with the once again fashionable fields of animal awareness, animal intelligence, and animal thinking—these topics not to be confused (as they all too frequently are) with one another, let alone with the question of animal "language"—revived and refocused in this country chiefly by Donald Griffin and in England by Lawrence Weiskrantz. Curiously, this problem area has not progressed much beyond anecdotal evidence since publication of the work of G. J. Romanes, in 1892, and thus Otto Koehler's stringent experiments of many decades ago still stand as the benchmark to which modern workers must continue to aspire.

How have the conference participants responded to Wilton Dillon's four questions of twenty years ago? Spectacular—if neither conclusive nor debate-free—progress has been reported on some aspects of the mechanisms that underlie facets of social behavior. Is man unique? Are creatures similar? Yes. Discontinuities in nature delimit each species from every other, while this surface diversity expresses variation of the deep intrinsic invariance that permeates all terrestrial life. Dillon's last question—whether apocalyptic or tongue-in-cheek—is at once the most nebulous: "endure" how, in what form, and for how long? Given that, on an astronomical scale, our progeny is doomed to the extent that it remains earthbound, I come up with the same short-range answer as Lynn Margulis did in 1986: through "the commingling of human and manufactured parts in new life-forms," a cybersymbiotic process that will enable us to rebuild our species.

Toward the end of my paper, "What Is an Animal?," I departed from my text to remark that the ideal zoo of the future will be an ecological park exhibiting not just samples of animals but exemplars of all forms of life—prokaryotic and eukaryotic—in their dense traffic with one another and with their enveloping atmosphere, hydrosphere, and lithosphere. Dr. Robinson, in his article, "Building the BioPark: Thoughts on the Zoo's Centennial, 1889–1989," published in the National Zoological Park's *Zoogoer,* Vol. 17, No. 6, Nov./Dec. 1988, gave voice to a kindred vision. To this I would now add that biotechnology, computers, robots, and other information-processing machines in their accreting interactions with humans now assuredly belong in the same park.

Acknowledgments

Michael H. Robinson

The Special Smithsonian Symposium, Man and Beast Revisited, was designed as a sequel to the 1969 intellectual landmark symposium, the proceedings of which were published by the Smithsonian Press in 1971 as *Man and Beast: Comparative Social Behavior* (editors, John F. Eisenberg and Wilton S. Dillon). The 1969 original and Man and Beast Revisited were both directed by Wilton S. Dillon. The idea for the sequel originated with Professor Thomas Sebeok, Indiana University, while he was a regents fellow of the Smithsonian Institution.

Administration for Man and Beast Revisited was handled by the staff of the Office of Interdisciplinary Studies, then the Office of Smithsonian Symposia and Seminars: Carla Borden, the late Dorothy Richardson, Helen Leavitt, and Sandra Seales. Their superb creative style of management met all challenges and resulted in another historic symposium. They were assisted by Cameron Knight and Harris Dillon, volunteers. Wilton Dillon masterminded and inspired the entire conference. His contributions were distinguished by the warmth of his personality and the depth of his intellect. Judith Gradwohl of my office assisted in these efforts and skillfully developed and coordinated the program content.

For special events, reception arrangements, and publicity, Robert Hoage, National Zoological Park chief, Office of Public Affairs, and his staff are commended for the outstanding preparation and success of these events. Grateful acknowledgment is extended to the NZP Office of Design and Exhibit Planning staff for their assistance, particularly Herman Krebs for the creative design of the conference program brochure and poster, and Jessie Cohen for photographic coverage.

Dr. Chris Wemmer, Jack Williams, and the staff of the Conservation and Research Center deserve special accolades for the excellent meeting facilities, arrangements for the meals and snacks, and the pleasant, cordial atmosphere which made us feel so welcome. The site was very suitable for this symposium, and the ambience made for a memorable occasion.

During the editing of the manuscript we incurred a debt to Sue Ruff for her excellent editorial assistance. Sue read and reviewed each essay. Appreciation and warmest thanks go to Carla Borden, Gail Hill, and Delores Bethea, who so efficiently took control of the multitude of administrative details involved. My thanks to them for preventing any blunders at this crucial stage. Especially acknowledged is the exemplary management by Carla Borden of financial arrangements with donors and authors and her negotiations with contractors for the symposium and publication of the book. Special thanks go to Marty Rogers for administrative coordination between contributors and principals involved in final editorial review of the manuscript.

The Smithsonian Institution gratefully acknowledges contributions from the following in support of the symposium and volume:

The British Council

The Commonwealth Fund

Century Healthcare Corporation

Geraldine R. Dodge Foundation

Fluker's Cricket Farm

The Harry Frank Guggenheim Foundation

Kal Kan Foods, Inc.

The Raymond John Wean Foundation

Wenner-Gren Foundation for Anthropological Research

World Wings International, Inc., Chesapeake Bay Chapter

Michael H. Robinson

Introduction

Lionel Tiger and Michael H. Robinson

The essence of the scientific story is that it insists on rewriting its endings and reevaluating its beginnings and middles. While to the outsider such implacable self-criticism may appear dispiriting or abrasive, to participants in the ongoing drama it is both just and intriguing. This book enters the modest pageant of study of the relations between biology and social science after a particularly lively and rich period of work and controversy. The book *Man and Beast* to which it is the sequel was in fact rather significant in the entire process, since it appeared at a critical time and involved a cast of characters who continued to play discernibly significant roles during the two decades which have followed the original conference at the Smithsonian Institution in 1969. Perhaps at no period since the original publication of Darwin's work has the consideration of the sources and fixity of human behavior enjoyed or endured such acrimony, ambitious speculation, empirical bounty, and a sense that the answer to the question What is human nature and is there one? has such moral and political meaning.

For example, even our book's title, *Man and Beast Revisited,* would not be acceptable were it not for its necessary evocation of the original volume. The use of *Man* as a symbol for both males and females would imply insensitivity to a significant shift in scientific understanding which resulted from the fact that for a very long time, when social scientists (and others, too) wrote *man,* they usually meant *men.* As Phyllis Dolhinow explains in her contribution, this was not only a semantic bias but a procedural one as well which resulted in possibly poor and certainly inadequate scientific attention to the circumstance and process of female behavior in many species including, so obviously, our own.

And *Beast,* would we use *beast* were our title page fresh and without a predecessor? No, because attitudes to the rest of the animal species with whom we share the planet have become almost drastically more sympathetic and egalitarian. The animal rights movement, which has been propelled by such writers as Peter Singer, Mary Midgely, and Tom Regan, represents a broader sense of kinship with animals and greater commitment to their rights and sensitivities than existed in 1969. (It is almost an amusing paradox that while the furor about whether or not humans share behavioral characteristics with other primates continues unresolved in some circles, there is increasing consensus around the view that other animals share *our* characteristics, particularly those associated with legal rights, individual dignity, and the avoidance of physical and increasingly psychological pain. It seems also the case that the interest groups supporting protection for humanlike attributes of animals boast much the same personnel as the groups opposing any suggestion of animal-like attributes to people.)

The subtitle of the first *Man and Beast* volume was *Comparative Social Behavior,* which clearly implied the editors' view about the continuity between people and animals. By the time of the second symposium, comparative social behavior was still a focus, formidably represented by John Eisenberg's thorough discussion in this volume. But it was only one of several foci. In this context, the preface to the book of the first symposium makes interesting reading. It was written by S. Dillon Ripley, the polymath secretary of the Smithsonian Institution and himself a distinguished ornithologist. Ripley was very concerned about aggression. At the time, there was a major concentration on the subject of aggression and violence, its dramatic subcategory. This had all been stirred by Konrad Lorenz's challenging assertions in *On Aggression;* by Anthony Storr; by the literate, provocative, and still much underrated Robert Ardrey (who else, as early as 1961, had put together such a seemingly disparate array of data and theories so coherently if controversially as Ardrey did in *African Genesis*?); and by the opposition to their views, as best reflected by Ashley Montagu and his colleagues in *Man and Aggression.*

Perhaps the concern with aggression was partly due, in America at least, to the Vietnam War and its profound implication for American society. Nevertheless, twenty years later, the subject is of less scientific salience, even though the world is as strife-torn, violent, and dangerous as in 1969—if not more so, when one considers the far broader ownership of far more lethal weapons by far more governments and even by individuals as well as criminal groups. As Robin Fox discusses aggression in this volume, the subject remains vital theoretically, since it is part of the larger question about the sources of behavior. One of the great foci of the first symposium was on the mechanisms that ultimately determine or circumscribe behavior, particularly of our own species. Ripley wrote: "Should the study of man be based on man alone? . . . do genes control how we hunt, protect our young, affiliate, cooperate, fight or claim territory? . . . The study of the inheritance of traits which affect culture is much needed" (Ripley 1969).

Essentially at that time there was a major interest in the behavioral part of the nature/nurture debate. In particular, ethology had stressed the instinct/learning dichotomy, and this had yielded a fervid argument. Fox and Lionel Tiger, who both participated in the first symposium, sought to solve the dilemma with their concept of a behavioral biogrammar that united the notion of universal grammar of Chomskyean linguistics with the acknowledgment of the enormous cultural variety in human arrangements—a variety akin to the array of many languages in the context of one Chomskyean language (Tiger and Fox 1971, 1989). They also had a rudimentary appreciation of the significance of William Hamilton's absolutely fundamental insights into the linkage of genetics and kinship. And when Edward O. Wilson, who met Hamilton at the Man and Beast symposium, incorporated this vital insight into his unusually broad and synoptic perspective, this was to become "The New Synthesis," which was to become sociobiology when his book of that name was published in 1975. Clearly, Wilson's chapter in *Man and Beast* was an overture to that glorious main symphony. One of the principal insights that has emerged from all this is that the study of human society, of which cultural variation is so important a component, had to be informed by the study and possible influence of biological determinants. Ripley seized on the significance of this with typical prescience: "I liked Edward O. Wilson's phrase, 'anthropological genetics' " (Ripley *op. cit.*).

Michael H. Robinson is an unapologetic descendant of "old guard" ethology who sees the essential basis of sociobiology in the work of Niko Tinbergen, Lorenz, and their colleagues and students who with such productivity studied animals in environments as natural as possible. They were thus able to add to the results of psychologists working in labs their observations about the broad social lives of animals, the animals' links to environment, and—particularly important for the complex, relatively long-lived primates—how the life cycle affected long-term developments in social structure. Just before the symposium, Desmond Morris, that brighter-than-bright Tinbergen student (and then curator of mammals at the London Zoo) had published his *Naked Ape,* while in the same month as the symposium, Tiger published his *Men in Groups.* (In fact, Tiger had been invited by Morris to spend a year at the zoo as a kind of "social scientist in residence.")

The ethological tradition represented by such work and a wealth of other publications was a critical part of the intellectual critical mass that the symposium represented. There was a general sense of excitement and of impending discovery and even of the promise of clarity. As well, there was an innocence about all this, a cheerful assumption that the world was waiting for the announcements of scientists about the nature of nature and of human nature. Who could object? One of the most illuminating results of our revisit to Man and Beast was Wilson's personal analysis of the genesis of his book and its reception. It was fascinating to be told that he did not expect the hornets to emerge from the nest as fiercely buzzing as they had and that they would dive-bomb in such large numbers.

His account seems to reveal the real innocence of the earlier time and not merely *post hoc* ingenuousness. Now we know how threatening to much of anthropology and sociology, and to the broad belief in human optionality and unfetteredness of industrial society in general, was any effort to draw a picture of natural *Homo sapiens,* who enters the world not as a wholly malleable tabula rasa but as an appetitive creature with a set of general capacities and needs, who in social groups is likely to act in broadly and very generally predictable ways.

Need such predictability, if it does exist, suppress human freedom and political imagination? Of course not. As Spinoza asserted, freedom is the recognition of necessity. And anyone who wants to change a system should understand it first. As for the canard that notions of old human nature are attractive to oppressive politicians who will harass citizens in the name of this old nature, modern history at least is rather more replete with examples of indefatigably dictatorial regimes who harass citizens in the name of the new human nature that their particular ideology—together, of course, with a wholly controlled environment—will produce in their extraspecial utopia. Stalin's most influential biothinker was Lysenko.

Aggression, instinct, and sociobiology have passed to the *passe* as far as current fashions in science go, though the interesting analysis by Helen Fisher of worldwide divorce rates is a worthwhile example of the uses of biology in interpreting even very broad social trends. What is now center stage in biological thinking? At last, biology itself, it appears. Some of the major controversies revolve around such stimulating issues as those Richard Dawkins raised in *The Selfish Gene* and his recent assertions about Darwinian theory in *The Blind Watchmaker.* On another tack is a group, the punctuated equilibrium camp, which was unfortunately not represented at the second Man and Beast symposium. In a sense their idea takes theory back to James Hutton and uniformitarianism. Where will it stand in twenty years should there be a third symposium?

Darwin was himself so prolific that the implications of his many insights seem over and over again to reward attention. One of his central ideas, about the role of sexual selection, was not directly treated at the second symposium, and we thought the omission sufficiently serious to ask Mary Jane West-Eberhard, one of the most articulate masters of this body of material, to contribute the gem of an essay which follows. Both Richard Potts and Sherwood Washburn confront the difficult issues which the study of the evolutionary record provokes among scholars of the story of human evolution. Washburn's essay adds to this his own account of, and role in, some of the most momentous episodes in the development of modern sophistication about primate/human evolution.

An area of science which has developed robustly since the first symposium has been the biology of cognition and consciousness. If sapience is indeed a marker for our species, what are its characteristics? Here Martin Moynihan, Robert Trivers, John Crook, and Richard Restak explore matters ranging from the relationship between meditation and the silent motionlessness of the hunter, to the role of self-deception in forming the military policies of fiercely powerful societies. In between are an array of insights into the process of communication and its impact on social behavior and arrangements.

The first symposium did not adequately examine the relationships between man and beast, an extraordinarily interesting area of study. Biology itself is, in many ways, and for many biologists, not merely an intellectual discipline or a descriptive science but an outcome of this relationship. For many it springs deep-rooted as an expression of the fascination that the living world holds for humans. Robinson tries to capture some of this essentially affectional response in his autobiographical contribution. But there is something even more significant in the relationship's fundamental contribution to our history, in its contribution to the origins, development, and form of our civilizations. We are a species that alone in the living world has utterly transformed other species to meet our needs for food, sources of power and mobility, and companionship. Our first dogs enhanced our hunting abilities; then came sheep and goats to enhance our foraging and accumulate energy in their tissues. Consider how we have used domestic animals as living storehouses of plant foods in seasonal environments and how we have used the work power of horses and oxen for most of our history (the use of steam and gasoline power has occurred within a blink of time compared to this). Consider how the mobility of horse and camel made possible the exploration and conquest of our lands. Domestication and cultivation made our present burgeoning numbers possible and, in turn, led to the large-scale modification of the world's ecosystems. The dog, domesticated as a hunting aid, now, as a companion animal, requires a pet-food industry larger than the entire economy of medieval Europe. The cat, deified in ancient Egypt as a vermin control device, now numbers more than 65 million in the United States alone. These facts speak of the crucial place of the man and beast relationship even in the twentieth century. The setting of our symposium, the National Zoological Park, was itself a reminder of the fact that in an urbanized society humans still crave contact with the world of other animals. More people visit zoos in the United States than attend field sports; what that tells us must be significant.

It is clear, in retrospect, that there should have been a historian of this relationship in our midst at the symposium. Our attitudes toward animals are crucial to the future, but they clearly have their origins deep in the past. The first things that humans created as art, in the misty morning of history, were paintings of animals, and these images persist from Altimira, through hieroglyphs, to Disney and Gary Larson. The man and beast interaction was not illumined at our symposium by a historian, but nonetheless Leo Bustad, Alan Beck and Aaron Katcher, and Andrew Rowan reveal the fascination of the subject matter, outline the considerable body of material available for study, and suggest some rather practical effects of the man and beast encounter.

Finally, a defect of the first symposium, emphatically noted by Ripley in his preface, was the absence of any reference to problems of conservation and the environmental crisis. This has become a much more imminently crucial issue in the intervening years, to the discussion of which Stephen H. Schneider and Norman Myers bring both technical information and a healthy if somewhat despondent sense of realpolitik and realeconomik. And all the deliberations acquired a sense of appropriate scale from their placement after Irwin Shapiro's terse announcement about how the universe began and how noisy was the big bang.

1. The Cosmic Setting for Man and Beast

Evolution from the Big Bang to the Brontosaurus

Irwin I. Shapiro

I address a fundamental question: Am I man or beast? After considerable reflection, I have come down on the side of the beast. Otherwise, how could I have the temerity to write on so broad a subject about which I know so little? My ignorance is so vast that it was only last week I discovered the Brontosaurus not only has vanished from the earth but has also been banished from our vocabulary. It turns out the term is redundant. Someone else got there first, and Brontosaurus must now bow out in favor of the earlier Apatosaurus—the unreal lizard.

Terminology aside, I will now concentrate on telling a story, more accurately a collection of myths, the myths of our time. I would be willing to bet a large Brontosaurus bone, if one can pardon that use of obsolete terminology, that future generations, should there be any of humans, will view our thoughts on the origin and evolution of the universe with about the same amount of amusement as we view those of the ancient Greeks. My reasoning is simple: the world is so enormously complicated that it is virtually impossible to figure out all the "right answers."

The myths begin, at least today's myths begin, with what is called the "big bang." What is the big bang? It is a descriptor for the birth of the universe, the belief that between 10 and 20 billion years ago, the universe, now so vast and seemingly serene, burst forth with the release of an unbelievably large amount of energy from an inconceivably small region of space. And yet, according to the latest theories, when the universe was only a few winks old, the temperature of this enormous concentration of energy was bounded from above by a value that man has the temerity to claim to be able to calculate.

The myths that describe the evolution of the universe, from the big bang through the lives of Brontosauri or Apatosauri, are rather complicated and cannot be discussed here in detail, since I must be very succinct to be able to cover about 700 million years per page. Luckily, the myths are fuzzy enough that one loses little by not dwelling on the details.

The physical conditions that existed in the universe just after its birth are so far beyond anything we can achieve in the laboratory that to treat them we must stretch—enormously—the application of the laws of physics as we have established them here and now. Even so, we cannot tell in detail what these laws predict under those conditions because quantitative calculations are too complicated. Qualitatively, then, what happened next? The next myth of major importance is the entering of the universe into a phase of very rapid expansion called inflation. This phase resembles somewhat the familiar transition of a substance from a liquid into a gas.

After this enormous expansion, which took place in a small fraction of a second, the universe slowed to a "normal" rate of expansion. At this epoch, the universe is believed to have been made up of exotic particles with even stranger names. But as it expanded, the universe cooled, and the zoo, if I may use that expression, of elementary particles was winnowed. We have here our first example of mass extinctions. The particles left after this initial winnowing were mostly protons, neutrons, and electrons.

At that time, when the universe had cooled to a balmy billion degrees or so, collisions took place which led to the creation, from these elementary particles, of the nuclei of the lightest elements: hydrogen, a trace of deuterium, and helium. The universe was then approximately three minutes old. It kept expanding and cooling and, after a half-million years, was cool enough for atoms of hydrogen and helium to form; the electrons combined

Fig. 1. A few of the approximately 100 billion galaxies in the universe, as photographed by a moderate-sized telescope. The elongated objects are the galaxies. Courtesy National Optical Astronomy Observatories.

with the nuclei to form these elements, or atoms, as we know them now. The radiation, or light, present, which interacted strongly with the electrons before atoms formed, decoupled and proceeded on its way in the universe, unimpeded by the matter, cooling as it went, to lower and lower temperatures.

The following phase, which I shall skip over, took much longer, maybe up to a billion years. The details are even fuzzier, but somehow this collection of matter managed through gravitational instabilities of some sort, to collect into clumps which we call galaxies. The mass of all the material involved in each clump was perhaps about 10^{12}, or a thousand billion, times the mass of our sun. These entities are illustrated in figure 1: a collection of galaxies as seen through a moderate-sized telescope. The fuzzy objects, with different shapes and orientations, are the galaxies; the little dots are mostly foreground objects, stars in our own galaxy.

If we were able to tell the distances from us of all these objects, that is, their distribution in the third, or depth, dimension, we could determine how

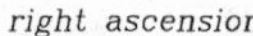

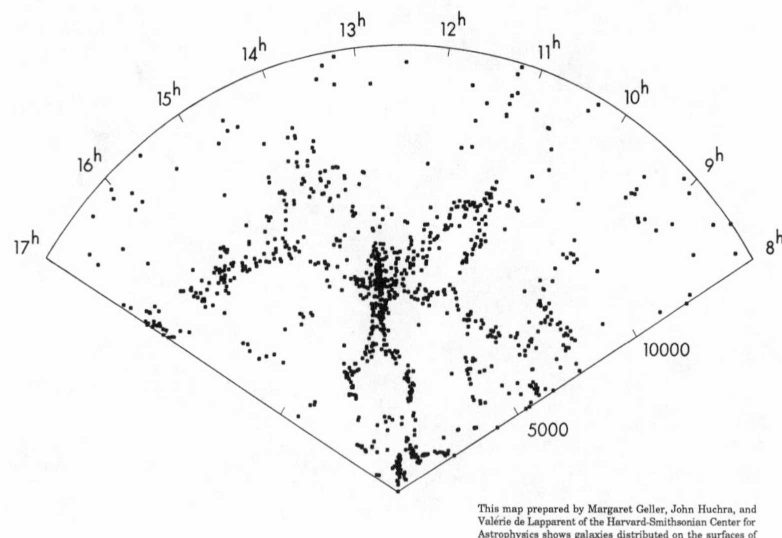

Fig. 2. A drawing of the distribution of galaxies, brighter than a certain magnitude, in a "slice" of the universe. Our position is at the point of intersection of the two straight-line segments. The distance of a galaxy from us is proportional to its distance in the drawing from that point (see text). Drawing courtesy of Margaret Geller and John Huchra, Harvard-Smithsonian Center for Astrophysics.

they are distributed in space. By using an elementary, but clever, technique based on the fact that the universe is expanding, one can determine this distribution. In figure 2, I show just a slice of the universe; the point on the bottom represents us, and radii emanating from it correspond to distance from us. Distribution in direction on the sky is represented in the left to right sweep of the figure. Each bright dot represents a galaxy, and as one can see, these galaxies are concentrated on the borders of great voids. If one looks a little deeper in the other (perpendicular) direction on the sky, it is apparent that the galaxies are distributed on the surfaces of "bubbles" with little or nothing being visible within them. This discovery, made just this past year, is a rather remarkable revelation about the distribution of galaxies in the universe. Theoretical explanations of this structure are still rather primitive and are represented in figure 3.

From closer up, galaxies can be seen to exhibit a wide variety of internal

Fig. 3. A caricature of the state of present theories of the origin of the "bubble" structure of the universe (see text). From *Bizarreries and Fantasies of Granville,* ©1974, Dover Publications.

structures; one example is shown in figure 4. They are usually rather complex collections of stars, dust, and gas. Many believe that the gas and dust, through gravitational instabilities on a smaller spatial scale, collapsed into smaller clouds and then into stars. However, there are others who believe the stars may have formed before the galaxies. Even something as seemingly simple as the order of formation of stars and galaxies is still controversial.

Where does life fit into this uncertain picture? Nowhere. Life was clearly

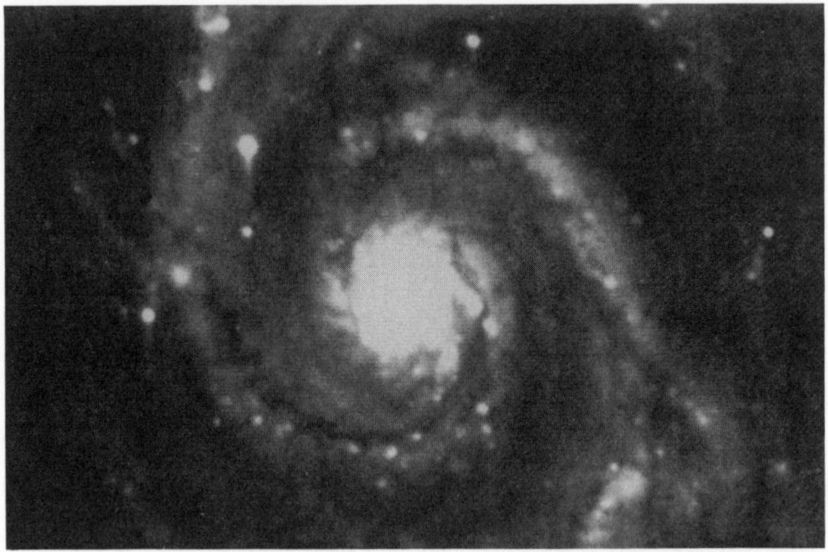

Fig. 4. Photograph of a spiral galaxy, viewed nearly "face on." Courtesy Smithsonian Astrophysical Observatory.

impossible at this time. The only atoms present then, according to our current myths, were hydrogen, helium, and a trace of deuterium. No one has yet been able to conceive of life of a form anything like we know it being made from just those building blocks. So we have to understand where the rest of the elements came from, in particular those that seem essential for life. Where *did* we come from in this fundamental sense? Enter here the life cycle of stars. We must consider how stars form, evolve, and die before we can obtain a clue as to where the stuff of life came from.

Let us then look very briefly at how a star is formed. Gas and dust, as I said, by some magic mechanism, are able to collapse. The potential energy released as all this material collapses into a smaller region creates high temperatures and pressures, and sets off nuclear, in particular hydrogen, burning. Nuclei of atoms actually burn in the center of these objects called stars. In this burning, hydrogen turns into helium. Then carbon is made. Then oxygen. Now we are getting someplace as far as life is concerned. Many of the needed building blocks result from nuclear burning in the cores of stars. But we would not expect to find much in the way of life at the heart of stars. The temperature there is on the order of millions of degrees, a little uncomfortably warm. We do not know even hardy enough bacteria that could survive under those conditions. So, though we have many of the building blocks, we cannot have life because the building blocks are buried in this rather uncomfortable environment.

On average, after a few billions of years, the nuclear fuel is more or less exhausted, and the inside of the star cools. But the star is kept from collapsing in the first place by the high temperature—the rapid motion of the materials—which fights against the gravitational pull, inexorably tending to make the star smaller. When the star cools sufficiently, the gas can no longer support itself against gravity and it collapses in a rapid fashion, taking only a very, very short time, on the order of seconds, to do so in many cases. In collapsing, the gas releases enormous amounts of energy. Paradoxically, this release of energy heats the gas to high enough temperatures to once again allow nuclear burning, but now because of the enormous temperatures, the burning reaches the point where heavier atoms, like iron and nickel, can be created. Moreover, in the explosive death throes of many stars, which occur after cooling and collapse, very heavy elements, like uranium, can also be created.

Many of these creations take place during a gigantic explosion that we call a supernova. Supernovas are so intense that the brightness of only one can often exceed the total brightness of the nearly hundred billion ordinary stars that might populate the same, run-of-the-mill galaxy in which the supernova occurs. And the explosion occurs, relatively speaking, in just a twinkling. As a result of such explosions, many of the newly created atoms spread out into interstellar space. This space is thereby enriched with heavy elements, although they represent only a very tiny fraction of the total amount of material present there. Most of the material is hydrogen, with about a quarter of the total being helium and maybe a few percent being atoms of these heavier elements—the stuff of life. This myth is probably the most profound one I have told: where we all came from. Supernovas are, in effect, our ancestors. Figure 5 shows a picture of a supernova remnant, the Crab nebula, whose name derives from its constellation. This remnant is of rather recent origin; in fact, its progenitor explosion is recorded in Chinese records from A.D. 1054. Of course, much earlier supernovas gave rise to the atoms in our bodies.

Back to our story line. We now have floating around between the stars, in

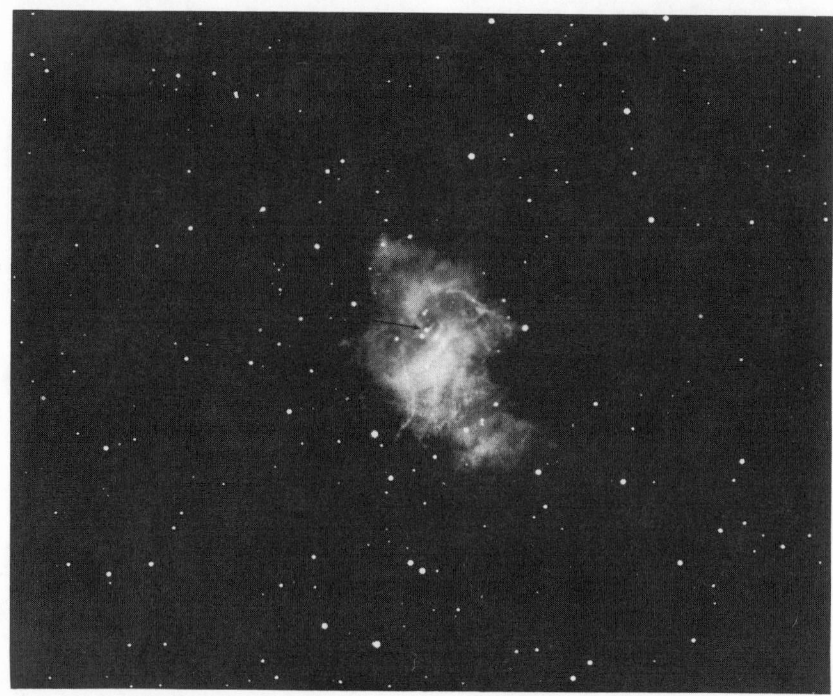

Fig. 5. Photograph of the Crab nebula, the remnant of a supernova explosion in A.D. 1054. Such explosions distribute in space the heavy elements that make life possible. Courtesy Smithsonian Astrophysical Observatory.

interstellar space, the atomic ingredients needed to make life. What happens next? According to our myths, there is a second generation of star formation. This new material, with a small fraction of heavy atoms, swirling between the stars, cools and forms dust and gas condensations. These big swirls of dust and gas collect into what are called nebulas, or clouds, which gradually collapse through another series of complicated maneuvers. The collapses lead to massive central condensations—suns—with rings of dust around them which gradually coalesce and form planets and satellites. Very few, if any, of these processes are understood in detail.

We are making progress. We have a sun, a second-generation star, and we have planets, including, magically, the earth, fully formed in all its beauty and complexity (see figure 6 for a later view). Somehow, somewhere, life

Fig. 6. Photograph of the earth as seen from space. Courtesy National Aeronautics and Space Administration.

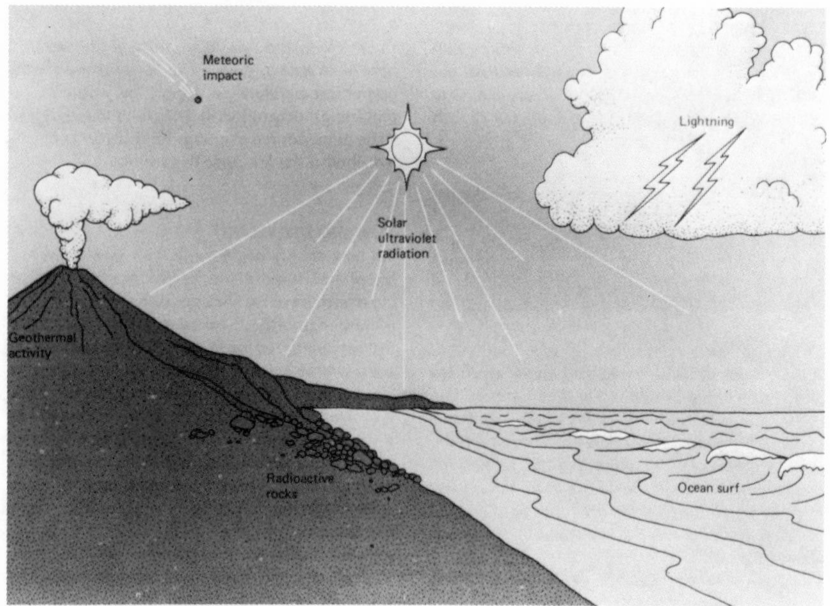

Fig. 7. Cartoon illustrating the ingredients thought to have been essential for the creation of life on earth. From *Exploring the Cosmos,* by Louis Berman and J. C. Evans, ©1983, Scott, Foresman and Company.

emerged on it. Even our myths do not tell us how that happened. We believe that the combination of earth, water, lightning, and perhaps some volcanic and other activity, all stirred well, led to life. Figure 7 is another cartoon, which illustrates the progress at about the level of detail of present theories. It is a rather complicated business; even describing the lightning alone theoretically is beyond our capabilities. But somehow, someway, the earth passed from a primitive, nonbiological environment to one containing a magnificent creation, the double helix, or DNA, the basis for replicating life. All of that from supernovas, in only a billion years or so.

Now we are practically home free. We have an earth with life thriving on it. In fact, though, we do not know that life originated on the earth. Perhaps, as some theorists believe, life came ready-made and just dropped down on earth. But that scenario just pushes the problem to a different time and place; we must then figure out where it was made, how it was made, and by what means it traveled here intact.

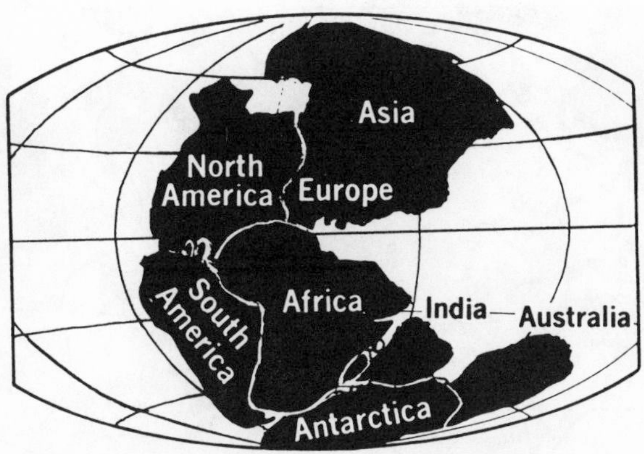

Fig. 8. Reconstruction by geologists and geophysicists of the positions of the continents about 225 million years ago. Courtesy Walter Sullivan, adapted from Dietz and Holden. From *Continents in Motion,* McGraw Hill, 1974.

In any event, life proliferated on the earth, yielding complex and baffling varieties. We find in the fossil record that, along the way to the present, erratic extinctions, mass extinctions, took place in many different eras. New species grew and left their mark; older ones disappeared. Finally, dinosaurs developed, perhaps over the order of 100 million years, from very small lizardlike animals.

Meanwhile, the earth itself was undergoing slow but inexorable changes, as illustrated in figure 8. The surface of our planet went through different stages; the continents formed and moved around, as shown by measurements and described by the theory of plate tectonics. The continents have been rearranging and renewing themselves over 100-million-year time scales, new material coming from the inside of the earth, its mantle, and old material going back under the crust of the earth to the mantle. The process is still going on, as illustrated in figure 9. Here is the earth more or less as we know it, but viewed in a slightly peculiar projection. The arrows show the directions of motion of the various plates that make up the crust of the earth. They are moving at the dramatic relative speeds of one to ten centimeters per year. And, believe it or not, we can now measure such motions in only one year with our modern techniques.

The earth's surface is not only made up of distinct parts in constant,

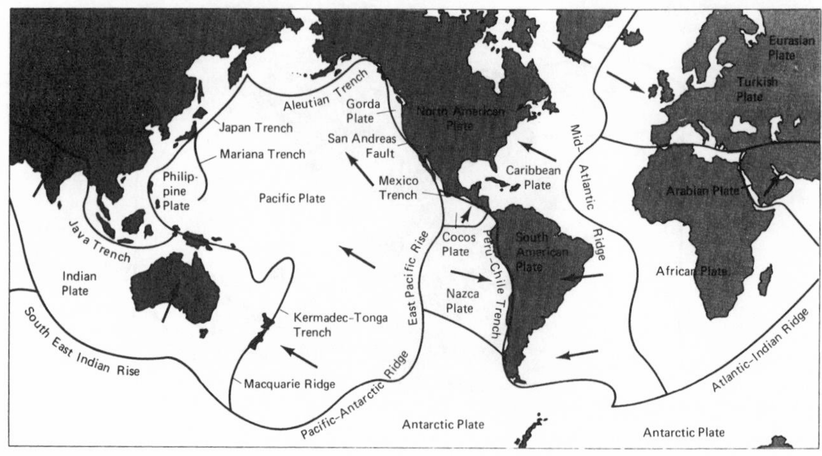

Fig. 9. Estimates of the present directions of motion of the "plates" that constitute the surface of the earth. From *Exploring the Cosmos,* by Louis Berman and J. C. Evans. ©1983, Scott, Foresman and Company.

although somewhat slow, relative motion, it occasionally entertains visitors from outer space (fig. 10). Even though everything on earth usually looks orderly and unchanging, occasionally something rather dramatic happens when people are not looking (sometimes even when they are); earthquakes, landslides, and meteorite impacts are common examples.

Finally, we come to the last point in my story: the dinosaur extinction. What happened to the Apatosaurus and all of his or her friends? This subject has fascinated scientists and laymen alike for at least a century, since dinosaur bones were first discovered and recognized as such. In this century, we

Fig. 10. Cartoon illustrating the occasional impacts of large meteorites on the earth. By permission of Johnny Hart and Creators Syndicate.

determined that dinosaurs vanished from the fossil record about 65 million years ago. Why did they disappear? There have been many conflicting theories proposed to explain this extinction. Nevertheless, I can say rather definitively that no one before today has blamed man, perhaps because man is known not to have appeared until about 60 million years after the dinosaurs disappeared. So the connection has proven hard for many to draw.

Lately, the topic of dinosaur extinction has seen a new renaissance. It stemmed from a very "small" fact. Discovered in the stratum of the geological record from about the time of the dinosaurs' extinction was an anomaly in the elemental composition of the material in that layer. Residing there was an unexpectedly large amount of iridium, an otherwise relatively rare metal on the surface of the earth. The concentration of this iridium in that thin layer which marks the geological boundary of 65 million years or so ago, was far higher, about a thousandfold higher, than was anticipated, based on the average concentration of iridium on the surface of the earth.

It is amazing what complicated theories and controversies have been spawned by this one observation. First came the theory that an asteroid of some 10 kilometers in diameter struck the earth. Asteroids are known, from meteorites which we can study, to have a much higher concentration of iridium than is found in indigenous materials on earth. This impact scenario goes as follows: The asteroid hit the surface of the earth, causing a tremendous explosion. Dust and other material, including the vaporized iridium that entered with the asteroid, were thrown upward in the air. The impact led to the spreading of dust all over the atmosphere, creating what has been termed the equivalent of nuclear winter. The weather and, relatedly, the environment, were putatively changed so significantly that creatures like dinosaurs could not survive and disappeared. Gradually, the iridium drifted down from the atmosphere and contributed to the layer recently discovered in the geological record.

There are a number of problems with this hypothesis, some perhaps fatal. One clear problem is illustrated by a question: Where is the enormous crater that would have been created by this collision of the asteroid with the earth? There should be some record, some smoking gun. None has yet been found. We do have a record of less impressive collisions that occurred much longer ago, as illustrated in figure 11. This crater is about 65 kilometers in diameter and is believed to have been formed by the impact of an extraterrestrial object

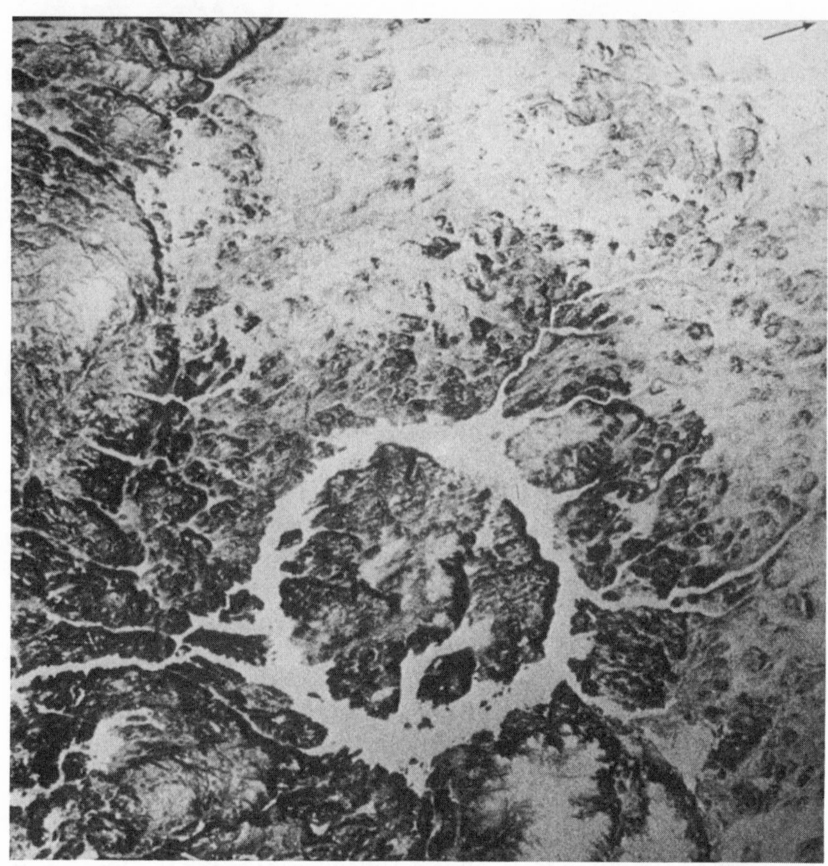

Fig. 11. Ring structure, 65 km in diameter, in Quebec, Canada, believed to have been caused by the impact of a large meteorite over 200 million years ago. Courtesy National Aeronautics and Space Administration.

on the earth over 200 million years ago during the Triassic geologic era. But for the epoch of 65 million years ago that marks the boundary between the Cretaceous and Tertiary eras, we have found no record of such an impact. One possible explanation: Maybe the crater is on the bottom of the ocean and is just not visible. Another possibility is that the impact region subsequently slid under the earth's surface into its mantle, as part of the tectonic processes that continue to affect the earth.

Scientists, being a very imaginative lot, have also come up with another explanation, namely, that the iridium came from deep within the earth

Fig. 12. Photograph of a recent volcanic eruption. Courtesy Smithsonian Institution.

through especially intense volcanism that brought up material from far below the surface. Recently, measurements in a volcanic region in Hawaii have shown the presence below of far larger concentrations of iridium than on the surface. Such concentrations could conceivably have given rise to this iridium layer. Unusually large amounts of volcanic activity could, in this scenario, have produced circumstances similar to those attributed to the asteroid and thus been responsible for the dinosaurs' demise.

We show in figure 12 what the volcanologists think may have happened. This picture is of a volcano of very recent origin, 1970, not from 65 million years ago. The camera had not quite been invented then. It is obvious that this volcanic action was a rather dramatic event, but still tame stuff compared to what must be called upon to produce the events leading to the extinction of the dinosaurs. In India a lava plain has been identified which might have resulted from tremendous volcanism that could have caused the traumatic events of about 65 million years ago.

For some years now the argument has raged between the proponents of

Fig. 13. Photograph of a scene in Tunguska, Siberia, after the impact there in 1908 of what is believed by many to have been a comet. Photograph by Leonid Kulik from SOVPHOTO.

The real reason dinosaurs became extinct

Fig. 14. Illustration of an alternative theory of the cause of the disappearance of dinosaurs. "The Far Side" cartoon by Gary Larson is reprinted by permission of Chronical Features, San Francisco, Calif.

the impact theory of mass extinction and the volcanic theory. Few theorists give up their ideas easily, and there have been new twists added to the asteroid impact theory by its proponents. Instead of an asteroid, they now call upon a swarm of comets to have collided with the earth, with each also hypothesized to have been extra rich in iridium. None of the individual comets would, it is supposed, have led to a sufficiently large explosion for a recognizable mark to have been left on the earth's surface. Figure 13 shows what happened in 1908 at Tunguska, Siberia, which may be considered as a model for the results from an impact of one of the possible swarm of comets; these latter might have hit the earth and left devastation on a scale we cannot easily comprehend, and might well have been buried without a trace after 65 million years. The cumulative effect could, it is hypothesized, do all the required damage; but the smoking gun would not, so to say, be expected to have remained smoking.

I would like to add yet another theory. While this argument—whether asteroid impacts, comet impacts, enormous volcanism, or something else was responsible for the dinosaur's demise—has been in progress between noted scientists, a very little known, but perceptive scientist has proposed a different cause of the dinosaur's demise, shown in figure 14. Contrary to the implication of my previous statement, in this story man *is* to blame.

Let me finish with one more statement. The amazing complexity of the myths about which I have written has been created from a relatively few fundamental observations made from a tiny corner of the universe. And yet it pales, this complexity, next to the real complexity found in the universe, and even in the small part of it that we occupy.

2. The Evolution of Man and Beast

Darwin Triumphant

Darwinism as a Universal Truth

Richard Dawkins

If we are visited by superior creatures from another star system—they will have to be superior if they are to get here at all—what common ground shall we find for discussion with them? Shall we overcome the barriers simply by learning one another's language, or will the subjects that interest our two cultures be so divergent as to preclude serious conversation? It seems unlikely that the star travelers will want to talk about many of our intellectual stocks-in-trade, about literary criticism or music, religion or politics. Shakespeare may mean nothing to those without human experiences and human emotions, and if they have a literature or an art, these will probably be too alien to excite our sensitivities. To name two thinkers who have more than once been promoted as Darwin's equals, I rather doubt whether our visitors will have much interest in talking about Marx or Freud, other than perhaps as anthropological curiosities. We have no reason to suppose that these men's works are of more than local, parochial, human, earthly, post-Pleistocene (some would add European and male) significance.

Mathematics and physics are another matter. Our guests may find our level of sophistication quaintly low, but there will be common ground. We shall agree that certain questions about the universe are important, and we shall almost certainly agree on the answers to many of these questions. Conversation will flourish, even if most of the questions flow one way and most of the answers the other. If we discuss the histories of our respective cultures, our visitors will surely point with pride, however far back in time, to their equivalents of Einstein and Newton, of Planck and Heisenberg. But they won't point to an equivalent of Freud or Marx any more than we, visiting a hitherto undiscovered tribe in a remote forest clearing, would nominate our civilization's equivalent of the local rainmaker or gully-gully man. One does not have to disparage the local achievements of Freud and Marx on this planet to agree that their findings have no universality.

What about Darwin? Will our guests revere another Darwin as one of their great thinkers of all time? Shall we be able to have a serious conversation with them about evolution? I suggest that the answer is yes (unless, as a colleague suggests to me, their Darwin is on the expedition and we are his or her Galapagos). Darwin's achievement, like Einstein's, is universal and timeless, whereas that of Marx is parochial and ephemeral. That Darwin's *question* is universal, wherever there is life, is surely undeniable. The feature of living matter that most demands explanation is that it is almost unimaginably complicated in directions that convey a powerful illusion of deliberate design. Darwin's question, or rather the most fundamental and important of Darwin's many questions, is the question of how such complicated "design" could come into being. All living creatures, everywhere in the universe and at any time in history, provoke this question. It is less obvious that Darwin's *answer* to the riddle—cumulative evolution by nonrandom survival of random hereditary changes—is universal. It is at first sight conceivable that Darwin's answer might be valid only parochially, only for the kind of life that happens to exist in our own little clearing in the universal forest. I have previously (Dawkins 1983, 1986) made the case that this is not so, that the general form of Darwin's answer is not merely incidentally true of our kind of life but almost certainly true of all life, everywhere in the universe. Here let me for the moment make the more modest claim that, at the very least, Darwin's bid for immortality is closer to the Einstein end of the spectrum than to the Marx end. Darwinism really matters in the universe.

When I was an undergraduate in the early nineteen sixties, we were taught that although Darwin was an important figure in his own time, modern neo-Darwinism was so much further advanced that it hardly deserved the name Darwinism at all. My father's generation of biologist undergraduates read, in an authoritative *A Short History of Biology* (Singer 1931), that "the struggle of living forms leading to natural selection by the survival of the fittest, is certainly far less emphasized by naturalists now than in the years that immediately followed the appearance of Darwin's book. At the time, however, it was an extremely stimulating suggestion." And the generation of biologists before that could read, in the words of perhaps the dominant British geneticist of the time: "We go to Darwin for his incomparable collection of facts [but] . . . for us he speaks no more with philosophical authority. We read his scheme of Evolution as we would those of Lucretius or Lamarck. . . . The transformation of masses of populations by imperceptible steps guided by selection is, as most of us now see, so inapplicable to the fact that we can only marvel . . . at the want of penetration displayed by the advocates of such a proposition" (Bateson 1913, quoted in Mayr 1982).

And yet the editors of this volume can commission an article with the title "Darwin Triumphant." I do not normally like writing to titles that others have proposed, but I can accept this one without reservation. In the last quarter of the twentieth century, it seems to me that Darwin's standing among serious biologists (as opposed to nonbiologists influenced by religious preconceptions) is rightly as high as it has been at any time since his death. A similar story, of even more extreme eclipse in earlier years followed by triumphant recent rehabilitation, can be told of Darwin's "other theory" of sexual selection.

It is only to be expected that, a century and a quarter on, the version of his theory that we now have should be different from the original. Modern Darwinism is Darwinism plus Weismannism plus Fisherism plus Hamiltonism (arguably plus Kimuraism and a few other *isms*). But when I read Darwin himself, I am continually astonished at how modern he sounds. Considering how utterly wrong he was on the all-important topic of genetics, he showed an uncanny gift for getting almost everything else right. Maybe we are neo-Darwinists today, but let us spell the *neo* with a very small *n*! Our neo-Darwinism is very much in the spirit of Darwin himself. The changes that Darwin would see if he came back today are in most cases changes that, I venture to suggest, he would instantly approve and welcome as the elegant and obviously correct answers to riddles that troubled him in his own time. Upon learning that evolution is change in *frequencies* within a pool of *particulate* hereditary elements, he might even quote T. H. Huxley's alleged remark upon reading the *Origin* itself, "How extremely stupid not to have thought of that!"

I referred to Darwin's gift for getting things right, but surely this can only mean right as we see it today. Shouldn't we be humble enough to admit that our right may be utterly wrong in the sight of future scientific generations? No, there are occasions when a generation's humility can be misplaced, not to say pedantic. We can now assert with confidence that the theory that the earth moves round the sun not only is right in our time but will be right in all future times even if flat-earthism happens to become revived and universally accepted in some new dark age of human history. We cannot quite say that Darwinism is in the same unassailable class. Respectable opposition to it can still be mounted, and it can be seriously argued that the current high standing of Darwinism in educated minds may not last through all future generations. Darwin may be triumphant at the end of the twentieth century, but we must acknowledge the possibility that new facts may come to light which will force our successors of the twenty-first century to abandon Darwinism or modify it beyond recognition. But is there, perhaps, an essential core of Darwinism, a core that Darwin himself might have nominated as the irreducible heart of his theory, which we might set up as a candidate for discussion as potentially beyond the reach of factual refutation?

Core Darwinism, I shall suggest, is the minimal theory that evolution is guided in adaptively nonrandom directions by the nonrandom survival of small random hereditary changes. Note especially the words *small* and *adaptively. Small* implies that adaptive evolution is gradualistic, and we shall see why this must be so in a moment. *Adaptive* does not imply that all evolution is adaptive, only that core Darwinism's concern is limited to the part of evolution that is. There is no reason to assume that all evolutionary change is adaptive (Williams 1966). But even if most evolutionary change is not adaptive, what is undeniable is that enough of evolutionary change is adaptive to demand some kind of special explanation. It is the part of evolutionary change that *is* adaptive that Darwin so neatly explained. There could be any number of theories to explain nonadaptive evolution. Nonadaptive evolution may or may not be a real phenomenon on any particular planet (it probably is on ours, in the form of the large-scale incorporation of neutral mutations), but in any case it is not a phenomenon that awakes in us an avid hunger for an explanation. Adaptations, especially complex adaptations, awake such a powerful hunger that they have traditionally provided one of the main motivations for belief in a supernatural Creator. The problem of adaptation, therefore, really was a big problem, a problem worthy of the big solution that Darwin provided.

R. A. Fisher (1930) developed a case, which did not make any appeal to particular facts, for the armchair deducibility of Mendelism. "It is a remarkable fact that had any thinker in the middle of the nineteenth century undertaken, as a piece of abstract and theoretical analysis, the task of constructing a particulate theory of inheritance, he would have been led, on the basis of a few very simple assumptions, to produce a system identical with the modern scheme of Mendelian or factorial inheritance." Is there a similar statement that could be made about the inevitability of the core of Darwin's scheme of evolution by natural selection? Although Darwin and Wallace themselves were field naturalists who made extensive use of factual information to support their theory, can we now, with hindsight, argue that there should have been no need for the *Beagle,* no need for the Galapagos and Malay Archipelagos? Should any thinker, faced with the problem formulated in the right way, have been able to arrive at the solution—core Darwinism—without stirring from an armchair?

Part of core Darwinism arises almost automatically from the problem that it solves, if we express that problem in a particular way, as one of mathematical search. The problem is that of finding, in a gigantic mathematical space of all possible organisms, that tiny minority of organisms that is adapted to survive and reproduce in available environments. Again, Fisher (1930) put it with characteristically powerful clarity. "An organism is regarded as adapted to a particular situation, or to the totality of situations which constitute its environment, only in so far as we can imagine an assemblage of slightly different situations, or environments, to which the animal would on the whole be less well adapted; and equally only in so far as we can imagine an assemblage of slightly different organic forms, which would be less well adapted to that environment."

Imagine some nightmarish mathematical menagerie in which is found the all but infinitely large set of conceivable animal forms that could be cobbled together by randomly varying all the genes in all genomes in all possible combinations. For brevity, although it is not as precise a phrase as its mathematical tone leads one to think, I shall refer to this as the set of all possible animals (fortunately the argument I am developing is an order-of-magnitude argument which does not depend on numerical precision). Most of the members of this ill-favored bestiary will never develop beyond the single-cell stage. Of the very few that manage to be born (or hatch, etc.), most will be hideously misshapen monstrosities who will early die. The animals that actually exist, or have ever existed, will be a tiny subset of the set of all possible animals. Incidentally, I use *animal* purely in deference to the title of this book. By all means substitute *plant* or *organism.*

It is convenient to imagine the set of all possible animals as arrayed in a multidimensional genetic landscape. *Distance* in this landscape means genetic distance, the number of genetic changes that would have to be made in order to transform one animal into another. It is not obvious how one would actually compute the genetic distance between any two animals (because not all animals have the same number of genetic loci); but again the argument does not rely upon precision, and it is intuitively obvious what it means, for instance, to say that the genetic distance between a rat and a hedgehog is larger than the genetic distance between a rat and a mouse. In the world of real animals that actually exist we can think of genetic distance as approximately the quantity that molecular taxonomists measure. All that we are doing here is to place as well, in the same multidimensional system of axes, the very much larger set of animals that have never existed. We are including those that could never have survived even if they had come into existence, as well as those that might have survived if they had existed but as a matter of fact never came into existence.

Movement from one point in the landscape to another is mutation, interpreted in its broadest sense to include large-scale changes in the genetic system as well as point mutations at loci within existing genetic systems. In principle, by a sufficiently contrived piece of genetic engineering—artificial mutation—it is possible to move from any point in the landscape to any other. There exists a recipe for transforming the genome of a human into the genome of a hippo or into the genome of any other animal, actual or conceivable. It would normally be a very large recipe, involving changes to many of the genes, deletion of many genes, *de novo* synthesis of many genes, and radical reorganizations of the genetic system. Nevertheless, the recipe is in principle discoverable, and obeying it can be represented as equivalent to taking a single giant leap from one point to another in our mathematical space. In practice, viable mutations are normally relatively small steps in the landscape: children are only slightly different from their parents even if, in principle, they could be as different as a hippo is from a human. Evolution consists of step-by-step trajectories through the genetic space, not large leaps. Evolution, in other words, is gradualistic. There is a general reason why this has to be so, a reason that I shall now develop.

Even without formal mathematical treatment, we can make some statistical statements about our landscape. First, in the landscape of all possible genetic combinations and the "organisms" that they might generate, the proportion of viable organisms to nonviable organisms is very small. "However many ways there may be of being alive, it is certain that there are vastly more ways of being dead" (Dawkins 1986). Second, taking any given starting point in the landscape, however many ways there may be of being slightly different, it is obvious that there are vastly more ways of being very different. The number of near neighbors in the landscape may be large, but it is dwarfed by the number of distant neighbors. As we consider spheres of ever increasing size, the number of progressively more distant genetic neighbors that the spheres envelop mounts as a power function and rapidly becomes for practical purposes infinite.

Incidentally, the statistical nature of this argument points up an irony in the claim, frequently made by lay opponents of evolution, that the theory of evolution violates the second law of thermodynamics, the law of increasing entropy or chaos within any closed system. The truth is opposite. If anything appears to violate the law (nothing really does), it is the *facts,* not any particular explanation of those facts! The Darwinian explanation, indeed, is the only viable explanation we have for those facts which shows us how they could have come into being *without* violating the laws of physics. The law of increasing entropy is, in any case, subject to an interesting misunderstanding, which is worthy of a brief digression because it has helped to foster the mistaken claim that the idea of evolution violates the law.

The second law originated in the theory of heat engines, but the form of it that is relevant to the evolutionary argument can be stated in more general statistical terms. Entropy was characterized by the physicist Willard Gibbs as the "mixed-upness" of a system. The law states that the total entropy of a system and its surroundings is very unlikely to decrease. Left to itself, without work being contributed from outside, any closed system (life, of course, is not a closed system) will tend to become more mixed-up, less orderly. Homely analogies—or they may be more than analogies—abound. If there is not constant work being put in by a librarian, the orderly shelving of books in a library will suffer relentless degradation due to the inevitable if low probability that borrowers will return them to the wrong shelf. We have to import a hard-working librarian into the system from outside, who, Maxwell's-Demon-like, methodically and energetically restores order to the shelves.

The common error to which I referred is to personify the second law, to invest the universe with an inner urge or drive toward chaos, a positive striving toward an ultimate nirvana of perfect disorder. It is partly this error that has led people to accept the foolish notion that evolution is a mysterious exception to the law. The error can most simply be exposed by reference to the library analogy. When we say that an unattended library tends to approach chaos as time proceeds, we do not mean that any particular state of the shelves is being approached, as though the library were striving toward a goal from afar. Quite the contrary. The number of possible ways of shelving the N books in a library can be calculated, and for any nontrivial library it is a very very large number indeed. Of these ways, only one, or a very few, would be recognized by us as a state of order. That is all there is to it. Of all possible states, the ones that we recognize as ordered are overwhelmingly outnumbered by the ones that we recognize as disordered. Far from there being any mystical urge toward disorder, it is just that there are vastly more ways of being recognized as disorderly than of being recognized as orderly. So, if a system wanders anywhere in the space of all possible arrangements, it is almost certain—unless special, librarianlike steps are taken—that we shall perceive the change as an increase in disorder. In the present context of evolutionary biology, the particular kind of order that is relevant is adaptation, the state of being equipped to survive and reproduce.

Returning to the general argument in favor of gradualism, to find viable life forms in the space of all possible forms is like searching for a modest number of needles in an extremely large haystack. There are, to be sure, plenty of ways of being alive, but even this large number is negligible compared with the size of the search space. There are so many more ways of being dead. The chance of happening to land on one of the needles if we take a large random mutational leap to another place in our multidimensional haystack is very small indeed. But one thing we can say is that the starting point of any mutational leap has to be a viable organism—one of the rare and precious needles in the haystack. This is because only organisms good enough to survive to reproductive age can have offspring of any kind, including mutant offspring. Moreover, the immediate neighbors of any organism in the space resemble it more than its more distant neighbors. Finding a viable body-form by random mutation may be like finding a needle in a haystack, but given that you have already found one viable body-form, it is certain that you can hugely increase your chances of finding another viable one if you search in the immediate neighborhood rather than more distantly.

The same goes for finding an improved body-form. As we consider mutational leaps of decreasing magnitude, the absolute number of destinations decreases but the proportion of destinations that are improvements increases. Fisher (1930) gave an elegantly simple argument to show that this increase tends toward 50% for mutational changes of very small magnitude. His argument seems inescapable for any single dimension of phenotypic variation considered on its own. Whether his precise conclusion (50%) generalizes to the multidimensional case I shall not discuss, but the direction of the argument is surely indisputable. The larger the leap through genetic space, the lower is the probability that the resulting change will be viable, let alone an improvement. Gradualistic, step-by-step walking in the immediate vicinity of already discovered needles in the haystack seems to be the only way to find other and better needles. Adaptive evolution must in general be a crawl through genetic space, not a series of leaps.

But are there any very special occasions when saltations, or macromutations, are incorporated into evolution? Macromutations certainly occur in the laboratory. Our theoretical considerations say only that *viable* macromutations should be exceedingly rare in comparison with viable micromutations. But even if the occasions when major saltations are viable and incorporated into evolution are exceedingly rare, even if they have occurred only once or twice in the whole history of a lineage from Precambrian to present, that is enough to transform the entire course of evolution. I find it plausible, for instance, that the invention of segmentation occurred in a single macromutational leap, once during the history of our own vertebrate ancestors and again once in the ancestry of arthropods and annelids. Once this had happened, in either of these two lineages, it changed the entire climate in which ordinary cumulative selection of micromutations went on. It must have resembled, indeed, a sudden catastrophic change in the external climate. Just as a lineage can, after appalling loss of life, recover and adapt to a catastrophic change in the external climate, so a lineage might, by subsequent micromutational selection, adapt to the catastrophe of a macromutation as large as the first segmentation.

This, as Professor M. S. Bartlett has reminded me, might be less unlikely if a competition vacuum had opened up in a previously virgin, uncolonized geographical area such as a new continent (not literally a continent in the case of segmentation itself, since segmentation was certainly invented in the sea!). And the great thing is that this kind of macromutational incorporation only has to happen once in the whole of geological time, in order for its effects to be still with us. We can therefore contemplate it without abandoning the needle-in-a-haystack argument that macromutational incorporation must be exceedingly rare.

In the landscape of all possible animals, our segmentation example might look like this. A wild macromutational leap from a perfectly viable parent lands in a remote part of the haystack, far from any needle of viability. The first segmented animal is born, a freak, a monster none of whose detailed bodily features equip it to survive its new, segmented architecture. It should die. But by chance the leap in genetic space has coincided with a leap in geographical space. The segmented monster finds itself in a virgin part of the world where the living is easy and competition is light. What can happen when any ordinary animal finds itself in a strange place, a new continent, say, is that, although ill-adapted to the new conditions, it survives by the skin of its teeth. In the competition vacuum its descendants survive for enough generations to adapt, by normal, cumulative natural selection of micromutations, to the alien conditions. So it might have been with our segmented monster. It survived by the skin of its teeth, and its descendants adapted, by ordinary micromutational cumulative selection, to the radically new conditions imposed by the macromutation. Though the macromutational leap landed far from any needle in the haystack, the competition vacuum enabled the monster's descendants subsequently to inch their way toward the nearest needle. As it turned out, when all the compensating evolution at other genetic loci had been completed, the body plan represented by that nearest needle eventually emerged as superior to the ancestral unsegmented body plan. The new local optimum, into whose vicinity the lineage wildly leapt, eventually turned out superior to the local optimum on which it had previously been trapped.

This is the kind of speculation in which we should indulge only as a last resort. The argument stands that only gradualistic, inch-by-inch walking through the genetic landscape is compatible with the sort of cumulative evolution that can build up complex and detailed adaptation. Even if segmentation, in our example, ended up as a superior body form, it began as a catastrophe that had to be weathered just like a climatic or volcanic catastrophe in the external environment. It was gradualistic, cumulative selection that engineered the step-by-step recovery from the segmentation catastrophe, just as it engineers recoveries from external climatic catastrophes. Segmentation, according to the speculation I have just given, survived not because natural selection favored it but because natural selection found compensatory ways of survival *in spite of it.* The fact that advantages in the segmented body plan eventually emerged is an irrelevant bonus. The segmented body plan was incorporated into evolution, but it may never have been favored by natural selection.

But in any case gradualism is only a part of core Darwinism. A belief in the ubiquity of gradualistic evolution does not necessarily commit us to Darwinian natural selection as the steering mechanism guiding the search through genetic space. It is highly probable that Kimura (1983) is right to insist that most of the evolutionary steps taken through genetic space are unsteered steps. To a large extent the trajectory of small, gradualistic steps actually taken may constitute a random walk rather than a walk guided by selection. But this is irrelevant if—for the reasons given above—our concern is with adaptive evolution as opposed to evolutionary change per se. Kimura himself rightly insists that his "neutral theory is not antagonistic to the cherished view that evolution of form and function is guided by Darwinian selection." Further, "the theory does not deny the role of natural selection in determining the course of adaptive evolution, but it assumes that only a minute fraction of DNA changes in evolution are adaptive in nature, while the great majority of phenotypically silent molecular substitutions exert no significant influence on survival and reproduction and drift randomly through the species'' (Kimura 1983, xi). The facts of adaptation compel us to the conclusion that evolutionary trajectories are not all random. There has to be some nonrandom guidance toward adaptive solutions because nonrandom is what adaptive solutions precisely are. Neither random walk nor random saltation can do the trick on its own. But does the guiding mechanism necessarily have to be the Darwinian one of nonrandom survival of random spontaneous variation? The obvious—only?—alternative class of theory postulates some form of nonrandom, i.e., directed, variation.

I tentatively suggest ''only'' because nonrandom, in this context, *means* directed toward adaptation. It does not mean causeless. Mutations are, of course, caused by physical events, for instance, cosmic ray bombardment. When we call them random, we mean only that they are random with respect to adaptive improvement (Dawkins 1986, 306–11). It could be said, therefore, that as a matter of logic, some kind of theory of directed variation is the only alternative to nonrandom selection as an explanation for adaptation. Obviously, combinations of the two kinds of theory are possible.

The theory nowadays attributed to Lamarck is typical of a theory of directed variation. This is normally expressed as two main principles. First, organisms improve during their own lifetime by means of the principle of use and disuse; muscles that are exercised as the animal strives for a particular kind of food enlarge, for instance, and the animal is consequently better equipped to procure that food in the future. Second, acquired characteristics—in this case acquired improvements due to use—are inherited, so as the generations go by, the lineage improves. Arguments offered against Lamarckian theories are usually factual. Acquired characteristics are not, as a matter of fact, inherited. The implication, often made explicit, is that if only they were inherited, Lamarckism would be a tenable theory of evolution. Mayr (1982), for instance, wrote, ''Accepting his premises, Lamarck's theory was as legitimate a theory of adaptation as that of Darwin. Unfortunately, these premises turned out to be invalid.'' Crick (1982) showed an awareness of the possibility that general, a priori arguments might be given, when he wrote, ''As far as I know, no one has given general theoretical reasons why such a mechanism must be less efficient than natural selection.''

I have since offered two such reasons, preceded by an argument that the inheritance of acquired characteristics is *in principle* incompatible with any system of embryology that is *epigenetic* rather than *preformationist.* I shall simply list these arguments briefly, since they have been spelled out elsewhere (see Dawkins 1982, 174–76; 1983; 1986, Chap. 11).

First, acquired improvements can in principle be inherited only in organisms whose embryology is preformationistic rather than epigenetic. Preformationistic embryology is blueprint embryology. The alternative is recipe, or computer-program, embryology. The important point about blueprint embryology is that it is in principle reversible. If you have a house, you can, by following simple rules, reconstruct its blueprint. But if you have a cake, there is no set of simple rules that enable you to reconstruct its recipe. All living things on this planet grow by recipe embryology, not blueprint embryology. The rules of development work only in the forward direction, like the rules in a recipe or computer program. They cannot be put into reverse. You cannot, by inspecting an animal, reconstruct its genes. Acquired characteristics are attributes of the animal. In order for them to be inherited, the animal must be scanned and its attributes reverse-transcribed into the genes. There may be planets whose animals develop by blueprint embryology. If so, acquired characteristics might there be inherited. This argument is not an argument against the possibility, in principle, of Lamarckian inheritance. It is an argument that ties Lamarckian inheritance to preformationistic embryology. It says that if you want to find a Lamarckian form of life, don't bother to look on any planet whose life forms develop by epigenesis rather than preformationism. I have an intuitive hunch that there may be a general, a priori argument against preformationistic, blueprint embryology, but I have not developed it yet.

Second, most acquired characteristics are not improvements. There is no general reason why they should be, and the principle of use and disuse does not really help here. Indeed, by analogy with wear and tear on machines, we might expect the principle of use and disuse to be positively counterproductive. This point has been noted before. If acquired characteristics were indiscriminately inherited, organisms would be walking museums of ancestral decrepitude, pock-marked from ancestral plagues, limping relics of ancestral misfortune. How is the organism supposed to "know" how to respond to the environment in such a way as to improve itself? If there is a minority of acquired characteristics that are improvements, the organism would have to have some way of selecting these to pass on to the next generation, avoiding the much more numerous acquired characteristics that are deleterious. Selecting, here, really means that some form of Darwinian process must be smuggled in. Lamarckism, I argue in the works referred to, cannot work unless it has a Darwinian underpinning.

Third, even if there were some means of choosing which acquired characteristics should be inherited, which discarded at the current generation, the principle of use and disuse is not powerful enough to fashion adaptations as subtle and intricate as we know them to be. A human eye, for instance, works well because of countless pernickety adjustments of detail. Natural selection can fine-tune these adjustments because any improvement, however slight and however deeply buried in internal architecture, can have a direct effect upon survival and reproduction. The principle of use and disuse, on the other hand, is in principle incapable of such fine-tuning. This is because it relies upon the coarse and crude rule that the more an animal uses a bit of itself, the bigger that bit ought to be. Such a rule might tune the blacksmith's arms to his trade, or the giraffe's neck to the tall trees. But it could hardly be responsible for improving the lucidity of a lens or the reaction time of an iris diaphragm. The correlation between use and size is too loose to be responsible for fine-grained adaptation. I argue that Darwinism relies upon a necessarily perfect correlation, the correlation between survival and survival.

I shall refer to these three arguments as the "Universal Darwinism" arguments. I am confident that they are arguments of the kind that Crick was calling for, although whether he or anyone else accepts these three particular arguments is another matter. If they are correct, the case for Darwinism, in its most general form, is enormously strengthened.

I have been made painfully aware that many biologists are hostile to what they call "armchair" arguments, lacking in empirical content. One critic has applied the epithet "philosophical," intending his biological readership to understand this as an insult. To be cynical, there may be those who are prepared to be impressed by armchair "philosophical" reasoning, but only if it is incomprehensible. Armchair arguments are certainly not valueless in themselves. We should scarcely attack Euclid because he did not sally forth with ruler and protractor to measure a statistical sample of triangular and circular objects in the field or the laboratory. There are three legitimate charges that might be leveled against a particular armchair argument: first, that it is wrong; second, that it is right but too obvious to need spelling out; third, that even if right and nonobvious, it is trivial and of no importance. I shall examine these three charges for the case of my Universal Darwinism arguments.

First, is any of them wrong? If so, I should like to hear about it. No refutation has so far been offered, in the literature, in personal communications to me, or in any of the many published reviews of the books in which they are summarized. The Universal Darwinism arguments may be philosophical and other terrible things, but nobody seems to have suggested that they are wrong.

Second, are the Universal Darwinism arguments correct but so obvious that they do not need spelling out? That this is not the case can be empirically demonstrated! You have only to survey human beliefs. The Universal Darwinism arguments, if valid, demonstrate that the Lamarckian theory of evolution, even if it were not ruled out by the facts, could not have any general importance. But among informed people today, a sizable minority will be found to espouse some form of Lamarckian theory. Until recently, a form of Lamarckian theory was state orthodoxy in the Soviet Union, and leading geneticists were imprisoned or exiled for refusing to accept it. If the Universal Darwinism arguments were all that obvious, this tragedy could hardly have happened.

Are they, then, correct and nonobvious but of trivial importance? One could say that this charge has already been answered by the previous paragraph, but let me offer another reply to it. If it could be shown that the Universal Darwinism arguments were "devoid of information content," I would have some sympathy with the attack. The information content of a statement, such as a scientific statement, can be measured as the reduction in prior uncertainty that it fosters (Shannon & Weaver 1949). If, before a piece of research is done, our ignorance allows us to entertain two equiprobable alternatives, and if the research then rules out one of these two prior possibilities, the research has contributed one bit of information to the store of human knowledge. How much prior uncertainty do the Universal Darwinism arguments reduce?

If we limit ourselves strictly and puritanically to empirical research, our uncertainty about life in the universe at large is, if not infinite, some positive function of the enormous number of other planets that exist. Armchair arguments, of the kind of which my own three Universal Darwinism arguments are tentative and preliminary specimens, are potentially capable of very substantial reductions in our prior uncertainty about life all over the universe. They do not require us actually to visit other planets or, indeed, to know any facts about them at all.

There is no need to feel affronted by this cavalier attitude to facts. If I say that Pythagoras's Theorem is as valid on all planets as it is on earth, you would hardly retort: "How do you know? Have you been to any other planets to see?" The Universal Darwinism arguments are not, of course, in the same class as Pythagoras's theorem. They do not add up to a deductive proof that all life, everywhere, has to have evolved by Darwinian means. They make the more modest though still substantial claim that, of all the theories that members of our species have ever proposed, core Darwinism is the only one that is *in principle* capable of solving that most difficult of problems posed by life anywhere in the universe, namely, the problem of the existence of adaptive complexity. If the Universal Darwinism arguments are valid, they add up to a substantial reduction in our prior uncertainty. This therefore constitutes a genuine finding with high information content. It actually tells us something important about the universe that we did not previously know. If that is not empirical research, it performs the same role as empirical research in building up our store of information about the universe.

I suspect that other armchair arguments about the nature of life all over the universe, more powerful and watertight than mine, are waiting to be discovered by those better equipped than I am to discover them. I hope that empirically minded, white-coated, or gum-booted biologists will not prejudice themselves out of the running. I, in turn, shall undertake not to forget that Darwin's own triumph, for all that it *could* have been launched from any armchair in the universe, was in fact the spin-off of a five-year circumnavigation of this particular planet.

Acknowledgments

I am grateful to Michael Robinson and Wilton Dillon for the invitation to participate in the second Man and Beast Symposium, and to Marian Dawkins, Helena Cronin, and Alan Grafen for criticizing the manuscript.

References

Crick, F. H. C. 1982. *Life Itself.* London: Macdonald.

Dawkins, R. 1982. *The Extended Phenotype.* San Francisco: W. H. Freeman (Oxford University Press paperback).

______. 1983. Universal Darwinism. In *Evolution from Molecules to Men,* ed. D. S. Bendall, 403–25. Cambridge: Cambridge University Press.

______. 1986. *The Blind Watchmaker.* New York: W. W. Norton.

Fisher, R. A. 1930. *The Genetical Theory of Natural Selection.* Oxford: Clarendon.

Kimura, M. 1983. *The Neutral Theory of Molecular Evolution.* Cambridge: Cambridge University Press.

Mayr, E. 1982. *The Growth of Biological Thought: Diversity, Evolution, and Inheritance.* Cambridge: Harvard University Press.

Shannon, C. E., and W. Weaver. 1949. *The Mathematical Theory of Communication.* Urbana: University of Illinois Press.

Singer, C. 1931. *A Short History of Biology.* Oxford: Clarendon.

Williams, G. C. 1966. *Adaptation and Natural Selection.* Princeton, N.J.: Princeton University Press.

Untying the Knot

Evolution of Early Human Behavior

Richard Potts

Studies of human origins which emanate from the behavioral and geological sciences seek to define the evolutionary trajectory that has made *Homo sapiens* unique. The paleontologist searching for fossil remains, the archeologist excavating stone artifacts, and the primatologist observing chimpanzees—all tend to converge upon a series of behaviors or factors generally construed to have been fundamental to this trajectory: bipedalism, stone technology, enlarged brains, culture and language, altricial birth, hunting, eating meat, home bases. Comparisons between modern humans and other primates help to define such elements which, by their presence in humans or by the degree to which they are present, reflect the uniqueness of *H. sapiens* in the zoological world. These elements are raw materials for the narrative of hominid evolution and define salient areas of debate within the field of human origins research.

Evolutionary studies, of course, emphasize not only derived or unique features of taxa but also the continuities, especially shared features which make bridgeable the apparent gaps between living species and make descent of species from common ancestors obvious to the evolutionary biologist. Traditionally, it is supposed that varied diets that include meat, the manufacture of tools, and a facility with language are distinctively human traits separating us from other species. However, research has clearly documented the omnivorous diets of many primates, tool-making activities in the wild by chimpanzees, and the ability of apes to manipulate symbols in the laboratory in possibly languagelike ways. This research emphasizes that all distinctively human traits are extensions of the behavioral capacities of other primates, and this is just one illustration that *H. sapiens* shares an evolutionary background with other mammals and most recently with the hominoid primates.

Still, consider language and how much the ability to manipulate symbols and to generate an infinite array of thoughts separates people from other primates. Or consider the fact that we humans demonstrate the capacity to congregate in groups over 100,000 strong to see conspecifics walk or dance bipedally down a pavement, or to yell emotionally at padded men crashing together with a combination of gracefulness and ferocity on a football field. The next time the reader finds himself as one in a long line of drivers confined to a steel-framed box waiting in a New York or Nairobi traffic jam, he might think of us as just hominids, individuals of a certain species of primate. Some of us never cease to be astonished, amused, and enlightened by that perspective.

Leaving aside such very recent manifestations of human behavior, the defining characteristics of our species (fig. 1) seem so extraordinary and so much a part of a distinctively human nature that there is a strong tendency to view most of them as an integrated package which arose a very long time ago. Indeed, most traditional renditions of human evolution recognize a common set of factors or causes woven together to explain how we became the way we are. These aspects of the explanation and narrative, by virtue of their presumed interdependence (traits had mutual influence on one another), have come to be viewed as an inseparable set of causes for human evolution. This set of elements—"the knot" as I refer to it here—has been ascribed to the earliest phases of hominid evolution in most previous scenarios. The origin of some of these traits (e.g., bipedalism) marked the split of the human lineage from that of the African apes. These initial traits quickly set into motion the conditions which favored other elements, as portrayed around the border of the knot represented in figure 2. The other traits were

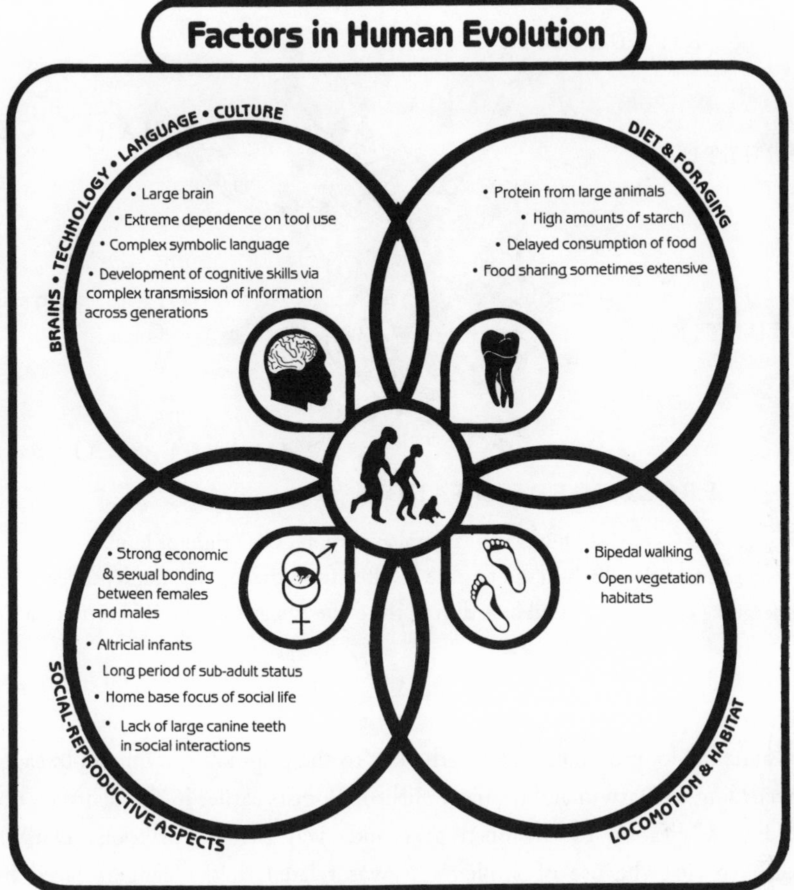
Factors in Human Evolution
BRAINS • TECHNOLOGY • LANGUAGE • CULTURE
• Large brain
• Extreme dependence on tool use
• Complex symbolic language
• Development of cognitive skills via complex transmission of information across generations
DIET & FORAGING
• Protein from large animals
• High amounts of starch
• Delayed consumption of food
• Food sharing sometimes extensive
• Strong economic & sexual bonding between females and males
• Altricial infants
• Long period of sub-adult status
• Home base focus of social life
• Lack of large canine teeth in social interactions
SOCIAL-REPRODUCTIVE ASPECTS
• Bipedal walking
• Open vegetation habitats
LOCOMOTION & HABITAT

Fig. 1. A list of major features which distinguish modern humans from our closest biological relatives. These elements emerged during human evolution.

added by natural selection to the repertoire of very early human ancestors. The origin of one trait provided the conditions for the selection of other traits, which in turn favored the evolution of still other elements. Due to this mutual dependence, these traits emerged together during the early phases of human biological history.

Darwin, in *The Descent of Man* (1871), speculated about this process. To Darwin, and to researchers since, one of the most significant shifts in human evolution was the fact that we left the trees. The shift from forest to open

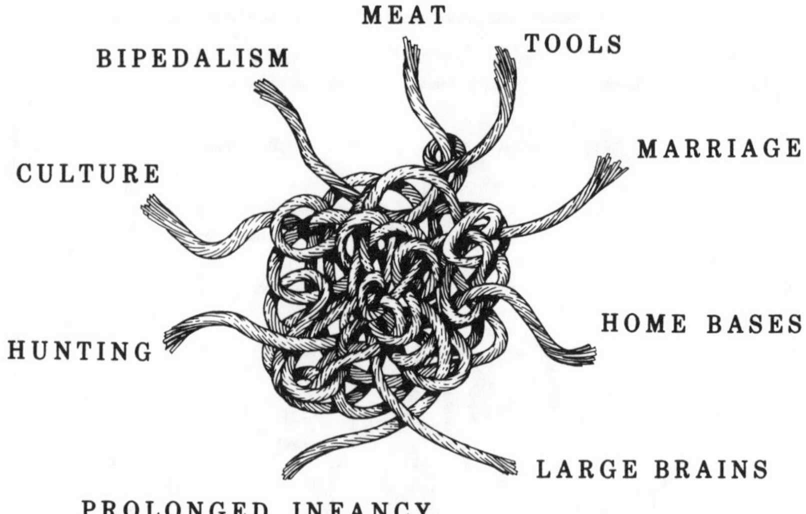

Fig. 2. The "knot" of human behavioral evolution. The origin of human characteristics is traditionally believed to have resulted from the highly interdependent emergence of the traits listed here during the earliest phases of hominid evolution.

savanna has long been considered the key to the origin of the human lineage. According to Darwin and to many anthropologists earlier in this century, the leading adaptation to the open grasslands was the use of tools. Darwin reasoned that the use of implements was related to the dangers faced by protohumans in the open savanna, particularly predators. Since tools required carrying, walking on only two legs was crucial in that it freed the hands. These two factors—tools and bipedal walking—are traditionally thought to be two prime movers in human evolution, and they touched off extraordinary changes in a wide variety of areas, including changes in diet and reduction in the size of the canine teeth (which were no longer used for defense because of tools). Bipedalism and tool use also set the stage for major shifts in social life and for enlargement of the brain. While Darwin mentioned these other factors, it has been left to anthropologists earlier in the century, especially in the 1950s and 1960s, to tie together all of these diverse elements of human evolution. Paleoanthropologists have often posited that these factors were strongly linked by positive feedback; i.e., they worked to reinforce one another and thus they evolved together. Some researchers lay emphasis on changes in hominid sociality; others have stressed the importance of hunting and eating meat. Nonetheless, in most scenarios the shift to open terrestrial habitats provided the initial situation requiring adaptation. The web of elements illustrated in figure 2 became, then, the answers that evolution provided. And thus we became human.

In orthodox interpretations not *all* of the elements in the knot are attributed to the earliest hominids, who existed at least 4 million years ago. Some of the elements typically are, such as bipedalism and prolonged infancy. Yet others—such as living at home bases, large brains, hunting, eating meat, and the regular manufacture of tools in standard, cultural patterns—are now generally ascribed to a later phase, coincident with the origin of *Homo* about 2.5 million years ago. Given this view, the knot (or perhaps two knots) of elements in human evolution implies several things. First, it implies that these basic features of humanity are at least 2 million years old. Second, they have undergone natural selection for lengthy periods of time; in other words, any genetic influences on these traits have been acted upon for millions of years. Finally, the early origin of these traits established a fundamentally human way of life; in the past 2–4 million years these traits have mainly been subject to fine tuning by natural selection and by cultural developments. Darwin suggested that the features which separated the human lineage from the apes' were critical in establishing not only a new lineage but also the behaviors that are most distinctively human. Anthropologists have tended to follow that lead. Thus, searching for traces of the earliest hominid has, erroneously I believe, become tantamount to seeking evidence for *the* fundamental transition in becoming human.

Untying the Knot

Over the past decade researchers who deal directly with the fossil record have begun to dissect this knot. Paleoanthropologists have taken hold of some of the threads in this tangle of elements and have followed them toward particular lines of paleontological and archeological evidence. As a result, many standard ideas about human evolution have been called into question. A new synthesis seems to be emerging, not just an ephemeral trend in interpretation. The remainder of this essay outlines new ideas and evidence pertaining to each of the elements denoted in figure 2.

Indeed, fossil footprints from Laetoli and several hundred fossil finds from Ethiopia and Tanzania demonstrate that two of the earliest innovations in hominid evolution were bipedal walking and the possession of small canines (i.e., less sexually dimorphic canines in males and females compared with those of apes). The Laetoli footprints record a moment in time in which hominids walked across the landscape (of at least equal symbolic significance to the footprints on the moon). The morphology of the pelvis, knee joint, foot, and vertebrae document that by 4 million years ago a new anatomy had been established in an ape. This anatomy reflected habitual locomotion on two legs, and that ape we traditionally separate from the other African apes by placing it in the taxonomic family called Hominidae.

Darwin and later anthropologists were remarkably insightful about the importance of changes in locomotion and canine size in the separation of hominids from other apes. Yet information about Miocene environments, 5–20 million years ago, and about the anatomy of the earliest hominid fossil samples, is beginning to provide new slants on old interpretations. About 20 million years ago climatic patterns began to shift in Africa, where hominid ancestors evidently thrived. Pronounced wet and dry seasons were established by the effect of the East African highlands on climatic belts. As a result, the expanse of forest did begin to break up, but by no means did it disappear. In fact, in areas where hominid fossils are found, there is evidence (fossil pollen, microfauna, and macrofauna) that only about 2.4 million years ago did major expanses of savanna grassland replace forest in East Africa. The traditional view that open grasslands quickly replaced forests does not appear now to be correct. In fact, it was never based on *data* about ancient environments; rather, in order to make hominids become bipedal, it simply made sense to assume that open terrain was the novel and dominant opportunity presented by changes during the Miocene. In contrast, a more favored reconstruction now places the earliest hominids in the proximity of trees used for foraging and shelter. Moreover, detailed studies of the limb bones of *Australopithecus afarensis* have shown definite signs that arboreality was not abandoned by hominids between 3 and 4 million years ago. Curvature of the hand and foot bones and certain details of the pelvis indeed do not contradict the fact that these hominids walked bipedally on the ground, but they also strongly suggest the agility of these hominids when in trees.

These findings about environmental settings and anatomy of the earliest hominids suggest that major anatomical characteristics which facilitate bipedalism originated before hominids had given up living and foraging in forests or woodlands. Accordingly, rather than an adaptation to living in open savannas (as has been the orthodox interpretation), bipedalism may now be viewed as initially a means to preserve a way of life in forests (Hill 1987). The change in habitat confronted by apes of the late Miocene, 5–10 million years ago, was that forest was becoming confined to patches, albeit probably quite large, which were farther apart from one another. To facilitate movement from one forested patch to another, bipedalism evidently was one of the experiments, and in the long run it thrived in at least one group of apes that tried it.

The idea that upright striding was one attempt to maintain a way of life in forested areas is an intriguing twist on the traditional view that bipedalism was a response specifically to living exclusively in open terrain. This new interpretation awaits testing with additional data about ancient vegetation patterns and analyses of fossil skeletal material. Nonetheless, it illustrates revised ways of thinking suggested recently by information from the fossil record. It strongly implies that modern-type bipedalism did not evolve full-blown with the first hominids but may have originated over several periods of change during hominid evolution. Based on skeletal fragments attributed to *H. habilis* from Olduvai, changes in locomotor anatomy may have occurred between 1.8 and 1.6 million years ago (Johanson *et al.* 1987; Susman and Stern 1982). Trinkaus (1984) posits that important modifications in hominid anatomy with locomotion and energetics occurred as late as the Upper Pleistocene, 60,000–40,000 years ago. In light of a nearly complete pelvis of a Neanderthal recently found at Kabara, Israel, biomechanical studies of Neanderthal pelvic remains further suggest that the bipedal locomotion of archaic hominids of the genus *Homo* was not precisely the same as that of humans today (Rak & Arensburg 1987). It now seems apparent that the original development of habitual bipedalism, regular habitation of open savannas, and the evolution of anatomically modern bipedalism were significantly separated from one another in hominid evolution.

One of the most significant shifts in thinking about early hominids concerns developmental rates. Hominid infants are born in an altricial state, at an earlier phase of skeletal and neurological development than are the infants of chimpanzees or gorillas. Altricial birth is a result, at least in part, of the large size of human crania; if infants were born at a developmental stage equivalent to that of apes, the human infant's cranium would never be able to pass through the birth canal. Furthermore, the period of human infant and childhood maturation is longer in absolute number of years than it is in the apes or other primates. Delayed maturation, or slower rate of development relative to that in apes, thus characterizes humans.

According to traditional interpretations, the change from an ape-like to a human pattern of development occurred very early in human evolution. The view that *Australopithecus* had essentially a humanlike rate of maturation is noted in most textbooks, suggesting that many of the important changes in human origins had already occurred in the earliest hominids. Scenarios of human evolution consistently link delayed maturation rates of infants with hominid social strategies, especially dependence on cultural learning, the need for other nurturing adults in addition to the mother, and the unusual degree of economic bonding typically seen in humans. A study by Mann (1975), which concluded that australopithecines show a modern human pattern of dental eruption, has played a crucial role in attributing these characteristics to the earliest hominids.

However, an array of new studies indicates that hominids prior to *Homo erectus* (1.6 million years ago) had dental maturation rates like those of apes, not humans. Although there is still debate on this matter (Mann *et al.* 1987), the evidence from dental eruption sequence and rates of formation of teeth now strongly suggests that somatic development in early hominids, possibly including early members of *Homo,* was more rapid than in people today and more like that seen in apes (Bromage & Dean 1985; Smith 1986; Beynon & Wood 1987; Conroy & Vannier 1987; Bromage 1987). Moreover, an independent study of the pelvis of *A. afarensis* (exhibited by "Lucy") indicates that few of the changes in the female pelvic canal associated with birth of altricial infants had occurred by 3 million years ago (Tague & Lovejoy 1986).

This suggests that the changes in developmental timing responsible for the altricial state of human neonates had not evolved as early as *A. afarensis.* Together, these recent analyses of hominid fossil material indicate that altricial birth and a human pattern of infant development originated later than previously believed, possibly less than 2 million years ago. The exact timing of these changes is still speculative, and they may not have occurred all at once.

Manufacture of tools

The earliest evidence for the manufacture of stone tools is 2.5 million years old. Unfortunately, tools made of materials such as wood are unlikely to be preserved; thus, it is uncertain whether the earliest bipeds consistently used perishable tools. With respect to implements of stone, patterns of technology 2 million years ago were simple and idiosyncratic, largely involving the production of sharp-edged flakes and cores by stone-on-stone percussion (Toth 1985; Potts 1988). If, by 2 million years ago, hominids did make use of stone tools on a regular basis, they left no evidence of any effort to improve or simply to change this basic stone technology over hundreds of thousands of years (Leakey 1971).

Brain size

By two million years ago hominid brain size had significantly expanded (and is one of the characteristics of *Homo*). Brain size increase is not confined to this period of hominid evolution but continues throughout the last 2 million years of hominid evolution. Clearly, major changes in hominid adaptation were occurring between 2.5 and 2.0 million years ago: the earliest stone tools and the origin of a large-brain *Homo* approximately coincided, if indeed *Homo* extends back to nearly 2.5 million years ago. The association of *Homo* with stone tools has been assumed for a long time (e.g., Leakey *et al.* 1964), and this association has suggested an intimate connection between stone technology, brain size, and overall mental function in our hominid ancestors (Gowlett 1984). However, during the next 2 million years, brain size continued to increase while stone tool technology changed very little. A few new implement types (e.g., stone hand axes) were added to the tool kits. Yet during long stretches of the Pleistocene, no directional change can be seen in stone technology despite the fact that brains get larger. Brain size in the earliest specimens of *H. erectus,* for example, is approximately 25% smaller than brain size 1.2 million years later among the latest specimens of this species; yet during this same period of time, stone tool kits, spread over three continents, were extremely homogeneous, dominated either by hand axes or by small cores and flakes. Consequently, the assumption that brain size and stone tool technology are tightly coupled may have to be reconsidered. The implications of the slow pace of change in lithic technology are further addressed below.

Home bases

Perhaps the most detailed scenario of early human adaptation to derive from the study of archeological sites is the home base interpretation. This idea maintains that by 2 million years ago, hominids possessed the basic socioecological characteristics of hunter-gatherers, especially the transport of food to a home base where food was processed and which also served as the spatial focus of social life. Hunter-gatherers today organize their social and foraging activities around a home base, the location of which shifts from time to time. The home base, or campsite, represents a safe refuge where the young and also sick and elderly individuals can reside. It is also the place to which food is returned for sharing and where other social functions take place. Economic interdependence among adults, especially the division of labor into hunting (mainly by men) and gathering (mainly by women), has also played a significant role in the concept of the home base and its application to early hominid sites. Economic interdependence between men and women characterizes marriage and distinguishes the human reproductive bond from that in the great apes and from the sort of pair-bonding which occurs in many species of primates and other mammals. Hence, home bases, division of labor, and marriage have typically been considered a related package.

Archeological sites 2 million years old and older have long been believed to show that hominids by this time were organized socially in this same manner. This widespread view has helped to propagate the idea that the basic elements of a hunter-gatherer way of life have existed for a long time without much change. Due to the hominids' long period of natural selection as tropical hunter-gatherers, human sociality and anatomical, physiological, mental, and emotional makeup have been shaped by the hunter-gatherer way of life (e.g., Washburn & Lancaster 1968).

However, the home base interpretation of early archeological sites, which has been used to support the hunter-gatherer scenario, has recently met extreme criticism from a number of studies. The best evidence for Plio-Pleistocene home bases was believed to derive from the sites in Olduvai Gorge, 1.85–1.70 million years old. The author's own study of these sites indeed began with the assumption that they were hominid campsites but, ultimately, produced evidence in conflict with the home base interpretation (Potts 1984, 1988). In brief, evidence of bone damage and of the ecological context of these archeological sites indicates that both hominids and large Carnivora were attracted to the same specific places on the ancient Olduvai landscape.

An important change in hominid foraging had occurred by this time which involved the seeking of meat from large animals. At Olduvai there is evidence of hominid tool marks and carnivore damage to the bone remains excavated from archeological sites, and both hominid- and carnivore-made bone accumulations are evident. The bones recovered from these sites show not only that hominids and large carnivores overlapped considerably in the kinds of meaty parts they processed for food, but they also overlapped in use of the same sites and the same animal carcasses. This overlap in the activities of hominids and carnivores suggests that the sites of animal bone (and stone tool) accumulation at Olduvai did not serve as safe refuges or as the primary foci of hominid social life. These sites certainly were places to which hominids brought parts of animals to process with stone tools, but there is no hint of the functions (e.g., safe refuge) which are fundamental to the home bases of modern humans. The recent critique of the home base interpretation of Olduvai implies that only later in time did an ecological separation between hominids and carnivores occur which allowed hominids to create safe home bases, i.e., to organize their social life around the primary spots to which animal bones and stone tools were brought. Recent field research in southern

Kenya suggests that such an ecological separation occurred by about 700,000, at least in eastern Africa (Potts 1988).

Hunting and eating meat

A second important issue concerning early hominid hunter-gatherers concerns whether the tool makers were, in fact, hunters. Did hominids two million years ago obtain carcasses of antelopes and other large mammals primarily by hunting? An affirmative answer to this question has been widely held, propounded in the popular literature, for example, by Ardrey (1961, 1976). Ardrey maintained that humans owe their uniqueness in the primate world to an evolutionary history of hunting and use of weapons stretching back at least 3 million years.

Over the past decade extensive research has been carried out on this issue, focusing on the fossilized animal remains excavated from early archeological sites such as those at Olduvai (e.g., Binford 1981; Bunn & Kroll 1986; Potts 1984; Shipman 1987). Among those who have studied the fossil remains a consensus is emerging that scavenging of dead animals was an important means by which hominids obtained meat and marrow. This inference does not mean that hunting was never practiced. Nonetheless, on the basis of archeological evidence, it appears possible to rule out behavioral specialization for hunting for most of the Pleistocene (see Tooby & DeVore [1987] for a dissenting opinion based on theoretical supposition). The earliest clear evidence for systematic hunting of a single species does not occur before about 100,000 years ago in southern Africa (Klein 1984) and perhaps not before the Upper Paleolithic in Europe (after 30,000 years ago). While there is some evidence that opportunistic hunting of animals occurred before this time, the potential for exclusive reliance on hunting, as opposed to scavenging, for animal protein now appears to have arisen later than originally supposed, almost certainly after 1.5 million years ago.

Ideas about the primacy of hunting in the evolution of humans have also stressed the importance of meat in the early hominid diet. The presence of tool cut marks on animal bones from 2-million-year-old sites is clear evidence that hominids had access to meat (Potts & Shipman 1981; Bunn 1981). The assumption has been that the large clusters of bones at these sites were accumulated in a brief period of time, analogous to the seasonal occupations of hunter-gatherers at campsites. If that had been the case during the Plio-Pleistocene, meat indeed formed a major component in the diet of these hominids. One recent insight into this issue is provided by the evidence of weathering of animal bones, which under certain stratigraphic contexts helps to measure the time over which bones were brought to sites and left exposed to the air. As a bone sits out on the landscape, it develops cracks and begins to peel in a characteristic set of stages (Behrensmeyer 1978). This information has recently been applied to fossil bone assemblages at Olduvai and shows that animals bones were introduced to these sites over a period of at least 5–10 years (Potts 1986). There is no doubt that hominids 2 million years ago occasionally sought meat from large animals; an important shift in foraging and diet had occurred by this time. However, the evidence of bone weathering and the fact that both hominids and carnivores fed off the animal bones at these early archeological sites means that we can no longer assume that hominids sought and consumed meat at a rate comparable to modern hunter-gatherers (typically 20%–40% of the diet by weight of tropical foragers). Methods have yet to be developed to estimate the significance of meat in the diets of Plio-Pleistocene tool makers.

Culture and language

It has been commonplace for anthropologists to equate the making of tools with culture, nongenetic transmission of information from generation to generation. Some anthropologists have claimed that the mere existence of flaked stone tools means that *language* had existed at least 2–2.5 million years ago. Yet, as remarked recently by J. Desmond Clark, a distinguished professor of African archeology, if the stone tools tell us that hominids had language during the early Pleistocene, those hominids must have been saying the same things over and over again for a very long time. As noted above, stone tool assemblages prior to the Upper Paleolithic were quite homogeneous and exhibited slow rates of change (often no clear directional development over vast periods). Stability and uniformity in stone tool shape over time and space characterized 99% of the Paleolithic.

In contrast, after about 100,000 years ago in southern Africa and about

30,000 years ago in Europe, tool kits become typified by striking heterogeneity in time and space. Innovations in stone and bone technology are associated with the first clear expressions of symbolic representation on preservable objects (e.g., cave paintings and mobile sculptures). Most such examples date back to about 20,000 years before the present. The archeological record of this period, the Upper Paleolithic, is consistent with modern cultural transmission, in which behavior is compartmentalized into distinctive cultures, and preservable technology tends to vary spatially and is susceptible to rapid innovation. The division of human behavior, at least styles of tool production, into distinctive and discrete units is evident during the Upper Paleolithic. Prior to 100,000 years ago, the lack of diversity in tool kits and in the nature of archeological sites seems to reflect the lack of processes of innovation that characterize culture in the modern sense of the term (Conkey 1978; White 1982; Chase & Dibble 1987).

This evidence contrasts with the long-held assumption that once tools appear in the prehistoric record, culture with many or all of the basic elements of modern human transmission of information (e.g., language) also appears. As is clearly the theme of these new studies I have summarized, important behaviors associated with modern humans—in this case, capacities for generating enormous behavioral variation—do not seem to have arisen until much later in the time scale of human evolution than originally believed.

New approaches to the archeological and fossil record suggest that significant shifts in human behavior and way of life occurred in a mosaic fashion over the past 4 million years, not all at once and probably not confined to the first half of human evolution. By dissecting the tangle of elements and causes typically considered in the investigation of hominid evolution, it is evident that several sets of features once believed to be highly interdependent now have to be decoupled. The development of systematic hunting and of tool making, for example, do not appear to coincide. Bipedalism, on the one hand, and delayed infant maturation or hunting, on the other, similarly must be disassociated from one another. Eating meat and the existence of home bases may also have to be separated even though a decade ago these two aspects of early hominid adaptation were viewed to be intimately related (Isaac 1978). Tool manufacture and innovations characteristic of modern culture must also be decoupled. Many of these features arose later in the evolutionary history of humans than originally assumed. Most of the ideas noted here require further tests against fossil evidence, and much more work needs to be pursued in dating the appearance of these various components of the human evolutionary story. Nonetheless, evidence is mounting rapidly that significant shifts involving the diverse elements portrayed in Figure 2 were spaced over much of the time scale of human prehistory.

Several implications need to be considered. First, as noted earlier, several influential views of human nature are founded on the idea that selection has had a long period of time to act on fundamental aspects of human behavior. That is, certain characteristics of human behavior, such as the universal elements considered in this essay, are deemed to be deeply imbedded or inherent by virtue of having undergone millions of years of natural selection. The hunting hypothesis mentioned earlier and the idea that we have spent 99% of the past 2.5 million years living as hunter-gatherers are examples of this particular view (e.g., Lee & DeVore 1968; Ardrey 1976). In contrast to this outlook on human nature and evolution, recent scrutiny of the various causal threads and events of hominid evolution documents that salient elements of human behavior entered considerably later into our evolutionary history than previously assumed. The late-appearing elements in hominid evolution are not necessarily any less distinctive or characteristic of people today. However, the view that distinctive features of human life are biologically inevitable by virtue of millions of years of selection will have to be abandoned.*

---

*Recent paleontological and molecular genetic evidence is relevant to this point. Such evidence suggests that major anatomical and genetic transitions took place in a confined population within the last 100,000–300,000 years. Late Pleistocene fossil hominids from southern and eastern Africa currently represent the oldest *Homo sapiens* that possess a modern morphology. An increasing number of paleontologists see sub-Saharan Africa as the region where modern humans evolved (e.g., Brauer 1984; Rightmire 1984; Stringer and Andrews 1988). According to this view, fully modern skeletal morphology and presumably the genetic bases for other characteristics dispersed from Africa over the Old World during the past 100,000 years. Moreover, genetic comparisons of populations over the world suggest that the mitochondrial DNA found in all modern humans derives from a dramatic population bottleneck within the past 300,000 years and that this event probably took place in sub-Saharan Africa (Cann *et al.* 1987). While not all researchers agree with these findings, these new interpretations do suggest that rapid genetic changes in behavioral capacities (and their rapid spread) could have occurred quite late in human evolution. In other words, we cannot automatically assume that behaviors (social, foraging, etc.) that are specific to or universal among *H. sapiens* today reflect the behaviors of the earliest hominids or early *Homo*.

Moreover, the presumed functional interdependence among the critical elements of human evolution ("the knot") needs serious reconsideration. Strong feedback relationships among these elements implied that human characteristics originated from a highly integrated, continuous regime of natural selection. The various parts of the whole of human adaptation fit together by virtue of having emerged together, or at least in an intimate succession of innovations in which the emergence of one element immediately set the conditions for the evolution of others. Now, however, we need to envision a mosaic pattern of behavioral change in which the elements are not functionally interrelated to the degree construed by the traditional feedback scenario of human evolution. High levels of selection for the biological bases of certain traits (e.g., delayed maturation, language) may have taken place quite independently of one another (in different time periods, under different environmental constraints and selection regimes), especially independently of traits honed by natural selection at an earlier time (e.g., bipedalism). Unless stabilizing selection acted stringently, variations in earlier evolved traits (e.g., in bipedal locomotor anatomy) may have persisted ("hitchhiked") due to a spurious association with independent variations (e.g., slower maturation rates) that apparently met with intense periods of selection later in time.

Finally, the approaches to the fossil record outlined in this essay are relatively new in the study of human ancestry. Undoubtedly, they are less well known than the discovery of hominid fossils and the consequent debates about family trees, which enjoy an enormous following. Nonetheless, studies that focus on the behavior, ecology, and developmental characteristics of hominids—and the debates they, too, engender—are certainly no less important. The emergence of human characteristics over the entire time scale of hominid evolution implies that the earliest hominid no longer represents the one main event in the origin of humans, as it traditionally has, at least in the popular imagination. Rather, traces of the events and processes involved in becoming human span the entire fossil history of hominids. Those events at the end of this history are no less fundamental than those at the beginning. This realization undoubtedly will continue to revolutionize the study of human origins.

References

Ardrey, R. 1961. *African Genesis.* New York: Dell.

______. 1976. *The Hunting Hypothesis.* New York: Bantam.

Behrensmeyer, A. K. 1978. Taphonomic and Ecologic Information from Bone Weathering. *Paleobiology* 2:150–62.

Beynon, A. D., and B. A. Wood. 1987. Pattern and Rates of Enamel Growth in Molar Teeth of Early Hominids. *Nature* 326:493–96.

Binford, L. R. 1981. *Bones: Ancient Men and Modern Myths.* New York: Academic.

Brauer, G. 1984. A Craniological Approach to the Origin of Anatomically Modern *Homo sapiens* in Africa and Implications for the Appearance of Modern Europeans. In *The Origins of Modern Humans,* ed. F. H. Smith and F. Spencer, 327–410. New York: Alan R. Liss.

Bromage, T. G. 1987. The Biological and Chronological Maturation of Early Hominids. *Journal of Human Evolution* 16:257–72.

Bromage, T. G., and M. C. Dean. 1985. Re-evaluation of the Age of Death of Immature Fossil Hominids. *Nature* 317:525–27.

Bunn, H. T. 1981. Archaeological Evidence for Meat-Eating by Plio-Pleistocene Hominids from Koobi Fora and Olduvai Gorge. *Nature* 291:574–77.

Bunn, H. T., and E. M. Kroll. 1986. Systematic Butchery by Plio-Pleistocene Hominids at Olduvai Gorge, Tanzania. *Current Anthropology* 27:431–52.

Cann, R. L., M. Stoneking, and A. C. Wilson. 1987. Mitochondrial DNA and Human Evolution. *Nature* 325:31–36.

Chase, P. G., and H. L. Dibble. 1987. Middle Paleolithic Symbolism: A Review of Current Evidence and Interpretations. *Journal of Anthropological Archaeology* 6:263–96.

Conkey, M. W. 1978. Style and Information in Cultural Evolution. In *Social Archaeology,* ed. C. L. Redman et al., 61–85. New York: Academic.

Conroy, G. C., and M. W. Vannier. 1987. Dental Development of the Taung Skull from Computerized Tomography. *Nature* 329:625–27.

Darwin, C. 1871. *The Descent of Man.* New York: Modern Library.

Gowlett, J. 1984. Mental Abilities of Early Man. In *Hominid Evolution and Community Ecology,* ed. R. Foley, 167–92. London: Academic.

Hill, A. 1987. Causes of Perceived Faunal Change in the Later Neogene of East Africa. *Journal of Human Evolution* 16:583–96.

Isaac, G. L. 1978. The Food-Sharing Behavior of Protohuman Hominids. *Scientific American* 238:90–108.

Johanson, D. C., et al. 1987. New Partial Skeleton of *Homo habilis* from Olduvai Gorge, Tanzania. *Nature* 327:205–9.

Klein, R. G. 1984. Mammalian Extinctions and Stone Age People in Africa. In *Quaternary Extinctions,* ed. P. S. Martin and R. G. Klein, 553–73. Tucson: University of Arizona Press.

Leakey, L. S. B., P. Tobias, J. Napier. 1964. A New Species of the Genus *Homo* from Olduvai Gorge. *Nature* 202:7–9.

Leakey, M. D. 1971. *Olduvai Gorge,* vol. 3. Cambridge: Cambridge University Press.

Lee, R. B., and I. DeVore, eds. 1968. *Man the Hunter.* Chicago: Aldine.

Mann, A. 1975. *Paleodemographic Aspects of the South African Australopithecines.* University of Pennsylvania Publication in Anthropology, no. 1. Philadelphia.

Mann, A., M. Lampl, and J. Monge. 1987. Maturational Patterns in Early Hominids. *Nature* 328:673–74.

Potts, R. 1984. Home Bases and Early Hominids. *American Scientist* 72:338–47.

______. 1986. Temporal Span of Bone Accumulations at Olduvai Gorge and Implications for Early Hominid Foraging Behavior. *Paleobiology* 12:25–31.

______. 1988. *Early Hominid Activities at Olduvai.* Hawthorne, N.Y.: Aldine.

Potts, R., and P. Shipman. 1981. Cutmarks Made by Stone Tools on Bones from Olduvai Gorge, Tanzania. *Nature* 291:577–80.

Rak, Y., and B. Arensburg. 1987. Kebara 2 Neanderthal Pelvis: First Look at a Complete Inlet. *American Journal of Physical Anthropology* 73:227–32.

Rightmire, G. P. 1984. *Homo sapiens* in Sub-Saharan Africa. In *The Origins of Modern Humans,* ed. F. H. Smith and F. Spencer, 295–325. New York: Alan R. Liss.

Shipman, P. 1987. Studies of Hominid-Faunal Interaction at Olduvai Gorge. *Journal of Human Evolution* 15:691–706.

Smith, B. H. 1986. Dental Development in *Australopithecus* and Early *Homo. Nature* 323:327–30.

Stringer, C. B., and P. Andrews. 1988. Genetic and Fossil Evidence for the Origin of Modern Humans. *Science* 239:1263–68.

Susman, R., and J. Stern. 1982. Functional Morphology of *Homo habilis. Science* 217:931–33.

Tague, R. G., and C. O. Lovejoy. 1986. The Obstetric Pelvis of A. L. 288-1 (Lucy). *Journal of Human Evolution* 15:237–55.

Tooby, J., and I. DeVore. 1987. The Reconstruction of Hominid Behavioral Evolution through Strategic Modeling. In *The Evolution of Human Behavior: Primate Models,* ed. W. G. Kinzey, 183–237. Albany: State University of New York Press.

Toth, N. 1985. The Oldowan Reassessed: A Close Look at Early Stone Tools. *Journal of Archaeological Science* 12:101–20.

Trinkaus, E. 1984. Western Asia. In *The Origin of Modern Humans,* ed. F. H. Smith and F. Spencer, 251–93. New York: Alan R. Liss.

Washburn, S. L., and C. S. Lancaster. 1968. The Evolution of Hunting. In *Man the Hunter,* ed. R. B. Lee and I. DeVore, 293–303. Chicago: Aldine.

White, R. 1982. Rethinking the Middle/Upper Paleolithic Transition. *Current Anthropology* 23:169–92.

Biochemical Insights into Our Ancestry

Sherwood L. Washburn

Human beings and other animals have been intensively studied for so many years that it may come as a surprise to many that there has been major progress in the last few years. Wilton S. Dillon wrote of the "wide net" that the organizers had used to catch the scientists who might help us to understand the changes and their implications. He wrote that "unanimity is not useful in the building of new knowledge or reaffirming the old."

Unanimity has surely not been a hallmark of studies on human evolution. Even among scientists there has been no agreement on which primates are our closest relatives or on the causes and implications of human evolution. Bowler (1986) has given an excellent review of many of the theories, and one is left with a strong feeling that emotional debate has been more characteristic of human comparative studies than any general unanimity. It is particularly in the interpretation of behavior that many disagreements arise, and this may be why lively discussions played so large a part in the Smithsonian symposia.

But the discussions of today have very different characteristics from those of a few years ago. In the 1920s and early 1930s theories centered on how long the human lineage had been separate from that of other primates. Were our closest relatives prosimians, primitive monkeys, or apes? Was the time of separation the Oligocene, Early Miocene, or some much later date? The commonest point of view was a separation of at least 20 million years. In terms of behavior, particularly social behaviors, the main point of interest in the Smithsonian symposia, this meant that humans were unique and no close approximation to any other primates was to be expected. Granted millions of years of separation and remarkably few fossils (compared to baboons, for example), perhaps we should wonder that such definite conclusions were drawn on the relations and the behaviors of our ancestors.

The problems of interpreting human evolution were well stated by William L. Straus (1949, in Howells 1962), who concluded that the line leading to humans became independent at a relatively early date, no later than the end of the Oligocene, and that humans had never passed through an ape-like stage as suggested by Huxley, Keith, and Gregory.

I call particular attention to this paper by Straus because it is a useful summary of a long stage in the study of human evolution and because the anatomical facts set forth (pp. 83–94) are used to prove that humans are generalized and not ape-like. Most references on human evolution either give the author's opinion or a very limited set of facts. Straus gives enough detail so that the reader can see the way the comparative information was ordered and how it was related to the various theories.

His conclusions that humans had never passed through an ancestral stage which might be called ape-like seemed inescapable. Yet in 1984 Sibley and Ahlquist published a major paper based on DNA hybridization showing that the order of the relations of human beings to other primates is: chimpanzee, gorilla, orangutan, and gibbon. The African apes are very close to humans, and the Asiatic apes are more substantially removed. The monkeys are much less closely related. The order of the relationships and the distance correspond very closely to the conclusions of Goodman (1967), Wilson (1969), and Sarich (1969, 1971), using immunological methods which have been available for many years.

The new molecular methods show that some of the anatomists had been right in their assessment of relations, but many others were not, as so clearly

Distances from Humans by DNA Hybridization

Humans to:	Chimpanzees	Gorillas	Orangutans	Gibbons	Monkeys
Distance:	1.8	2.4	3.6	5.2	7.7
Millions of years:	4	5	10	12	20

Source: DNA information from Sibley and Ahlquist (1984).
Note: Estimates of millions of years are the shortest probable estimates from a variety of sources.

argued by Straus. The difference between the molecular methods and the traditional anatomical ones is that the molecular methods offer quantitative proof which remains the same no matter who performs the test or in which laboratory it is performed. The anatomical comparisons failed to provide convincing proof of any particular theory, and although I happen to think that Gregory (1934) was correct, he did not succeed in convincing many highly informed scientists. It was not that particular scientists were right or wrong, but the methods of anatomy were unable to settle the issues.

It should be stressed that an enormous intellectual effort went into the attempt to determine human relations. For more than 100 years classification was the major topic in biology, and the study of human beings was only a single case in an anatomically ordered biology. The central issue was such that biology could not make the sort of decisions that scientists relied on. What was needed were methods which could check the anatomical conclusions, showing which were useful and which were not. Molecular biology has provided such controls. The information given in the preceding table is of an entirely different order than the opinions of scientists, no matter how knowledgeable they may have been.

The same basic confusions were encountered in the estimates of how long human beings had been separate from other kinds of primates. In 1900 the whole age of the earth was estimated at less than 100 million years, and the age of the mammals at only 3 million years. It was only after the discovery of radioactivity and its use in determining the dates of geologic ages that evolution could be put in a useful relationship to time. It is easy to forget that the principal theories of human evolution *all* had their origins before the radioactive methods of dating. For example, Keith (1931), in a widely used diagram, estimated the whole age of the mammals at a little over 2 million years—or about the same as the present estimate of the age of Bed 1, Olduvai.

Just as the molecular methods replace traditional anatomy, so a number of new methods replace the estimates of time based on traditional geology. Carbon 14 analysis has revolutionized archeology, and potassium argon and time scales based on magnetic reversals have been particularly useful in estimating time in the Miocene and Pliocene. As in the case of anatomy, it is not that the scientists were wrong, but that there were no adequate methods. Keith's dates were reasonable, but they were shown to be wrong by the advances in geological methods.

It has taken both the development of radioactive time scales and molecular biology to give an adequate framework for human evolution. There has been a strong tendency in our culture to place blame on individuals. For example, was Dart wrong in 1924? Or was Leakey wrong in 1934? The issue is not the changes in personal opinions, but in the methods which produced the recent dates. We can now say that humans were bipedal at 3.5 million years because of the fossil footprints discovered by Mary Leakey and co-workers and because of the potassium argon dates (Curtis 1981).

Perhaps no change signals the modern world more clearly than plate tectonics. At one time everyone "knew" that continents could not drift, that they were in fixed positions, and Wegener was ridiculed. But modern methods showed that he was right. Africa and South America were not as far apart as had been thought. Perhaps the molecules were right in suggesting that African and South American monkeys were not so far apart either.

It is not only creationism which is wrong. The science of only a few years ago is almost equally misleading. The new techniques suggest new interpretations of the fossil record. Is adaptation as dominant as was thought only a few years ago? How important is the neutral theory? Issues such as this will not be settled by individuals but by technical advance. Is biological evolution gradual, punctate, or both? It is not a question of who is right or wrong, but what are the critical methods? What questions will help us to build toward the future?

The comparisons of human beings to other animals now take place in an intellectual world which is radically different from the world of Keith, Straus, or Hooton. For example, one of the widely accepted theories of human evolution was that *Homo sapiens,* anatomically like us, was very ancient. This theory was reasonable when the age of the mammals was estimated at 3 million years, but it became increasingly unreasonable with the discovery of the new methods of measuring time and relationships. It should be remembered that the key "fossils" supporting the theory were the Galley Hill skeleton, London skull, and Piltdown (a burial, a mistake, and a fake). Yet the theory is still alive today. And the reliance by some scientists on anatomical comparisons is unshaken by the molecular evidence which shows that they are frequently wrong.

I think that the molecular methods have settled the problem of which primates are most closely related to human beings. But we must remember Dillon's remark that "uniformity" is not necessarily useful. It has taken many years for the molecular methods to be accepted (Sarich 1983), and even now, acceptance is by no means universal.

The essential point is that techniques derived from molecular biology (DNA hybridization, immunology, sequence of amino acids in proteins, electrophoresis) give objective, quantitative answers, and anatomy does not. The difference between the answers from molecular biology and those from anatomy may be made clear by an example. It has long been recognized that the anatomy of the human arms and trunk is very similar to those of the apes (pongids). The similarity is shown in the general proportions and in much greater detail in the sternum, sterno-clavicular joint, shoulder, elbow, forearm, and wrist. The similarity is so great that it has been very difficult to see how anyone could think that all these similarities were due to parallel evolution. Yet the possibility of an ape-like origin of human beings has been specifically and repeatedly denied. And it has been claimed that the evolutionary line leading to humans "must" have separated from that of the apes in the Oligocene, well before that leading to the gibbons.

I am not concerned here with summarizing all the numerous arguments for regarding humans as primitive with a very long ancestry separate from other primates. This point has been made on the basis of an enormous amount of anatomy and the investment of many scientific lifetimes. All this vast amount of research was not as useful as the molecular biology of the last few years. A molecular biochemist in a few afternoons can provide solutions to the problems of human ancestry which are more likely to be correct and useful than all the studies of comparative anatomy.

The molecular methods give us the classification—what is closest to what. They do not tell us about the behaviors of the ancestral form. The solutions of the problems listed by Wilton S. Dillon on page 7 of his introduction to the Man and Beast Revisited symposium program (bipedalism, language, brain, cooperation, fighting . . .) do not stem automatically from classification. Much of the understanding of the human past is locked in the fossil record and in the behaviors of contemporary primates. If molecular biology had been discovered before anatomy, it would have prevented the waste of time, and it might have increased our desire to understand behavior and the events of human evolution. The danger now is that biochemical sophistication may replace anatomy to such a point that little effort will be made to understand the evolutionary events, the behaviors which determined success or failure.

How molecular biology and anatomy supplement each other can be demonstrated by looking at human hands, which have been regarded as primitive (generalized) or specialized (Napier 1970). The long flexor muscle of the thumb is always large in human beings but is small or absent in more than half of chimpanzees, three-fourths of gorillas, and nine-tenths of orangutans (Straus 1949, in Howells 1962). No simple conclusion can be drawn from this information, but DNA analysis shows that chimpanzee and human are the closest.

The long flexor muscle of the thumb is not only always present in human beings but is large and powerful. Many human males can grip more than 60 kilos, and females about half that. There is no suggestion that strength of this order is necessary for picking up seeds or other small objects. Tanner (1964, 328) suggests that the male is adapted to hunting, fighting, and manipulating heavy objects. In spite of the close similarity of human and chimpanzee, it is clear that the human thumb has evolved under very different selection pressures in recent time. The difference is illustrated by Swindler and Wood (1973, 38). I think that grip is of the greatest importance in human beings, that it accounts for the terminal phalange of the thumb being so much larger in human than in ape, and that it may help to account for the origin of bipedal locomotion. The remarkable size of the cortical representation of the human thumb is diagrammed in Penfield and Rasmussen (1950, 25).

It used to be thought that bipedal locomotion came first and that this was followed by the freeing of the hands, but what if the evolution of the hands and of locomotion were parts of the same adaptation? Throwing, hunting, hand strength, and bipedal locomotion were probably a single complex. The evolution of a unique way of locomotion would then be a part of an adaptive complex which is unique. This would account for the differences between human and ape and show why this complexity in both hand and locomotion might have evolved in a very short period of time, as is suggested both by the DNA and the fossil record. Goodall's remarkable 1984 book summarizing many years of her own and her assistants' studies of chimpanzees, mentions many behaviors which would be aided by the evolution of a powerful grip. Throwing stones, hitting with sticks, hunting, fighting—all could be done more efficiently with a powerful grip than with the weak chimpanzee thumb.

In summary, the usual behaviors of the contemporary great apes may have led to a reduction in the muscles of the thumb and a decrease in the power of grip. In humans, selection may have been in the opposite direction, for a powerful grip made possible by powerful thumb muscles; such muscles are small or even absent in the apes. The evolution of the powerful thumb laid the background for the evolution of the locomotor changes leading to bipedal locomotion. Increase in the size of the thumb and its musculature is anatomically much less complex than the changes in the pelvis, hip muscles, and the anatomy of bipedal locomotion.

I would like to stress two points. First, without the molecular proof that chimpanzees and humans shared common ancestors at some recent time, there would be no reason to regard human hands as particularly ape-like, and many have not done so. Second, the discussion as presented here has two distinct parts. It accepts the molecular analysis and the consequences of a close relationship between human and ape. It builds a traditional anatomical narrative on the basis of that relationship. The molecular analysis simply makes some reconstructions more probable and eliminates others entirely. It gives no information on the evolutionary events. This must come from anatomy and fossils, ordered by some narrative and theory of evolution.

Even if all the "facts" are used (molecular biology, recent evolutionary theories, anatomy, fossils), a theory of human evolution still has a large narrative element. As Landau (1984) has pointed out, both the traditionally defined events of human evolution (coming to the ground, etc.) and the relations of the events vary from one account to another. Further, the evolutionary story shows how the difficulties which faced the species were overcome. Evolutionary progress led to civilization, and often holds promise for a better future. The narrative has come a long way from the facts.

In the discussion at the Man and Beast Revisited symposium, it was often difficult to tell whether statements were offered as "facts" or as parts of much less provable narratives. For example, only human beings can speak, and so in a very real sense the whole symposium was a tribute to the uniqueness of human beings. Among all the hundreds of species of primates, thousands of species of mammals, and millions of species of vertebrates, only human beings can communicate using a code of relatively few sounds. It is this phonetic code which gives human behaviors their uniqueness. The phonetic code has the characteristic of other codes: only a few elements are needed to carry an almost infinite amount of information. Surely the biology which makes the phonetic code possible is the most important part of the biology which separates man from beast. My hope is that this last separation will be understood by the time of the next Smithsonian symposium.

References

Bowler, P. J. 1986. *Theories of Human Evolution: A Century of Debate, 1844–1944.* Baltimore: Johns Hopkins University Press.

Curtis, G. H. 1981. Establishing a Relative Time Scale in Anthropological and Archaeological Research. In *The Emergence of Man.* London: The Royal Society and the British Academy.

Goodall, J. 1986. *The Chimpanzees of Gombe.* Cambridge: Harvard University Press.

Goodman, Morris. 1967. Effects of Evolution on Primate Macromolecules. *Primates* 8:1–22.

Goodman, Morris. 1968. Phylogeny and Taxonomy of the Catarrhine Primates from Immuno-diffusion Data: A Review of the Major Findings. In *Taxonomy and Phylogeny of Old World Primates with References to the Origin of Man,* organized by B. Chiarelli. Turin, Italy: Rosenberg & Sellier.

Gregory, W. K. 1934. *Man's Place among the Anthropoids.* Oxford: Clarendon Press.

Howells, W., ed. 1962. *Ideas on Human Evolution.* Cambridge: Harvard University Press.

Keith, A. 1931. *New Discoveries relating to the Antiquity of Man.* London: Williams & Norgate.

Landau, M. 1984. Human Evolution as Narrative. *American Scientist* 72:262–68.

Napier, J. 1970. *The Roots of Mankind.* City of Washington: Smithsonian Institution Press.

Penfield, W., and T. Rasmussen. 1950. *The Cerebral Cortex of Man.* New York: Macmillan.

Sarich, V. M. 1971. Hominid Origins Revisited. In *Climbing Man's Family Tree,* eds. T. D. McCown, K. A. R. Kennedy. Englewood Cliffs: Prentice-Hall.

Sarich, V. M. 1983. Retrospective on Hominoid Macromolecular Systematics (Appendix). In *New Interpretations of Ape and Human Ancestry,* ed. R. L. Ciochon and R. S. Corruccini. New York: Plenum.

Sibley, C., and J. E. Ahlquist. 1984. The Phylogeny of the Hominoid Primates, as Indicated by DNA-DNA Hybridization. *Journal of Molecular Evolution* 20:2–15.

Swindler, D. R. and C. R. Wood. 1973. *An Atlas of Primate Gross Anatomy.* Seattle: University of Washington Press.

Tanner, J. M. 1964. In *Human Biology,* ed. G. A. Harrison *et al.* New York: Oxford University Press.

Wilson, A. C., and Sarich, V. M. 1969. A Molecular Time Scale for Human Evolution. *Proceedings of the National Academy of Science,* Vol. 63.

Professor Washburn has been at the very center of the enormous changes in information and theory about primate evolution and has been a critical figure in interpreting this emerging material for scholars interested in our own species. To our knowledge Washburn has not recorded any extensive autobiographical commentary on his experience in this process, and we thought it would be of interest to readers, revisiting man and beast, to have the opportunity to share his own circumstances with him.

Professor Washburn kindly provided the following remarks which with gratitude we have added herewith to his original contribution. THE EDITORS.

Current Views on the Evolutionary Process

In discussing the problems of understanding human evolution, I have found that it is most difficult to get people to realize that over the last few years everything has changed. There are new theories, new fossils, and above all, new techniques. The difficulties which loomed so large a few years ago have changed their form or have effectively disappeared.

For example, Lord Kelvin, one of the greatest physicists of the nineteenth century, ''proved'' that evolution was impossible because there simply was not enough time. The earth itself was thought to be less than 100 million years old, so how could all the forms of life have evolved in this amount of time? Yet many scientists thought that they had. I stress *scientists* because the problems of accepting the theory of biological evolution are often blamed on religion and the creationists, but confusions about evolution, and particularly human evolution, were by no means limited to the Church. In the 1920s Sir Arthur Keith, one of the most influential students of human evolution, believed that monkeys, apes, and humans had all evolved from a common ancestral stock in less than 1 million years. And surely that was reasonable *if* the whole earth were less than 100 million years old.

But science was making rapid progress, and the discovery of radioactivity soon led to a very different assessment of the age of the earth. In 1931 a committee of the National Academy of Science published a report suggesting that the age of the earth was more than 2 billion years, and estimates of the age of the earth are now over 4 billion years. The unaided human mind is not adapted to understand time measured in millions of years, and a graph may clarify the issues. Suppose we make a graph with a scale of one million years to a mile. Let the graph start out in the middle of the Atlantic Ocean and move west to the Pacific Ocean. Such a graph might represent the time from the beginning of the earth to now, some 4,500 million years, and human beings would be present only for the last 4 or 5 million years. Thus our existence would start only 4 or 5 miles from the Pacific Ocean.

Looking back, it is easy to see why humans had great difficulty in understanding geologic time measured in millions of years, and it was only after the age of the rocks had been measured by radioactive methods that biological evolution started to become an understandable process.

A further complication came with the idea of plate tectonics. In 1912 Wegener suggested that the continents had drifted from their original positions to where they are now. Almost to a man scientists repudiated this idea, and it was not until the movements of the continents could be measured in the 1960s that the idea of continental drift was generally accepted.

I stress situations in which most scientists were mistaken, because in our culture science is treated as if it were necessarily right, not as if it were the complex of thoughts and techniques which by slow degrees is helping human beings to escape from the errors of the human past. It is particularly when we approach the problems of comparing man and beast that we are likely to be caught in the rich traditions of the common sense of our ancestors. Of course, continents could not drift. But they did. Of course, we could not be closely related to apes or monkeys. But we are. The lessons from the past are clear. Human understanding only progresses when it is based on technical progress, and the techniques are based on the discoveries in a wide variety of sciences. This is why controversy is an inevitable part of progress. This is why the relation of man and beast takes no simple, stable form.

One of the controversies which is very much alive today deals with the problems of human ancestry. Were our ancestors similar to the African apes (chimpanzee and gorilla) or was the separation of man and ape much further back? Both points of view were supported by distinguished scientists who had access to the same information but came to radically different conclusions. Since I lived through that controversy and played a small part in its solution, some history may help us to understand our evolutionary past and why many of the old mistakes may easily be repeated.

There were two major points of view. The first was that our ancestors had been very similar to the contemporary African apes. This theory was supported by the detailed similarity of ape and human as outlined in numerous papers. The other point of view was that the apparent similarity between ape and human was due to parallel evolution and that in fundamental anatomy, humans were more like monkeys. William Straus (1949) outlined the two contrasting points of view, and he believed that he had presented a firm case for an early separation of monkey and ape. But Straus used what MacLean has called emotional cerebration. Paul MacLean pointed out that in science "as in politics" emotional cerebration may stand on either side of any question.

On the Asiatic Primate Expedition organized by Harold Coolidge in 1936, I had the opportunity of watching quadrupedal monkeys and gibbons (small apes) going through the very same trees. Later I had the chance of dissecting some of them and making direct comparisons. The anatomy of the gibbons seemed remarkably human compared to that of the monkeys. So in my emotional cerebration, ape and human seemed human, precisely the opposite of Straus's conclusion. Obviously Straus knew far more anatomy than I did, but seeing the living animals locomoting through the trees made a lasting impression on me. In later years Straus and I discussed comparisons of ape and monkey, trying to see why we differed so much in our interpretations.

In retrospect, it is easy to see that we were both wrong, or at least badly misled by the nature of the anatomical material. Just as geology unaided by modern science could not determine the age of the earth, so comparative anatomy unaided by modern biology could not determine the relation of apes and humans. New techniques were needed to settle the old problems.

In the period 1960 to the present, molecular biology provided the techniques. According to Morris Goodman and Vincent Sarich, immunological experiments show that humans are very closely related to the African apes. Comparisons of the DNA give the same results. According to Charles Sibley and Jon Ahlquist (1984), DNA hybridization gives the following distances: humans to chimpanzees 1.8, to gorillas 2.4, to orangutans 3.6, to gibbons 5.2, and to monkeys 8. The numbers will vary depending on the technique used, but the order of relations is the same. The results are the same no matter who performs the tests. *One* immunological test gives more useful results than all comparative anatomy.

The problems of human relation to other animals seem settled. The new information is far more definitive than anything that was available before 1960, but the conversion of molecular distances into time is still a matter of debate. Possible time of the separation of human beings from other primates might be (in millions of years): from African apes 4–6 million, from orangutans 10 million, from monkeys 20 million. But more fossils and geological dates are needed before the record can be accurately quantified.

With regard to the way the molecular information was accepted by students of human evolution, the simplest statement is that it was *not* accepted. The similarity of ape and human was denied, and no group of creationists could have asserted ancient truths with more fervor than some paleoanthropologists. The study of human evolution shows repeatedly that scientists are not unbiased, waiting for each new truth. As to whether the new discoveries were troubling to me, I can state, "Not at all." This was because, following William K. Gregory, our ancestors had been ape-like forms, long separated from other primates. The anatomical bases for these beliefs were stated in several papers (Washburn 1950, 1963, 1968, 1982; Moore 1980). I only mention these papers to indicate that over my whole life I believed that comparative anatomy correctly stated the relations of humans and other primates. But this was by no means a universal opinion. Naturally, I was delighted when the immunological studies showed that humans and African apes were not only related, but very closely related. It was easy for me to accept the new because it gave the same results as the traditional anatomy, but only if the anatomy was interpreted in one way. If one believed that apes and humans were not closely related, then one simply had to look for mistakes and misinterpretations in molecular biology, a game which has become increasingly unpopular in the last few years.

In my opinion molecular biology has laid a new foundation for approaching the problem of man and beast. The apes can no longer be dismissed by postulating a very long period of ape and human separation. At the symposium a close relationship was often implied, even if the evidence was not discussed. But in spite of all the new human fossils, comparative behavior, and new theories, many of the major problems remain. The behaviors related to speech, social behavior, hand skills, and complex tools still separate man and beast. Is human intelligence something new and different or is it easily evolved from what is seen in the behaviors of the nonhuman primates? When biological analysis has been carried as far as possible, will humans be satisfied or will this only increase the desire to understand culture and all the events of human history?

3. Social Behavior

Sociobiology and the Test of Time

Edward O. Wilson

The past seventeen years have been an exhilarating experience for me but also an education in the sociology of science. The 1960s were a tumultuous time in the biological sciences. Evolutionary biology and ecology were then trying to cope with the triumphalism of molecular biology. The prevailing doctrine was that explanations at the molecular level could, with appropriate change here and there, be extended all the way up to the levels of the organism and population, rendering "old-fashioned biology" unnecessary. It was a period of extreme philosophical as well as methodological reductionism.

A small group of evolutionary biologists thought otherwise. They believed that studies of populations and ecosystems could be made much more rigorous if some of the methods of the physical sciences were emulated but at a level higher than the molecular. As a member of that group, which also included Richard Lewontin, Richard Levins, and Robert MacArthur, I moved from a nearly exclusive study of ants to larger issues of population biology. MacArthur and I took deliberate aim at a field which at that time seemed especially old-fashioned and muddled, namely, biogeography. We used a top-down approach to produce the theory of island biogeography, which postulated equilibria of species diversity in isolated ecosystems as a balance of immigration and extinction. Thoughts about immigration and extinction led us to a reconsideration of the basic processes of demography, including natality, mortality, and dispersal. Thus, the theory of island biology was built at the intersection of biogeography and ecology.

Soon afterward, in 1967, I returned to the ants as I thought of synthesizing knowledge of these and other social insects on the framework of the new theories of population biology. The result was *The Insect Societies,* published in 1971. The last chapter was entitled "The Prospect for a Unified Sociobiology." I described sociobiology as the study of the biological basis of social systems, especially complex social systems, in terms of the most rigorous concepts and methods of population biology that might be devised.

I saw, in 1971, that the literature on social vertebrates was technically less difficult and voluminous than the literature on social insects. So, with the help of a number of specialists, some of whom were in the process of formulating sociobiology in their own fashion, I learned as much as I could about the social organization of these organisms. I then went on to publish *Sociobiology: The New Synthesis,* in 1975. In writing this book, I felt I had to include human beings, because I believed I'd be faulted if I didn't. It also seemed to me that a lot of the knowledge of animal sociality might be applied to human studies in a new and fruitful way. I thought that social scientists would say, "Yes, population biology and sociobiology are of use in the social sciences, and we will learn and integrate some of this interesting material that the biologists have provided, and it will be done quietly." Believe it or not, I did not expect the book would be controversial.

It was controversial, of course, in ways I never dreamed. One of the outcomes was that I was soon to be tutored in basic Marxism by my Harvard colleague Daniel Bell. I realized by this time that a great deal more was at issue than biology and social organization. Anyone speaking of genes and culture necessarily strikes a deep chord in philosophy and social theory. No one can stay truly neutral; no one can write in wholly value-free prose.

So, still undaunted, I set out to write my next book, *On Human Nature* (1978), in order to sketch the larger issues of philosophy and social theory as I understood them. I thought this work would have a calming effect and help turn sociobiology from a blood sport into a more conventional discipline. But an even bigger storm broke around my head. By this time I (and a few others) realized that we were entering a new terrain about which almost nothing was known: the relation between biological evolution and cultural evolution, or what we later called gene-culture coevolution. Much of the controversy, in other words, was due to ignorance.

We knew at least this much: biology affects cultural evolution in important ways. We also understood that human biological traits, including especially the forebrain, evolved in a largely cultural context during the past two million years. But how the two processes are linked was still mostly unknown.

In 1979 there appeared at Harvard a young theoretical physicist named Charles Lumsden who was so bright and insistent about sociobiological studies that I dropped my research on ants to collaborate with him. We produced two books on gene-culture coevolution at the same time that several research groups were making independent advances in the same direction. Of course, the *sapiens* curse followed me here as well: gene-culture coevolution also proved very controversial.

At the present time I have temporarily stopped work on human sociobiology and have just published a treatise on ants with Bert Hölldobler of Harvard (1990). I am also involved with biogeography again, an interest from the 1960s, but this time with new emphasis on the worldwide problem of accelerating species extinction.

The 1969 Man and Beast symposium accomplished several things, but for me it was an early milestone in the development of sociobiology. For the first time it brought together scholars who had been contributing to this subject from radically different directions, it suggested that a common language was possible, and it added a needed cachet to the enterprise. I was personally encouraged by the event, and I made friendships that have persisted through the years.

The naturalistic philosophy held by most of the 1969 participants has grown steadily more prevalent among scholars. Evolutionary, adaptive interpretations of social behavior, including that of human beings, now dominate the literature of animal behavior. They have gained credence within anthropology and psychology and, to a lesser extent, political science, economics, and sociology. These interpretations are routinely cited in the popular press, although only rarely with much depth or technical competence. The approach has had a new impact on ethical philosophy and epistemology as more philosophers have come to ask the question of *why* human beings feel and think in such and such a way and not some other.

Five journals in sociobiology have been launched since 1969, and a large amount of research has been published, much of it first-rate. Research and teaching in the field has spread worldwide, with the formation of the European Sociobiological Society, for example, and an increasing number of contributions from socialist countries. The divisions that seemed at first to exist along the lines of political ideology have faded. The "controversy" today is largely over the relevance of evolutionary biology to various of the enterprises of the social sciences. Does culture really have a biological basis in any sense that can be expressed in the language of present-day biology? Incest avoidance and color vocabularies can be explained in part with existing biological models, but is the same possible for ten-year economic cycles and military coups? In my opinion one of the great unsolved problems of science is the relation between biological and cultural evolution, or gene-culture coevolution. We know that almost all of human social behavior is transmitted by culture. We also know that cultural transmission is greatly affected by the idiosyncrasies of human biology—which in turn has evolved in the human cultural environment. When enough light is shed on the linkage between these two processes, a new era will begin in biology and the social sciences. That might be the subject of the next Man and Beast symposium.

Reference

Hölldobler, B., and E. Wilson, 1990. *The Ants.* Cambridge: Belknap Press of Harvard University Press.

Aggression

Then and Now

Robin Fox

My first task is to interpret the intent of my essay title. *Then* presumably means the time of the first Smithsonian Man and Beast symposium, in 1969, and I shall indeed look at the state of the art then and now. But I shall take advantage of the title's vagueness to suggest another chronological contrast. For the moment, however, I shall not reveal the *then* or the *now.* What I shall do is disavow any attempt at a survey of research on aggression (and/or violence) over these nearly two decades. I have been involved in much of it both directly and as a sponsor, but such a survey is more appropriate to a technical journal. What is needed here, and what will be more in the spirit of the undertaking, is an assessment of the meaning of all this research. Where do we stand now? What do we know and what can we say about human aggression and its beastly counterpart?

One position on this might be that we still know pitifully little, that we need to conduct even more expensive and more elaborate research before we can evaluate, much less recommend, ameliorative measures. I could argue that looking for a ''cure'' for aggression is infinitely more difficult than looking for a cure for cancer, and equally massive funds should be expended on the search for it. Such a position obviously suits those engaged in either the conduct or sponsorship of such research. But I beg to differ. I cannot see what we would gain except marginal increments in knowledge, from further research. The increments are not without interest, but they will not affect any fundamental issue. The word is in on aggression. There was only ever a "problem" because of the way we phrased the questions, formulated the issues. The "problem" stems from our very human capacity to create problems, not from anything about aggression per se. I worked for twelve years for a foundation dedicated to the hopeless premise that if we collected enough scientific information on the subject, we would eventually be able to lessen violence and stop wars. I finally parted company with these well-meaning people because (among other things) I wanted to diversify and investigate a wide range of topics only loosely connected to aggression proper. There was no future that I could see in pouring resources into "aggression research" with this pious end in mind. Let me elaborate on this with reference to *then* and *now*.

Then the issue was variously phrased, but predominantly it was a quarrel between the "original sin" mafia and the "perfectibility of man" crew (henceforward the "sinners" and the "perfectionists"). The latter were dedicated to the liberal-environmentalist position: either man was basically without instincts at all, and hence by definition without aggressive ones, or he was innately good and cooperative. In either case, aggression was "caused" by external forces that knocked him off his neutral or kindly balance. "Frustration" was popular as an external cause, and "crowding" rapidly gained ground as a favorite. The resurgence of Marxism (*soi-disant*) made "exploitation" and "alienation" strong candidates. Much energy was expended in looking for causes of aggression and war, and again the assumption was that in the absence of such causes man would not be aggressive or warlike.

It is perhaps hard *now* to imagine that such views were seriously promulgated, but they were, and versions of them are still around and kicking. I have linked them to the ultimate premise of the perfectibility of man, and indeed they were solidly in that Enlightenment tradition, with its nineteenth-century counterpart of inevitable progress. This Rousseauist tradition has a remarkably strong grip on the post-Renaissance occidental imagination.

It is feared that without it we shall be prey to reactionary persuasions by assorted villains, from social Darwinists to eugenicists, fascists, and new-right neo-conservatives. To fend off this villainy, the argument goes, we must assert that man is either innately neutral (tabula rasa) or innately good and that bad circumstances are what make him behave wickedly. Ergo, remove the bad circumstances and human perfectibility is possible.

It is only by understanding the power of this paradigm that we can understand the hysterical reaction of its promulgators (in all the behavioral sciences, as well as philosophy, history, and some, but not all, life sciences) to the original sin movement. This was basically neo-Darwinian. Its premises had been around since Darwin, but they had been eclipsed with the decline of instinct theory and the triumph of behaviorism and environmentalism. Ironically, their resurgence after World War II was greeted with cries of welcome from Christian theologians (man was indeed a fallen creature), which was a stark contrast to the Church's original reaction to Darwin himself. It did not help, in the eyes of the perfectionists, that the strongest scientific claims of this movement came out of Germany, since that was where genetic theories had been distorted in the service of precisely the kind of regime the liberals feared most. But it was not exclusively German and ethological, even if Konrad Lorenz was its leading popular exponent; it was equally South African (which didn't help with the liberals either) and anthropological, with Raymond Dart as its main scientist and Robert Ardrey as his prophet.

What it said that was so heretical was somewhat as follows: natural selection has programmed man to be aggressive, in part a heritage from his animal (primate) ancestry and in part a special development of his own evolutionary history as a weapon-using hunter. This aggression is intimately linked with reproductive success (the basic Darwinian process) and hence with dominance and territory, and it serves constructive and adaptational functions rather than purely destructive ones. Indeed, it is hard to see how natural selection could have worked without it. It is mitigated and constructively channeled by the tendency to ritualize (this was a central idea), to substitute displays, threats, and ceremonies for the real thing. It gets out of hand and destructive when such ritualization cannot work, as, for example, with weapons and killing at a distance, or in cases of crowding, where organisms cannot exhibit normal spacing behavior.

Looking back from the *now* vantage point, with the proverbial 20/20 hindsight, it is hard to see what all the fuss was about. The two positions were not all that different. Both acknowledged that external conditions could aggravate aggression and violence. They differed only in that the perfectionists did not want to admit any aggressive content to human nature, whereas the sinners insisted that there must be at least an aggressive potential. Otherwise, how come aggression at all? There was, I suppose, a real difference at one level of argument. Even if the perfectionists were willing to admit an aggressive potential, it was an essentially passive potential which had to be hit from the outside to be activated; the sinners, on the other hand, saw an appetitive quality to aggression, which made it, like sex or hunger, a drive seeking satisfaction. What is more, the drive had a low threshold of activation; it didn't take much to set it in motion. The analogy with sex was obvious. People obviously have a sex drive, and while this does not mean that everyone all the time is running around looking for sex, they nevertheless are easily aroused by the appropriate erotic stimuli (external) or hormonal conditions (internal) or a combination of the two. Clearly, it is of great adaptive advantage to have these drives (hunger, sex, aggression) in a state of readiness just below the surface so that they can easily be brought into play to serve the organism's reproductive interests. But equally important is the fact that they can easily be inhibited (sublimated, ritualized). Timing is everything in comedy and evolution; organisms must avoid inappropriate surges of eating, copulating, and violence, or risk expulsion from the gene pool.

I have found it necessary (although it shouldn't be) to repeat the caution that these potentials for aggressivity are not uniform but are normally distributed in any population. Thus, in any naturally occurring population, only about 1% of the individuals will be hyperaggressive. To anticipate a future argument, let me say that this presents few problems for a small group. In a primate group such individuals will as often as not be driven out. In the small human groups in which we evolved (50 or so members), only 1 or 2 might be hyperaggressive. They would again either be driven out or found some useful role in fighting against other groups. Even if the group rose to 5,000 (the outer limits of the Paleolithic linguistic tribe), 50 or so individuals do not raise a very large problem, and the small, tight social system could either constrain or channel their hyperaggressivity without difficulty, as ethnography testifies. But when we come to large heterogeneous societies of 50 million or more, then we are speaking of 500,000 individuals loose in a relatively anonymous setting without the inbuilt constraints of the small group. The amount of damage that half a million hyperaggressive people can do in a society of 50 million is way out of proportion to that done by 50 people in a society of 5,000. Yet nothing about the organisms has changed; the only change is in the absolute numbers. But this alone can cause such a violent change in the conditions of violence that we can have a new problem of gigantic proportions. The important thing to note, however, is that it is not the innate violence that has caused the problem—that was always there. It is the new numbers game. (How typical it is that people only look for causes of things they don't like. They look, for example, for the causes of divorce but never think of asking for the causes of marriage. Similarly, they will look for the causes of destructiveness but seldom for the causes of creativity. Creativity is simply assumed to be spontaneous and somehow self-rewarding for creative individuals. Why cannot destructiveness [which in the case of people like Alexander or Napoleon is hard to separate from creativity] be also looked at as spontaneous and self-rewarding? Because it frightens us to think this way, that's why. We ask what sinister thing causes people to actually find enjoyment in bullfighting. But we assume that the enjoyment of great music is natural, normal, and self-rewarding. Our comfortable, civilized, bourgeois prejudices have a lot to do with the way we pose, and hence beg, these "scientific" questions.)

Nevertheless, if we put all this together, we come up with a very plausible picture of aggression that fits our commonsense and systematic observations of aggressive behavior in humans and other animals, as well as an accumulation of scientific evidence on the internal states associated with aggression and violence. I stress *commonsense,* here meaning observations not clouded by one of the intense ideological positions on the topic. To deeply committed liberal-perfectionist-environmentalists—and they are still with us—any suggestion of the innate quality is abhorrent. That such suggestions came at a time when the perfectionists were engaged in furious (and often very aggressive!) combat with forces of militarism and racial oppression (regarding Vietnam and the civil rights movement) made the ideological battle all the more irrational. That their intellectual opponents largely shared their position on these issues should have told them something. But they were obsessed with the fear that had haunted Locke, Mill, Hobhouse, and the liberal-reformist tradition: that to admit innate content to human nature was to give aid and comfort to political reaction. Again, "now" we can see that this is simply not true. It does not follow from the sinners' view of aggression that anyone should feel impelled to support any particular status quo or become a raving militarist. Quite the contrary. In the same way that one can provoke high or low levels of sexual arousal by controlling the external stimuli to sex, so one can provoke high or low levels of aggression. Take away the stimuli of glory, excitement, gain, immortality, xenophobia, or whatever, and one will surely lower levels of aggression and violence. That the Church regarded sin as innate and ineradicable did not mean it did not actively campaign against it and try to remove those things that would lead us into temptation. Calvin Coolidge, that man of few words, was asked on returning from church about the subject of the sermon. "Sin," he replied. When asked further about the preacher's message on the subject, he said, "He was agin' it."

But this cautionary tale does point up a basic difference between the perfectionists and the sinners. If we lower levels of external sexual stimulation, we will still get sexual behavior because the internal stimuli, plus the inevitable existence of the two sexes, will move the organism to appetitive satisfaction. If aggression is analogous (and this is compatible with physiological findings), then we will always get some aggressive behavior, no matter what we do with the environment. The internal potential is there, and there will always be enough frustration, rivalry, greed, gain, etc., no matter what the social system. And as we have seen, there will always be a low proportion of individuals with a very low threshold of aggressive arousal who can cause problems out of all proportion to their numbers. Consequently, it is pie in the sky to wish to abolish aggression. Those societies paraded as examples of such abolition always return to embarrass the paraders (Pueblo Indians, Eskimos, Bushmen—all with high levels of personal aggression). On this argument, it would be as personally and socially impossible to abolish aggression as to abolish sex.

Here there is a real difference between the two views. But note that none of the perfectionists ever proposed abolishing sex. Despite their principles, their common sense would have told them this was impossible. But they did seriously propose trying to abolish aggression: remove the stimuli and it will go away. They never did adequately answer the objection (which goes back at least to George Bernard Shaw's Fabian Tract 45, "The Impossibilities of

Anarchism'' [1893], that such an argument fails to explain how we get the aggressive response in the first place. You cannot stimulate aggression if there are not internal mechanisms already in place to be stimulated.

We *now* know what these internal mechanisms are, and the tabula rasa theory is no longer even minimally respectable here, any more than it is in linguistics or cognition, for example. It can only be understood or sympathized with if one first understands its tenacious (if false) premises in the history of ideas and ideologies, and how desperately essential these appeared to be in combating reactionary, racist, and militarist evils. To this list were eventually added sexist evils, and the same tedious argument ensued over sex differences, with the same non-issues preponderant.

Calmer times bring calmer minds. But even so, some hangover from the great debate is still with us in an age of terrorism, soccer violence, sectarian killings, and crime in the streets. Here we can perhaps turn to the second implication of ''then and now.'' But before that, let us note something positive that emerges—a convergence of views—from the debate. Whichever position you espouse, if a lessening of violence is at issue, as opposed to its abolition, then the conclusion is that a lowering of the intensity of the stimuli to violence will be effective. But paradoxically, the original sin position offers something more, namely, the effectiveness of ritualization or sublimation (*pace* Freud) of aggressive drives. If ritualization, for example, is as innate as aggression itself, then we have a powerful related drive, already geared to the control of aggression, to call upon. This was Lorenz's great hope, and the much maligned Robert Ardrey firmly agreed. He used to hand out little desk plaques to people with a quotation from his own work engraved on them: ''If there is hope for men, it is because we are animals.'' Our wonderful intelligences may not save us, but our animal propensity to ritualize just might.

Which leads us back to the second chronological contrast and its implications. Aggression now, that is to say in the twentieth century, is something very different from aggression in the context of our Environment of Evolutionary Adaptedness (EEA)—aggression then. The EEA of any species is easily determined as that environment in which the major adaptations leading to its distinctiveness as a species occurred. For *Homo sapiens/erectus* this is the preagricultural hunting, gathering, and scavenging environment of ninety-nine percent of our history, which culminated in the truly astonishing cultural achievements of the Upper Palaeolithic. (See, e.g., the stone tool industries, the carvings, and the cave paintings of Altamira and Lascaux.) *Now* in this context is really the period after the Neolithic revolution, circa 10,000 B.P. (before the present).

In what way is *now* different from *then* regarding aggression? The organism is not different. Only some minor changes (mainly in teeth) have occurred. Hence the basic aggressive and ritualizing mechanisms are still in place. What is different is this: these mechanisms were the result of the slow molding of the preceding primate mechanisms to the EEA of the genus *Homo,* and in this environment they worked. Thus aggression was able to perform its constructive functions, and ritualization was equally able to contain the aggressive inclinations. Aggression was no more a problem in this context than it is in the context of a primate group with its dominance and breeding hierarchies, or a bird colony with its breeding territories, or a lion pride with its competing males. It was a perfectly natural extension of primate aggression, mediated by the evolving human capacities for language and symbolic expression, which served both to facilitate and inhibit aggression in the newly emerging "human" context. There was aggression, there was violence, there was ritualization; but there was no problem, unless one wishfully imagines that there should not be any such drives in *Homo.* Aggression performed the same services here—even if "culturalized" with weapons, war paint, martial songs, magic, and myths—as it did for other species: territorial spacing, formation of breeding hierarchies, distribution of resources, sexual selection, etc., etc. Within communities violence was ritualized in many forms (law, customs, kinship, dueling); and even between communities, when ritualization (treaties, truces, trading, single and ceremonial combat, ceremonial cooperation, competitive sports, intermarriage) failed, the sanguinary consequences were limited by the crudity of weapons and the relatively small numbers involved. Not only was the species not threatened by all this aggressivity, it may well have benefited from the selection pressures for intelligence, foresight, strength, courage, cooperation, altruism, comradeship, and sociality that this organized intercommunal violent activity involved.

This is not a happy picture for committed pacifists. But neither are the goings-on in a primate group. It cannot be helped. This is the way things are. It was fashionable in the late sixties and seventies for the perfectionists to use the friendly and amiable chimpanzees as a model for protohuman behavior, as against the aggressive and irascible baboons favored by the sinners. But more and more recent research has shown our friends the wild chimpanzees to be irascible, sexist, territorial, hierarchical, carnivorous, predatory, cannibalistic, and given to extreme intergroup violence to the point of genocide. It may well be that *Homo sapiens sapiens* (us) was only carrying on the traditions of its closest primate relatives when it exterminated its hominid cousins *Homo sapiens neanderthalensis* (them). This is much disputed. But they did disappear, and we are still around. However, we must realize that this happened toward the beginning of the end of our period in the EEA. Population expansion was already leading to serious competition for hunting territories and the destruction of the mammalian megafauna. And thereby hangs the tale.

The "population explosion" of the early Neolithic, following the shift from hunting to domestication, was of the order 1.5 million to 100 million within a millennium. One hundred million is not, in absolute terms, very large. But relatively, and in the restricted areas where it occurred (the Fertile Crescent and near the Ganges, Indus, and Yellow rivers), it was an enormous leap entailing a drastic change of environment. Let us recapitulate: the basic organism was almost totally unchanged—certainly the deeply programmed systems of sex and aggression were not changed. But heretofore these had not been a "problem." From 10,000 B.P. on, however, it had to operate in an ever more radically changing context for which it had not evolved. It was what the changed context did to the essentially unproblematic basic mechanisms that began to constitute the "problem of violence." Thus the "problem" was not aggression per se, any more than it was sex per se. The problem was with the development of cities, states, slavery, castes and classes, bureaucracies, armies, universalistic religions, ideologies, nationalism, science, economic exploitation, increasingly sophisticated weaponry, and above all, sheer increase in numbers. And all of this occurred in a fraction of 1% of the time that we have existed as a distinct genus.

Those then who hold that the causes of war and large-scale violence lie in class antagonism, xenophobia, ideological fanaticism, or any other external factor are quite correct. They are only incorrect when they insist that this in turn "causes" human aggressivity. The human aggressivity is there to start with. These external factors simply bring it into play in unprecedented ways.

The external-cause argument, as we have seen, was advanced to counter the equally erroneous argument that the innate aggressivity caused the wars and violence! If the reader can now see how my argument takes neither of these positions, then we have come a long way to understanding my original statement that as far as aggression is concerned, there is nothing to find out; there is no problem. The problem, to repeat at risk of being tedious, is a problem of social organization and change, not of human nature. It is not clear, therefore, how further investigations of mechanisms of human or animal aggression will help with the "problem," interesting as they may be as additions to human knowledge. Nor is it clear how massive sociological or social psychological research will help either. We know what the triggers for aggression and violence are. We have seen them over and over again throughout history. What more do we need to know? Once we have grasped that our problems are conceptual rather than real, perhaps we can begin to talk sense on the subject.

Thus, if Marxists maintain that the abolition of class society and the withering away of the state will lead to an absence of violence, they are probably wrong. These are only two of the stimuli to violence, and before they existed, there was violence anyway. But their absence would certainly remove two occasions for (I prefer this to "causes of") large-scale violence. If overcrowding and economic exploitation are associated with (again better than "causes of") violence, then their removal will add to the list of defunct triggers. But this will only reduce the incidence, not abolish the phenomenon. Why is this not enough? I was asked by the chairman of the President's Commission on Violence (1968), Milton Eisenhower, if gun control laws would mean less violence. I said probably not, but they might mean fewer people would shoot each other, which was surely a worthy result in any case.

One of the problems in interpreting the so-called causes of violence and wars is the shortsightedness of the social, behavioral, and even historical sciences. They are trapped in the *now*—that is, post 10,000 B.P. And one of the main things to grasp about the *now* is that in the perspective of the species' evolution, it is a peculiar, aberrant, violent, unnatural time. Despite the triumph of various relativisms since Nietzsche, we cannot seem to shake off our Enlightenment/Victorian notions of progress. Thus, for almost all theorists, *human behavior* means post-Neolithic behavior; before this was savagery—"the primitive." It is emotionally inconceivable that the pre-

Neolithic could be essentially the normal equilibrium time of human behavior, and all that goes under the heading of civilization an aberration—an inhuman and inhumane state of frenetic change and violent deviation from a "human" norm. (And this is not a revamping of Freud's *Civilization and Its Discontents.* I do not see the discontents stemming from repression. There was repression in the Paleolithic.) We find this inconceivable because we are trapped within the assumptions of this historic period. We label what went before as "prehistory"—a sublime arrogance. To regard at least 2 million (and even upwards of 5 million) years of human history as "pre-," as simply a run up to the real thing, is a pure value judgment for which we have no authority. Before we knew better—before we knew the human time scale—there was perhaps an excuse; but there is no longer. We still talk of "early man," and this is man for 99% of his existence! If we changed our terms and called ourselves "late man," as opposed to "man" proper, we might begin to get a glimmer of our colossal mistake. The theorists want to explain history, but their explanations take history for granted. They do not question the very phenomenon of history.

Let us do just that for a moment. Let us take history to be a late development of the human trajectory—so late that it is still in its experimental stage and has by no means established its inevitability. It is a blip at the end of the trajectory—a blip that may well disappear as things return to normal. If we treat history as a possible mistake or disease, then it is a deviation from some norm; and that norm can only be the culmination of the species' EEA—the Upper Paleolithic at the latest. Let us then view history as a series of divergences—swings of the pendulum—from this norm, rather than as a linear progressive improvement or a series of cyclical returns. The diagram illustrates my own view of the major termini of the major swings of the historical pendulum. Others might come up with different points of departure, but the overall picture is the same: wider, faster swings away from the norm. Of course, the items listed here as major deviations can only be rough summaries which require an essay each for justification; but I think the readers can make their own adjustments. Thus I do not list *capitalism* and *socialism,* since these are both included under *industrialism,* and so on.

What intrigues me is that the major violent upheavals that have formed the modern world (which is why the Franco-Prussian War and the American Civil War are there) all took place on one or other of the great swings of the

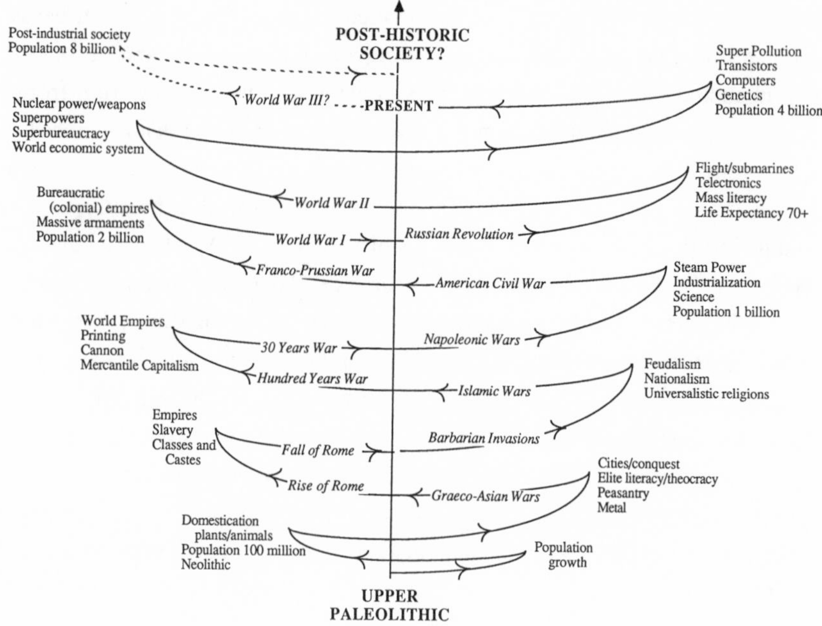

pendulum. This makes intuitive sense; the more wildly we swing away from the norm, the more violently we react. The most violently effective swings have occurred in the West, which biases our diagram in that direction. But this is a fact of history that has given rise to a whole industry of interpretation. Here then is the possibility of a "theory of war," if one wants one. The penultimate swing was so rapid that no major deadly quarrel occurred, but that may just be an artifact of my choice of conditions for that arc. I do not know whether World War III will come on the way to the prophesied postindustrial society or will be a consequence of our achieving that state. "Post-historical society" is of course just wishful thinking, but it puts me in good company. Spelling out this theory in detail is a whole other task. I offer it here as a first try at looking differently at human history and human violence—a try that seems to me more compatible with what we know about ourselves in the post-Darwinian world.

What hope is there, I am often asked, for a future of peace and nonviolence, in this view? The answer is obviously: not much. But then, I ask in return, what hope is there for a future of chastity and nonsexuality? Not much, either. What can we do about violence? Perhaps we can learn to live with it, since we don't seem to have much choice. And this may not be too bad. We know we can lessen the stimuli to violence, and we know that we can inhibit some violence with the threat of greater violence. We can try these things. But unless we can totally dismantle the world as we know it now and return to the EEA equilibrium, we must accept that our huge industrial world society is bound to provoke high levels of violent response, not because we are killer apes seeking blood and mayhem, but because we are apes that easily resort to violence as a solution. And if we are constantly presented with situations in which violence seems to be the only solution, then we will resort to it with a measure of courage, sadness, dignity, grim determination, cool efficiency, religious devotion, and sheer insane glee. For we can imbue violence with all the shades of meaning our imagination is capable of. And in the end it is our violent imagination rather than our innate violence that will determine the issue one way or the other. But there is no sense berating violence. It is history that is the disease, not violence. If you wish to cure the sickness, abolish history.

But for the sake of an upbeat ending to this apparently pessimistic essay, let me offer the following: In looking at the perturbations of history with a view to fleshing out the details of my diagram, I am struck by one singular fact: The actual amount of killing per capita in human sanguinary contests is relatively small. However large the number of those killed, it is small as a proportion of the populations involved. What is more, the amount of energy expended in actual fighting is equally small as a proportion of the total energy expended in any war. Further, the amount of time expended in ''diplomacy''—widely interpreted—is greater than that expended on the wars themselves. In going a little beyond Clausewitz, it sometimes appears to me thus: War is diplomacy's way of creating more diplomacy. Men love the treaties at least as much as the battles. And is this so strange in an animal that had to evolve inhibition as well as facilitation of aggression in its long evolutionary history? The cultural expression of inhibition is rules. We are as geared to rules and their keeping as to mayhem and zero-sum outcomes. This is one of our versions of the universal ritualization function. Perhaps we can capitalize on this. We can take some heart from the observation that given the awesome possibilities of violence today, we may just be living in the best of all possible worlds.

Monogamy, Adultery, and Divorce in Cross-Species Perspective

Helen Fisher

A*nthropomorphizing:* The charge of my critics. My countercharge: There is a sense in which, when we cease to anthropomorphize, we cease to be men, for when we cease to have human contact with animals and deny them all relation to ourselves, we . . . cease to anthropomorphize ourselves—to deny our own humanity. We repeat the old, old human trick of freezing the living world and with it ourselves.'' Loren Eisley wrote these words on January 22, 1970.

Since then, a revolution in the biological sciences has occurred. Sparked in 1975 by Edward O. Wilson's landmark book, *Sociobiology: A New Synthesis,* zoologists have documented altruism, deceit, the roots of nationalism, nepotism, and many other complex human behaviors in other creatures, from ants to antelope. Evolutionary biologists have developed mathematical principles grounded in impeccable genetic logic to explain why individuals of different species behave alike. And primatologists have recorded chimpanzees kissing, hugging, and bowing to each other; using tools and weapons; mourning dead relatives; warring on chimp neighbors; even praticing primitive dentistry. Eisley's conviction that we share some behavior patterns with other creatures is gaining adherents around the world.

Yet despite careful examination of the social and sexual activities of other creatures, little of these data have been used to understand human mating and parenting tactics, what biologists call our "reproductive strategy." Are we nature's only beings that philander and desert each other? Do other creatures fall in love? Where in the animal community is monogamy prevalent and why? Can the mating games of wolves or robins tell us anything about divorce? Although our human reproductive maneuvers are, in part, the product of culture, a survey of worldwide patterns of marriage, adultery, and divorce illustrates a constellation of cross-cultural characteristics that have uncanny parallels in other animals.

Over 90% of American men and women in every birth cohort marry; records go back to the mid 1800s (Cherlin, 1981). The 1982 *United Nations Demographic Yearbook* (United Nations 1984, chart 24; Fisher 1989) lists the number of women and men who have married by age 49 in 97 industrial and agricultural societies. Between 1972 and 1981, the sample average proportion of women who married was 93%, while 91% of men married by middle age. Although no worldwide tabulations have been taken on the percentage of people who wed in gathering/hunting, pastoral, fishing, and horticultural societies (where people garden with a hoe rather than a plow), the ethnographic literature confirms that marriage is a pancultural custom (Murdock 1949; Hawthorn 1970). In nonindustrial communities, bachelors and spinsters are rare (Lévi-Strauss 1985).

The most conspicuous trait we share with other creatures is our propensity for monogamy, a term anthropologists have borrowed from naturalists to describe one of our marriage systems: marrying one person at a time. Men tend to marry one woman, *mono-gyny,* and women tend to marry one man, *mon-andry.* The terms for these variants of monogamy—monogyny and monandry—are useful because they enable one to dissect the reproductive tactics of men and women separately. And this is important; women and men are different subspecies, with slightly varied marriage patterns. For example, in the 853 societies for which data are available, only 16% require monogyny for men (van den Berghe 1979). The balance of human cultures, 84%, permit a man to take several wives simultaneously—polygyny (van den Berghe 1979). In some African societies, as many as 70% of men have more than a single wife at once at some point in their lives (Isaac, pers. comm.). But even though polygyny is permitted in most human cultures, it is much less practiced (Murdock 1949). In the vast majority of societies where men are permitted to have several wives simultaneously, only about 10% take more than one wife at once (van den Berghe 1979). The balance, about 90%, marry a single woman at a time. And because polygyny in humans is regularly associated with rank and wealth, Daly and Wilson (1983) propose that monogyny was even more prevalent in unstratified, hunting/gathering societies of the past.

Women exhibit a less-variable marriage pattern. Where monogamy is law, women marry only one man at once—monandry. Where polygyny is permitted, women also marry only one man at a time, even though they may have co-wives. In fact, of the 853 societies on record, only .5% permit polyandry—marrying several husbands simultaneously; the remaining 99.5% prescribe that a woman take only one husband at a time (van den Berghe 1979). For women, monogamy—or pair-bonding—is even more common than for men.

Men and women also form pair-bonds without marrying. These relationships are difficult to compare cross-culturally, however, because "living together" in Western cultures and unmarried partnerships among other peoples are not systematically tabulated. But popular literature and anthropological sources suggest that these unions are regularly monogamous relationships. Thus available data on worldwide matrimony and partnerships between unwed people indicate that monogyny and monandry—the formation of a social/sexual/economic unit with only one individual at a time—is standard for the human species.

Monogamy is not a common reproductive strategy in other mammals. About 3% form a pair-bond, a mating relationship with only a single individual at a time (Kleiman 1977). Of the "higher" nonhuman primates (monkeys and apes), 12% are monogamous (Kinzey 1987). The only close biochemical and phylogenetic relatives of humankind that exhibit monogamy are the gibbons and siamangs. Species of wolves, foxes, coyotes, jackals, beavers, elephant shrews, and two little antelope, the klipspringer and the dik-dik, are among the few other monogamous mammals (Kleiman 1977; Wittenberger & Tilson 1980). Monogamy is much more common in birds. Of some 9,000 species, over 90% are monogamous (Lack 1968).

This is not to suggest, however, that either people or other monogamous creatures are sexually faithful to their partners. The *Oxford English Dictionary* defines monogamy as having one spouse at a time. Nowhere does it say that spouses are necessarily sexually faithful to one another. The zoological definition of monogamy does not imply sexual fidelity either. As Kleiman (1977, 39) writes: "The concept of monogamy implies exclusivity in mating, i.e. a given male and female will mate only with each other. This requirement, of course, has yet to be proven to exist for the vast majority of birds and mammals which are said to be monogamous. Only biochemical or long term behavioral evidence could demonstrate mating exclusivity. Thus, monogamy is generally recognized in the field and in captivity by a variety of less stringent characteristics."

So in the dictionary and in scientific parlance, monogamy does not imply fidelity. Moreover, monogamy and adultery regularly coexist in nature. Americans are a good example. In the United States, every man and woman who marries takes a single spouse; bigamy is against the law. Polls suggest that approximately 50% of American men and women today are adulterous, however (Lampe 1987; Wolfe 1981). And adultery occurs in societies around the world, regardless of whether people are bankers, merchants, farmers, herders or hunters, and collectors, and regardless of their beliefs about fidelity or their penalties for adultery, which may include death (Fisher, in press).

Monogamy and adultery are also seen in tandem in other species. In a study of red-winged blackbirds, some males were vasectomized; despite this, many of the females that nested on the territories of vasectomized males laid fertile clutches, leading Daly and Wilson (1983) to conclude that female red-winged blackbirds copulate with more males than just their mates. Wolves live in a pack. The highest ranking male and female often form the only breeding unit. But as the female comes into estrus, she copulates with other pack members; only at the height of her sexual receptivity—when she is most likely to conceive—does her mate guard her (Klinghammer, pers. comm.). A female gorilla lives in a harem with several other females, but she has only a single mate—monandry. During her monthly period of heat, she copulates only with him. After she is pregnant, however, she may court and copulate with other group males (Fossey 1983). So monogamy and adultery are separate but related aspects of a *mixed* sexual strategy seen in animals and people.

Another hallmark of humanity is divorce. There are very few societies in the world that do not permit divorce. The Roman Catholic church banned divorce in the Dark Ages. The ancient Incas did not permit divorce either (Murdock 1965). But with these and a few other exceptions, peoples from Amazonia to Siberia see divorce as a secular act, have rules about divorce, have means to obtain divorce, and do divorce. In many societies the frequency of divorce is much higher than in America today (Friedl 1975; Textor 1967; Barnes 1967; Murdock 1965; Ackerman 1963). Moreover, divorce has counterparts in the rest of the animal community. But before one can compare desertion in man and beast, one must establish our primary human patterns of divorce.

Since 1947, census takers in places as culturally different as South Africa, the Soviet Union, Greenland, Venezuela, and the United States have gathered information about divorce. These data, compiled by the United Nations Statistical Office for dozens of agricultural and industrial societies in specific years between 1947 and 1981 (United Nations 1984; 1982; 1977; 1969; 1959; 1949), exhibit three specific configurations that have echoes in the animal community (Fisher 1989).

Most relevant are data on the duration of marriage that ends in divorce (see table of divorce patterns). Among the 58 societies for which data are complete, divorces exhibit a skewed distribution characterized by the occurrence of a divorce peak early in marriage—often on or around the fourth year—and a gradual, long-tailed decline in divorce following this peak. Finland is a good example. In 1950 the highest frequency of divorce (the peak, or mode) occurred during the fourth year of marriage. In 1966 the number of divorces peaked during the third year of marriage. Finnish divorces once again clustered around a four-year pinnacle in 1974 and 1981 (table; figs. 1–4; Fisher 1989).

When these divorce peaks, recorded for every society in every year for which data are available (table, column 4; Fisher 1989), are compiled on a master chart (fig. 5; Fisher 1989), it becomes evident that among these 58 varied peoples—with different religions, economies, household arrangements, per capita incomes, and ethnic backgrounds—there is a worldwide divorce peak during and around the fourth year of marriage. There are exceptions, of course. In Egypt in 1978 the highest frequency of divorce occurred during the first few months of marriage, whereas Italy in 1980

Table 1. Divorce Patterns for 58 Countries, Areas, and Ethnic Groups Based on Available Data for the Years between 1947 and 1982

	Year	No. of Divorces	Modal No. Yrs. Married at Time of Divorce	Decay Rate (% Divorces within 7 Yrs.)	Age at Divorce (Mode) F/M	Divorces by Age 45 F/M
Australia: Whites	1967	9,688	7	23%	25–29 / 40–44	74% / 65%
	1981	41,412	4	39%	25–29 / 30–34	83% / 77%
Austria	1957	8,177	3	53%	30–34 / 30–34	82% / 71%
	1967	8,880	2	62%	25–29 / 25–29	85% / 80%
	1975	10,763	2	58%	20–24 / 20–24	98% / 97%
	1980	13,327	2	52%	25–29 / 30–34	88% / 83%
Belgium	1966	5,826	8	28%	30–34 / 30–34	83% / 77%
	1975	10,977	6	33%	25–29 / 25–29	84% / 79%
	1979	13,381	6	34%	25–29 / 30–34	83% / 78%
Brunei	1972	57	1	63%	25–29 / 20–24	84% / 79%
	1976	68	4	71%	20–24 / 20–24	91% / 84%
Bulgaria	1967	9,652	<1	72%	20–24 / 20–24	— / —
	1974	11,567	<1	68%	20–24 / 25–29	— / —
	1980	13,110	<1	64%	25–29 / 25–29	— / —
Byelorussian SSR	1975	23,443	3–4	—	25–29 / 25–29	— / —
	1981	30,848	3–4	—	25–29 / 25–29	86% / 84%
Costa Rica	1957	169	7	43%	30–34 / 25–29	83% / 74%
	1966	202	3	32%	30–34 / 30–34	78% / 68%
Cuba	1963	7,480	1	55%	20–24 / 25–29	82% / 71%
	1972	26,037	1	—	<20 / 20–24	98% / 96%
	1978	25,397	2	69%	<20 / 20–24	77% / 78%
Czechoslovakia	1966	20,244	2	50%	20–24 / 25–29	84% / 77%
	1973	29,458	2	53%	25–29 / 25–29	85% / 79%
	1981	34,595	3	53%	25–29 / 25–29	89% / 83%

Denmark	1955	6,771	4	—	25–29 / 30–34	82% / 74%
	1966	6,726	4	49%	25–29 / 25–29	80% / 73%
	1973	12,637	3	49%	25–29 / 25–29	84% / 75%
	1981	14,425	4	45%	30–34 / 30–34	85% / 77%
Dominican Republic	1956	827	1	57%	25–29 / 30–34	74% / 62%
	1967	2,137	4	54%	30–34 / 30–34	48% / 43%
	1974	9,421	3	72%	30–34 / 35–39	57% / 53%
	1976	9,017	3	73%	30–34 / 25–29	47% / 51%
Ecuador	1974	1,542	2	40%	25–29 / 30–34	65% / 59%
	1979	2,279	2	45%	25–29 / 30–34	83% / 77%
Egypt	1947	75,404	<1	—	20–24 / 25–29	94% / —
	1973	75,487	<1	80%	20–24 / 25–29	87% / 78%
	1978	78,023	<1	85%	20–24 / 25–29	87% / 80%
El Salvador	1957	451	6	55%	25–29 / 30–34	82% / 77%
	1966	677	3	48%	25–29 / 30–34	57% / 55%
	1974	1,109	3	46%	25–29 / 25–29	78% / 76%
	1980	1,549	3	43%	25–29 / 25–29	77% / 74%
England/Wales	1966	39,067	4	33%	20–24 / 30–34	99% / 75%
	1973	106,003	4	35%	25–29 / — —	79% / —
	1981	145,713	3	39%	20–24 / 20–24	98% / 98%
Federal Republic of Germany	1967	62,835	3	54%	25–29 / 25–29	85% / 79%
	1975	106,829	3	48%	25–29 / 30–34	87% / 82%
	1981	109,520	5	39%	25–29 / 30–34	86% / 80%
Guam	1974	207	4	53%	35–39 / 35–39	74% / 70%
	1980	489	6	44%	30–34 / 30–34	82% / 79%
Finland	1950	3,687	4	51%	25–29 / 35–39	81% / 75%
	1966	4,856	3	45%	25–29 / 25–29	79% / 75%
	1974	10,019	4	45%	25–29 / 25–29	83% / 79%
	1981	9,497	4	37%	30–34 / 30–34	82% / 77%
France	1954	28,664	7	41%	30–34 / 30–34	79% / 70%
	1967	29,321	3	37%	30–34 / 35–39	79% / 72%
	1972	39,861	5	43%	25–29 / 25–29	83% / 77%
	1978	61,729	4	44%	25–29 / 30–34	85% / 80%

Table 1. Divorce Patterns for 58 Countries, Areas, and Ethnic Groups Based on Available Data for the Years between 1947 and 1982

	Year	No. of Divorces	Modal No. Yrs. Married at Time of Divorce	Decay Rate (% Divorces within 7 Yrs.)	Age at Divorce (Mode) F/M	Divorces by Age 45 F/M
German Democratic Republic	1966	27,949	2	63%	25–29 / 25–29	86% / 82%
	1975	41,632	2	55%	20–24 / 30–34	89% / 87%
	1981	48,567	2	58%	25–29 / 25–29	90% / 87%
Greece	1980	6,684	4	45%	25–29 / 30–34	— / —
Greenland	1981	130	4	48%	30–34 / 35–39	94% / 88%
Guatemala	1965	436	5	39%	25–29 / 25–29	79% / 74%
Honduras	1957	243	3	65%	25–29 / 25–29	95% / 88%
Hungary	1956	12,479	3	57%	25–29 / 25–29	85% / 77%
	1967	21,078	2	52%	25–29 / 25–29	84% / 77%
	1975	25,997	2	53%	20–24 / 25–29	84% / 77%
	1981	27,426	3	52%	25–29 / 25–29	87% / 81%
Iceland	1966	192	6	38%	25–29 / 30–34	82% / 75%
	1975	397	3,5	50%	25–29 / 25–29	90% / 86%
	1980	441	5	50%	25–29 / 25–29	88% / 82%
Israel	1956	1,944	<1	66%	20–24 / 25–29	83% / 70%
	1966	2,237	1	56%	20–24 / 25–29	80% / 69%
	1975	3,100	1	56%	25–29 / 25–29	77% / 71%
	1981	4,629	2	49%	25–29 / 30–34	86% / 79%
Italy	1980	11,844	9	—	— / —	— / —
Jamaica	1972	598	6	22%	20–24 / 20–24	— / —
	1978	748	8	21%	20–24 / 25–29	— / —
Japan	1966	44,255	<1	73%	25–29 / 25–29	94% / 89%
	1975	74,227	<1	75%	25–29 / 25–29	92% / 88%
	1981	99,170	<1	—	30–34 / 30–34	89% / 83%

Jersey/Channel Isles	1967	78	8	45%	25–29 / 25–29	90% / 85%
	1971	140	5	37%	25–29 / 30–34	80% / 74%
Jordan	1967	1,391	1	83%	20–24 / 25–29	94% / 88%
	1974	2,064	<1	82%	20–24 / 25–29	95% / 88%
	1980	2,733	1	86%	20–24 / 25–29	95% / 88%
Kuwait	1979	1,708	<1	—	20–24 / 25–29	93% / 83%
Luxembourg	1957	93	7	28%	30–34 / 30–34	70% / 81%
	1967	198	7	32%	25–29 / 35–39	89% / 81%
	1974	268	5	38%	25–29 / 25–29	90% / 87%
	1980	582	3,4	40%	25–29 / 25–29	82% / 76%
Martinique	1970	188	4	—	25–29 / 30–39	— / —
Morocco	1955	498	5	43%	30–34 / 30–34	60% / 52%
Netherlands	1947	8,847	5	39%	30–34 / 30–34	80% / 74%
	1967	7,464	3	42%	25–29 / 30–34	75% / 67%
	1975	20,093	4	39%	25–29 / 25–29	74% / 68%
	1981	28,509	2	37%	30–34 / 30–34	79% / 72%
Netherlands Antilles	1966	184	8	41%	30–34 / 25–34	86% / 74%
	1971	297	1	44%	25–29 / 30–34	81% / 80%
New Zealand	1967	2,047	5	23%	20–24 / 20–24	97% / 95%
	1975	4,761	7	31%	20–24 / 20–24	97% / 96%
Norway	1956	2,071	6	43%	30–34 / 30–34	77% / 70%
	1967	2,876	4	44%	25–29 / 25–29	77% / 71%
	1974	5,156	4	44%	25–29 / 25–29	82% / 76%
	1981	7,136	5	35%	25–29 / 30–34	84% / 76%
Panama	1967	624	4	46%	30–34 / 30–34	58% / 52%
	1974	864	2	56%	25–29 / 25–29	80% / 72%
	1980	1,116	3	51%	25–29 / 30–34	66% / 63%
Poland	1953	12,814	<1	—	20–24 / 25–29	93% / 89%
Portugal	1957	811	6	22%	30–39 / 40–44	65% / 56%
	1967	722	6	26%	30–34 / 30–34	70% / 61%
	1974	777	7	37%	25–29 / 25–29	73% / 68%

Table 1. Divorce Patterns for 58 Countries, Areas, and Ethnic Groups Based on Available Data for the Years between 1947 and 1982

	Year	No. of Divorces	Modal No. Yrs. Married at Time of Divorce	Decay Rate (% Divorces within 7 Yrs.)	Age at Divorce (Mode) F/M	Divorces by Age 45 F/M
Reunion	1970	118	1	—	25–29 / 30–34	— / —
Romania	1966	25,804	1	69%	20–24 / 25–29	91% / 87%
	1974	17,951	8	46%	25–29 / 30–34	88% / 82%
Scotland	1957	1,516	8	30%	25–29 / 30–34	84% / 76%
	1967	2,765	5	36%	25–29 / 25–29	88% / 82%
	1975	7,795	4	41%	25–29 / 25–29	89% / 84%
	1981	9,895	4	36%	25–29 / — —	84% / —
South Africa: Asians	1977	364	4	59%	25–29 / 25–29	90% / 83%
Blacks	1967	775	4	—	30–34 / 30–34	78% / 73%
	1972	900	5	34%	30–34 / 30–34	79% / 72%
	1977	1,165	6	40%	25–29 / 25–29	83% / 76%
Whites	1951	3,951	3	—	25–29 / 30–34	82% / 74%
	1967	5,833	2	—	25–29 / 25–29	73% / 66%
	1972	8,432	3	48%	25–29 / 25–29	74% / 67%
	1977	9,864	2	55%	25–29 / 25–29	84% / 78%
Sweden	1956	8,608	4	41%	30–34 / 30–34	80% / 72%
	1967	10,722	3	41%	25–29 / 25–29	79% / 72%
	1975	25,085	9	34%	30–34 / 30–34	79% / 70%
	1981	20,019	3	39%	35–39 / 35–39	79% / 71%

Switzerland	1956	4,293	4	45%	30–34 / 30–34	78% / 70%
	1966	4,944	4	44%	25–29 / 30–34	80% / 70%
	1975	8,917	5	46%	25–29 / 30–34	85% / 78%
	1981	11,131	3	38%	30–34 / 30–34	84% / 77%
Tunisia	1972	4,930	1	—	20–24 / 25–29	90% / 82%
Ukrainian SSR	1974	156,703	3–4	—	20–24 / 25–29	— / —
	1981	185,818	3–4	—	25–29 / 25–29	82% / 82%
United States*	1970	708,000	2	—	20–24 / 25–29	67% / 63%
	1979	589,723	2	—	<20 / 20–24	82% / 81%
USSR	1967	646,295	3–4	—	25–29 / 25–29	— / —
	1981	929,537	3–4	—	25–29 / 25–29	85% / 83%
U.S. Virgin Islands	1973	299	3	48%	30–34 / 25–29	71% / 66%
Venezuela	1966	2,253	5	43%	25–29 / 30–34	81% / 72%
	1974	4,018	6	46%	25–29 / 25–29	66% / 59%
	1979	4,852	4	53%	25–29 / 25–29	55% / 49%
Yugoslavia	1956	19,336	2	—	25–29 / 25–29	89% / 83%
	1966	23,042	1	58%	25–29 / 25–29	87% / 82%
	1974	24,802	2	—	20–24 / 25–29	86% / 81%
	1979	9,895	1	—	25–29 / 25–29	83% / 78%
58 Peoples	150 Cases†	*Mode:*	4 Yrs.	45%	25–29 / 25–29	82% / 77%
		Median:	—	45%	—	83% / 77%
		Mean:	—	48%	—	82% / 75%
		Range:	<1–9 Yrs.	21%–86%	—	47%–100% / 43%–100%

Source: Demographic Yearbook, United Nations, 1982, chart 38; 1976, chart 39; 1968, chart 41; 1958, chart 29.

*From Vital Statistics of the United States 1970; 1979.

†Two cases have two modes; these cases are excluded from analysis of modal duration of marriage that ends in divorce in the text and Fig. 1.

— Data not available.

exhibited the highest frequency of divorce during the ninth year of marriage (table, column 4; Fisher 1989). The 1979 United States divorce peak occurred between the second and third year of marriage (fig. 6; Fisher 1989). These variations are not surprising; given the tremendous variety in worldwide opinions about divorce and procedures concerning divorce, it is remarkable that cross-cultural patterns appear at all. Yet they do. Worldwide divorces cluster around a peak during the fourth year of marriage.

Age at divorce also has a pattern. The 23 societies for which data are available from 1966 to 1981 illustrate that divorce risk is greatest among men in the age category 25–29; among women, the two age categories of equally highest divorce risk are 20–24 and 25–29 (United Nations 1982, chart 40, 38; United Nations 1977, chart 41, 39; fig. 7; Fisher 1989). After age 29 the risk of divorce systematically decreases with increasing age. Thus worldwide divorce is most frequent among men and women in their twenties—the height of reproductive and parenting years.

The third divorce pattern seen in the United Nations data concerns the number of children per divorce. Unfortunately, because there are no data to compare the number of children in marriages that do not end in divorce with the number of children in marriages that do end in divorce, it is impossible to establish whether a couple is at greater risk of divorcing when childless, after having a single infant, or after bearing several offspring. But the raw data on 45 societies for which information is available between 1950 and 1981 illustrate that 40% of divorces occur among couples with no children, 26% of divorces occur among couples with one dependent child, 18% of divorces occur among couples with two dependent children, 7% of divorces occur among couples with three dependent children, and the number of divorces among couples with four or more children becomes increasingly slight (United Nations 1982, chart 39; United Nations 1977, chart 40; United Nations 1969, chart 39; United Nations 1959, chart 27; Fisher 1989). How pertinent these figures are is difficult to say; the number of children per divorce may be an artifact of the short duration of many marriages or the young age of most divorcées. But divorce counts peak among couples with one or no children.

A final contingent of divorce is remarriage. The United Nations Statistical Office records the number of remarriages for specific peoples in specific years, but it does not tabulate the percent of divorcées that remarry. Remarriage is

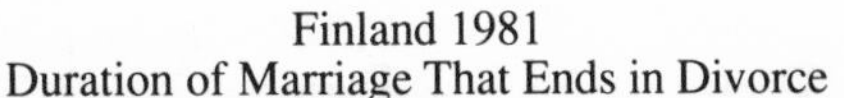

Finland 1981
Duration of Marriage That Ends in Divorce

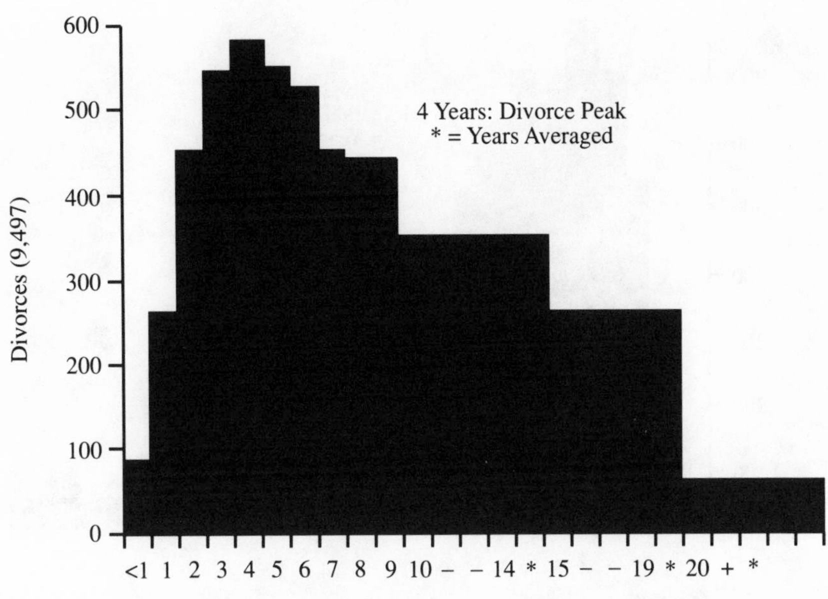

Fig. 1 illustrates the divorce profile for Finland in 1981 (*Demographic Yearbook,* United Nations 1984, chart 32). There were 587 divorces during the fourth year of marriage, the year during which the highest frequency of divorce occurred. Data on divorces occurring between 10 and 14 years of marriage and between 15 and 19 years of marriage are averaged because the raw data lump them together. Data on divorces occurring after 20 or more years of marriage are also lumped in the raw data. Because of the long-tailed distribution of divorce in the 20+ category (with divorces occurring among peoples aged 70+), this category was designated 20–40 years married and averaged in order to draw this histogram. In actuality, divorce steadily declines with increasing number of years of marriage.

frequent, however, in those places for which data are available. Cherlin (1981) estimates that 75% of American women and 80% of American men who divorce remarry. Similar data are available for Canada (Kuzel & Krishnan 1979), and England and Wales (McGregor 1957) for specific years since 1950; in all these cases, the majority of those who divorce while in their twenties take another spouse.

So in many industrial and agricultural societies, a high frequency of men

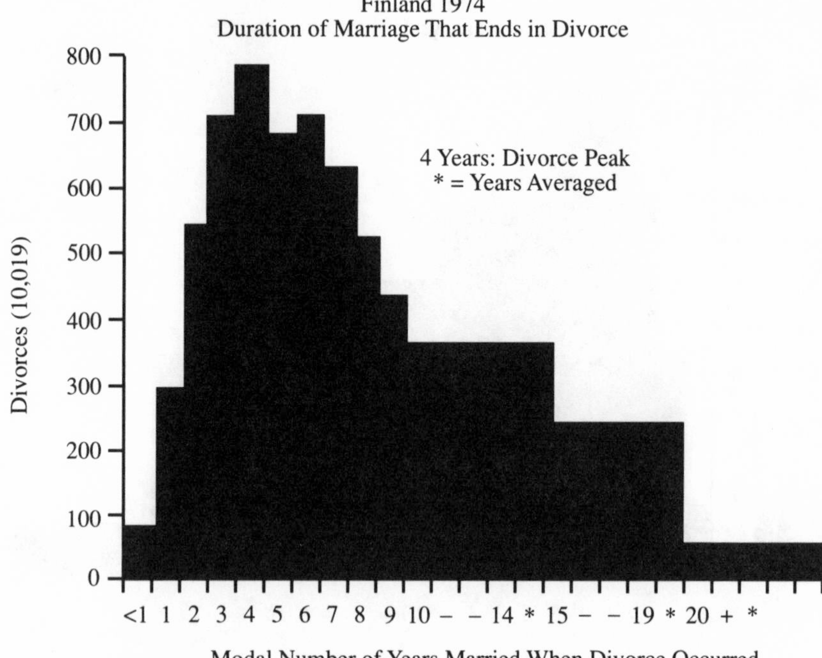

Figs. 2–4 illustrate the divorce profile for Finland in the three previous decades (*Demographic Yearbook,* United Nations 1977, chart 39; 1969, chart 41; 1959, chart 29). As can be seen the divorce *pattern* shows little change—with a divorce peak on or around the fourth year of marriage—despite steadily increasing divorce *rates* during these decades.

and women form a pair-bond with one individual, remain pair-bonded for about four years, dissolve their pair-bond and bond again—what is commonly known as serial monogamy. It will be interesting to establish which sex divorces more frequently, but who divorces whom is impossible to establish. Although laws and customs often dictate which spouse begins divorce proceedings, which individual actually initiates emotional, physical, and legal separation is not quantifiable. After all the arguing and tears are over, sometimes even the parties involved are not sure who left whom.

Data on serial pair-bonding are not available for most of the societies that lack official census takers—peoples that live along the headwaters of the Amazon, on coral atolls in the Pacific, and in other remote parts of the world. Anthropologists have collected relevant material in a few of these

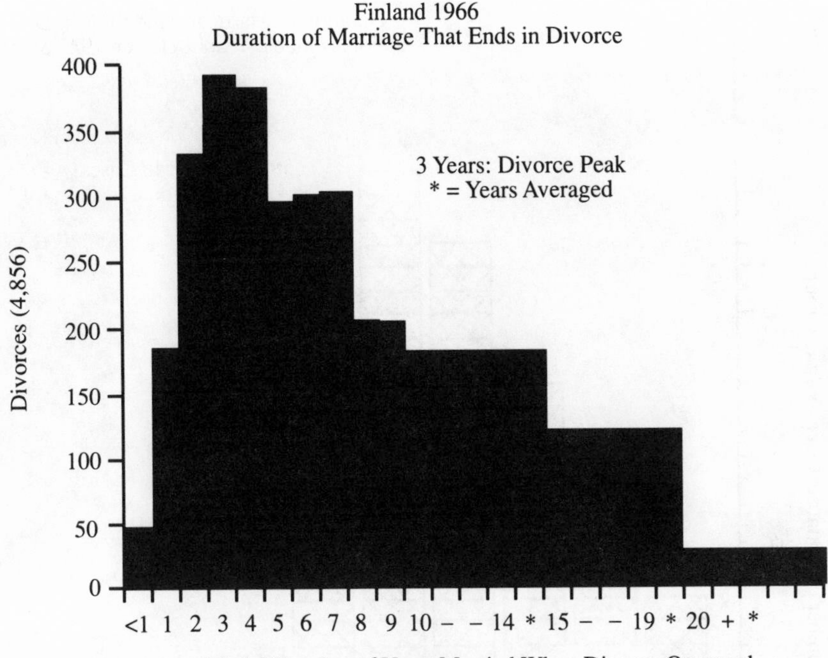
Finland 1966
Duration of Marriage That Ends in Divorce
400
350
300
250
200
150
100
50
0
Divorces (4,856)
3 Years: Divorce Peak
* = Years Averaged
<1 1 2 3 4 5 6 7 8 9 10 – – 14 * 15 – – 19 * 20 + *
Modal Number of Years Married When Divorce Occurred

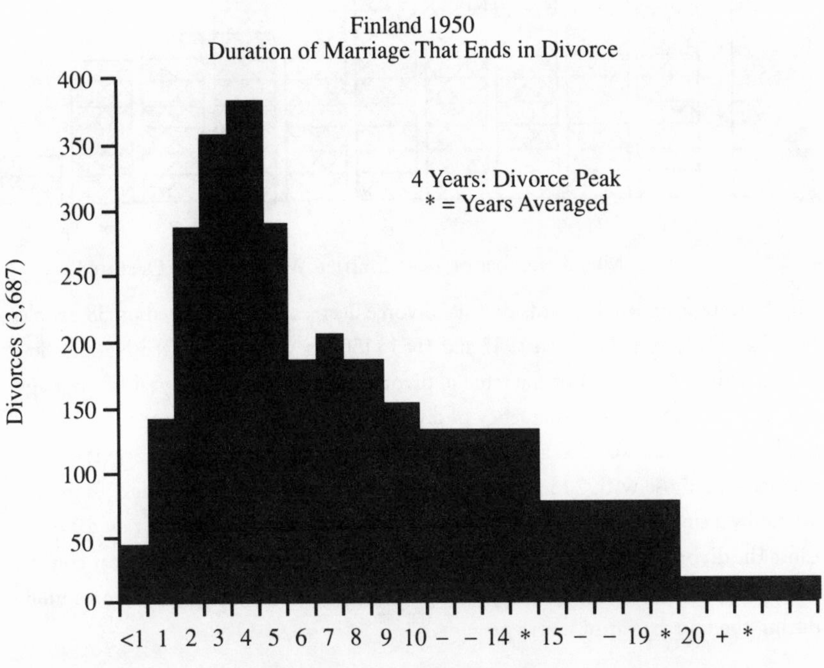
Finland 1950
Duration of Marriage That Ends in Divorce
400
350
300
250
200
150
100
50
0
Divorces (3,687)
4 Years: Divorce Peak
* = Years Averaged
<1 1 2 3 4 5 6 7 8 9 10 – – 14 * 15 – – 19 * 20 + *
Modal Number of Years Married When Divorce Occurred

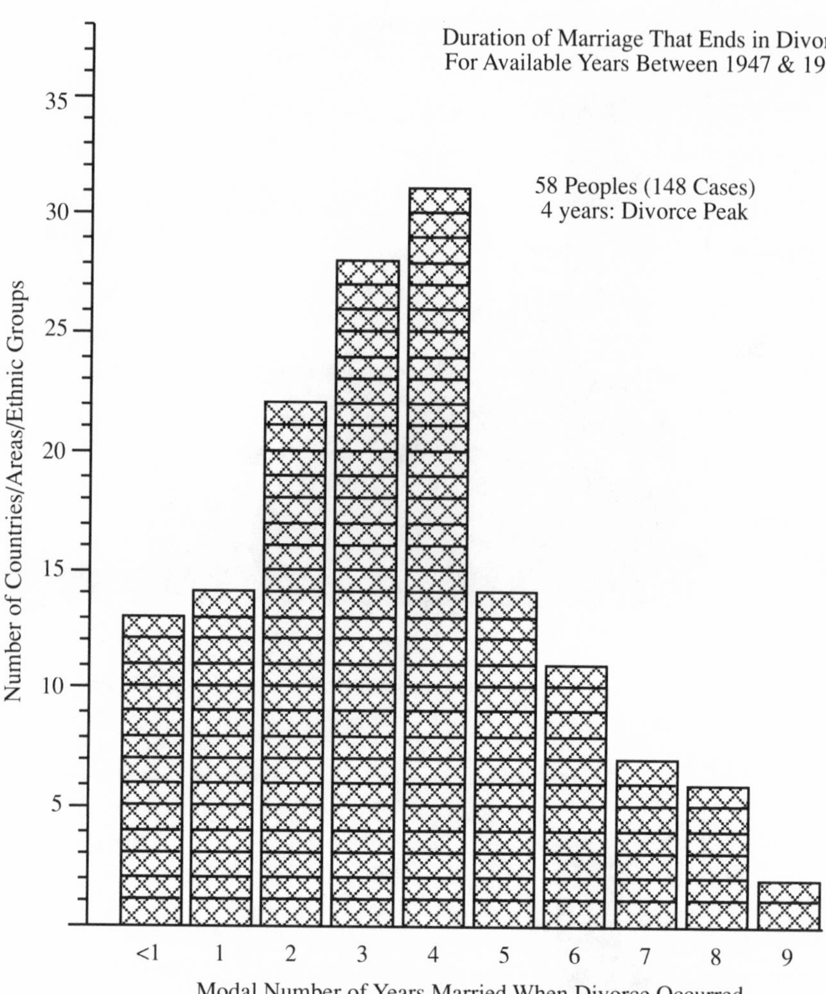

Fig. 5. Data from legal records on final divorce decrees were compiled on 58 peoples for all available years between 1947 and 1981 (150 cases) by the United Nations Statistical Office. Column 4 of the table of divorce patterns shows the year of marriage during which the highest frequency of divorce occurs for every society and year available; societies excluded are those in which fewer than 50 divorces occur; cases excluded are those with 2 modes (2 cases). Each of these "divorce modes" is represented by a single square in Fig. 5. Russian census takers lumped their raw data; because the divorce mode was 3–4 years in all 6 cases, 3 boxes are in the 3-year column and 3 boxes are in the 4-year column. Fig. 5 illustrates a cross-cultural divorce mode during the fourth year of marriage.

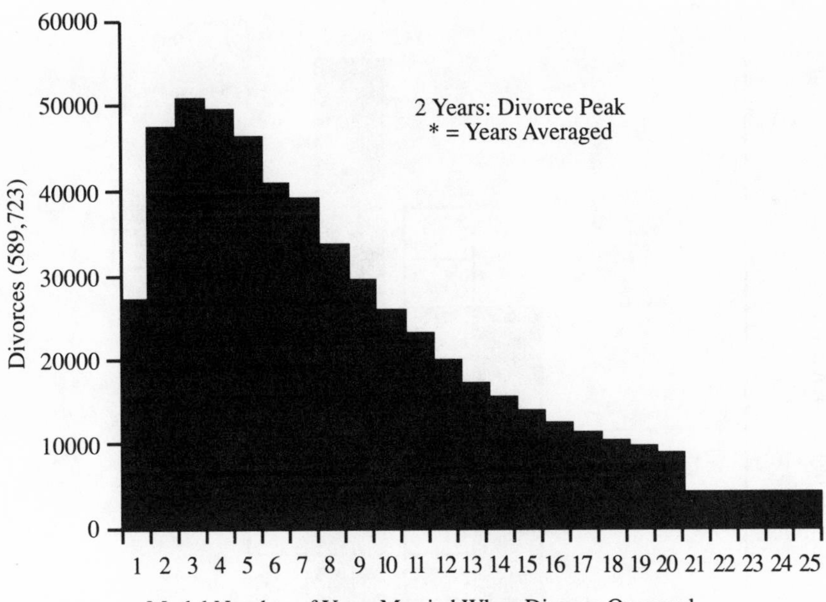

Fig. 6 illustrates the divorce profile for the United States in 1979. (*Vital Statistics of the United States, 1979*.) Because of the long-tailed distribution of divorce in the 20+ category, this category was designated 20–40 years married and averaged in order to draw this histogram.

cultures, however. In studying the decay rate of the nuclear family in 13 Yanomamo villages of the Upper Orinoco region of Venezuela, Chagnon (1982) reports that nearly 100% of children aged less than five years live with their natural mother; the majority have their natural father living with them, too. But the co-residence of both biological parents declines sharply after the child reaches age five. And although may of these marriages terminate because of death in this society rife with warfare, the balance are the result of divorce. Among the Trukese of the Pacific, marriages are brittle among people in their twenties but become more stable after this period (Murdock 1965), and divorce is also frequent among young couples in several other horticultural (gardening/hunting) societies (Friedl 1975). Although the ethnographic literature does not provide statistical data on remarriage, it does

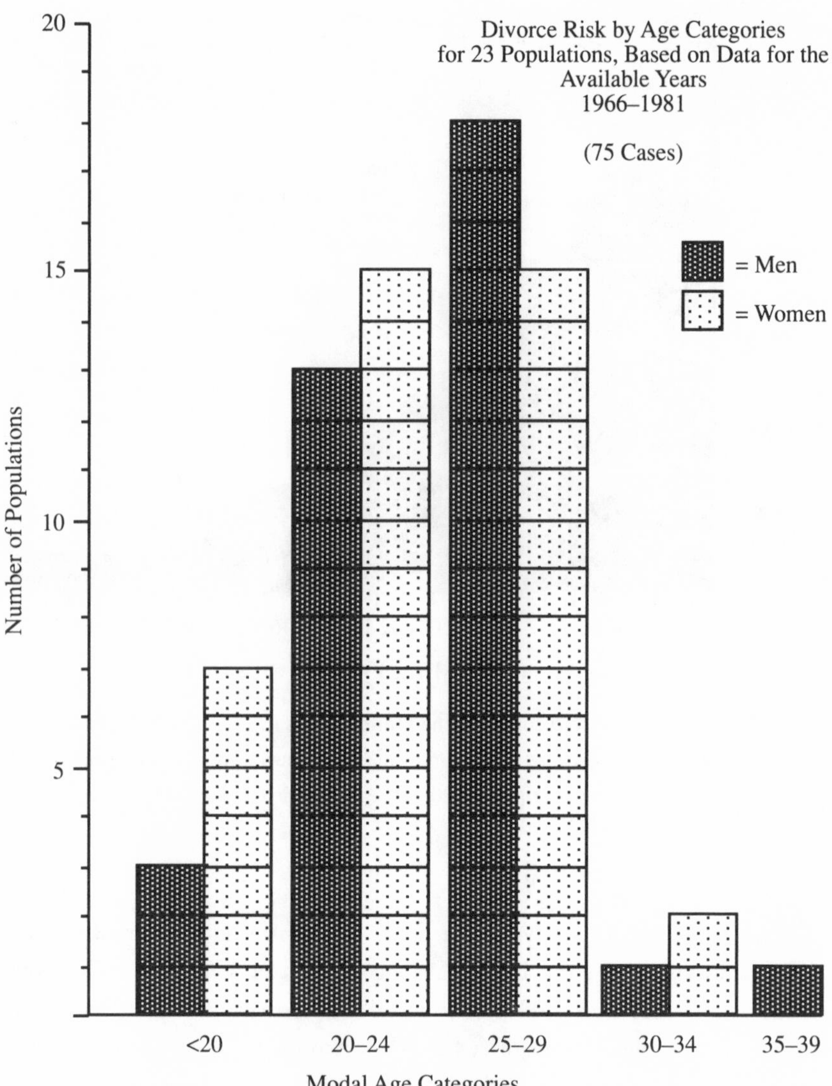

Fig. 7. Age at highest divorce risk, or the percent of married men and women who divorce in specific age categories, is tabulated for all 23 societies for which data are available on selected years (75 cases) between 1966 and 1981 (Fisher 1989). In Fig. 7 the age category of highest divorce risk in each case is represented by a single square, designated male or female. Fig. 7 illustrates that within this sample, divorce risk is greatest among men in the age category 25–29; divorce risk for women is equally greatest in age categories 20–24 and 25–29.

indicate that individuals of reproductive age wed again. Almost no young men or women remain single long. These data are consistent with the general divorce patterns seen in the societies tabulated through the demographic yearbooks of the United Nations.

Among the Kanuri, a Moslem people of Nigeria, a different pattern occurs (Cohen 1971). Divorces peak prior to the first full year of marriage, not during or around the fourth year. This early divorce peak, Cohen reports, is because "young girls tend not to stay with first husbands whom they are forced to marry by parents" (Cohen 1971, 135). The same pattern of high divorce among couples within months of marriage is seen among the Dobe !Kung of southern Africa, where arranged marriages are also common (Howell 1979), and among couples of arranged marriages in several other societies studied by anthropologists (Friedl 1975).

This pattern of divorce within months of wedding is also seen in the United Nations sample, although it is the exception rather than the rule. Bulgaria, Egypt, Israel, Japan, Jordan, Kuwait, and Poland all exhibit a divorce peak prior to the first full year of marriage (table; Fisher 1989). Curiously, Egypt, Japan, Jordan, and Kuwait also have a high incidence of arranged first marriages. Further research is necessary to establish the possible correlation between arranged marriages and quick divorces and other variations off the norm found in the United Nations sample. Suffice it to say that despite these exceptions, a four-year divorce peak occurs. Why?

The answer does not have to do with divorce rate. Among the Yanomamo, the divorce rate is low, while it is high among the !Kung, the Kanuri, and other horticultural peoples; yet these peoples share some similar patterns of divorce. In the United Nations sample, the divorce rate varies dramatically from one society to the next (United Nations 1982, chart 24, 35; United Nations 1955, chart 35; Fisher 1989) and independently of the cross-cultural divorce peak (Fisher 1989). Divorce rates also vary within the same society over time without affecting the divorce peak. For example, in Finland the divorce rate doubled between 1950 and 1981 (United Nations 1955, chart 35; United Nations 1982, chart 24; Fisher 1989); throughout those three decades, however, the divorce peak remained on or around the four-year mark (Figs. 1–4; Fisher 1989).

These patterns of divorce are not the function of child conception either. In the dozens of societies canvassed between 1936 and 1981 by the United

Nations, without exception the highest frequency of births occur during less than a year of marriage or during the first full year of marriage (United Nations 1949, chart 18; United Nations 1982, chart 37; Fisher 1989). There is no correlation between the period of time it takes to conceive a child and the four-year divorce peak. In fact, it is only when one examines monogamy in other species that these patterns of divorce become understandable.

Kleiman (1977) defines two types of monogamy in animals: Type I monogamy (facultative monogamy), in which adult pairs have overlapping territories but do not travel regularly in family groups, and Type II monogamy (obligate monogamy), in which adult pairs are commonly observed in family groups. She reports that obligate monogamy is favored in evolution in one or both of the following situations: "1) whenever the carrying capacity of the habitat is not great enough to permit another female simultaneously to raise a litter in the same home range, or 2) whenever more than a single individual (the female) is needed to rear the young" (Kleiman 1977, 51).

These circumstances, individually or in combination, as well as other circumstances (Wittenberger & Tilson 1980), could contribute to the incidence of monogamy in *Homo sapiens* and other species. But Kleiman's second reason for obligate monogamy may be particularly important. Several canid species bear large litters and/or infantile pups, and they regularly form a pair-bond and cooperate to raise their young (Kleiman & Eisenberg 1973). For example, a female red fox forms a pair-bond in mid-winter, and together the mated pair raise their young during the summer months. But when the young begin to wander in the autumn, parents split up to forage independently. The pair-bond lasts only through the breeding season, and individuals do not always form a pair-bond with the same mate in successive breeding periods (Gage 1979; Rue 1969). Among wolves, the alpha male and alpha female often form the only breeding unit, and their pair-bond can last for several years. But if the male is deposed, the female will form a new pair-bond with a different male in a subsequent breeding season (Klinghammer, pers. comm.). In canid species, serial monogamy occurs, and it occurs in association with a breeding season.

Formation of a pair-bond during the breeding season is a common reproductive strategy in birds (Kleiman 1977). Most of these species bear highly immature, helpless, altricial young or young that for other ecological reasons need the support of two adults, and over 90% of 9,000 species of birds form pair-bonds. But Eugene Morton (pers. comm.) estimates that in at least 50% of these species, the pair-bond does not last for life. For example, a male and female robin form a pair-bond and raise their young together. But after the fledglings fly, mates split up. They will not form another pair-bond until the next breeding season; most likely they will not mate with one another (Kleiman 1977).

These data on monogamy in other creatures lend perspective to divorce, because human beings share two critical characteristics with foxes, robins, and other serially monogamous animals. First, women bear babies that need the care of more than a single individual, the female. Like the young of many avian species, human infants are helpless, infantile, altricial. All of the primates bear altricial young, and the degree of altriciality increases from prosimians, to monkeys, to apes. But there is a significant increase in the degree of altriciality in hominids relative to apes (Trevathan 1987; Lindburg 1982), known as hominid secondary altriciality.

Second, we tend to form pair-bonds that last about four years—and four years may have been the length of our ancestral breeding season. Howell (1979) notes that among the traditional !Kung San of southern Africa, continuous breast-feeding inhibits ovulation for up to three years, creating a pattern of four-year birth spacing. The same pattern of four-year birth intervals is seen in traditional Australian aborigines (Birdsell 1979). Infants are generally weaned among the Yanomamo of Amazonia (Hames, pers. comm.), among the Netsilik Eskimo (Briggs 1970), and among the Lepcha of Sikkim (Gorer 1938) during the fourth year, suggesting a four-year pattern of birth spacing among these peoples also. These data have led Lancaster and Lancaster (1983) to propose that four-year intervals was the regular pattern of birth spacing in ancestral hominid populations.

Thus the modern human pattern of serial monogamy—with a peak marriage duration of four years—conforms to what could be the traditional period between successive births. Like pair-bonding in foxes and robins, human serial monogamy may have evolved in the hominid lineage to raise successive cohorts of highly dependent young. The "seven year itch," recast as a four-year reproductive cycle, may be a biological phenomenon.

No one knows when monogamy evolved. Human pair-bonding could have originated over 3.5 million years ago, when our first hominid ancestors began to adapt to a woodland/grassland environment by walking on two legs on the ground from one food source to the next (Fisher 1975, 1982, in press). The evolution of bipedalism would have required females to carry infants in their arms rather than on their backs, increasing their "reproductive burden." Coupled with increased predation pressure, these vicissitudes could have selected for Kleiman's second type of obligate monogamy: a situation in which "more than a single individual (the female) is needed to rear the young" (Kleiman 1977, 51).

The evolution of secondary altriciality of the hominid infant also could have contributed to the female's reproductive burden and triggered the evolution of monogamy. But no one knows when this occurred. A standard explanation is that hominid secondary altriciality developed when smaller maternal pelvic diameters, in association with the corresponding larger diameters of the fetal cranium, no longer permitted successful parturition—favoring delivery of the fetus at an earlier stage of development (Washburn 1950; Montagu 1961; Gould 1977). Martin (quoted in Lewin 1982) and Berge et al. (1984) independently conclude that by 2 million years ago selection for altricial young must have taken place in the species *Homo habilis.* But because different altricial traits could have been acquired at different times (Lewin 1985), because it is unclear when the complete suite of human characteristics attributed to secondary altriciality evolved, and because there is evidence that the evolution of hominid secondary altriciality is not associated with cephalopelvic disproportion (Lindburg 1982), these data lend few insights into the evolution of pair-bonding.

Another trait which may be linked to the origin of human monogamy is the evolution of hominid growth rhythms. Human beings have a much longer childhood than do the apes, and we continue to feed our juveniles long into teenage—unlike the apes, who do not feed their offspring after weaning them (Lancaster and Lancaster 1983). Lancaster and Lancaster (1983) and Lancaster (forthcoming) propose that human pair-bonding evolved in tandem with extended childhoods and that along with this shift in the hominid life course came other hallmarks of human social life, including the evolution of male hunting and female gathering, the division of labor between the sexes, and the sharing of food at a home base. But the development of these cultural traits is also hard to pinpoint. From the balance of archeological evidence, Lancaster (forthcoming) concludes that the long hominid juvenile period and parental partnerships could have evolved as early as 1.5 million years ago or as recently as the last glaciation, beginning about or less than 100,000 years ago.

Other data give conflicting inferential evidence for the evolution of monogamy, too. Information derived from fossil teeth suggests that the extended juvenile period could have evolved as early as 2 million years ago among australopithecines (Mann 1975), or much later (Conroy & Vannier 1987; Bromage & Dean 1985; Smith 1986). The postcranial bones of *Homo habilis* peoples living 2 million years ago exhibit extreme sexual dimorphism in body size, a trait normally associated with polygyny, whereas later *Homo erectus* fossils show a reduction in sexual dimorphism in body size resembling modern male/female ratios (Lewin 1987). Until several lines of investigation converge, it is impossible to establish exactly when ancestral females began to need a mate to help them raise their young.

Nevertheless, monogamy did indeed evolve at some point in human evolution; we see pair-bonding around the world today. And I propose it evolved under the same conditions that monogamy originated in foxes and robins—when more than a single individual (the female) was needed to rear the young (Kleiman 1977, 51). But why did these early pair-bonds need to be permanent? Permanent monogamy is not universal to people. Long marriages take work. Many men and women around the world divorce, sometimes several times. Moreover, there are several reasons why serial pair-bonds—lasting at least long enough to raise one child through infancy, about four years—could have had genetic payoffs for both ancestral men and women.

Individuals that conceived offspring by more than one partner would have borne more varied young, producing genetic vitality in their individual lineages. We see this behavior pattern regularly today—women who bear children by more than one man, and men who produce sons and/or daughters by more than one woman. Producing variety in one's lineage has survival value; in times of extreme selection pressure, most young will die, but some will live. Serial monogamy could have had other biological benefits in the past. A male that dissolved one partnership for another would have had the opportunity to select a younger mate more likely to deliver more viable offspring; an ancestral female that dissolved an unsatisfactory relationship had the opportunity to choose a mate that provided better protection, food, and nurturance to her, her children, and to forthcoming infants, increasing her chances of raising offspring to maturity. These strategies are also commonplace today. Men often take a younger, second wife, and women who replace their spouse try to pick a more compatible companion that provides more goods and services.

But was it to a male's reproductive advantage to abandon his own genetically related children to raise new young with a different partner, thereby possibly acquiring responsibilities for the unrelated children of the new consort? Likewise, one must consider whether it was to a female's reproductive advantage to subject her children's welfare to the whims of a "stepfather" when she changed consorts. One could argue, however, that in modern Western cultures—where children are normally the responsibility of only two adults and the costs of education and entertainment are high—the genetic disadvantages of stepparenting may be considerably higher than in hunting/gathering cultures of the past, in which children past the age of four grew up in multi-age play groups under the auspices of several adults and the costs of education and entertainment were low. Suffice it to say that whatever the disadvantages of serial pair-bonding were, they were not adequate to have produced a human reproductive strategy of universal lifelong monogamy. Dozens of sources confirm that serial pair-bonding is a common cross-cultural practice.

This is not to suggest that lifelong monogamy had no advantages in prehistory or that human beings are incapable of maintaining long-term pair-bonds. Although almost half of American marriages fail (Cherlin 1981), the balance last for life; human beings can maintain permanent marital relationships. But these are much more common in some societies than in others. Lifelong pair-bonds are particularly prevalent in agricultural peoples such as in preindustrial India (Fernando 1981), preindustrial China (Wolf 1981), nineteenth-century America (Cherlin 1981), and preindustrial European societies (Dupaquier et al. 1981). Not surprisingly, lifelong monogamy is also more clearly understood from the cross-species perspective.

As reported above, Type II monogamy, or obligate monogamy, also occurs "whenever the carrying capacity of the habitat is not great enough to permit another female simultaneously to raise a litter in the same home range." Gibbons and siamangs may have evolved monogamy primarily for this reason. These lesser apes live in Southeast Asia in forests of dispersed resources. Here food is so spread out that several females cannot raise their young in the same home range; they must split up. So a male and female form a pair-bond soon after puberty and defend a territory containing an adequate number of fruit trees and sleeping sites. Both partners are tied to the real estate and to one another; the pair-bond regularly lasts for life. Monogamous New World monkeys also exhibit this pattern of dispersed resources, exclusive territories, and lifelong monogamy (Kinzey 1987).

This mosaic configuration is also seen in agricultural societies. Like gibbons, siamangs, and monogamous New World monkeys, a man and woman living on a farm characteristically raise their young in a defined, and defended, area with a limited but continuously renewing food supply. And in agricultural societies, where marriage is a fundamental exchange of property between families and these between-family ties are the warp and woof of social life, men and women are bound to the land and to one another. Marriages normally last for life (Fisher 1987, in press).

Sociologists, psychologists, and cultural anthropologists have proposed several variables that contribute to marital stability (Cohen 1971). But the United Nations data suggest two patterns of long-term monogamy that have an evolutionary ring. One is increasing chronological age. In the 58 cultures tabulated over 4 decades via the demographic yearbooks of the United Nations, the frequency of divorce continues to decline after age 30. Eighty-two percent of divorces occur among women before age 44; 75% of divorces occur among men prior to age 44 (Fisher 1989). These data indicate that long-term monogamy has adaptive advantages for men and women after they pass the height of reproductive and parenting years. Perhaps these bonds served grandparenting and reciprocal care-giving services in prehistory.

The United Nations data also demonstrate that divorce counts peak among couples with two or fewer children (Fisher 1989), suggesting that couples that produce three or more issue normally remain married for life. This is logical; couples that remain together are probably more compatible and thus more likely to bear additional young. And from a Darwinian perspective, the reproductive burden of several offspring probably obliged ancestral couples with several children to remain together to raise them, a trend that continues to this day.

When all these data on worldwide divorce are examined together, they lead me to an unprovable, multipart theory. In hunting/gathering societies of the past, several reproductive strategies may have operated simultaneously: young, childless couples frequently deserted one another; couples with one child frequently remained together at least long enough to raise their baby through infancy; couples with several children frequently remained pair-bonded for life to raise several young; older couples frequently remained together to raise grandchildren (and other young of the community) and to help one another in old age.

Only one of these speculations is arguable at this time, however. Because there is a cross-cultural divorce peak during and around the fourth year of marriage, because the proposed period between successive births in past populations is four years, and because there is an association between serial pair-bonding and the rearing of highly dependent young through infancy in several other mammalian and avian species, it is parsimonious to conclude that pair-bonding evolved in humankind concurrent with an increased female reproductive burden and that the modern cross-cultural four-year divorce peak reflects an ancestral adaptive strategy to remain pair-bonded at least long enough to raise a single infant through the period of lactation.

But why, if pair-bonding is critical to the survival of our young, do men and women engage in adultery? Philandering is a legitmate cause for divorce in many cultures (Murdock 1965), and male sexual jealousy is the leading cause of spousal homicide and wife beating in much of the world today (Daly & Wilson 1983). Yet people indulge in adultery with avid regularity. Infidelity probably had Darwinian payoffs for both sexes in the past. For ancestral hominid males, adultery would have produced extra young, increasing their genetic fitness. Adultery could have been advantageous to hominid females, too. Hrdy (1981) points out that female primates of several species apparently engage in nonreproductive sexual behavior to confuse paternity, thereby encouraging several males to behave "paternally" toward infants and discouraging infanticide by males during times of group social upheaval. It seems logical that a similar mechanism to confuse paternity would have served the same useful functions for ancestral hominid females. But because open promiscuity would have jeopardized the pair-bond, perhaps with the evolution of monogamy, overt promiscuity evolved into covert adultery.

Nisa, a traditional !Kung San woman living in the Kalahari Desert of southern Africa, summed up this female strategy succinctly. "There are many kinds of work a woman has to do, and she should have lovers wherever she goes. If she goes somewhere to visit and is alone, then someone there will give her beads, someone else will give her meat, and someone else will give her other food. When she returns to her village, she will have been well taken care of'' (Shostak 1981, 271). Adultery may have provided ancestral women with the same perquisites it does for Nisa and females of other species—supplementary support and protection to the adulterous female and her young.

American scientists and laymen are convinced that men are more adulterous than women, and our polls confirm our belief (Kinsey et al. 1948; Kinsey et al. 1953; Hunt 1974; Lampe 1987). Yet in several cultures where no sexual double standard exists, wives appear to philander just as regularly as their husbands (Fisher, in press). The study of adultery is not a science; we may never know which sex philanders more often. But as with all other aspects of male and female sexuality, a host of cultural, ecological, *and* evolutionary factors probably contribute to the frequency of adultery in so malleable an animal as a human being.

But we do exhibit a few regularities to our sexual tactics; men and women exhibit a ''mixed'' reproductive strategy. Although polygyny is more prevalent among men than is polyandry among women, monogyny and monandry are the norm; the vast majority of men and women around the world have one spouse at a time. Some remain married to the same person throughout life, while others remarry once or several times. And some men and women are adulterous in every society for which data are available. Breeding programs in zoos support the conclusion that this mosaic reproductive strategy—serial (or lifelong) monogamy and clandestine adultery—is, at least in part, genetically determined, selected during human evolution.

The consequences have been enormous. Our human concepts of *husband, father, wife,* and *family;* our worldwide customs about marriage, divorce, and remarriage; the myriad cross-cultural traditions of courtship; mankind's punishments for adultery; Western beliefs about morality and sin; patterns of family violence stemming from jealousy and desertion; our great love stories; our mournful songs and seductive dances; and millions of other cultural artifacts—all stem from the human propensity to make and break pair-bonds with one another. But the most provocative result of this human sexual revolution may lie in the brain.

In some highly speculative work, Liebowitz (1983) theorizes that the attraction phase of love is associated with heightened levels of, or increased sensitivity to, phenylethylamine and/or other neurotransmitter substances in the brain, chemicals that create the sensations of euphoria, elation, optimism, and sleeplessness normally associated with infatuation. But he suggests that, with time, nerve endings in the limbic system become either saturated by, or increasingly insensitive to, these neurotransmitters, causing a cessation of the attraction phase of love. As he writes, "If you want a situation where you and your longterm partner can still get very excited about each other you will have to work at it because in some ways you are bucking a biological tide" (Liebowitz 1983, 200). Money (1980) and Tennov (1979) report that the sensation of infatuation is typically at its peak for two to three years.

Liebowitz (1983) also theorizes that the second stage of human love, the attachment phase, is associated with brain physiology, specifically the endorphins, neurotransmitters that seem to play an important role in attachment in other animals. He does not speculate on how long this second stage lasts, but he proposes these two different chemical systems evolved in human evolution for distinct and specific reasons. "For primitive man two aspects of relating to the opposite sex were important for survival as a species. The first was to have males and females become attracted to each other for long enough to have sex and reproduce. The second was for the males to become strongly attached to the females, so that they stayed around while the females were raising their young" (Liebowitz 1983, 90).

This controversial proposal by Liebowitz is raised here for an important reason. We have long known that some emotions are correlated with bodily reactions; for example, adrenaline is generally associated with fear and rage. And although anthropologists often speculate on the evolution of human behavior patterns, such as the use of home bases, male parental investment, and male/female division of labor, they are regularly unable to suggest the *physical* mechanism by which selection could have favored these behavior patterns. The above data, although speculative at present, provide a possible physiological locus on which selection could have acted to produce modern patterns of pair-bonding. And to go one step further, I would not be surprised if we someday learned that the same physiological mechanisms underlie patterns of attachment and desertation in other animals. The feelings of infatuation, devotion, and sexual boredom may not be unique to men and women.

As Stendhal wrote, "Love is like a fever that comes and goes quite independently of the will." If human male/female attraction and attachment during reproductive years is a cyclic process, grounded in brain physiology, that evolved millennia ago to insure the survival of the young through infancy, then no wonder peoples from New Guinea to New York have rules about marriage, adultery, and divorce; no wonder men and women become captivated by one another then struggle to contain a restless spirit; no wonder Loren Eisley saw continuity between beast and man.

Acknowledgments

Thanks to Judy L. Andrews and Sue S. Carroll for their research assistance. All errors in this manuscript are those of the author.

References

Ackerman, C. 1963. Affiliations: Structural Determinants of Differential Divorce Rates. *American Journal of Sociology* 69:13–20.

Barnes, J. 1967. Divorce Rates in Tribal Society. In *The Craft of Social Anthropology,* ed. A. Epstein. London: Tavistock.

Berge, C., R. Orban-Segebarth, and P. Schmid. 1984. Obstetric Interpretation of the Australopithecine Pelvic Cavity. *Journal of Human Evolution* 13:573–87.

Birdsell, J. B. 1979. Ecological Influences on Australian Aboriginal Social Organization. In *Primate Ecology and Human Origins: Ecological Influences on Social Organization,* ed. I. S. Bernstein and E. O. Smith, 177–252. New York: Garland.

Briggs, J. L. 1970. *Never in Anger: Portrait of an Eskimo Family.* Cambridge: Harvard University Press.

Bromage, T. G., and M. C. Dean. 1985. Re-evaluation of the Age at Death of Immature Fossil Hominids. *Nature* 317:525–27.

Chagnon, N. 1982. Sociodemographic Attributes of Nepotism in Tribal Populations: Man the Rule Breaker. In *Current Problems in Sociobiology,* ed. B. Bertram, 291–318. Cambridge: Cambridge University Press.

Cherlin, A. J. 1981. *Marriage, Divorce, Remarriage.* Cambridge: Harvard University Press.

Cohen, R. 1971. *Dominance and Defiance: A Study of Marital Instability in an Islamic African Society.* Washington D.C.: American Anthropological Association.

Conroy, G. C., and M. W. Vannier. 1987. Dental Development of the Taung Skull from Computerized Tomography. *Nature* 329 (no. 6140):625–27.

Daly, M., and M. Wilson. 1983. *Sex, Evolution, and Behavior.* Boston: Willard Grant.

Daly, M., M. Wilson, and S. J. Weghorst. 1982. Male Sexual Jealousy. *Ethology and Sociobiology* 3:11–27.

Dupaquier, J., E. Helin, P. Laslett, M. Livi-Bacci, and S. Sogner, eds. 1981. *Marriage and Remarriage in Populations of the Past.* New York: Academic.

Fernando, D. F. S. 1981. Marriage and Remarriage in Some Asian Civilizations. In *Marriage and Remarriage in Populations of the Past.* J. Dupaquier, E. Helin, P. Laslett, M. Livi-Bacci, and S. Sogner, eds., 89–93. New York: Academic.

Fisher, H. E. In press. *The Evolution and Future of Marriage, Sex, and Love.* New York: W.W. Norton.

______. 1989. Evolution of Human Serial Pairbonding. *American Journal of Physical Anthropology* 78:331–54.

______. 1987. The Four-Year Itch. *Natural History Magazine* 96 (no. 10): 22–33.

______. 1982. *The Sex Contract: The Evolution of Human Behavior.* New York: William Morrow.

______. 1975. *The Loss of Estrous Periodicity in Hominid Evolution.* Ann Arbor Michigan: University Microfilms International.

Friedl, E. 1975. *Women and Men: An Anthropologist's View.* New York: Holt, Rinehart and Winston.

Gage, R. L. 1979. *Fox Family.* New York: Weatherhill/Heibonsha.

Fossey, D. 1983. *Gorillas in the Mist.* Boston: Houghton Mifflin.

Gorer, G. 1938. *Himalayan Village: An Account of the Lepchas of Sikkim.* London: M. Joseph.

Gould, S. J. 1977. *Ontogeny and Phylogeny.* Cambridge: Harvard University Press.

Hawthorn, G. 1970. *The Sociology of Fertility.* London: Collier-Macmillan.

Howell, N. 1979. *Demography of the Dobe !Kung.* New York: Academic.

Hrdy, S. B. 1981. *The Woman That Never Evolved.* Cambridge: Harvard University Press.

Hunt, M. 1974. *Sexual Behavior in the 1970's.* Chicago: Playboy.

Kinsey, A. C., W. B. Pomeroy, and C. E. Martin. 1948. *Sexual Behavior in the Human Male.* Philadelphia: W. B. Saunders.

Kinsey, A. C., W. B. Pomeroy, C. E. Martin, and P. H. Gebhard. 1953. *Sexual Behavior in the Human Female.* Philadelphia: W. B. Saunders.

Kinzey, W. G. 1987. Monogamous Primates: A Primate Model for Human Mating Systems. In *The Evolution of Human Behavior: Primate Models,* ed. W. G. Kinzey, 105–14. New York: State University of New York Press.

Kleiman, D. G. 1977. Monogamy in Mammals. *Quarterly Review of Biology* 52:39–69.

Kleiman, D. G., and J. F. Eisenberg. 1973. Comparisons of Canid and Felid Social Systems from an Evolutionary Perspective. *Animal Behaviour* 21:637–59.

Kuzel, P., and P. Krishnan. 1979. Changing Patterns of Remarriage in Canada, 1961–1966. In *Cross-Cultural Perspectives of Mate-Selection and Marriage,* ed. G. Kurian, 391–400. Westport, Conn.: Greenwood.

Lack, D. 1968. *Ecological Adaptations for Breeding in Birds.* London: Methuen.

Lampe, P. E. 1987. *Adultery in the United States.* Buffalo, N.Y.: Prometheus.

Lancaster, J. B. Forthcoming. Parental Investment and the Evolution of the Juvenile Phase of the Human Life Course. In *The Origins of Humanness,* ed. A. Brooks, Washington, D.C.: Smithsonian Institution Press.

Lancaster, J. B., and C. S. Lancaster. 1983. Parental Investment: The Hominid Adaptation. In *How Humans Adapt: A Biocultural Odyssey,* ed. D. J. Ortner, 33–65. Washington D.C.: Smithsonian Institution Press.

Lévi-Strauss, C. 1985. *The View from Afar.* New York: Basic.

Lewin, R. 1987. The Earliest "Humans" Were More Like Apes. *Science* 236:1061–63.

______. 1985. Surprise Findings in the Taung Child's Face. *Science* 228:42–44.

______. 1982. How Did Humans Evolve Big Brains? *Science* 216:840–41.

Liebowitz, M. R. 1983. *The Chemistry of Love.* Boston: Little, Brown.

Lindburg, D. G. 1982. Primate Obstetrics: The Biology of Birth. *American Journal of Primatology Supplement* 1:193–99.

Mann, A. 1975. *Paleodemographic Aspects of South Africa Australopithecines.* Philadelphia: University of Pennsylvania Press.

McGregor, O. R. 1957. *Divorce in England: A Centenary Study.* London: Heinemann.

Money, J. 1980. *Love and Love Sickness.* Baltimore: Johns Hopkins University Press.

Montagu, A. 1961. Neonatal and Infant Immaturity in Man. *Journal of the American Medical Association* 178:56–57.

Murdock, G. P. 1965. Family Stability in Non-European Cultures. In *Culture and Society.* Pittsburgh, Penn.: University of Pittsburgh Press, 312–23.

______. 1949. *Social Structure.* New York: Macmillan.

Rue, L. L. 1969. *The World of the Red Fox.* Philadelphia: J. B. Lippincott.

Shostak, M. 1981. *Nisa: The Life and Words of a !Kung Woman.* Cambridge: Harvard University Press.

Tennov, D. 1979. *Love and Limerence: The Experience of Being in Love.* New York: Stein and Day.

Textor, R. B. 1967. Divorce (Table FC 272). In *A Cross-Cultural Summary,* comp. R. B. Textor. New Haven, Conn.: HRAF Press.

Trevathan, W. R. N. D. 1987. *Human Birth: An Evolutionary Perspective.* New York: Aldine.

Statistical Office of the United Nations. Department of Economic and Social Affairs. 1984. *United Nations Demographic Yearbook: 1982.* New York: United Nations.

Statistical Office of the United Nations. Department of Economic and Social Affairs. 1982. *United Nations Demographic Yearbook: 1981.* New York: United Nations.

Statistical Office of the United Nations. Department of Economic and Social Affairs. 1977. *United Nations Demographic Yearbook: 1976.* New York: United Nations.

Statistical Office of the United Nations. Department of Economic and Social Affairs. 1969. *United Nations Demographic Yearbook: 1968.* New York: United Nations.

Statistical Office of the United Nations. Department of Economic and Social Affairs. 1959. *United Nations Demographic Yearbook: 1958.* New York: United Nations.

Statistical Office of the United Nations. Department of Economic and Social Affairs. 1955. *United Nations Demographic Yearbook: 1954.* New York: United Nations.

Statistical Office of the United Nations. Department of Economic and Social Affairs. 1949. *United Nations Demographic Yearbook: 1948.* New York: United Nations.

van den Berghe, P. L. 1979. *Human Family Systems: An Evolutionary View.* Amsterdam: Elsevier.

Vital Statistics of the United States, 1979. 1984. Vol. 3, *Marriage and Divorce.* Hyattsville, Md.: U.S. Department of Health and Human Services, Tables 2–21.

Washburn, S. L. 1950. The Analysis of Primate Evolution with Particular Reference to the Origin of Man. *Cold Spring Harbor Symposia on Quantitative Biology* 15:67–78.

Wittenberger, J. F., and R. L. Tilson. 1980. The Evolution of Monogamy: Hypotheses and Evidence. *Annual Review of Ecology Systematics* 11:197–232.

Wolf, A. P. 1981. Women, Widowhood, and Fertility in Pre-Modern China. In *Marriage and Remarriage in Populations of the Past*, ed. J. Dupaquier, E. Helin, P. Laslett, M. Livi-Bacci, and S. Sogner. New York: Academic.

Wolfe, L. 1981. *Women and Sex in the 80s: The "Cosmo" Report.* New York: Arbor House.

Mammalian Social Organizations and the Case of *Alouatta*

John F. Eisenberg

Since the last Man and Beast Symposium, research on the social behavior of animals has made significant advances. Indeed, whole new directions in research orientation have been established. After the 1950s the study of animal behavior by Western scientists had begun to undergo a revolution. It was then appreciated that the study of animal behavior, or for that matter human behavior, involved a crucial first step. An observer had to record objectively the behavior of the subjects in a natural context. It was impossible to study the variations in behavior patterns unless it was known beforehand what the norm was from which the variants depart (as paraphrased from P. Medawar, in Chapple 1970, 4).

In 1969, ethology (the study of behavior) was on the threshold of a new synthesis. Natural selection was recognized to have played a role in shaping the behavior of animals. It was established that the dichotomy between learning and instinct was an artificial one. That "species typical" behavior could be described as a norm or an average was recognized, but the variation of behavior from a norm, and its underlying causes, was still a relatively unexplored domain. That animals could communicate with each other was firmly established, but we did not know exactly what information was conveyed. Finally, we were beginning to appreciate how altruistic behavior could evolve under natural selection and thus account for the evolution of animal societies (see Eisenberg & Dillon 1971).

Aspects of interspecific sociality could, of course, be discussed, but this would lead us into the realm of community ecology. I will limit my comments to intraspecific sociality, a difficult task at best. A social system is, above all, a communication system. It consists of senders and receivers whose roles may be interchangeable. It was recognized by early naturalists that methods of communication could involve vastly different signal types depending on the perceptual organs involved (Uexküll 1909). Thus at the minimum we could have chemical signals, visual signals, auditory signals, and tactile signals. In the early years of analyzing animal communication, the description of the signals themselves took on paramount importance. Thus inventories according to the sense organs for which these signals were intended were drawn up, and a physical description, where possible, was rendered for the signal types (Marler & Hamilton 1966, chaps. 10–12).

The second approach to communication analysis involved a consideration of the significance of the signal to the communicant. This task was accomplished initially by inferences based on the nature of the receiving animal's response. A recent area of great interest in communication analysis involves the meaning of a signal (Smith 1977). In this approach the signal can express more than a fixed category of denotation and may convey a connotation to the receiver allowing the receiver to assign a specific meaning to the signal. Some significant progress has been made by analyzing antipredator calls in an attempt to discover if variations in call structure might in fact indicate to the receiver a specificity of the predator type (see Seyfarth 1987).

It was recognized by ethologists that there are different degrees of sociality, usually defined by the number and classes (age and sex) of individuals constituting a group showing some cohesion in space and time. Thus an aggregation was a group of interacting organisms that associated either because of some particular environmental circumstance or because they had come together by chance. Aggregations based on an environmental variable were held up in contrast to true social organizations in which the members actively sought to maintain different types of relationships. It was also recognized that for any given species, the degree of sociality and the type of sociality may be phasic. Thus, migratory birds might move seasonally in large flocks but, when resident, could exhibit territorial behavior and, in the case of breeding, pair formation on territory. Intraspecific relationships were actively described for a wide range of organisms within the animal kingdom. Deegener (1918) perhaps made one of the most heroic efforts to classify the social systems, but this led to a complex terminology and confusion between a functional classification and a descriptive one.

Descriptions of social organizations focused on how individuals were dispersed in space, the age and sex classes within a group, the manner in which space was utilized, the degree of cohesion shown by group members, whether the group was permeable to outsiders or not, and finally, the form of the relationships among individuals constituting the group, such as social dominance—that is, the direction of aggression and to whom aggressive displays were performed (Eisenberg 1966; Wilson 1975).

In 1966, I published on the convergence in the form and feeding strategies of primates, comparing the New World, Old World, and Madagascan radiations. Crook and Gartlan (1966) attempted to arrange primate societies into evolutionary grades and to correlate each of their five grades with the ecological adaptations exhibited by the species. Subsequent to that effort, two colleagues and I attempted in 1972 to classify primate social systems into five grades. We focused on the degree of male involvement within the social life of the troop and the mechanisms of social control employed by males in regulating their access to females. By focusing on the role of males in troop life, we were able to generate some correlations between group size, the dominance system, and spacing behavior. Behavioral mechanisms displayed by females were not as rigorously analyzed. There was a growing awareness, however, that a static classification was not enough in terms of an adequate description and that fruitful approaches could be based on functional models.

In recognition of the fact that social groupings exhibited by a species may be divided into phases, I proposed in 1981 that the classification of mammalian social organizations could be based on a consideration of four functional phases: (1) the mating system; (2) the rearing system; (3) the foraging system; and (4) the refuging system. Further, I felt it was convenient to view the social organization of males as one subset and that of females as another. Finally, I treated antipredatory behavior by a group or individual as a separate issue, since selection by predators contributes to the form of the rearing system, mating system, etc.

Most primate species were shown to exhibit a high defense of their refuging area, a moderate to high defense of feeding areas, and a moderate to high defense of mates. In an annual cycle, primates usually exhibit a relaxed synchrony of reproduction, and their rate of reproduction tends to be low. Parental investment may fall solely to the female or, in monogamous species, may be shared by both sexes. In any event, parental care is a reasonably high priority. Antipredator strategy in higher primates tends to be based on group defensive actions. Their mating systems are somewhat variable, as are their rearing systems.

The work of W. D. Hamilton (1964) set the stage for another direction of research, namely, how social systems evolve. If we assume that a certain amount of an animal's behavior derives from the influence of its genotype and that social organizations are the outcome of individual interactions, then it follows that genetically controlled behavior would also influence the ultimate form of a species' social organization. Hamilton addressed himself to the problems of the evolution of nonfertile castes in social insects and this paradox: How could such a system evolve when most notions of natural selection involve the idea of increasing individual fitness in the Darwinian sense? His solution was to propose inclusive fitness as a term to describe colonies of social insects in which donating care to the next reproductive generation, whether a given insect reproduces or not, is compensated for by the degree of relatedness to the recipient. Thus the excitement of the mid-to-late sixties generated whole hosts of questions concerning how social units evolved, how they functioned, and what types of questions needed to be asked to further our understanding of the evolution of social behavior in animals (Wilson 1975).

I would now like to turn to the howler monkey (*Alouatta*) as an example. The genus *Alouatta* is included within the family Cebidae. Howlers are distributed from southern Mexico to northern Argentina. This distributional range is among the broadest of any New World primate. The genus is divisible into six species. Most of my comparisons will be between *A. palliata* and *A. seniculus*. The genus has adapted to a wide variety of habitats from rain forests to tree savannas. They are the most folivorous (i.e., leaf eating) of the New World primates and can derive most of their water from the moisture contained in the leaves they eat. Thus, they are not bound to areas in the proximity of permanent water, and in this feature they resemble some of the more xeric (i.e., dry forest) adapted, Old World langurs (e.g., *Presbytis entellus*).

The adult male is larger than the female, but size dimorphism is most pronounced in *A. seniculus* (Thorington et al. 1979). *A. caraya* and *A. fusca* show sexual dimorphism with respect to coat color (Thorington et al. 1984). The other species show no such color dimorphism, although there may be distinctive differences in the appearance of the external genitalia. For example, in *A. seniculus* testicular descent is very early, and young males can easily be distinguished from young females at six months of age. Such is not the case of *A. palliata*, whose young males' genitalia mimic those of females.

The males of all species have a modified hyoid bone and generate a resonant, low-frequency, loud, long call with the fundamental frequency around 400 CPS. The low roars or long calls give rise to the common names: howler monkeys, Allouador. Long calls may be directed at adjacent troops and toward intruding transient bands. In the wild, longevity of males can exceed 25 years and females somewhat over 20 years. The typical number of young at birth is one; gestation is approximately 190 days. Although breeding can take place in any month, usually a population demonstrates a birth peak, and the birth peak can be exceptionally pronounced in those habitats that show a seasonal pulse in primary productivity by the plant community.

One of the consequences of the howlers' specialization for folivory is that they exist on a very tight energy budget. Leaves are ubiquitous but offer a low energy return because much of the leaf structure is indigestible. Although they can exploit a readily available food resource, there are also the attendant problems of detoxification. Leaves are rich in mildly toxic secondary compounds, a costly process for complete digestion. In general, howler monkeys have relatively small home ranges because their food resource is plentiful. They have the possibility for resource defense of their home range, and the vocalizations are involved in spacing between adjacent troops (Milton 1980; Sekulic 1982).

In 1934, C. R. Carpenter published his classic study on the behavior of howler monkeys (*A. palliata*) on Barro Colorado Island, Panama. This was a benchmark work because Carpenter, by direct observation and by very objective recording of behavior, had for the first time described in great detail the social organization of a nonhuman primate in the wilds. Carpenter's work pointed out that howler monkeys tended to live in groups of varying sizes (8–23) and that the groups consisted of adult males and females and their various-aged progeny. Groups of howlers tended to move and rest in a cohesive fashion, and when encountering adjoining troops, they would roar at one another, thereby maintaining some sort of exclusivity with respect to their home-range use patterns. Their diet consisted of both leaves and fruits. The existence of several adult males within a troop was remarked upon because of the seeming noncompetitiveness among males for access to estrous females. Later commentators on his work remarked on the peaceful vegetarians of the treetops.

The howler monkeys of Barro Colorado have been studied off and on from the time of Carpenter's pioneer work until the present time. There was one notable hiatus in studies, namely, during the years 1937–1951. But a world war and other great events had interrupted the course of much biological research in the world. With renewed interest in primate field studies, however, other populations of *A. palliata* and other species of howler monkeys began to be examined. Most notable in the recent howler research was the effort initiated by R. Rudran on the red howler monkey (*A. seniculus*) in Venezuela. Prior to Rudran's effort it had been noted that the so-called red howler tended to live in smaller groups than *A. palliata* (7–9). Furthermore, it had been noted that red howlers tended to have a single adult male in a troop, although exceptions had been recorded. Apparently there were important differences between the two species, and it was with this in mind that Rudran and I embarked upon a program of research on the red howler monkey.

The environment where *A. seniculus* was studied in Venezuela shows a pulsed, primary productivity. Rainfall tends to be concentrated between May and November, and a distinct drought period occurs from December to April. However, when one examines the climatic patterns for this particular study area, one notes a high variability from year to year (Eisenberg et al. 1979). In short, the length and monthly distribution of rains during the rainy season is highly unpredictable. This results in lean years and fat years, and can translate into annual variations in primate density.

The study area permits another comparison which is rather instructive. On the east side the forest abuts a river system and the forest is taller. On the west side of the study area the forest is extremely open and almost savannalike. Mean troop size in the west was 8.7, ranging from 5 to 17. The mean troop home range was approximately 10 hectares. Troops tended to have a single adult male, or if more than one male, they tended to be graded in age. Males that leave their natal troop may form groupings, and such coalitions will attempt to take over stable troops and evict the resident male (Rudran 1979).

In contrast, at the beginning of our study the mean troop size in the east was 5.4. Troop structure was strongly skewed toward a unimale condition. Home ranges were larger, nearly 20 hectares; but during the course of our research we have watched the population on the east side reach troop sizes and composition characteristic of those on the west. However, the home ranges continue to remain large. We have had an opportunity thus to witness a population at reasonable stability to slight expansion on the west side, and a population obviously in a rapid expansion phase on the east side (Crockett and Eisenberg 1987).

Rudran (1979) made a number of important discoveries during his field work. Since the howler population on the west side of the study site was expanding, certain behavioral traits changed. The population increase was accompanied by emigration from established troops, and both sexes emigrated, although there was a higher probability that the males would emigrate upon reaching sexual maturity than would their sisters. Emigrating animals tended to form new troops or, in the case of all-male bands, loose coalitions that attempted to displace resident males from established troops. Takeovers, when they were successful, often involved severe combat and occasionally the death of a male. Finally, emigrant males in a new troop invariably killed infants under eight months of age. We have now gone from the peaceable society portrayed by interpreters of Carpenter's data from Barro Colorado Island to a very different form of society involving conflict, male-male competition, and infanticide.

Infanticidal behavior was not a new phenomenon to Rudran, who had described male takeovers and subsequent infanticides for the purple-faced langur (*Presbytis senex*) in Sri Lanka. The phenomenon had previously been reported for *P. entellus* on peninsular India. Now, of course, a whole symposium volume has been published on the phenomenon (Hausfater and Hrdy 1984). Considerable discussion revolves around how such a behavior could evolve. It is seen as advantageous to males to terminate lactation by killing a female's infant, thereby resulting in the rapid return to an estrus condition and permitting the new male to sire offspring. But it is of considerable disadvantage to a female to lose her investment, namely, the infant, after a seven-month gestation and many months of lactation. It is further of great interest to note the relative frequency of infanticidal behavior as a function of population density. Some years ago, Rudran (1973) had proposed that infanticidal behavior could be phasic and exhibited under peak population densities with high emigration rates by subadults from their natal troops.

Crockett and Sekulic (1984) note that the formation of coalitions among males who are not necessarily close relatives may be important to the success of displacing a resident male. But Saavedra (1984) has evidence to indicate that coalitions among nonrelated males may be shaky indeed and that a certain amount of disharmony and reduced reproductive success can occur if relationships between males are not amicable. Theresa Pope (pers. comm.) further notes that in most cases of multimale troops, the males are related, and even where there is more than one male in the troop, usually only a dominant male mates with the females.

Troop size, recruitment, and emigration are ultimately controlled by primary productivity, and much of the variation seen when troops of the same population are compared from year to year may be related to variations in plant productivity deriving from annual variations in rainfall (Crockett & Eisenberg 1987). One of the intriguing facts that we have discovered in our long-term study of howler monkeys is that troop size, troop structure, and social dynamics may be quite different at differing population densities.

It was not fully appreciated at the onset of the study to what extent densities could fluctuate over time. When we began our studies of howler monkeys on the west side of Masaguaral, the population appeared to be at approximately the same density as when Melvin Neville studied it in the late sixties; but during the course of our study, from 1975 to 1982, the population first showed a slow but demonstrable increase, only to go into a gradual decline during the last two years. The population on the east side, on the other hand, was at a very low density at the beginning of the study but increased throughout the course of the study until troop sizes approximated those of the west. The home ranges of the eastern troops are still larger, however, than those of the western troops.

The difference in home-range size may relate to genuine differences in the carrying capacity of the two habitats, since figs, a major food resource, are extremely abundant in the west habitat. On the other hand, *Cebus olivaceous* is present in the east habitat and absent from the west, and the coexistence of the two species may have resulted in a new equilibrium density deriving from the fact that both compete for fruit at certain times of the year (Eisenberg 1979). As the density increased on the west side, infanticidal frequency increased, suggesting to us that the rate of takeovers by alien males, displacement of the resident male, and subsequent killing of infants less than six months of age is density dependent. In the east, at the beginning of the study, when there were very low densities and small troops, infanticide was not noticed nor was the frequency of takeover by alien males detectable. However, this changed with the demographic changes during the subsequent seven years, and the eastern troops now resemble those on the west in aggressive behavior.

Clearly our picture of red howler society is somewhat different from the picture derived from observations of mantled howlers. More important, our focus now is not to describe a modal social organization for a given species but rather to examine the variation shown within a population with respect to social structure and reproductive success. Only long-term field studies can answer these types of questions, but at this time we can draw the following conclusions: At low population densities, there is little emigration and there is relative stability of male tenure within troops. As the population expands, emigration rate increases and so does the formation rate of new troops. The establishment of new troops is dependent on available habitat. Thus in a situation where most habitat is occupied, the possibility for establishing a new troop is grim. The success rate of new troops at high population densities is usually rather low, but if an area can be staked for foraging, a newly formed troop may persist for a considerable period of time, moving in the interstices between established troop ranges. Well-established troops have home ranges of great stability. Some troop ranges on the west side have been stable over a 15-year period. During a period of population growth, as troop size increases, the males of the troop tend to be related descending from one father. During periods of high population density with increased emigration rates, in part forced by takeovers, groups of males may assemble that are not related. If a group of unrelated males invades, evicts the resident male, and takes over a troop, one will have a situation of more than one adult male; but usually their behavioral interactions are qualitatively different and there is a high probability for a subsequent breakdown in the troop structure (Saavedra 1984).

What can we say concerning the differences between *A. palliata* and *A. seniculus*? There are genuine differences when one compares the two species. It is possible to make the generalization that the troop size of *seniculus* is smaller than that of *palliata,* and there are more adult males on the average within a troop of *A. palliata* than there are in a troop of *A. seniculus.* The number of adult females per adult males in each species' troops is, however, rather similar, as one might have predicted (Crockett & Eisenberg 1987). Usually, there is one adult male per two adult females. It is perhaps no coincidence that what appears to be contributing the most to the differences between the two species is the fact that *A. seniculus* consistently averages a smaller troop size. The reason for the smaller troop size in *A. seniculus* is not at all obvious, since small troop sizes characterize the species over a wide range of habitats and densities. It is known, however, that adult females have a hierarchy and the top female has priority of access to prime feeding sites. Perhaps the energetic constraints mandate, over much of the red howler's habitat, a small home range and thereby sets an upper limit on the number of females that can coexist. During favorable times in population increase, it may be that the only option a daughter of a low-ranking female has for reproductive success is to emigrate.

Long-term demographic studies are exceedingly important in helping us to interpret the dynamics within a troop or a population. Variation in structure between troops is highest at high population densities. Troop structures are much more similar within populations at low densities. Within the system in Venezuela, rainfall drives primary productivity, and this in turn sets the carrying capacity. Long-term climatic trends can profoundly influence the carrying capacity and thus the density that the populations can achieve. The modal troop structure and composition for a population will ultimately depend on whether the population is at carrying capacity, has exceeded carrying capacity, is declining, or is at an extremely low ebb in density.

The preceding paragraph has implications for human history. The behavior of human societies can change rapidly when population densities increase and when the age structure changes markedly. The creation of empires through historical time has often been associated with profound demographic shifts within the aggressive society such as increase in population and a preponderance of young individuals. Perhaps it is time to take an ecological view of history such as that portrayed by Colinvaux (1980).

References

Carpenter, C. R. 1934. *A Field Study of the Behavior and Social Relations of Howling Monkeys* (Alouatta palliata). Comparative Psychology Monographs, vol. 10, no. 48. Baltimore: Johns Hopkins University Press.

Chapple, E. D. 1970. *Culture and Biological Man.* New York: Holt, Reinhart and Winston.

Colinvaux, P. 1980. *The Fate of Nations: A Biological Theory of History.* New York: Simon and Schuster.

Crockett, C. M., and J. F. Eisenberg. 1987. Howlers: Variations in Group Size and Demography. In *Primate Societies,* ed. B. B. Smuts, D. L. Cheney, R. M. Seyfarth, R. W. Wrangham, and T. T. Struhsaker, 54–68. Chicago: University of Chicago Press.

Crockett, C. M., and R. Sekulic. 1984. Infanticide in Red Howler Monkeys (*Alouatta esniculus*). In *Infanticide: Comparative and Evolutionary Perspectives,* ed. G. Hausfater and S. B. Hrdy, 173–91. New York: Aldine.

Crook, J. H., and J. S. Gartlan. 1966. Evolution of Primate Societies. *Nature* 210:1200–1203.

Deegener, P. 1918. *Die Formen der Vertgesellschaftung im Tierreiche.* Leipzig: Verlag von Veit.

Eisenberg, J. F. 1966. The Social Organization of Mammals. *Handbuch de Zoologie,* VII(10/7), Lieferung, 39:1–92.

______. 1979. Habitat, Economy, and Society: Some Correlations and Hypotheses for the Neotropical Primates. In *Primate Ecology and Human Origins: Ecological Influences on Social Organization,* ed. I. S. Bernstein and E. O. Smith, 215–52. New York: Garland.

______. 1981. *The Mammalian Radiations.* Chicago: University of Chicago Press.

Eisenberg, J. F., and W. Dillon, eds. 1971. *Man and Beast: Comparative Social Behavior.* Washington, D.C.: Smithsonian Institution Press.

Eisenberg, J. F., N. Muckenhirn, and R. Rudran. 1972. The Relationship between Ecology and Social Structure in Primates. *Science* 176:863–74.

Eisenberg, J. F., M. A. O'Connell, and P. V. August. 1979. Density, Productivity, and Distribution of Mammals in Two Venezuelan Habitats. In *Vertebrate Ecology in the Northern Neotropics,* ed. J. F. Eisenberg, 187–207. Washington, D.C.: Smithsonian Institution Press.

Hamilton, W. D. 1964. The Genetical Evolution of Social Behavior. Parts I, II. *Journal of Theoretical Biology* 7:1–16, 17–52.

Hausfater, G., and S. B. Hrdy, eds. 1984. *Infanticide: Comparative and Evolutionary Perspectives.* New York: Aldine.

Marler, P. R., and W. J. Hamilton III. 1966. *Mechanisms of Animal Behavior.* New York: John Wiley.

Milton, K. 1980. *The Foraging Strategy of Howler Monkeys.* New York: Columbia University Press.

Rudran, R. 1973. Adult Male Replacement in One-Male Troops of Purple-Faced Langurs (*Presbytis senex*) and Its Affect on Population Structure. *Folia Primatologica* 19:166–92.

———. 1979. The Demography and Social Mobility of a Red Howler (*Alouatta seniculus*) Population in Venezuela. In *Vertebrate Ecology in the Northern Neotropics,* ed. J. F. Eisenberg, 107–27. Washington, D.C.: Smithsonian Institution Press.

Saavedra, C. J. 1984. The Spatial and Social Relationships of Males in Two Groups of Red Howler Monkeys. M.S. thesis. Department of Zoology, University of Florida.

Sekulic, R. 1982. Daily and Seasonal Patterns of Roaring and Spacing in Four *Alouatta* Troops. *Folia Primatologica* 39:22–48.

Seyfarth, R. M. 1987. Vocal Communication and Its Relation to Language. In *Primate Societies,* ed. B. B. Smuts et al., 440–51. Chicago: University of Chicago Press.

Smith, W. J. 1977. *The Behavior of Communicating.* Cambridge: Harvard University Press.

Thorington, R. W., Jr., R. Rudran, and D. Mack. 1979. Sexual Dimorphism of *Alouatta seniculus* and Observations on Capture Techniques. In *Vertebrate Ecology in the Northern Neotropics,* ed. J. F. Eisenberg, 97–106. Washington, D.C.: Smithsonian Institution Press.

Thorington, R. W., Jr., J. C. Ruiz, and J. F. Eisenberg. 1984. A Study of a Black Howling Monkey (*Alouatta caraya*) Population in Northern Argentina. *American Journal of Primatology.* 6:357–66.

Uexküll, J. von 1909. *Umwelt und Innenwelt der Tiere.* Berlin: Springer.

Wilson, E. O. 1975. *Sociobiology.* Cambridge: Harvard University Press, Belknap Press.

Tactics of Primate Immaturity

Phyllis Dolhinow

Popular accounts of immaturity, especially those focusing on the very young, tend to stress dependency and helplessness. The "needy" infant receives attention and care; and although it is usually credited with participation in the relation that builds between it and its mother, it is seldom portrayed as an active and often skillful, persistent, opportunistic manipulator of its social world. Immaturity usually is also considered to be a time of preparation for maturity. The events of infancy are like seeds that may bear fruit at a later time—given appropriate tending. There is truth in both views: the youngster depends on others for care, and there is much that it must do and experience if it is to progress normally into the years of maturity. Knowledge and skills are carried forward and consolidated as a primate ages, but emphasizing early years as mainly preparation for the future may detract from a full appreciation of how the immature survives, first as an infant and later as a juvenile. A critical armamentarium, the tactics of immaturity, is in place to help ensure survival; the infant needs to be skilled in what it does, from day one.

The tactics of immaturity include the multitude of ways infants and juveniles respond to and manipulate their social environments to gain individual advantage, to survive as successfully as possible. It is argued that in the long run biological success, fitness, is measured by reproduction (Daly & Wilson 1983; Hamilton 1964; Williams 1966; Wilson 1975), but here our concern is with success in surviving immaturity and specifically with the quality of life during that portion of the life span. To evaluate individual success and to measure whether the tactics used gain the desired goals, we need to know what an animal wants. An interesting aspect of this calculus eventually will be to evaluate how realistic an immature's wants are. There are obviously dramatic changes in what an animal wants as it matures, and a central part of socialization is the realization that wants must be tempered by social realities and that others place strict limits on what a youngster may do with impunity. These limits change drastically with maturation, and to be unaware of them can cause not only pain but peril.

Much has been written about the tactics of adulthood, the choices, plans, and maneuvers that may lead to increased success or fitness. In surprising contrast very little has been written about the tactics used to structure daily life situations during immaturity. After all, infants must be sensitive to their surroundings, make choices, express their feelings, and make plans to gain what is desired. Most youngsters are quick to learn how to manipulate their social environment to advantage, but there is a tremendous range in how fast these abilities are acquired and how effectively they are used.

Infancy is the most critical time of the entire life span, and all neonates must have adequate care to survive. The degree of dependency at birth depends upon the kind of primate, with human and great ape infants relatively helpless and slow maturing in comparison with monkeys. But all require food, warmth, protection, and transport, and must also experience an array of activities and relations and learn an impressive amount about their physical and social environment. Rates of maturation in primates vary, from the mouse lemur (*Microcebus murinus*), reaching reproductive maturity within the first year of life, to a chimpanzee giving birth at 11. Immaturity is a time of rapid and profound change in all aspects of life—social, emotional, and physical. Monkeys mature earlier than apes, and both mature sooner than humans. There are few visible physical markers that herald maturity. Rather, profiles of behavior, or what an animal does with its time, change gradually, and observers must scan many months of records to determine when the gradual transitions from childhood to adolescence and then adulthood occur.

This essay looks closely at a few social abilities characteristic of most young nonhuman primates and at how these skills, suited to gain advantage when infants are denied what they want, are practiced. There are many paths to maturity, and we are far from understanding the importance of early experiences and the mechanisms by which they become part of adolescent and then adult life patterns (Bateson 1981, 1982; von Bertalanffy 1968; Oyama 1985). This is not a survey of our substantial knowledge of the lifeways of young primates; rather, examples will be selected from several Old World species to illustrate general tactical abilities and their consequences (for accounts of development for different primates, see baboons: Altmann 1980; Ransom & Rowell 1972; Nash 1978a, 1978b; Young & Bramblett 1977; patas: Chism 1986; rhesus: Suomi 1977, 1982; chimpanzee: Goodall 1986; and for a discussion of ontogeny and socialization, see Hinde 1974; McKenna 1979b; Poirier 1972). The Old World primates are selected because they are more closely related to us than are the New World monkeys. A few details of langur monkey (*Presbytis entellus*) behavior will be offered as examples because I have observed them in India or in captivity for more than 18 years. Langurs are quite representative in many ways of most Old World monkeys, and they have been well studied in the field (Jay 1962, 1963, 1965; Boggess 1976; Bishop 1975; Mohnot 1971; Vogel 1976; Hrdy 1977).

Young Infants

Primate infants are quite variable. Size, strength, sensory acuity, emotionality, reactivity to different physical and social stimuli, alertness, and perseverence are a few characteristics that vary within and among species. Color identifies infants in species in which the infants are born with natal coat and/or skin color strikingly different from adults (Wolfheim 1983). All infant primates require substantial tending, and each must be able to stimulate this care. Newborns can signal pleasure or displeasure by quality of movement and by sound. Movement from slight to thrashing tells much about comfort, and vocalizations, from barely audible to shrieks, make the infant's feelings known. Neonates can and do stimulate others to provide care, and in most species, they do it from the first day of life (Lewis & Rosenblum 1974; Levine 1982). Among many colobines (McKenna 1979a, 1979b) and a few cercopithecines (Chism 1986; Nicolson 1987), adults other than the mother can provide some care for the infant, and the additional attention is not without cost to the infant (Dolhinow & Murphy 1982; Hrdy 1976; Paul & Thommen 1984; Quiatt 1979; Lancaster 1985). An infant's ability to object to and stop allomothering could prevent harm to itself.

And what of care givers in general? The messages—movement, struggles, whimpers, or screams—of the passive to assertive newborn may seem to fall on deaf ears if the mother fails to respond. The maternal half of the equation traditionally has been considered to be the most important, and our bets on infant survival are generally based on the probability of her appropriate responses. The actions of the most sensitive and expressive of infants will accomplish nothing if the mother is not receptive and willing to perform. Maternal style, difficult to quantify in scientifically acceptable units, yet generally recognized and often described, is critical not only to whether an infant survives but also to the quality of its survival. Mothers can be permissive, restrictive, gentle, punishing, attentive, ignoring, and much more (Dolhinow & Krusko 1984; Johnson et al. 1979; Nicolson 1987). Some mothers do not tolerate independence-seeking behaviors, while others ignore them. Individuals may show distinct preferences for newborns, others for older infants; and style is not necessarily consistent for one female throughout adulthood (Dolhinow & Krusko 1984).

Female style may have more to do with the events and relations in her life than the attributes of her infant (Dolhinow & Krusko, 1984). Maternal social status or rank may have profound effects on her offspring (on macaques, see Kawai 1958; Kawamura 1958; Missakian 1972; Sade 1967; Silk et al. 1981; on baboons see Lee & Oliver 1979; Nash 1978b; Hausfater et al. 1982). A high-ranking mother may provide a protected context for her infant that the lowest on the ladder cannot. The latter may shrink fearfully from social interactions and do her best to restrict the movement of her infant so as not to attract the attention of others in the group (personal observation; Altmann 1980). The mother's social relations, status, and temperament have tremendous consequences for the offspring, as measured by both physical and psychological calibrations.

From the day it is born, a langur monkey neonate attracts the attention of most group females, and it is held by many for as long as 5 hours a day and may be nursed by females other than the mother (Dolhinow & Murphy 1982; McKenna 1979b). Most transfers of an infant from one female to another are gentle, although at times there may be a tug-of-war with the infant between two females, each eager to hold, nuzzle, and groom the youngster. When a very young female takes a newborn, the results are not always appreciated by the latter, which may be held upside down or bumped along the ground between carrier's ventrum and the hard surface. Regardless of the tending female's age, if a neonate does not like the way it is handled, every animal within earshot knows it. Shrieks of protest are heard long before a neonate is able to make anything resembling an efficient protest gesture.

Although the first flush of intense interest fades quickly, infant langurs continue to be passed among females for 5 to 6 weeks after birth. I strongly suspect that if we could ask infants whether they would like the females to stop, the would shout yes. Infants definitely prefer certain adults, and when a disliked female gains possession, an infant screeches and struggles. It takes a very motivated and persistent female to hold a flailing infant. And what, you may ask, about the mother during these minutes of adversity? Some mothers respond instantly to the slightest signal of infant distress, whereas other mothers pay no attention. Most mothers monitor their infants fairly casually but seem to know when intervention is required to avoid trauma.

As with most kinds of infant monkeys, young langurs are afforded a substantial degree of protection by the group. A newborn langur's poor motor coordination prevents it from getting into too much trouble, but this changes rapidly. Week 5 is almost magic, for then the youngster climbs! (Dolhinow & Murphy 1982). This signals a profound change in its ability to investigate all it can see as well as a sudden increase in management problems for its mother. Even before it could climb, it had become manipulator, explorer, player, attacker, hider, and seeker. First bursts of activity are used to practice the basic motor skills of getting somewhere and getting milk. With increased competence, getting there becomes focused and the goal of moving about becomes doing things. As with most nonhuman primates, maternal vigilance wanes gradually and the behaviors of the pair become less synchronized. In general, cooperation and compromise are far more common than conflict. The extent of the mother's availability and responsiveness remains exceedingly important to the infant in times of stress or danger, and this continues to be the case until weaning.

Attachment

Life's first and most important relationship is with the mother (see Emde & Harmon 1982 for review), and it is a complex bond actively forged as much by the infant as by the mother. The infant is an active manipulator in transactions with its mother, and here, as elsewhere, the tactics of immaturity are critical. This and all other attachment relationships are based on feelings, the same basic emotions of limbic origin that serve all primates. The complexities of perception are such that it is impossible to state with any certainty what it is about each of the pair that serves to activate strong feelings in the other. Because from day one of life langur monkeys have a great deal of prolonged and intimate contact with most adult females in their group, langurs were excellent candidates for a study of attachment relations comparable to studies on bonnet and pigtail macaques (Kaufman 1977; Kaufman & Rosenblum 1967; McKinney 1985), other Old World monkeys. In our investigation using langurs living in stable, normally constituted, captive social groups, we wanted to answer questions such as what happens to an infant that loses its primary attachment figure, the mother. How does an infant cope with loss? Do some infants manage loss better than other, similarly bereft infants? It was hoped that answers would lead to more understanding of the role an infant plays in attachment relationships. Mothers of several 8 month olds were removed from the infants' social group for two weeks (Dolhinow 1980; Dolhinow & Murphy 1983). When the infants noticed the mothers were missing, all infants were distressed, from a little to a lot. Responses to loss were neither simple nor predictable, and the variability was instructive. Most youngsters quickly compensated for the missing mother and gained both contact and comfort with their chosen mother substitute. Youngsters with the least and briefest distress were those most persistent and opportunistic in their efforts to find an adult female to adopt as a mother substitute (Dolhinow & DeMay 1982).

The basis for choice of maternal replacement remains obscure. An intensive study of relationships in the first months of life, when infants are passed from female to female, led to the disappointing conclusion that early contacts and interaction patterns in the first 3 months of life did not help predict either which infants would adopt or which females they would choose. The adult females that infants chose were those who had been approached least frequently of all group members in the month before the mother disappeared. Infants were not choosing females they approached frequently or spent much time with. Most infants strongly preferred certain females as mother substitute, but these females had little in common with each other except that they were willing to be co-opted by infants needing contact and comfort. Adopted females did not actively care for their adoptees; the latter sought them out and remained nearby or in contact. Persistence was the critical factor in gaining and keeping a mother substitute, especially when the targeted female was less than enthusiastic about having an infant companion. The more persistent the youngster, the greater the probability that an adult female would allow it to sit in contact or to cling. When the adult was reluctant or rejecting, an infant that watched and waited for an opportune time to press its demands was usually rewarded. The infant's timing and sensitivity was critical to success. Regardless of the amount of distress it showed, no infant was ever adopted spontaneously. The infant always initiated and carried out the entire process; and with only one exception, the adult adopted was a female. One young male infant adopted the group's alpha male, a very tolerant young adult male whose initial astonishment was soon overcome and replaced by acceptance of the following or clinging youngster (Dolhinow & Taff, in preparation).

Signals of Independence

Early in life it is the infant that initiates escape from maternal control and surveillance; but this changes, and gradually the tables are turned and the mother actively discourages attachment behaviors. Increasing independence comes with maturation (Bolwig 1980; Kaufmann 1966; Rheingold & Eckerman 1970; Suomi 1976). The same infant that struggled to escape maternal restraint does its best to sit next to her, timing its approaches to minimize her rejection. For both monkeys and apes this period of rejection marks the start of weaning. Timetables differ depending upon the kind of primate, but for most monkeys weaning starts toward the end of the first year of life. Weaning is a process, not an event, and is best measured by changing frequencies of many behaviors. It is a signal of independence that proceeds by fits and starts as the infant is rejected or succeeds in temporarily postponing rejection.

Not all maternal behaviors between the mother and young disappear with weaning, but the nature of the relationship definitely changes. Months before weaning begins, the infant directs much of its attention away from the mother and toward peers and others in the social group. By the time the mother begins to object to its demands for attention, contact, or being nearby, it no longer needs her constant care, milk, or attentive support. What the infant still seems to want from her, and on demand, are the psychological components of the relationship that come from being close or touching. It would be inaccurate to describe langur weaning as a battle, because although there are noisy confrontations, each immature knows precisely what to expect from its mother. It knows the limits of her patience, reaction times, and the patterns of her rejection.

Timing and intensity of weaning are the result of both maternal style and infant response. Some females wean firmly and quickly but are not necessarily harsh, while others waver between leniency and firmness. For whatever reasons, perhaps mainly infant persistence, mothers may retreat from firm rejection and allow a nagging infant to cling. This usually produces vigorous protest when she resumes rejection. Maternal response to an aggressive infant is predictably swift and strong, and if the infant does not switch tactics, she forces it to retreat. Infant response to rejection can be subtle and opportunistic. Its early whining, nagging, and contact gained by force are quickly replaced by careful visual monitoring of the mother and well-timed approaches when she is most likely to be tolerant of touching and being in contact. The youngster is rewarded for learning to modulate its attempt to be near or to cling to its mother.

A Comparison of Human and Nonhuman Primates

All primates act to shape their lives; none are merely acted upon by others. Each primate has its own set of tactics keyed to the experiences typical for its kind. Hence it is necessary to compare for humans and nonhumans some major attributes of their lives. For both, biological, psychological, and social processes and experiences are importantly interconnected throughout the life course (Rossi 1985; Oyama 1985; and many others), and if we focus on only a portion of this enormously complex web of relationships, our understanding will be as restricted as our field of view. There are many similarities among primates, including biological needs such as food, warmth, and protection. We share emotions generated from the limbic systems of our brains, and these feelings form the bases for our social relationships. The range of affects we hold in common certainly includes pleasure, pain, fear, rage, sadness, depression, and anxiety, to name a few. Some recent accounts of social behavior show increased sensitivity to patterns and qualities of, for example, friendship among the monkeys and apes (Strum 1987). Smuts describes baboons as showing to each other emotions resembling our feelings in comparable contexts of friendship (1985). We are social creatures and contact can comfort us, especially contact with familiar conspecifics. The presence of familiar others is calming and helps build an atmosphere in which play and learning occur. Many scholars of the human condition have recognized and learned from continuities with our primate past (for example, Bowlby 1969).

There are, however, very important differences between humans and the rest of the primates. Human mental capacity and cognitive skills developed late in our evolution, long after we shared a common ancestor with the African apes. For example, we are able to conceptualize events in distant times past and future as well as to understand and verbally articulate the relationship of events in the life course. The human mother typically anticipates and prepares for a birth, and her newborn becomes part of an extensive and complex web of real and/or fictitious relationships. The social network into which humans are placed after birth may be composed, wholly or in part, of biologically unrelated people, and yet all are defined as relatives. The monkey's or ape's social world is its mother, perhaps siblings, and other group members. The newborn monkey or ape may benefit or suffer from its mother's attributes, including temperament and status, and may feel these affects into adulthood. This direct translation of the effects of biological relatedness into an infant's life history is very different from the human condition, where society assigns status, religion, rights, property, kin, and many other attributes to the yet-unborn child. Human gender is assigned at birth, whereas the nonhuman assumes sex-specific activities only as it develops.

Human culture can prescribe the way we think, the contents of our thought, our attitudes and roles in life. Culture builds a support system for all members of human society and assigns responsibility for a child that can extend long past adolescence. Human language, based on our modern human brain, makes it possible for culture to do these things.

Culture defines critical aspects of our attachment relationships with infants, and these bonds can range from cherishment to neglect. Even a biologically based transaction such as nursing can be programmed by society. Mammalian mothers have nursed their infants for about the last 70 million years, but now humans can delegate the process, even using milk from other kinds of mammals. The circumstances and mechanics of nursing and even the appropriate time to stop are prescribed differentially, historically, and according to culture and class.

The nonhuman primate infant usually commences life with its mother and a few others in a small social group. Only the mother, however, has responsibility for providing its most basic needs. Both nonhuman and human mothers recognize their own infant by sight, but the human can also recognize hers by written label, or by assignment, as in the case of adoption. Human societies require that someone care for an infant if the mother is killed or incompetent. A baby cannot be discarded or killed except in those few cultures where infanticide is condoned (Dickemann 1984; Scrimshaw 1984). The survival of an infant monkey or ape depends on both its ability to stimulate appropriate care and on maternal attribute. If a mother monkey or ape lacks motiviation or ability, it is moot as to whether the infant is adequate; it pays for her incompetence with its life.

Human mother-offspring relationships can last a lifetime, whereas for most other primates the mother-infant relationship seldom lasts into adulthood and often ends shortly after weaning. Human weaning usually refers only to the end of nursing and rarely marks a major change in the attachment relationship between mother and offspring. Weaning may be stimulated by the arrival of the next child or dictated by a culture's timetable of appropriate stopping points. Biology, in contrast, sets the timetable for nonhuman primate weaning, and if there is a break in the regular production of infants, the last surviving infant might be able to enjoy continued close contact with its mother if it is persistent. The slow-to-mature human may have a number of dependent siblings while he or she is still dependent on parents; but the nonhuman primate is usually quite independent of the mother by the time a sibling is born. The chimpanzee is an exception, as a chimp mother may have 2 or 3 relatively dependent young (Goodall 1986). Whereas nonhuman primates assume adult social roles when they reach sexual (for the female) and physical (for the male) maturity, humans may remain dependent on parents or society long after adolescence. Preparation for assuming full adult responsibility in our society may take decades.

Because of the differences between human and nonhuman primates, many kinds of information from the nonhuman primates may be of very limited relevance to our diagnosis, understanding, or treatment of, for example, early human childhood developmental problems. The human child's cognitive, language-based world is so much more complex and different from that of the monkey or ape (this is the case from day one, long before the human infant is able to speak). There is much in our lives that has no counterpart for the nonhuman primate. For example, in our own society we obsessively evaluate and rank individuals with standardized tests that measure everything from physical to mental attributes. The stigma of being placed as an infant or child in the lowest percentiles can last a lifetime and serve to allow society to track the individual for continued failure or mediocrity. We often base our evaluations on selected abilities unique to modern Western society, abilities that might contribute precious little to success or survival elsewhere or in times past.

Paths to and Qualities of Success

It is not sufficient to note that normal psychological and physical development during immaturity produces adequate subadults and adults because there are many developmental paths through the early years and a resulting array of attributes, abilities, and degrees of success among adults. We are far from identifying specific paths and being able to say these qualities of youth lead to those kinds of adult behaviors. We can, however, identify some social skills available to a young primate and look closely at how they are used. From this overview it is obvious that very little of what needs to be done has been accomplished. Epigenetic studies including observation and experimentation are needed to identify developmental variables within and among species. Everything in our analysis is seen through human eyes, and it is important to be fully aware that what we consider to be options or choices of action may not be perceived as such by a monkey or an ape. Our window into the life of the immature nonhuman primate only enables us to see a portion of their reality. Nonetheless, we witness situations in which we can identify apparent choices, possible alternatives, and probable motivations. Primates have much in common; we feel the psychological pain of loss as well as the comfort of companions and the good feelings of satiety. In assessing the thoughts, feelings, and motivations of the nonhuman primate of any age, we have problems similar to those that arise in studying the prelanguage human. Although neither can tell us what it experiences, we assume each must handle many of the same challenges in daily life. Because human attitudes and thought processes are frequently ascribed to nonhuman animals (see cautions by Washburn 1978a, 1978b), we must remember that there may be significant differences in human and nonhuman interpretations of the actions of the nonhuman.

Nonhuman primate societies allow their immatures much greater latitude for error than they do their adults. This tolerance provides young a context for trial-and-error learning of the tactics they will need as adults when the stakes are high. Youngsters spend countless hours stretching their abilities, honing motor and social/psychological skills. They appear to find repetition and investigation pleasurable, and familiarization with new objects, movements, and situations leads to new knowledge. Even the minutest increments of increase in skill gained from constant repetition are investments in the future. Contrast this with adult behavior, in which something new is treated with caution or avoidance and is more likely to arouse anxiety than curiosity.

Much attention has been paid to adult dominance relations (Rowell 1974; Bernstein 1981; Mitchell & Maples 1985) but relatively little to the tactics of competition itself. Curtin (1981) emphasized the highly opportunistic nature of adult langur monkey competition, with success depending on the exploitation of temporary advantages. Infant langurs concentrate on the same tactics of opportunism and, as they mature, hone their skills in using them. There are many conflicts during development, including those with the mother over the extent of maternal investment and those with siblings, peers, and other group members over access to all manner of valued items from ripe fruit to huddling with another animal. For the most part these conflicts are neither serious nor prolonged. Juveniles often observe adults very carefully without actually interacting, which may give us the notion that they are peripheralized behaviorally when, in reality, although they are not interacting, they are learning a great deal (de Benedictis 1979). A more accurate description of primate immaturity emphasizes the patterns of cooperation and mutual adjustments that are important dimensions of all social relations (Altmann 1980; Bateson 1981; Dolhinow & Murphy 1982; Fedigan 1982).

To decide whether and how being a successful primate immature leads to being a successful adult requires following many animals through life, a daunting task. But without such long-term information many questions will remain unanswered and we will need to continue to state our ideas in terms of probabilities. In the meanwhile we can draw up a list of qualities taken from the tactical repertoires of typical nonhuman primate immatures. On this list would be perserverance, motivation, stubbornness, alertness, cooperativeness, accommodation, opportunism, sensitivity to moods of others, perceptiveness, ability to "read" and manipulate social responses accurately and quickly so as to stimulate maternal support, and a good sense of timing. Knowing when to press a demand or make a move is exceedingly critical and can make the difference between success and failure. Notice that neither size nor strength are on this list because both are much less important to an immature than the abilities to make sensitive calculations about a situation and to modify responses quickly. There are many combinations and permutations of these qualities and no immature can boast all. As though this weren't sufficiently complicated, in addition to these factors we must also recognize the impact of idiosyncratic features of personality and temperament (Suomi 1985). This "generalized" immature and its tactical abilities reflects, of course, my impressions after watching langur monkeys for more than 3 generations and macaques for years, both in the field and in captivity. Readers will amend this list according to their experiences. Having identified qualities, the next steps are to describe and measure each in a systematic and replicable manner, and we and others are working on just that. There also has been significant concern with, but relatively little information on, the appearance of behavioral sex differences among the primates in the field and in captivity (for example, on macaques see Gouzoules 1980; Fedigan 1982; on baboons, Altmann 1980; Mitchell 1968; Nash 1978a; Ransom & Rowell 1972; Young & Bramblett 1977; Young and Hankins 1979).

So far nothing has been said of failures, of the few that are the least successful. Depending upon why individuals fall into the lowest percentiles on scales predicting success, they may pursue an undistinguished career through immaturity to adulthood, they may survive marginally, or they may die. If the individual ranks at the bottom because it is, for example, too aggressive or gives inappropriate social responses, it will most likely not outlive immaturity. If it is too daring, it may fall and break its bones and die; or if, in quite a different scenario, it cannot muster sufficient maternal support for safety, it may fall prey to accident or predator. Other factors that affect the quality of early life may be beyond the infant's control, such as being born to a poor mother, having inadequate prenatal nutrition, or lacking a peer group with which to play and practice. However, most infants and juveniles share in the enjoyment that comes with even a modest degree of skill. Getting off to a bad start is not typical, and some of these unfortunate individuals may change if they survive and mature. There is a certain amount of pain for all young, as learning usually has a price, whether it is learning a social grace or a leaping maneuver, and it is probably never a painless transition from being a juvenile to an adolescent. A typical obstreperous male juvenile may become a peripheralized, wary adolescent, constantly monitoring the adults' whereabouts and activities, whereas a female's path through adolescence is much briefer and, in net, less traumatic than the male's.

Although each stage of life has its different challenges, there are many similarities, as, for example, the need to get along with others. Most of the tactics that are used to gain desired states, objects, and relationships, and also to forge the niceties of social life, were learned and practiced when young, and these abilities remain critical during adulthood. Individual variability surpasses our ability to predict adult behavior patterns by looking at the young, but we do know that the odds may change dramatically in favor of the primate that has learned its skills early in life and well.

Acknowledgments

Thanks to the Smithsonian for making possible the Man and Beast Revisited symposium and its stimulating discussions. In this paper, statements about langur monkey development are based on more than 1-1/2 decades of continuous work by many people and on countless discussions of the results and meanings of our study. I also thank J. McKenna, S. Sperling, F. Rickenback, and the editors of this volume for perceptive critical comments on this paper.

References

Altmann, J. 1980. *Baboon Mothers and Infants.* Cambridge: Harvard University Press.

Bateson, P. 1981. Ontogeny of Behaviour Patterns. *British Medical Bulletin* 37(2): 159–64.

______. 1982. Behavioural Development and Evolutionary Processes. In *Current Problems in Sociobiology*, ed. Kings College Sociobiology Group, 133–51. Cambridge: Cambridge University Press.

Bernstein, I. S. 1981. Dominance: The Baby and the Bathwater. *Behavioral and Brain Sciences* 4: 419–57.

Bertalanffy, L. von. 1968. *General Systems Theory.* New York: Braziller.

Bishop, N. H. 1975. Social Behavior of Langur Monkeys (*Presbytis entellus*) in a High Altitude Environment. Master's thesis. University of California, Berkeley.

Boggess, J. E. 1976. The Social Behavior of the Himalayan Langur (*Presbytis entellus*) in Eastern Nepal. Master's thesis. University of California, Berkeley.

Bolwig, N. 1980. Early Social Development and Emancipation of *Macaca nemestrina* and Species of *Papio Primates. Primates* 21: 357–75.

Bolby, J. 1969. *Attachment and Loss.* Vol. 1, *Attachment.* New York: Basic.

Chism, J. 1986. Developmental and Mother-Infant Relations among Captive Patas Monkeys. *International Journal of Primatology* 7 (1): 49–81.

Curtin, R. A. 1981. Strategy and Tactics in Male Gray Langur Competition. *Journal of Human Evolution* 10: 245–53.

Daly, M., and M. Wilson. 1983. *Sex, Evolution, and Behavior.* Boston: Willard Grant.

de Benedictis, T. 1979. Spatial and Behavioral Peripheralization in Subadult Male Monkeys: Observations of a *Macaca fascicularis* Colony. Ph.D. diss., University of California, Berkeley.

Dickemann, M. 1984. Concepts and Classification in the Study of Human Infanticide. In *Infanticide: Comparative and Evolutionary Perspectives,* ed. G. Hausfater and S. B. Hrdy, 427–37. New York: Aldine.

Dolhinow, P. 1980. An Experimental Study of Mother-Loss in the Indian langur Monkey (*Presbytis entellus*). *Folia Primatologica* 33: 77–128.

Dolhinow, P., and M. DeMay. 1982. Adoption: The Importance of Infant Choice. *Journal of Human Evolution*. 11: 391–420.

Dolhinow, P., and G. Murphy. 1982. Langur Monkey (*Presbytis entellus*) Development: The First Three Months of Life. *Folia Primatologica* 39: 305–31.

______. 1983. Langur Monkey Mother Loss: Profile Analysis of Variance with Multivariate Analysis of Variance for Separation Subjects and Controls. *Folia Primatologica* 40: 181–96.

Dolhinow, P., and N. Krusko. 1984. Langur Monkey Females and Infants: The Female's Point of View. In *Female Primates: Studies by Women Primatologists,* ed. M. Small, 37–57. New York: Alan Liss.

Emde, R. N., and R. J. Harmon, eds. 1982. *The Development of Attachment and Affiliative Systems.* New York: Plenum.

Fedigan, L. M. 1982. *Primate Paradigms: Sex Roles and Social Bonds.* Montreal: Eden.

Goodall, J. 1986. *The Chimpanzees of Gombe: Patterns of Behavior.* Harvard University Press, Belknap Press.

Gouzoules, H. 1980. Biosocial Determinants of Behavioral Variability in Infant Japanese Monkeys. Ph.D. diss., University of Wisconsin.

Hamilton, W. D. 1964. The Genetical Evolution of Social Behavior. Parts 1, 2. *Journal of Theoretical Biology* 7: 1–16, 17–52.

Hausfater, G., J. Altmann, and S. Altmann. 1982. Long-Term Consistency of Dominance Relations among Female Baboons (*Papio cynocephalus*). *Science* 217: 752–55.

Hinde, R. A. 1974. Mother/Infant Relations in Rhesus Monkeys. In *Ethology and Psychiatry,* ed. N. F. White. Toronto: University of Toronto Press.

Hrdy, S. B. 1976. The Care and Exploitation of Nonhuman Primate Infants by Conspecifics Other Than the Mother. In *Advances in the Study of Behavior,* vol. 6, ed. J. Rosenblatt et al. New York: Academic.

______. 1977. *The Langurs of Abu: Female and Male Strategies of Reproduction.* Cambridge: Harvard University Press.

Jay, P. 1962. Aspects of Maternal Behavior among Langurs. *Annals of the New York Academy of Science* 102: 468–78.

______. 1963. The Ecology and Social Behavior of the Indian Langur Monkey. Ph.D diss., University of Chicago.

______. 1965. The Common Langur of North India. In *Primate Behavior,* ed. I. DeVore, 197–249. New York: Holt, Rinehart and Winston.

Johnson, C. K., M. D. Gilbert, and G. H. Herdt. 1979. Implications for Adult

Roles from Differential Styles of Mother-Infant Bonding: An Ethological Study. *Journal of Nervous and Mental Disorders* 167(1): 29–37.

Kaufman, I. C. 1977. Developmental Considerations of Anxiety and Depression: Psychological Studies in Monkeys. In *Psychoanalysis and Contemporary Science*, ed. T. Shapiro, 317–63. New York: International University Press.

Kaufman, I. C., and L. A. Rosenblum. 1967. Depression in Infant Monkeys Separated from Their Mothers. *Science* 155:1030–31.

Kaufmann, J. H. 1966. Behaviour of Infant Rhesus Monkeys and Their Mothers in a Free-ranging Band. *Zoologica* 51: 17–28.

Kawai, M. 1958. On the System of Social Ranks in a Natural Group of Japanese Monkeys. *Primates* 1: 11–48.

Kawamura, S. 1958. Matriarchal Social Order in the Minoo-B Group: A Study on the Rank System of Japanese Macaques. *Primates* 1: 149–56.

King, F. A., C. J. Yarbrough, D. C. Anderson, T. P. Gordon, and K. G. Gould. 1988. Primates. *Science* 240: 1475–82.

Lancaster, J. B. 1985. Evolutionary Perspectives on Sex Differences in the Higher Primates. In *Gender and the Life Course,* ed. A. Rossi. Hawthorne, N.Y.: Aldine de Gruyter.

Lee, P. C., and J. I. Oliver. 1979. Competition, Dominance, and the Acquisition of Rank in Juvenile Yellow Baboons *(Papio cynocephalus). Animal Behaviour* 27: 576–85.

Levine S. 1982. Mother-Infant Relationships: Stress and Coping. *Annali Istituto Superiore di Sanita* 18(2): 223–30.

Lewis, M., and L. A. Rosenblum. 1974. *The Effect of the Infant on Its Caregiver.* New York: John Wiley and Sons.

McKenna, J. J. 1979a. Aspects of Infant Socialization, Attachment, and Maternal Caregiving Patterns among Primates: A Cross-Disciplinary Review. *Yearbook of Physical Anthropology* 22: 250–86.

______. 1979b. The Evolution of Allomothering Behavior among Colobine Monkeys: Function and Opportunism in Evolution. *American Anthropologist* 81: 818–40.

McKinney, W. T. 1985. Separation and Depression: Biological Markers. In *The Psychobiology of Attachment and Separation,* 201–21. New York: Academic.

Missakian, E. 1972. Genealogical and Cross-genealogical Dominance Relations in a Group of Free-ranging Rhesus Monkeys (*Macaca mulata*) on Cayo Santiago. *Primates* 13(7): 169–80.

Mitchell, G. D. 1968. Attachment Differences in Male and Female Infant Monkeys. *Child Development* 39: 612–20.

Mitchell, G., and T. L. Maple. 1985. Dominance in Nonhuman Primates. In *Power Dominance and Nonverbal Behavior,* ed. S. L. Ellyson and J. F. Dovidio, 49–66. New York: Springer-Verlag.

Mohnot, S. M. 1971. Ecology and Behavior of the Hanuman Langur, *Presbytis entellus* (primates: Cercopithecidae), Invading Fields, Gardens, and Orchards around Jodhpur, Western India. *Tropical Ecology* 12: 237–49.

Nash, L. T. 1978a. Kin Preference in the Behavior of Young Baboons. In *Recent Advances in Primatology,* ed. D. J. Chivers and J. Herbert, 71–73. London: Academic.

______. 1978b. The Development of the Mother-Infant Relationship in Wild Baboons *(Papio anubis). Animal Behaviour* 26: 746–59.

Nicolson, N. A. 1987. Infants, Mothers, and Other Females. In *Primate Societies,* ed. B. Smuts et al., 330–42. Chicago: University of Chicago Press.

Oyama, S. 1985. *The Ontogeny of Information: Developmental Systems and Evolution.* London: Cambridge University Press.

Paul, A., and D. Thommen. 1984. Timing of Birth, Female Reproductive Success, and Infant Sex Ratio in Semifree Barbary Macaques *(Macaca sylvana). Folia Primatologica* 42: 2–16.

Poirier, F. C., ed. 1972. *Primate Socialization.* New York: Random House.

Quiatt, D. D. 1979. Aunts and Mothers: Adaptive Implications of Allomaternal Behavior of Nonhuman Primates. *American Anthropolitist* 81: 311–19.

Ransom. T. W., and T. E. Rowell. 1972. Early Social Development of Feral Baboons. In *Primate Socialization,* ed. F. E. Poirier. New York: Random House.

Rheingold, H. L., and C. D. Eckerman. 1970. The Infant Separates Himself from His Mother. *Science* 168: 78–83.

Rossi, A. 1985. Gender and Parenthood. In *Gender and the Life Course,* ed. A. Rossi New York: Aldine de Gruyter.

Rowell, T. 1974. The Concept of Social Dominance. *Behavioral Biology* 11: 131–54.

Sade, D. S. 1967. Determinates of Dominance in a Group of Free-ranging Rhesus Monkeys. In *Social Communication among Primates,* ed. S. Altmann. Chicago: University of Chicago Press.

Scrimshaw, S. 1984. Infanticide in Human Populations: Societal and Individual Concerns. In *Infanticide: Comparative and Evolutionary Perspectives,* ed. G. Hausfater and S. B. Hrdy, 439–62. New York: Aldine de Gruyter.

Silk, J. B., C. B. Clark-Wheatley, P. S. Rodman, and A. Samuels. 1981. Differential Reproductive Success and Facultative Adjustment of Sex Ratios among Captive Female Bonnet Macaques *(Macaca radiata). Animal Behaviour* 29: 1106–20.

Smuts, B. B. 1985. *Sex and Friendship in Baboons.* Hawthorne, N.Y.: Aldine.

Strum, S. 1987. *Almost Human: A Journey into the World of Baboons.* New York: Random House.

Suomi, S. J. 1976. Mechanisms Underlying Social Development: A Reexamination of Mother-Infant Interactions in Monkeys. In *Minnesota Symposium on Child Psychology,* vol. 10, ed. A Pick. Minneapolis: University of Minnesota Press.

______. 1977. Development of Attachment and Other Social Behaviors in Rhesus Monkeys. In *Attachment Behaviors,* ed. T. Alloway, P. Pilner, and L. Krames, 197–224. New York: Plenum.

______. 1982. The Development of Social Competence by Rhesus Monkeys. *Annali Instituto Superiore di Sanita* 18(2): 193–202.

______. 1985. Response Styles in Monkeys: Experiential Effects. In *Biological Response Styles: Clincial Implications,* ed. H. Klar, L. J. Siever, 1–17. Washington, D.C.: Psychiatric Press.

Vogel, C. 1976. *Okologie, Lebensweise und Sozialverhalten der Grauen Languren in verschiedenen Biotopen Indiens.* Berline: Parey.

Washburn, S. L. 1978a. Human Behavior and the Behavior of Other Animals. *American Psychologist* 33(5): 405–18.

______. 1978b. What We Can't Learn about People from Apes. *Human Nature* (Nov.): 70–75.

Williams, G. C. 1966. *Adaptation and Natural Selection: A Critique of Some Current Evolutionary Thought.* Princeton: Princeton University Press.

Wilson, E. O. 1975. *Sociobiology: The New Synthesis.* Cambridge: Harvard University Press.

Wolfheim, J. H. 1983. *Primates of the World.* Seattle: University of Washington Press.

Young, G. H., and C. A. Bramblett. 1977. Gender and Environment as Determinants of Behavior in Infant Common Baboons (*Papio cynocephalus*). *Archives of Sexual Behavior* 6: 365–85.

Young, G. H., and R. J. Hankins. 1979. Infant Behaviors in Mother-reared and Harem-reared baboons (*Papio cynocephalus*). *Primates* 20: 87–93.

Sexual Selection and Social Behavior

Mary Jane West-Eberhard

Charles Darwin considered sexual selection a major feature of evolution. He distinguished it from "natural selection" and made it the subject of an entire book (*The Descent of Man and Selection in Relation to Sex*). Subsequent writers have denied both the major significance and the distinctiveness of sexual selection, and the study of man and beast had been seriously retarded as a result. The recent revival of sexual-selection theory amounts to a demonstration of Darwin's astuteness on the subject. Beginning in 1972 with the publication of *Sexual Selection and the Descent of Man, 1871–1971* (Bernard Campbell, editor), the revival has led to rapid advances in understanding, rendering certain patterns in nature which were not even perceived before, except by Darwin, suddenly obvious and "expected."

Sexual-selection theory ranks alongside molecular genetics and immunology as an area in which a biologist trained twenty years ago is likely to need an update. A student of human evolution, character diversity in any sexually reproducing organism, or sociality who does not have a basic understanding of sexual-selection theory is as crippled and anachronistic as a geneticist who would proceed today without a basic knowledge of the nature of DNA. The purpose of this essay is to explain why.

Sexual Selection Defined

There have been many definitions of sexual selection. Darwin himself made several descriptions of it. In one place (569) he referred simply to "the advantage of certain individuals over their rivals," in another (583) to "the advantages which favoured males derive from conquering other males in battle or courtship," and in another (568) to "the advantage which certain individuals have over others of the same sex and species solely in respect of reproduction." Using Darwin's terms we can make a composite definition that accurately circumscribes all of his illustrative examples: sexual selection is differential reproduction due to variable success in obtaining mates, via combat or courtship. This is in contrast to natural selection, which is differential reproduction due to variable success in "the struggle for existence"—escape or protection from harmful environmental contingencies, and acquisition of resources needed for growth, survival, and the rearing of young. Note that not all aspects of mating competition come under the heading of sexual selection—only social, or interactional, competition for mates. This is clear in an example given by Darwin (1871, 569). Referring to prehensile antennae used by certain male crustaceans to grasp females, he distinguished between "natural" and "sexual" selection as follows:

> We may suspect that it is because these animals are washed about by the waves of the open sea, that they require these organs in order to propagate their kind, and if so, their development has been the result of ordinary or natural selection. . . . if the chief service rendered to the male by his prehensile organs is to prevent the escape of the female before the arrival of other males, or when assaulted by them, these organs will have been perfected through sexual selection.

A concise definition, then, is that sexual selection is due to social (interactional) competition with conspecific rivals of the same sex for mates.

Although both intersexaual (''choice'') and intrasexual (combat) interactions may be involved, the *competition* that results in sexual selection is always fundamentally intrasexual. A ''battle of the sexes''—conflict of interests between males and females—arises only as a secondary consequence of sexual selection. For example, conflict may begin when males attempt to bypass female choice and ''coyness'' by force, or when females trap males into some investment in the young as a condition for mating. Thus it is not strictly correct to say that sexual selection is of two types, intra- and inter-sexual; rather, the *interactions* that give rise to sexual selection (differential success of rivals) are of two types. If there is no contest between rivals of the same sex, there is no sexual selection.

Kinds of Sexually Selected Interactions and Special Features of Their Evolution

The contests that evolve under sexual selection include physical fighting, ritualized threat, races, complex tracking of mates, sequestering, rape, and competitive courtship. The antics involved, and the morphological accoutrements that support them, are among the most beautiful and bizarre in nature; and if their precise effects on conspecifics are usually unknown, they have moved biologists to uncharacteristic poetic heights: ''Peculiar adornments are thrust into prominence: crests, wattles, ruffs, collars, tippets, trains, spurs, excrescences on wings and bills, tinted mouths, tails of weird or exquisite form, bladders, highly coloured patches of bare skin, elongated plumes, brightly hued feet and legs. . . . the display is nearly always beautiful. It is always striking'' (Armstrong 1965, 305, on sexually selected displays of birds).

Intrasexual interactions are usually male-male, and choice is almost always female choice. It is important to understand why this is so. The different precopulatory roles of the two sexes presumably originated in association with a dimorphism between male and female gametes: eggs are usually relatively large, nonmotile, and well-endowed with nutrients, whereas sperm are small and motile. Male and female individuals of both plants and animals usually have sexual roles that parallel those of their gametes. Males promote the movements and egg-seeking activities of the sperm, and females adopt a more sedentary, nutritive role. These specializations are in turn associated with sex differences in the amount of parental investment in offspring (see Trivers 1972). Females nurture the young, presumably because this is more profitable than attempting to replace costly unprotected young (see Williams 1975); and males usually invest relatively little in their offspring, presumably because they profit more by pursuing the motility and mate-getting function for which their relatively inexpensive gametes are so well suited. Furthermore, while a male's genetic stake in a particular diploid zygote is equal to that of the mother, its certainty of paternity may be less, since it does not so easily maintain contact with the fertilized egg. For these reasons it is the male that is "eager"—as Darwin put it—and the female that is coy. Males are more aggressive in combat with each other and in courting the opposite sex; and females are more discriminating in choice of mates.

I will simplify much of the following discussion by referring to "male-male combat" and "female choice" even though these sex roles can be varied and even reversed, especially when males contribute to the well-being of the mate or the young. A classic example of sexual role reversal is the phalaropes (*Phalaropus* species), colonially nesting birds, the males alone of which incubate the eggs and care for the young while the more brightly colored females "quarrel and display among themselves as well as courting the males" (Wynne-Edwards 1962, 238).

The distinction between intra- and inter-sexual interaction is more than a simple classification by interactants. The two kinds of competition may have different evolutionary consequences. According to sexual-selection theory (e.g., as envisioned by Fisher 1930), contests involving choice can lead to more extravagant traits because they are subject to "runaway" evolutionary change: if certain stimuli are favored under "choice" (that is, they elicit a favorable response from potential mates), then there should be selection on individuals of the choosing sex to favor superior performers of those stimuli as mates, due to the advantage of producing offspring who are superior performers. As first pointed out by Fisher (1930), this can lead to increasingly strong selection on performance ability, and the establishment of a genetic correlation of preference and performance greatly accelerating the evolution of both. The evolutionary elaboration of courtship signals is in theory limited only by selection in some other context (e.g., energetic cost or structural unwieldiness).

In the case of combat, the runaway process is expected to be checked by selection on opponents to detect true ability to fight, to call the bluff of superior signalers who are in fact weak fighters. Thus, even though sexually selected combat can be highly ritualized and abstract, with winners and losers decided without a blow, there should always be selection for the threat displays to be ''truthful'' in the sense of reflecting true relative strength or prowess.

''Female choice'' sounds anthropomorphic, and Darwin invited criticism by attributing it to the ''aesthetic sense'' of nonhuman animals as well as people. But female choice means simply differential responsiveness to different fertilization-inducing stimuli. For example, if tapping behavior by a courting male beetle causes a female to become immobile and therefore more susceptible (or ''receptive'') to insemination, effective tapping behavior can be said to affect ''female choice'' of mates. Sexual selection involving choice requires that (1) more than one potential mate be sampled (scanned or sensed), and that (2) variations in stimuli vary in their ability to evoke responses—behavioral or physiological—affecting the likelihood of successful fertilization. The female need not be choosing a mate who is genetically superior in other traits like escaping predators or parasites, acquiring food, etc., for female choice to proceed. As just explained, female preference means that males genetically disposed to perform the preferred stimuli automatically become genetically superior in the context of mate acquisition, if in no other way. Under female choice, the signal per se becomes a kind of commodity, apart from any value it may originally have had (or lacked) as an indicator of male quality.

Courtship does not stop when copulation begins, as evidenced by the bizarre and complex forms of animal genitalia. There is substantial evidence that genitalia are internal courtship devices used to manipulate physiological and behavioral responses of females. They could thus affect the probability that a given male's sperm will fertilize her eggs. Females may manipulate sperm during or following copulation in several different ways: by preventing complete intromission; by restricting sperm transfer within the reproductive tract; by inactivating, removing, and storing sperm; and by remating (Eberhard 1985). Genitalia may be the prototypical results of ''pure'' female choice. They usually are not wielded during male-male interactions as are so many structures used in courtship; they seem unlikely to indicate male quality in any other context; and they may evolve largely unchecked by natural selection in many organisms (e.g., insects), being small in proportion to body size (presumably inexpensive to produce) and, in many species, carried internally when not in use. The likelihood that females discriminate among males on the basis of genitalic characters suggests that females have the last word in deciding mating contests. But the "aggressive" manipulative nature of male genitalia (all are intromittent, and some are equipped with gafflike hooks, recurved spines, and barbs), and the females' convoluted reproductive tracts, which they must traverse, suggests an internal battle of the sexes that may sometimes be won by males. Particularly suggestive is the observation that in some leeches and bedbugs, males forcibly inject sperm directly into the body cavity by piercing the body wall with the genitalia. They completely bypass the female reproductive tract that remains as a vestigial reminder of ancestral affairs.

Both female choice and male-male combat can give rise to greatly exaggerated characters showing spectacular diversity among related species, a quality indicative of rapid evolution. Why does rapid and extensive change characterize the evolution of even sexually selected weapons, such as beetle horns, which are known to be wielded in battle, not courtship, and are therefore not subject to runaway change? Darwin (1871, 583) first suggested the answer which is still accepted today. Sexually selected characters are products of an unending evolutionary race.

> In regard to structures acquired through ordinary or natural selection, there is in most cases, as long as the conditions of life remain the same, a limit to the amount of advantageous modification in relation to certain special purposes; but in regard to structures adapted to make one male victorious over another, either in fighting or in charming the female, there is no definite limit to the amount of advantageous modification; so that as long as the proper variations arise the work of sexual selection will go on.

Thus, under sexual selection, as in the coevolution of predator and prey, parasite and host, each new evolved step sets the stage for another—except that in the case of sexual selection the coevolutionary race is intensified because the contestants belong to the same species. As a result, the interactions can become extraordinarily specialized, like those between a host-specific parasite and its host. By contrast, characters evolving under natural selection can usually approach some optimal solution. This is because they deal with aspects of the environment which either do not evolve in response (being inorganic in nature) or evolve only slowly because they must respond to a variety of species simultaneously.

The unending race and the runaway process help explain the relentlessness and rapidity of change. But they do not explain the great diversity and oddness of the evolved forms. Why do sexually selected characters change in so many different directions, even in species that seem to occupy very similar ecological niches? Attempts to explain diversity of sexually selected traits in terms of environmental differences alone have usually failed, beginning with Darwin's initial attempts to explain sexually selected human racial differences in terms of climate and ecology—an effort that led him to develop his ideas on sexual selection (see Darwin 1871, chap 7). I can think of three main reasons for the diverse directions of evolution under sexual selection, and there may be more. First, in courtship and in battle, novelty per se (or "surprise value") can be an advantage. For example, courtship in many species includes behavior by the male that causes the female to approach or to stop moving as a necessary step toward successful copulation. Any behavior by the male that happens to cause immobility or approach by females might therefore initially become part of courtship simply because of its oddness. It might be an arresting clicking noise, a sudden wave of a cheliped, or a flashing red feather. Individual courting males in many species employ a great variety of small repeated movements in a variety of different sequences, depending on female responses. Novel signals may be retained as part of an array of devices used to overcome female habituation (decline in response) to other repetitive courtship signals. Second, some signals appear to originate as "sensory traps," with males playing upon already existing, deeply ingrained responses of females or opponents. Males seem to take advantage of a large variety of responses evolved in other contexts, such as feeding, defense, timidity in the face of aggression, or brood care. They may give a brief threatening lunge, cry like a baby, mimic an alarm call, hop on one leg as if wounded, or (as in peacocks) peck at the ground as if food has been found. In beetles, immobility is commonly stimulated by tapping on the female's body, and this is performed by males of different species in nearly every conceivable way—by drumming with their antennae, their mouthparts, their feet, and their genitalia. Whichever appendage is used frequently becomes modified into some bizarre and species-specific shape. A simple challenge like inducing female (or opponent) immobility would have an array of possible solutions as great as the response repertoire of the individuals concerned multiplied by the stimulus-producing repertoire of the sexually selected sex. The resulting number of potential evolutionary directions would be very large indeed.

Still another set of signal changes can originate under selection for the ability to recognize the genetic or phenotypic superiority of the displayer. Courted females as well as fighting males are known to assess size, vigor, and quality via scrutiny of numerous indicators such as bodily bulk, size of antlers, rapidity of pursuit, success in observed contests with others, tone (pitch) of voice, and size of nuptial gifts. Again, a multitude of cues is possible for each desirable characteristic. And once established as a signal, each cue is subject to selection for improved effectiveness, a process that can continue for each element of an aggressive or courtship display until limited by selection in some other context. Signals are often elaborated in outlandish ways. For example, in 14 closely related species of fruit flies (of the *Drosophila adiastola* group), the male stands before the female, curves the abdomen forward, and vibrates it near the female's head. In 13 of the 14 species, there is no obvious modification of the abdomen, but in one (*D. clavisetae*) the male's abdomen is adorned with a brush of hairs which sweep over the female's head during the display. It is this embellishment of seemingly trivial signals that gives sexually selected displays their "extravagant" character. Colors and sounds are amplified in ways indicating that reaction to "supernormal" exaggerations of initially modest signals may play a role.

Given so many different potential influences on the direction and embellishment of signals, it is likely that reproductively isolated populations will adopt somewhat different signal characteristics. So it is no surprise that courtship and aggressive displays acquire great complexity and seem to evolve in all directions at once, even among closely related species.

In addition to fostering the proliferation of geographic variants among reproductively isolated populations, sexual selection contributes to the origin of organic diversity in another way. As in other cases of strong intraspecific competition, competition for mates often gives rise to alternative phenotypes which enable individuals losing out in the mainstream competitive mode to switch to a different tactic, thereby increasing their chances of success. Alternative mating tactics of males are extremely common, both in the pursuit of females and in the patterns of combat with other males. Species with dominant males in a position to monopolize females frequently contain "satellite" males which lurk near the dominants for a chance to copulate with females. Mating tactics of excluded males include sneaking copulations, migrating to other sites, simply waiting for a chance to dominate, adopting female coloration and/or behavior, and even (in some fish) changing sex. Species with fighting males (e.g., horned beetles and earwigs, among insects) often contain nonfighting forms. Darwin was the first to notice this as a general phenomenon. In his discussion of the great "variation" of sexually selected characters, he included male dimorphisms, along with geographic variation and transient, evolving forms. Thus, sexual selection gives rise not only to spectacular morphological diversity but to adaptive flexibility as well.

Many fine, detailed studies of the evolution of sexually selected displays, showing both their origins and the mechanisms of their effects, are found in the literature of classical ethology (e.g., in the writing of Lorenz, Tinbergen, Hinde, Eibl-Eibesfeldt, and their students). Although ethologists were not directly concerned with sexual selection theory and its predictions, their careful comparative studies constitute a largely untapped gold mine for modern students of sexual selection who wish to understand the sources and effects of sexually selected displays.

Social Selection

Sexual selection always involves *social* competition via direct interaction with conspecifics. Obviously, social competition for mates is just one subset of social competition for resources. Group-living organisms compete socially for all kinds of commodities—food, water, space, shelter, and allies. They do so by fighting, competitive seduction, and threat—the same means which under sexual selection control access to mates. Examples of nonsexual social competition include sibling competition for parental attention (e.g., the cheeping and gaping of nestling birds), feeding territoriality by both sexes in certain hummingbirds, dominance interactions among female social insects (Hymenoptera), battles for status among female primates, and the aggressive defense of shelters by both male and female mantis shrimp (stomatopod Crustacea).

Because nonsexual social competition, like sexually selected interaction, is a contest among members of the same species, it is expected to have the same evolutionary qualities: unending change, diversity of direction, and (if choice is involved) the potential for runaway change. This expectation is borne out by a survey of comparative data. Nonsexual social signals and associated morphology are often as species-specific as are sexually selected signals, indicating that they undergo similarly rapid diversifying evolution. Examples include the facial markings of nestling birds, the sexually monomorphically bright plumage of hummingbirds (*Amazilia* species) in which both sexes display aggressively, the dominance displays and pheromones of many social insects, and the aggressively displayed meral spots and intraspecifically defensive armor of telson in mantis shrimp. "Choice" analogous to female choice may occur in nonsexual social competition when one class of individuals can control a resource contested by another class. For example, in some social insects the "workers" (sterile helpmates of egg-laying "queens") select one or a few females from among many potential queens and kill or expel rejected individuals. This kind of behavior, or "worker choice," is accompanied by some of the most exaggerated displays known in insects; for example, the bending and shaking of certain tropical wasp queens and the high-pitched piping of honeybee queens. "Parental choice" may occur when solicitous adults are unable to rear an entire brood and eliminate some offspring. In such cases, if certain characteristics of the young form a basis for the parental decision, they would be expected to evolve under social selection for success in signaling per se, and could be subject to runaway change. Nonsexual social selection also produces alternative tactics and polymorphism, a spectacular example being the queen and worker "castes" of dominant and subordinate insect females.

There can be little doubt that both sexual and social selection have played an important role in the evolution of man, as they have in the evolution of other highly social, sexually reproducing species. In view of the commonness of strong selection and marked specialization of social signals in group-living organisms, it is reasonable to hypothesize that the human ability to imitate and influence peers via skillful use of language and costume has evolved under social selection; and this implies that social selection likely contributed importantly to the rapid evolution of the extravagantly developed human brain—the "peacock's tail" of human evolution.

Speciation

It is a remarkable fact that during the decades of amnesia regarding sexual-selection theory, the spectacular characters that Darwin took such pains to explain in terms of sexual selection—characters like peacocks' tails and the plumes of birds of paradise—came to be explained as products of natural selection, or the struggle for existence, although in a very roundabout way. The fact that these adornments are sex-limited in expression and wielded primarily during courtship did not escape notice, but courtship came to be seen as having a completely different function: species identification, in order to avoid breeding with individuals of an alien species. The reasoning was that the genomes of different species would presumably be selected for adaptation to different, geographically separate environments. Interbreeding would disrupt the genetic harmony achieved independently by the two populations and would handicap the offspring of the individuals concerned, putting them at a disadvantage in the struggle for existence. The species-recognition hypothesis fit so perfectly with contemporaneous ideas about the importance of allopatric divergence (assumed due to environmental differences or drift), speciation, and the importance of maintaining a finely coadapted gene pool, that it was scarcely questioned.

In cruel retrospect it seems surprising that the species-recognition hypothesis (like a subsequent "mate recognition," or mating efficiency, hypothesis) was so widely accepted. Why attribute long and complicated courtship displays primarily to species (or mate) recognition, when recognition, whose function is to prevent wasted effort and gametes, should be accomplished quickly and simply? In fact, many observations show that "recognition" does involve brief interaction early in (or prior to) courtship (see references in West-Eberhard 1983). And, when mating competition (sexual selection) is reduced (e.g., in the monogamous termites), fertilization devices are simple (see Eberhard 1985). An alternative explanation, in terms of sexual selection, predicts complexity, as well as species-specificity, of characters. The generation-to-generation constancy of sexual competition, and the many factors altering the direction of evolution of signals, should make sexually selected characters among the most rapidly evolving (and, hence, species-specific) traits in nature.

The belief in species recognition was so strong, however, that the species-recognition hypothesis was sustained even when observations militated against it. If sexual-display morphology or coloration diverged on isolated islands or in lakes lacking sympatric congeners, the necessary species were supplied by invoking the "lost neighbor" hypothesis—the possibility that divergence occurred in response to hybridization or confusion with similar species now extinct. Reproductive character displacement, a major prediction of the species-recognition hypothesis, proved to be uncommon although energetically sought in a variety of groups. This hypothesis states that courtship signals are expected to diverge most rapidly in areas where potentially interbreeding species overlap geographically. The rarity of character displacement contrasts sharply with the abundance of data to support the corresponding prediction of sexual-selection theory: marked geographic variation in sexual signals should be common in geographically isolated populations, with or without overlap with potentially hybridizing congeners. Such rapid divergence characterizes even sexually selected features of beetle horns which are known not to be involved in male-female interactions (and therefore could not be functioning in species recognition).

Under social selection, competition for mates (and other socially contested resources) may contribute to speciation by accelerating divergence of characters crucially affecting reproductive success, thus contributing to (1) the genetic incompatibility of subsequently hybridizing sibling populations, and/or (2) the likelihood of premating isolation due to social courtship incompatibility. Even slight divergence in key aspects of courtship behavior may be sufficient to put "misfit" males at a severe disadvantage under sexual selection, with female discrimination against them a secure barrier to interbreeding.

Was Darwin justified in setting apart sexual selection for special consideration? It now seems difficult to deny that he was. One of the salient contributions of sexual-selection theory is to point out that adaptation and character divergence are not invariably responses to ecological conditions. Sexual-selection theory argues that evolutionary change can occur outside the framework of adaptation to ecological contingencies; in other words, species diversity need not be based upon niche or habitat diversity, but could (especially in allopatry) begin with divergence in the characters used in competitive social and sexual displays, with ecological specializations (if any) a secondary result of speciation. This is an important insight for students of sexually reproducing and social organisms, in which interactions among conspecifics importantly affect success in intraspecific competition. In such species, including humans, social factors may be far more important than ecological factors in determining their most distinctive evolved characteristics.

Like all dichotomies, the natural-selection/sexual-selection distinction is artificial in some important ways. Both kinds of selection entail differential success in reproduction, as biologists use that word today (to mean "replication" rather than "mating," as it was often used by Darwin). In fact, the sexual-natural selection dichotomy was dissolved partly to make that separate point regarding the meaning of selection. It is unfortunate that defining selection in terms of reproductive success interfered with admitting that Darwin's two distinctive subcategories of selection could be involved.

Sexual-selection theory comprehends a set of relationships that allow working biologists to predict patterns of expected traits. For example, it is well established that unless other factors intervene (see Mayr 1972 for a discussion of some of them), increased male parental investment is associated with increased monogamy, increased male coyness (male choice), and decreased sexual dimorphism. One can also begin to predict which behavioral and morphological characters of adults will prove important in sexual displays, by their degree of sexual dimorphism (the criterion most often used by Darwin) and by the degree to which they show species specificity of form. Conversely, if a certain character is known to be wielded in courtship or combat, it is likely to be a useful taxonomic character at the species level. This generalization has long been recognized in practice by taxonomists in a wide variety of groups with regard to male genitalia and many other sexually selected traits.

Social competition within groups (including groups of sexually active adults) can largely determine individual reproductive roles and group structure—hierarchy, territorial spacing, division of labor, and distribution of crucial resources. Thus social and sexual selection are key concepts for understanding not only the origin of character diversity and speciation but also the nature of social organization and the "emergent" qualities of groups (see West-Eberhard 1979). The fact that the special predictions of sexual-selection theory apply as well to nonsexual social competition confirms Darwin's wisdom in recognizing conspecific interaction as a distinctive factor in the evolution of life.

References

Armstrong, E. A. 1965. *The Ethology of Bird Display and Bird Behaviour.* New York: Dover.

Campbell, B., ed. 1972. *Sexual Selection and the Descent of Man.* Chicago: Aldine de Gruyter.

Darwin, C. 1871. *The Descent of Man and Selection in Relation to Sex.* New York: Modern Library.

Eberhard, William G. 1985. *Sexual Selection and Animal Genitalia.* Cambridge: Harvard University Press.

Fisher, R. A. 1930. *The Genetical Theory of Natural Selection.* New York: Dover.

Mayr, E. 1972. Sexual Selection and Natural Selection. In *Sexual Selection and the Descent of Man, 1871–1971,* ed. B. Campbell. Chicago: Aldine de Gruyter.

Trivers, R. L. 1972. Parental Investment and Sexual Selection. In *Sexual Selection and the Descent of Man, 1871–1971,* ed. B. Campbell. Chicago, Aldine de Gruyter.

West-Eberhard, M. J. 1979. Sexual Selection, Social Competition, and Evolution. *Proceedings of the American Philosophical Society* 123:222–34.

______. 1983. Sexual Selection, Social Competition, and Speciation. *Quarterly Review of Biology* 58:155–83.

Williams, G. C. 1975. *Sex and Evolution.* Princeton: Princeton University Press.

Wynne-Edwards, V. C. 1962. *Animal Dispersion in Relation to Social Behavior.* Edinburgh: Oliver and Boyd.

4. Communication, Consciousness, and Intelligence

Deceit and Self-Deception

The Relationship between Communication and Consciousness

Robert Trivers

Everyone seems agreed that there is some kind of intimate connection between the topics of communication, on one hand, and consciousness, on the other. I think there are several good reasons for this. For example, as I shall discuss later, the ability to communicate directly with other animals may draw us much more quickly and deeply into their social lives, thereby giving added insight into their consciousness. But there is one relationship between communication and consciousness that I particularly wish to stress. This is the tendency for processes of deception *between* individuals to generate patterns of self-deception *within* individuals. That is, the way in which we communicate with others—the degree to which we attempt to deceive them—may affect our own degree of consciousness, the extent to which we apprehend reality *correctly*.

Deception Causes Unconsciousness

Just as biologists have long appreciated that deception is a pervasive feature of predator-prey relations, so we now see that deception may also be a widespread pervasive feature of communication within many social species (for a recent review with numerous references, see Trivers 1985, chap. 16). Since deception is usually costly to the victim, deception generates evolutionary powers for its own detection. A coevolutionary struggle is induced, with more skillful deception being matched by greater powers of detecting deception. We have good reason to believe that selection to spot deception may have improved cognitive capacity, including elementary abilities to count, but also including very subtle kinds of discriminations between two nearly identical forms (model and mimic).

In highly social species such as ourselves, spotting deception may involve close scrutiny of the behavior of another individual and of the apparent mind behind the behavior. The stress that accompanies consciously mediated deception may provide information useful to an observer. Quality of voice, eye movements, small movements of the extremities, may all provide information suggesting attempted deception. In this situation, there may be selection to render the fact of deception *unconscious,* the better to hide the attempt from others. As language arises, there may be new opportunities for self-deception, rendering various true facts and motives unconscious, the better to hide them from others. According to theory, then, the practice of deception may over a period of time engender unconsciousness *in the deceiver.* The deceiver begins by deceiving one and ends up deceiving two!

I pause to point out that emphasis on deception and self-deception gives little support to the notion that communication can be conceptualized solely in terms of "information." There was a period of time about fifteen years ago when for one wild moment it looked as though the concept of "information" was going to provide some key integrative function stretching from physics right through to complicated ecosystems, and including animal communication somewhere along the line and even computers and artificial intelligence as part of the whole achievement. Various mathematical definitions of information have been produced, useful in various contexts. In physics, the notion is that entropy, or lack of structure in the environment, can be defined in terms of lack of information.

One bar to the generality of information, at least where animal communication is concerned, is that along with selection for conveying "information" in the usual sense there must also be selection to convey misinformation and lack of information, to hide information, to give biased samples of information, and so on. Thus, to me, theoretical efforts to reduce communication to information transfer, mathematically defined and inferred by the change in behavior of the other organism, had a certain illusion of rigor and generality, but had very misleading connotations. In particular, without having thought about it very carefully, I felt that it tended to sweep deception and self-deception completely out of sight.

In evolutionary biology, incidentally, the sophisticated literature regarding deception has been the wonderful work, largely in entomology but spread throughout the living world, on the predator-prey relationship and the nearly endless variety of deception it has engendered (see Cott 1940, Wickler 1968, and Edmunds 1974, among many others). It is, of course, more difficult to study deception *within* a species, but with the rebirth in interest in individual reproductive success, much work is now pouring out on this subject (see Trivers 1985, Mitchell & Thompson 1986).

Self-Deception Can Be Studied Experimentally in Humans and Other Animals

Philosophers at times have been tempted to see some kind of deep paradox in the concept of self-deception, since there would seem to exist some active entity outside the self but still within the individual doing the deception. I believe the simplest way out of this is to equate the self with the conscious mind. I follow Gur and Sackeim (1979) in expecting to find three features in self-deception:

1. True and false information are simultaneously stored in the same individual.
2. The true information is in the unconscious, the false information in the conscious.
3. We can effect the form of an individual's self-deception by changing its relationship to others.

To demonstrate these three things experimentally, Gur and Sackeim made use of an interesting fact of human physiology: we respond to the sound of the human voice with increased arousal, as measured, for example, by the galvanic skin response (GSR); but this jump is especially large if we are hearing a tape recording of our own voice. Since we are unconscious of our own galvanic skin responses, Gur and Sackeim used them as a measure of unconscious self-recognition. To determine conscious self-recognition, they used verbal reports of self-recognition in response to the same voice stimuli (and interviews after the fact concerning whether mistakes had been made). A person listens to a master tape consisting of matched short segments of voices reading the same material and including some of the person being tested. For each little segment the individual must say whether the voice is his or her own voice or another's. At the same time, measurements of galvanic skin responses give an independent index of unconscious self-recognition. One part of the body has it right and one part has it wrong, and it turns out almost always to be the voice that has it wrong and the galvanic skin response that has it right. This immediately satisfies the first two criteria above: true and false information with a bias toward false information in the conscious mind. Finally, Gur and Sackeim showed that they could influence the kind of mistakes that were made. People told they had failed an exam tended more often afterward to *deny* their own voice some of the time and to *project* it after having been made to feel good about themselves.

I think this methodology could be applied to the study of self-deception in other species. Of course, we cannot ask the question in English, but we can train the animal to perform some task when it recognizes its own voice and take performance of this task as something the organism is likely to be conscious of. It is known that birds respond with greater arousal to the sound of their own species' song compared to those of others, and assuming the same difference is found between self and other *within* species, then we could train a bird to turn on a light when it hears its own voice and thereby see whether it makes mistakes, whether the bird's GSR has it right, and whether we can manipulate a bird to change its form of self-deception. You could subject your bird to a defeat or humiliation of some sort and see whether it tended to deny its own voice more frequently thereafter. So, in principle, it seems to me that processes of self-deception could be studied in other creatures.

This suggestion just scratches the surface of what can be done, and here I agree with Don Griffin on the marvelous dexterity possible in experimental work. You can never quite guess what ingenious experiment is going to turn up next. When early work showed that other animals often had episodes of REM sleep, suggesting dreaming (an observation which of course can be made on one's own dog), some diehards on the animals *un*consciousness side said, "Yes, but how do you know the animal sees movies like we do?" The matter never troubled me for a moment, but I still remember the delight of learning that some ingenious soul had then trained a monkey in a dark room to press a bar at the sight of visual images projected on the screen. Sure enough, during REM sleep its foot "involuntarily" began to bar-press!

The Split Between Conscious and Unconscious Precedes Self-Deception

I operate on the assumption that the split between conscious and unconscious evolved long before processes of deception and self-deception affected transfers of information between the two spheres. The split itself probably related to energy efficiency: consciousness is an energy-expensive state that permits much more concentrated mental attention. We can imagine that over long periods of evolutionary time the brain either turned a whole series of functions over to the unconscious or left them there. Thus, under normal circumstances, we run our heart rate, our breathing, and other internal processes unconsciously. We only choose to be conscious about them [by assumption] under conditions in which it makes sense to invest the extra energy and faculties to scrutinize something carefully.

The image I have of a conscious animal is one in which a light is on inside the organism. In this sense, insects are certainly conscious: there is a light turned on inside them when you interact with them. For example, I may try to countersing with a male or make a series of little threatening moves or even friendly ones, pseudofriendly ones. You can certainly see the insect cock its head and try to get a fix on me from several angles to figure out what on earth I am doing. So there appears to be a conscious entity in there, in this metaphorical sense.

But I do not assume from this anything about *self*-consciousness in the insect, or degree of self-deception. This has to be argued separately on both theoretical and empirical grounds. If within a species insects have been selected to pay close attention to the moves of others, such as opponents, the insects may indeed be selected to shunt some true information preferentially to the unconscious, the better to manipulate an opponent during an ongoing evaluation.

It is perhaps worth emphasizing that the hallmark of self-deception is a biased system of information transfer from conscious to unconscious and back. In an original world in which the conscious-unconscious split is based on energy conservation, I see no reason for storing true information preferentially in the *un*conscious. If anything, a bias would exist in favor of true information being found in the *conscious* mind, the better to make use of the special powers of consciousness. Self-deception involves the counterintuitive fact that the conscious actor is kept in the dark regarding relevant pieces of information. Our interpretation is that others are cueing in on the actions of the conscious actor, so that keeping it in the dark may be one's first line of defense from others. Notice the self-serving way in which this was just put. Given the aggressive nature of deception, I could as easily have argued for conscious ignorance as one's first line of offense!

There Are Levels of Consciousness

It follows from this kind of approach that consciousness should not be treated as some simple unitary concept; one must usually consider levels or degrees of consciousness: how deeply in the unconscious is something buried, how inaccessible is it? Sometimes this takes the form of: how much is the mind willing to deny in support of a given proposition? According to the concepts emphasized here, attitudes toward deception, degree to which it is practiced, and denial surrounding it may be central forces in organizing our level of consciousness. We can fail to practice deception. We can practice deception but fail to deny it to ourselves. We can practice deception, deny the deception, deny the denial, and so on. Indeed, at each stage we can challenge the organism and see whether it continues to deny. The logic of self-deception suggests there may be situations in which a growing pattern of denial must be blocking out successively deeper portions of reality!

Consider verbal behavior and consciousness. Certainly we hear ourselves talking most of the time. We are conscious of our words spoken, but not invariably so. I make linguistic slips, my audiences wrap themselves in laughter, and I have to figure out what it is I just said that is making them act that way. I have become so conscious of this predicament that I sometimes warn myself prior to a talk that I will almost certainly invert a phrase and should be on the lookout for unexpected hilarity on the part of the audience. My most memorable case occurred in 1975 at the Fifteenth World Entomological Congress, where I reviewed my work on the ratio of investment in the social insects, especially ants. As I followed a shapely and dear female friend of mine into the auditorium prior to my talk, I warned myself that I would surely invert a phrase; so when halfway through my talk the room erupted in unexpected laughter, I backed up in my mind and found the offending phrase. I had been trying to say "rear the brood," as in ants "raise the larvae." Instead, I had said "brood the rear." Perhaps it is really true in life that we have a greater need to slip sexual material into normal discourse than other kinds of unconscious material, but toward what end is an interesting question.

John Eisenberg mentioned the test in which you ask a person to say one word with forty different meanings. My favorite word for that test is the word *yeah.* It is not quite a full *yes* and always has, to my ears at least, a little bit of *no* in it. There are places in Maryland I am told where the word *yes* has disappeared entirely and people are capable of saying the word *yeah* almost so it sounds like a 100% *yes;* but you can always add some *no* to it. Using *yes* so as to add a *no* to it is more difficult, and one has to be inventive. For example, you can say "Yes, *sir*!" so that it sounds like "Yes, but up yours," metaphorically speaking. Incidentally, at the University of California at Santa Cruz I have the students under a heavy discipline which they do not like. I do not accept "yeah" as an answer in class or in person. I usually ask "yes or yeah?" and make them jump one way or the other.

Some people are conscious *after the fact* some of the time of the difference between *yeah* and *yes.* People are generally less conscious of just how they have said the word *yeah.* When asked to mimic their earlier usage, for example, they usually increase its resemblance to a complete *yes.* Thus people can be more or less conscious that pronunciation may have connotations. Some resist any association, however, whereas others are conscious both of the general principle and of their own usage. To me this suggests again that consciousness is a very layered kind of phenomenon, not all or nothing. We wish always to know what is rendered unconscious and where the exact limits of consciousness are.

Talking to Other Animals in Their Own Language

Martin Moynihan mentioned the value of talking to animals in their own language instead of just training them to understand English. I think this is a very important area of evolutionary biology, and one which I hope is going to be developed much more fully. There are several advantages to doing this. For one thing, it may allow you to slip inside the social system of the animal itself, becoming a participant and experiencing the social system from the inside. Communicating with other animals in their own language immediately changes your relationship with them, often in a dramatic way. We are usually trapped in a predator-prey relationship with other creatures, so that we only see of them as little as the potential prey can reveal. Adding binoculars may draw the creatures in closer, but the sight to them of a creature with greatly enlarged eyes may cause them to increase their distance in response, with little or no net gain. Thus studying bird behavior is often reduced to watching birds flicker from behind one bush to behind another at a distance of several hundred yards.

All of this was changed one day for me in what was my most vivid moment in nature to date. My friend and teacher, Bill Drury, invited me to go bird-watching one day on a small island off the coast of Maine. We left bird books and binoculars behind and strode to the nearest small tree growing alone in the open. He then made a series of high-pitched bird sounds and soon the tree began to fill up with birds, themselves making a series of calls. As the tree started to fill up, it seemed to attract more and more birds, so that as if by magic all small songbirds in the area were streaking toward the tree under which we were standing. By this time Bill was down on his knees, bent over, and most of the time making a deep kind of moaning sound. The birds actually appeared to wait in line to get the closest look at Bill they could; that is, they hopped from branch to branch until they rested on a branch about eight feet off the ground and not more than two feet from my face. As each bird hopped down, Bill, as if on cue, would introduce them. "This is a male, black-capped chickadee. You can tell because of the black along the neck and shoulders. I would guess he's about two to three years old. Can you see if there is yellow on his back between his shoulders? This is a good index of age."

For me the moment was utterly magical. In a matter of minutes Bill had reduced the distance between us and these birds by orders of magnitude, both physically and socially. Our relationship was so completely different that I was permitted individual introductions at a distance of a couple of feet. Obviously Bill was pulling some kind of trick and had induced some kind of trance through his bird song. Of course, as many of you know, Bill was at first only imitating the mobbing calls of a couple of the small passerines in the area and interspersing these with occasional owl hoots. The owl is deadly at night but is vulnerable in the daytime, and groups of songbirds will mob it in order (presumably) to run it out of their area, or even harass and kill it on the spot. This drew them into the tree at an ever-increasing rate, since mobbing assemblages gain in individual safety with each new arrival (as well as gaining in power to harass the owl). Once they landed in the tree, however, they could see two four-eyed human beings but could not see the owl. Bill's bending over and hooting from the ground was meant to suggest the owl was hidden underneath him. This drew them as close as they could get for a good look, which put them two feet from my face. Unlike some magic tricks, knowing how Bill's was done did not detract from my enjoyment. What remains vividly etched on my mind is a beautiful moment when I actually saw wild songbirds at the distance at which they might interact with each other.

Note that Bill had replaced the usual predator-prey relationship and its caution, concealment, and avoidance with a novel predator-prey relationship in which the predator feigned vulnerability so as to induce attack. To me this is the essence of communicating with members of other species, to replace the boring predator-prey relationship with something far more revealing. So I have been hooked on this line of research ever since. The results of my interactions are sometimes somewhat unexpected. A particularly memorable case concerns the time I made a squirrel paranoid or, perhaps better put, the time a squirrel made *me* even more paranoid. This happened about ten years ago when my son was a year of age. We were outside in Cambridge, and I spotted a squirrel in a tree while my son was in my arms. I was pointing out the squirrel to my son, but he could not spot it. The squirrel was not moving. So I started a very melodious, inviting sort of song, a siren song toward the squirrel. The squirrel was interested and apparently liked it, for it responded positively and crept toward us, which was what I expected it to do. But my son still had not spotted the squirrel, so I decided to reverse action and make a hostile gesture to the squirrel, expecting it to turn immediately and rush in the opposite direction, at which point my son would spot the movement and the squirrel. Of course, this would destroy my relationship with the squirrel, but I gave scant concern to the possible consequences and instead suddenly threatened the squirrel by stamping my foot and perhaps making a move in its direction. Well, the squirrel moved, but he came *toward* us at about a hundred miles per hour, rabid, chattering, and rushing out to the very edge of the branch nearest us, his sharp teeth unexpectedly close to my neck and my son's neck. The organism was not that large, but in its present state of mind I moved back thirty feet with my son before you could say, "Who, me paranoid?" By then my son had seen the movement; it was coming right at us.

So one realizes that there is a natural syntax to animal communication in which the order of presentation of positive and negative signals may signify different meanings. The squirrel expects you to act hostile or indifferent. If you keep to this mode, you will neither much surprise it nor, I believe, anger it. But if your first message is melodious, signifying that you are a friendly organism who would not dream of harming the squirrel's self-interest, you may, in fact, be intending to trap it, to kill it. There is the risk of deception. So when you turn around and reveal through your foolishness the underlying hostility of your posture, the organism comes straight at your throat, in this case because it has been, as I imagined, badly manipulated and hoodwinked. Put another way, there seems to be a moralistic or moral quality to the squirrel's anger. The squirrel seems to be saying with considerable feeling, "Your act of fooling me in order to harm me is not a morally neutral act." Incidentally, the squirrel reminded me rather vividly of the importance for a small creature of *agility* in aggressive encounters rather than brute force.

With a skillfully placed leap and a couple of rapid movements and bites to the right places, the squirrel could, in fact, have killed both myself and my son!

Another example of syntax in animal signals was observed by Irven DeVore and me in East Africa. As recounted in some detail elsewhere (Trivers 1985, 368–72), during a day of exceptionally memorable interactions between adult male baboons in a troop in Gilgil, Kenya, over access to a female in estrus, we saw one male send another male what looked like a double message. He was already threatening the animal from close quarters, sometimes with canines fully bared, because the other male had supported his opponent, now sitting nearby with the female in contention. Yet while threatening the male, the first male also turned his rear end toward the second male, a behavior which in another context appears to be submissive. The translation seemed to be: "Don't ever support my opponent again and, by the way, how about switching sides?" This immediately suggested to us that creatures without language (in the human sense) could nevertheless engage in complex strategic negotiations in which the *order* in which various signals were presented determined meaning: inviting followed by threatening suggested deception and required rabid counteraction, while threat followed by appeasement suggested the possibility of a new relationship.

I have been having a lot of fun trying to talk to birds (and even lizards) by whistling with them and, in the case of the birds, counter-singing to them. Unless you have a tape recorder and you try to fool them in a sophisticated way, any old whistle that is more or less the same pitch as the bird's own sound will do. It is, in fact, amazing how much males wish to counter-sing with a sound that is roughly like their own. I have gotten into extended bouts with mockingbirds at 2:00 in the morning outside my home in Santa Cruz. Shortly after you start singing back to a mockingbird, he is so delighted to have a competitor that he immediately floods the airwaves with a whole set of new sounds and you are sometimes forced to jump around to keep up with him. And you can just imagine the other birds laughing in the dark at my efforts to join mockingbird society.

While whistling, you must be highly conscious of what Eugene Morton has taught us about the importance of body size in determining the pitch of voice. Remember that the birds are very tiny and that they generate high-pitched sounds and hear such sounds best themselves. Since larger organisms naturally tend to produce deeper sounds, deep sounds have themselves evolved a signal function as threats, while high-pitched sounds indicate submission, as if the organism, in response to an attack, in effect squeals out, "I'm tiny, and therefore harmless." A very important application of this line of logic is that the pattern of pitch which conveys meaning in human conversation obeys a simple underlying logic. For example, questions end with the pitch going up because asking a question is a polite or submissive act compared to making an assertion, on which the voice may drop (Ohala 1984). This suggests immediately that the music in our everyday speech or in song may consist of a sequence of relatively positive (high) notes with relatively negative (low) ones. It also suggests immediately that other creatures may be sensitive to melodies and intonations much in the same way that we are.

In any case, enough of rationale. Let us amuse ourselves with some examples. Let us say that I have struck up a relationship with a bird or two in my yard, and Ed Wilson pays a visit, and I want to show him this little trick. Then I will stand outside with Ed and introduce him, in my mind, in English. In my mind I'll say, "Hi, this is Ed Wilson. He is my friend." Only the birds will not be able to hear it or make anything out of it in my own range, so I whistle it up there at about the range that I think goes with their size, and I emphasize the highs and the lows. So I go:

"Hi-i. This is Ed Wil-son. He is my fri-end."

Notice I start with a nice high "Hi," then my voice goes up when I mention Wilson and again when I mention friend. This suggests that Wilson is a positive force in my life. If I turn toward Ed as I introduce him, then there will be gesture coupled with the high notes, so that, it seems to me, the birds might reasonably quickly understand that I am introducing them to a friend.

Now I have actually done this with my son. I have taken him out when he was four or five (for some reason he has to suffer along with a lot of episodes of trying to talk with the lower orders), in which case I say:

"Hi-i. This is Jo-na-than. He is my so-n"

Notice again that my voice goes way up at the beginning of my son's name and then on the word *son.* The generally higher pitch of my voice is consistent with the fact that my son is smaller, relatively more subordinate to me than Dr. Wilson, and enjoys a closer relationship. Perhaps we whistle the words *son* and *friend* slightly differently as appropriate to their different weighting.

The assumption behind this, of course, is that birds are sensitive to this, that they will come to understand things and perhaps say something novel back. My son and I have even acted out sequences in which he will agree to answer to his whistled name so that the birds can connect my whistling of my son's name not only with hand gestures toward him but with his whistling back and then running toward me:

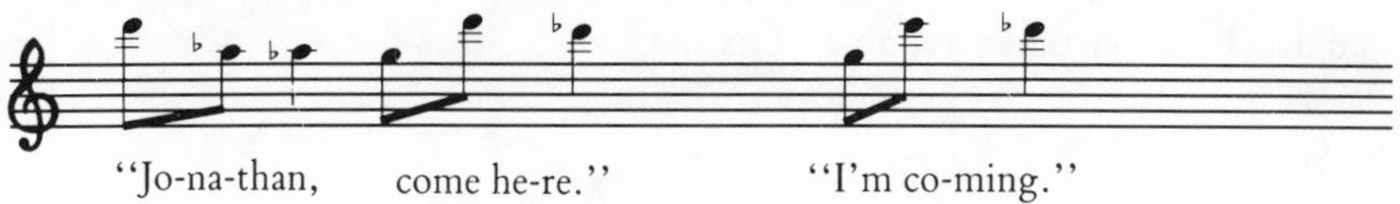
"Jo-na-than,
come he-re."
"I'm co-ming."

Sometimes these kinds of antics on my part elicit some countersinging. They almost always elicit intense interest but are frequently cut short by the nervousness of the birds. When this kind of thing goes well over a period of several weeks, you can believe that my arrival in the backyard is greeted by a good deal of interest from a variety of birds, and whether they make any more sense out of this than I, I cannot say. So I would say both on scientific grounds and as a way of raising one's own consciousness, being able to mimic the sounds of animals and attempting to communicate with them has a lot of value. On the scientific side, it is worth noting that some of our nicest evidence regarding reciprocal altruism in nature comes from playback experiments. It was playback experiments of territorial song that demonstrated reduced aggressive response to the sounds of neighbors *coming from the neighbor's territory.* This suggested the value of mutual restraint among neighbors. More to the point, sounds of the neighbor's voice from inside one's own territory elicited the full-scale aggressive response (see Trivers 1985). In a more dramatic usage, Seyfarth & Cheney (1984) played vervet alarm calls to other vervets within two hours of the time the alarm caller had groomed the target subject or at some other times. This device allowed them to show that unrelated vervet monkeys are more likely to orient toward an alarm call (which would be the first move in giving aid) when they have received a grooming from the caller within the preceding two hours than if no such interaction has occurred. Among related vervets prior grooming has no such effect.

Notice in principle that Cheney and Seyfarth could have made these observations without experimental manipulation. The problem is it would have taken several hundred years. Andre Dhondt (pers. comm.) in Belgium has recently shown that endurance while counter-singing in a songbird at one year of age correlates positively with life span. He did this by creating through tape recording a continuously counter-singing opponent. The time before a male in nature induced to counter-sing finally quit was taken as a measure of endurance. As Dhondt explained it to me, he is attracted to using playbacks because they can condense a lifetime of research into a few months. One is thus permitted in the short span given us to move much more rapidly and deeply in our understanding of nature.

Does Consciousness Require a Central Nervous System?

Griffin has proposed that consciousness depends upon the existence of a central nervous system. We can see that the area of consciousness has been a contentious one because when I suggest keeping an open mind on the subject of whether plants may have some form of consciousness, Griffin accuses me of being a pan-psychicist, which I am not. I just believe in keeping an open mind, especially where it is unclear exactly what position logic forces us to take. Of course, the cost of *not* keeping our minds open is always that there is some deeper, unconscious assumption, often biased, which may blind us more than the initial distinction helps us. I do not take a position on plants, but I do wonder sometimes. People in rural areas or people with gardens often say during a drought, "My plants are suffering." You see some dreadful phenotype that is obviously barely making it, and you wonder: is there any sense in which the word *suffer* could be used besides the obvious one that the morphology is in sad shape? When the rains come, we say, "The trees are happy." They certainly look good, leaves and branches once more reaching for the sky, color returning. But perhaps the happiness is entirely in ourselves. Perhaps inside the tree all is quiet and there is nothing resembling internal pleasure or satisfaction in the new state of affairs. Seems a shame, if true, but this sentiment itself may merely be the bias of a relatively sentient animal.

Incidentally, for feats of *un*consciousness on the subject of feeling pain, we can hardly do better than the medical profession. As recently as thirty years ago—in defense, for example, of the practice of greeting newborn sons by lopping off their foreskins—it was claimed that, since the cortex was not turned on or connected until several weeks later, *young infants feel no pain!* They may writhe, turn red, and scream until tears roll down their faces. But relax, inside everything is calm—blank, in fact. This rather supports the old adage that "there is no fool like an educated one." Call it the dark underbelly of instruction: education permits marvels of reality orientation (witness our knowledge of how to combat bacterial infections), but it gives its strengths to self-deception, as well, in the form of logic, evidence, and the backing of venerable authority (witness the wonderful body of knowledge in support of setting leeches upon individuals suffering from malaria).

Sea anemones are to us distantly related, mostly sessile animals, which lack a central nervous system. They do have nerve cells, however, and these are organized into at least one extensive nerve net permitting the organism rapid, coordinated action in certain circumstances (e.g., quick contraction when disturbed). It has been known for some time that in some anemones individuals will fight with members of their own species concerning space, using specialized structures to sting—and sometimes kill—neighbors. In several cases individuals discriminate between clone mates and nonclone mates, only attacking the latter, but they make no discrimination in regard to sex, attacking males and females alike. It was commonly assumed that these simple creatures were incapable of making the discrimination. Then Kaplan (1983) showed for one species, the plumose anemone, *Metridium senile,* males fight only males and females fight females (nonclone mates).

This startling discovery suggested the possibility that sexual selection may be operating in these lowly organisms, so Kaplan and I brought these sea anemones into the lab and set them up in little experiments that were designed to heighten any kinds of sexual concerns they might have had. Each individual sat touching two unrelated individuals of the opposite sex while a same sex member was seated diagonally opposed and within range of tentacles. The anemones were placed in their seating positions on the bottom of glass fish tanks, and they had a considerable amount of mobility on this surface. Movements were tracked for twenty-four hours, and intensive behavioral observations were made during the first two hours after release. We were amazed to see a pattern of sex differences emerging. Males seemed to be more mobile than females, a male more likely to follow a female or to lean over her and caress her with his tentacles. In some cases, when a male spotted that a female was next to him, he raised out pseudopods, or legs filled full of water, and extended these toward the female as if touching her. The female might lean away from this attention, and it all looked somewhat familiar on the great vertebrate-insect paradigm. So we certainly believe now that the sea anemones can apprehend sex, that they appear to act very differently toward male and female nonclone mates, and I would be inclined to imagine there is some internal representation of ongoing experience. When one plumose anemone is stung by another, it recoils sharply and shrinks in size very dramatically. Ocontia (small defensive filaments) extrude copiously from the body wall. Certainly it *looks* painful, watching it.

Consciousness and communication enjoy a complex relationship. For example, selection for deception may induce self-deception—the better to remain undetected—thus inducing a form of unconsciousness. The split between conscious and unconscious mental functioning almost certainly predates selection for deception and evolved as an energy-saving device, but once the split emerged, selection to hide deception must have favored biased transfers of information between the two spheres. Information may be held at different levels of consciousness, signifying the differing degrees to which the information is inaccessible to consciousness.

One of the best ways to get close to other creatures is to communicate with them in their own language or a facsimile thereof. Casual experiments in this vein suggest that there is a natural syntax in animal communication such that the order in which positive and negative signals are presented itself signifies meaning. In both animal and human communication high-pitched sounds are relatively positive, and low-pitched, negative. This suggests that whistling sounds which mimic human intonation during speech may be a vehicle for conveying complex information from humans to birds. Experiments on sexually directed behavior in sea anemones suggest that a central nervous system may *not* be a prerequisite for low orders of consciousness.

References

Cott, H. B. 1940. *Adaptive Coloration in Animals.* London: Methuen.

Edmunds, M. 1974. *Defense in Animals.* Essex, England: Longman.

Gur, C. R., and H. A. Sackeim. 1979. Self-Deception: A Concept in Search of a Phenomenon. *Journal of Personality and Social Psychology* 37:147–69.

Kaplan, S. 1983. Intrasexual Aggression in *Metridium senile. Biological Bulletin* 165:416–18.

Mitchell, R. W., and N. S. Thompson, eds. 1986. *Deception: Perspectives on Human and Nonhuman Deceit.* New York: State University of New York Press.

Ohala, J. J. 1984. An Ethological Perspective on Common Cross-Language Utilization of F_0 of Voice. *Phonetica* 41:1–16.

Seyfarth, R. M., and D. L. Cheney. 1984. Grooming, Alliances, and Reciprocal Altruism in Vervet Monkeys. *Nature* 308:541–43.

Trivers, R. 1985. *Social Evolution.* Menlo Park, Calif.: Benjamin/Cummings.

Wickler, W. 1968. *Mimicry in Plants and Animals.* New York: McGraw-Hill.

Structures of Animal Communication

Martin H. Moynihan

Communication is the conveyance of information from one organism to another organism. The subject has been of interest for a very long time, if not from the time of the Paleolithic, then at least from the time of Herodotus onward. There do not seem to be many original points that remain to be made as singular statements. Almost everything that could conceivably be said on the subject has already been said by someone, somewhere, somehow, at some time. Thus, the following comments cannot pretend to be original. They may, however, be useful insofar as they suggest that certain approaches and emphases could be remembered or recalled with profit.

Students of communication should respond to a number of general questions. Three are particularly important: (1) What is the information proffered for conveyance or transmission? (2) How is the information encoded for transmission? (3) How is the information or code perceived and interpreted?

The ultimate focus of this essay will be on nonhuman animals (I have worked with birds, primates, and cephalopods, doubtless introducing some bias, at least in the choice of examples), but no form of communication can be considered in isolation. Human and nonhuman are difficult to separate. Since we ourselves are human, some degree of anthropomorphism in the analysis of the communication systems of other species is inevitable. We should, however, try to distinguish between the sorts of anthropomorphism, comparisons of animals with humans, that are useful and revealing, and the other sorts that are merely confusing and nonproductive.

A point to be made is that the logical investigation of human language may tell us as much about the structure of nonhuman communication systems as the study of nonhuman systems can tell us about the evolutionary development of human languages.

The first question posed above (the content, or the "what") may be the most important of all. It addresses the basic problem directly but not very closely. Presumably the information proffered provides much of the material upon which natural selection has to operate, to choose or reject. I should like to argue, however, that the answers to this question are already known *in principle.* Of course, they are not known in actual facts in all cases. (An ethologist should never say "*Malheur aux détails!*"). It is fairly evident, nevertheless, that most statements of most animals indicate probabilities of attack, escape, feeding, sex, and other activities of comparable functional importance and, in a sense, simplicity (see also Marler [1961], Smith [1977], and Rand [1988]). It is unlikely that anything surprising or revolutionary for theory will come from further studies of content alone.

Some of the answers to the second question (forms of encoding) are less well known. They might, therefore, be more interesting. In this context of argument, one may provisionally discard the media of transmission. They will appear at a later stage of discussion. Communication can be visual, acoustic, vibratory, olfactory, tactile, electrical, or any combination thereof. Students have usually assumed that any stimulus produces an "automatic" response in particular conditions. This can hardly fail to be true at some level of analysis. As scientists, we should try to be as mechanist and reductionist as humanly possible (Ockham's razor!). But the conditions are complex, and there are both external and internal circumstances to be considered. Some facts are not in dispute. We do know, in a general way, what kinds of external stimuli induce what kinds of responses. We know something about hormones and physiology. We can trace correlations with aspects of external environments (*e.g.* Morton 1977). What we do *not* know is how statements are organized within themselves.

A subsidiary question can be posed. How much attention should be paid to the internal arrangements within any given statement? The answer is: probably quite a lot. Some relations are obvious. Positions in sequences have always been recognized to be relevant. Pattern A before B cannot transmit quite the same information as pattern B before A. Repetitions cannot be the same as first statements.

We should try to go further or deeper. It seems to me that students of animal behavior could profit from adopting, or putting emphasis upon, a "structuralist" approach. This approach has long been fashionable and influential in studies of linguistics, anthropology, literature, and (*sensu lato*) philosophy. It has not affected studies of animal behavior to any significant extent, except indirectly, via intermediaries (*e.g.* Zipf 1936; Cherry 1957) and occasional, usually unstated implication. Ethology is in some ways a backward or provincial science.

What is structuralism? The classic work in the field is that of Ferdinand de Saussure (his lectures as recollected by his students and first published in 1915; the edition before me is 1986). There is a point to the classics (*viz.* Darwin). I suppose that structuralism could be best, if vaguely, defined as the analysis of the relations among the objects or data being investigated (DeVitt & Sterelny 1987). As applied to the study of communication, it is the science of signs (semiotics, semiology) (see, for instance, Eco 1976) and the series edited by T. A. Sebeok entitled "Approaches to Semiotics." Saussure and many others were or are primarily concerned with human language. We do not need to follow all their arguments in all their complexity. We may, however, be able to use some of their insights and terminology. Mere terms can help to direct our views upon both objects and subjects.

Some parenthetical remarks may be inserted here. Human language, with its visual, written, and computerized derivatives, may be the most intellectually complex system of communication known to us. It is in some ways unique—largely learned and therefore variable, varying along certain lines over certain time spans. This does not mean that any given communication by a human being is more complex in physical form than any given communication by a nonhuman animal. Even whole repertories of nonhuman animals can be as complex in forms as those of humans. As an example, I can cite the Caribbean reef squid (*Sepioteuthis sepioidea*). The signal repertory of the species is almost entirely visual, including rapid color changes, often intricate, and distinctive movements and postures, all of which can be combined, simultaneously and/or sequentially, in an enormously large number of permutations (Moynihan & Rodaniche 1982; Moynihan 1985). An observer from another planet would take a long time to discover that the communication systems of the squids referred to fewer subjects, or referred to the same subjects less subtly, than did the communication systems of the humans on the nearby mainland. The physical forms of the signal repertories of some nonhuman animals are potentially capable of encoding anything.

Saussure claims that almost all the elementary units that appear and reappear in human language(s) are *arbitrary.* They do not usually reflect, extend, or mimic the "referents," the objects or external stimuli referred to. The words *arbor* and *tree* are different in sound. Yet, within their own systems, they mean exactly the same thing. Arbitrariness can be hypothetical. "The word 'dog' exists, and functions within the structure of the English Language, without reference to any four-legged barking creature's real existence" (Hawkes 1977).

There are, of course, exceptions to the prevalence of arbitrariness. Even Saussure excluded exclamations and onomatopoetic utterances. Other exceptions can be found, but the generalization still holds. The signals of nonhuman animals are only slightly less arbitrary than are those of humans. For conveying the signal of threat, it hardly matters if an animal turns black, swells up, roars, or ruffles its feathers. The information encoded, some probability of attack, can be essentially the same in all cases (see also Lorenz [1935, 1950]).

Arbitrariness per se is not a sacred tenet. But there are practical advantages, for certain analyses, in proceeding as if the signals discussed were or might be *abstract.* X, Y, and Z, so to speak. They should also be considered relational. The factors of simple sequences (A and B) and repetitions cited above are clear enough. Yet simple relations can become very complicated when they are numerous and controlled by arbitrary rules. A favorite Saussurian analogy is the game of chess. Perhaps we should think of wild chess in which the king can be captured—or even the game of *Go.* There are many dimensions. One is rather horrified to revert to "game theory" (references in Maynard-Smith 1979 and Moynihan 1982), but the reversion is only partial.

For the moment, we are concerned with the logical rules (regularities of occurrence) of communication among the players rather than with the goals achieved or failed. Unfortunately, these rules are precisely the features that remain most obscure to us.

All systems of communication are semantic. There are relations between the symbols used and the world to which they refer. Any complex system of signals must also be syntactic. There must be relations among symbols. We should like to know more about the structures of syntax in different species.

Saussure distinguishes between *langue* and *parole.* The former is a somewhat theoretical concept, perhaps best translated in English simply as "language" (*not* quite the same thing as the French *language*). *Parole* comprises actual performances of individuals in particular situations. For vocal animals like human beings, the term *speech* will do. The distinction between *langue* and *parole* is not very different from the distinction between *competence* and *performance* in more recent discussions (see, for instance, Chomsky 1980). None of the terms may be ideal, but they do seem to reflect a real dichotomy.

All that we can hear or see or feel or smell is *parole.* In the case of humans, with our own natural empathy and access to copious written accounts, we can hope to identify some aspects of *langue.* This is (even) more difficult to do for nonhuman animals. Yet the attempt should be made. There may be a "deep structure" to human languages. If so, there probably are comparable structures lurking below the surfaces of nonhuman signal systems. What are they? Are they the same in all species? If not, how do they differ from species to species? In what ways can they diverge? And why? What are the selection pressures?

The formal elements of speech can be defined by various criteria. An early and influential classification of human systems (Morris 1946) separated identifiers, designators, appraisers, prescriptors (modern spelling). This is fine, well put, convincing. It is, however, derived from assessment of the information contents, even the "purposes," of the parts. Could we recognize other categories irrespective of the information encoded? Can *different* messages be organized and controlled in the *same or parallel* ways?

A rather ambitious, if flimsy, attempt to identify syntax or even grammar was made in the study of Caribbean reef squids. It was suggested that the various color patterns, color changes, postures, and movements could be assigned to four categories: standards, signifiers (*not* the same as Saussure's *significants*), modifiers, and positionals. This was anthropomorphic. (The signifiers are equivalent to nouns and verbs, substantives. The modifiers are equivalent to adjectives and adverbs.) Was this the right or the wrong kind of anthropomorphism? Who can tell in the present state of our knowledge? We still are almost confined to human language(s) for comparison. We need to know more about more species.

The paucity of our current knowledge is remarkable. I can cite some areas of ignorance. The diverse vocalizations of some species of birds and mammals (primates) are physically discrete—hard, round glass marbles, so to speak. The vocal signals of other animals (sometimes closely related species) could be more fairly compared to barely distinguishable points along continua from smooth to harsh, short to long, soft to loud (Marler 1970; Morton *op. cit.*). Does this difference in acoustic properties imply a difference in syntax?

Some animals make statements in phrases or sentences. Instances that come to mind include the ''songs'' of many birds and the equivalent utterances of such primates as gibbons, *Hylobates* spp. (e.g., Marshall & Marshall 1976; Tembrock 1974; Tenaza 1976), and titi monkeys, *Callicebus* spp. (Moynihan 1966; Robinson 1979).

As usual, definitions are difficult. I would suggest that the term *sentence* be applied to any statement that has a *predictable* beginning and an *anticipated* end. This definition is simplistic, but it may still be useful. Consider a particular case. A young chimpanzee, nicknamed ''Nim,'' was taught some elements of human gestural sign language. The results are well described by Terrace (1981). But what were the implications? Terrace came to the conclusion that Nim did not utter sentences. For two reasons. Nim's statements were composed of only two or three signs, and they were influenced by human interlocutors. Neither criterion seems to me to be decisive, especially in the artificial circumstances of the experiment.

An absence of sentences or sentencelike structures is better documented in some other species in more nearly natural conditions. Again, Caribbean reef squids may be examples. Their various signals, and the combinations thereof, seem to start when they start, and to last as long as they last. An experienced observer can, perhaps, hazard a statistical prediction. Any particular *Sepioteuthis* pattern or combination may be slightly more likely to occur near the beginning of a sequence than toward the end, or vice versa. Still, prediction would be difficult and often insecure. There are no obvious "station identifications" at the start or definite "signoffs" immediately before or at the finish.

Whatever the descriptive terms used (and they are all awkward), the differences of organization between the songs of birds and the signals of some primates and the complex performances of squids is appreciable. To what can the differences be ascribed? There are various possibilities. They are not likely to be due to any great difference of information content. As far as a human observer can tell, squids "talk" about attack, escape, sex, etc., the usual subjects of discourse among many other animals. There is a complication. Cephalopods are both prey of larger animals and predators upon smaller ones. Their environments are often crowded with other species as well. Many kinds of interspecific relations are possible. Some cephalopod displays are almost certainly meant to be read correctly by conspecifics (and by friendly allies and associates of other species). At the same time, many of the same displays are designed to be overlooked or to be misread or to baffle possible predators upon the cephalopod performers. A certain amount of unpredictability of behavior can be useful to a potential prey. Unpredictability may be difficult to program. It is a sophistication of cephalopods. (They have larger brains than do fishes of comparable sizes [references in Packard 1972]).

Differences in media of transmission—visual vs. acoustic, aerial vs. aquatic—cannot be entirely irrelevant. It must be admitted, however, that the existing evidence is less than satisfactory. There are many special conditions. Consider the visual displays of anoline lizards (Greenberg & Noble 1944; Carpenter 1965; further references in Rand & Williams 1970). These patterns may be sentences as defined above. Yet the brevity of the utterances, frequently repeated as they often are, could be a simple consequence of physiology. Most reptiles use anaerobic rather than aerobic metabolism for mobilizing energy during intense activity. Some displays are intense. Being supported by anaerobic processes, they are necessarily brief. It is easy to imagine how or why brief statements could be most effective when they are most sentencelike. They have to be vivid in the time available. Both station identifications and sign-offs can be useful markers, calls or re-calls to attention. (It might be added that the acoustic performances of those Old World gekkos which vocalize at night are also short and sentencelike.)

Forced compression in time may be exceptional. There are suggestions that the visual displays of crabs on land (Crane 1975) and certain fishes in fresh waters, cichlids and sticklebacks (Baerends & Baerends van Roon 1950; van Iersel 1953; Morris 1958), are open-ended in some of the same ways as are the performances of squids. Again, I am citing only classic accounts in the hope that they will appear to be noncontroversial. Perhaps visual displays tend to be more complex than acoustic displays at any given moment because color changes, movements, and postures can be combined simultaneously, whereas sounds usually (not always) are produced only one at a time.

All this is inconclusive. The very inconclusiveness does, I think, serve to emphasize the need for further research on syntax. Ethologists could borrow procedures, as well as insights, from linguists. When attempting to decipher a statement in a foreign language, linguists first *transcribe.* They reproduce the material literally. A biologist studying another animal can do the equivalent by use of the naked eye or ear or by employing modern audiovisual recording techniques. After or along with transcription, linguists should, and often do, *parse* their material. They try to identify the various parts of speech, markers, verbs, tone groups, locatives, suffixes, negatives, allomorphs, or whatever other terms may be appropriate to the systems being studied. Only then do they attempt a translation, to give the meaning of the statement. At least in theory, ethologists should be able to do something similar for complex utterances and performances of nonhuman animals. (A good example of linguistic analysis that should be intelligible to ethologists is provided by Williams 1965.)

What we really need is more parsing. The three questions posed at the beginning of this essay are linked to one another, but they can be approached in sequence. If we can determine the codes, then we should be able to add precision to our already considerable knowledge of the information encoded. Without cracking the codes, we cannot get much further in discovering how information is perceived and interpreted.

Continuing progress in the study of animal communication will depend upon several factors: certainly improved technology but also a reordering of our own ideas on the subject. Detailed, intelligent, rigorous, and ruthless classification is the objective to be aimed for. The identification and comprehension of formal, logical structures and relations will be crucial.

References

Baerends, G. P., and J. M. Baerends van Roon. 1950. An Introduction to the Study of the Ethology of Cichlid Fishes. *Behavior,* Suppl. 1.

Carpenter, C. C. 1965. The Display of the Cocos Island Anole. *Herpetologica* 21(4): 256–60.

Cherry, C. 1957. *On Human Communication.* New York: Wiley.

Chomsky, N. 1980. *Rules and Representations.* New York: Columbia University Press.

Crane, J. 1975. *Fiddler Crabs of the World.* Princeton: Princeton University Press.

DeVitt, M., and K. Sterelny. 1987. *Language and Reality.* Oxford, England: Basil Blackwell.

Eco, U. 1976. *A Theory of Semiotics.* Bloomington: Indiana University Press.

Greenberg, B., and G. K. Noble. 1944. Social Behavior of the American Chameleon (*Anolis carolinensis* Voight). *Physiological Zoology* 17(4): 392–439.

Hawkes, T. 1977. *Structuralism and Semiotics.* London: Methuen.

Iersel, J. J. van. 1953. An Analysis of the Behaviour of the Male Three-spined Stickleback (*Gasterosteus aculeatus* L.). *Behaviour* Suppl. 3.

Lorenz, K. 1935. Der Kumpan in der Umwelt des Vogels. *Journal fuer Ornithologie* 83:37–213, 289–413.

______. 1950. The Comparative Method in Studying Innate Behaviour Patterns. *Symposium of the Society of Experimental Biology* 4:221–68.

Marler, P. 1961. The Logical Analysis of Animal Communication. *Journal of Theoretical Biology* 1:295–317.

______. 1970. Vocalizations of East African Monkeys. 1. Red Colobus. *Folia Primatologica* 13:81–91.

Marshall, J. T., Jr., and E. R. Marshall. 1976. Gibbons and Their Territorial Songs. *Science* 193:235–37.

Maynard-Smith, J. 1979. Game Theory and the Evolution of Behavior. *Proceedings of the Royal Society of London* B205:475–88.

Morris, C. W. 1946. *Signs, Language, and Behavior.* New York: Prentice Hall.

Morris, D. 1958. The Reproductive Behavior of the Ten-spined Stickleback (*Pygosteus pungitius* L.). *Behaviour* Suppl. 6.

Morton, E. S. 1977. On the Occurrence and Significance of Motivation–Structural Rules in Some Bird and Mammal Sounds. *American Naturalist* 111(981): 855–69.

Moynihan, M. 1966. Communication in the Titi Monkey, *Callicebus. Journal of the Zoological Society, London* 150:77–127.

———. 1982. Why Is Lying about Intentions Rare during Some Kinds of Contests? *Journal of Theoretical Biology* 97:7–12.

———. 1985. *Communication and Non-Communication by Cephalopods.* Bloomington: Indiana University Press.

Moynihan, M., and A. F. Rodaniche. 1982. The Behavior and Natural History of the Caribbean Reef Squid *Sepioteuthis sepioidea. Advances in Ethology* 25:1–150.

Packard, A. 1972. Cephalopods and Fish: The Limits of Convergence. *Biological Review* 47(2): 241–307.

Rand, A. S. 1988. An Overview of Anuran Acoustic Communication. In *The Evolution of the Amphibian Auditory System,* ed. B. Fritzch, 415–31. New York: John Wiley and Sons.

Rand, A. S., and E. E. Williams. 1970. An Estimation of Redundancy and Information Content of Anole Dewlaps. *American Naturalist* 104:99–103.

Robinson, J. G. 1979. An Analysis of the Organization of Vocal Communication in the Titi Monkey *Callicebus moloch. Zeitschrift fur Tierpsychologie* 49:381–405.

Saussure, F. de. 1986. *Cours le linguistique générale.* Paris: Payot.

Smith, W. J. 1977. The Behavior of Communicating. Cambridge: Harvard University Press.

Tembrock, G. 1974. Sound Production of *Hylobates* and *Symphalangus.* In *Gibbon and Siamang,* vol. 3, ed. D. M. Rumbough, 176–205. Basil, Switzerland: Karger.

Tenaza, R. R. 1976. Songs, Choruses, and Countersinging of Kloss' Gibbons (*Hylobates klosii*) in Sibernt Island, Indonesia. *Zeitschrift fur Tierpsychologie.* 40:37–52.

Terrace, H. S. 1981. *Nim: A Chimpanzee Who Learned Sign Language.* New York: Washington Square.

Williams, K. 1965. *A Grammar of the Kolokuma Dialect of Ijo.* West African Language Monograph Series, eds. Joseph H. Greenberg and John Spencer. Cambridge: Cambridge University Press.

Zipf, G. K. 1936. *The Psycho-Biology of Language.* Boston: Houghton Mifflin.

Consciousness and the Ecology of Meaning

New Findings and Old Philosophies

John Hurrell Crook

Basic to human understanding is the fact of experience. Consciousness itself is the root of being human and of humanity's knowledge of the nature of that being. Yet, paradoxically, consciousness is one of the most poorly understood of psychological phenomena, and a concept upon which scepticism and even abuse has been heaped by those scientists seemingly best placed to comprehend it. Within the last 100 years, consciousness has been seen as the fount of all experience (James 1950) only then to be denied any useful significance in a psychological science (Watson 1913). Today, once more, the theme of consciousness is granted central significance in attempts to understand the cognitive life of both humans and other higher animals (e.g., Griffin 1976; Crook 1980, 1983, 1987; Cranach & Harre 1982; Humphrey 1983). In this essay I aim first to show how consciousness can be understood scientifically and, second, to demonstrate how modern Western education tends to overdevelop some aspects of mind at a cost to us through neglecting aspects of ancient experience that have become rare in the modern world.

As described in the *Oxford English Dictionary, consciousness* refers to personal and mutual knowledge of the fact of experiencing. It is not, therefore, merely to be equated with experience, but it implies an awareness of experience; it implies not only cognition but metacognition. As such it is "prior" to knowledge, and taken in this way, its existence and function have, in the sciences of knowledge, simply been assumed. It is only when we ask, as eventually we must, what it is and how it originated that science runs into paradox, for the lamp then has to illuminate itself.

When an explanation is demanded in Western scientific thought, the usual procedure is to try to describe a phenomenon in terms of something better understood or to reduce it analytically to underlying processes at a lower causal level. This tradition, stemming originally from the ancient Greek attempt at understanding the world, has meant that theories of mind have tended to be expressed in terms of the most advanced machinery of control known to the modelers. While the Greeks themselves wisely focused on the link between mind and breathing, Descartes was fascinated by pipes and clockwork; contemporary thinkers (e.g., Sayre 1976) turn naturally to the computer for inspiration. Mind is thus "objectively" discussed in terms of performance and interpreted from the viewpoint of engineering. Yet, for you and me, mind also denotes experience. Scientists have had great difficulty in attempting to marry interpretations of mind couched in terms of physical or behavioral performance with other, equally rational viewpoints emphasizing subjective experience itself as basic. To put together, for example, a neurophysiology of psychoanalysis would be an uncommonly difficult endeavor, for knowing what brains do contributes little to understanding what people say.

The issues involved have been sharply emphasized by the resuscitation of an old problem first examined by von Uexküll (1909): do animals have consciousness, and if so, how much and of what form and to what extent in different species? In reviving this issue, the ethologist Griffin (1976) has also intensified the debate within psychology concerning the nature and importance of consciousness in attempts to understand the mind. As cognitive psychology and evolutionary ethology come to overlap in this area, exciting and far-reaching interpretations of the origin and nature of mind are emerging, some of which require us to take into account the psycho-philosophical understandings of mind within the experience of Eastern cultures as well as our own.

The Nature of Conscious Experience and Self-Awareness

Let us begin by asking what consciousness is. To have awareness of personal experience implies a process whereby action is reviewed so that an understanding of sequences of events can be constructed. What sort of a process can this be?

A number of psychologists have been impressed by the minor importance that consciousness appears to have in many activities. Even William James noted that "actions originally prompted by conscious intelligence may grow so automatic by dint of habit as to be apparently unconsciously performed." Many acts of communication are performed mindlessly. This is especially true of conventional social interactions heavily "scripted" through habitual use (Nisbett & Wilson 1977; Langer 1978; Berger & Kellerman 1983). Social performance is often run off with little involvement of higher cognitive reflection.

A number of functions do seem, however, to be facilitated by awareness, and among these are the formulation of intentions, control in the execution of projects, detection of inconsistencies in behavior, behavioral adjustment to context, the reconstruction and interpretation of otherwise unconscious conflicts, and effective responses to novelty (Baars 1983). A number of scholars agree that consciousness is present and is especially important where new learning and responses to arousal promoted by novelty are occurring, but consider it to be of lesser importance once conventional behavior has been established. In particular, Mario von Cranach and his co-workers (1982) have argued from their complex experimental program that the behavior of humans is characteristically goal oriented, verbally reportable, and therefore conscious, planned, and purposeful within social contexts of diverse kinds. Cognitions, they argue, become conscious when attention is focused upon them. Attention therefore moves cognition into awareness, where it becomes subject to verbal formulation and reporting to others, in a matrix of social exchange.

In my view, psychologists have underrated the importance of conscious awareness in the context of moment-to-moment adjustment in an individual's perception of the world. Consciousness appears to be part of the process whereby the world is monitored and performance made effective in relation to goals of importance to an individual. The need for adjustment varies in intensity with the demands of the moment, being least, for example, at a conventional happening but acute, perhaps, during foreign travel—getting off a train in Banaras (now called Varanasi), for example. Consciousness is based, I argue, on the feeding forward of expectations derived from mental representations of known circumstances. These expectations require confirmation or adjustment in new experience before actions can be carried out. The continuous presence of fed-forward expectations for match-mismatch analysis accounts, I believe, for the continuum of awareness as commonly perceived—the so-called stream of consciousness (Crook 1987).

Basic to such an approach is the important notion that individuals adjust to their worlds by constructing representations of them (MacKay 1965; O'Keefe & Nadel 1978; Inglis 1980). Craik (1952) pointed out that this was perhaps the prime function of the human brain with its extraordinary capacity for association. The sum of these representations amounts to a model of "reality"—strictly speaking, the only reality that a subject can actually know. Such a viewpoint takes the form of a "dissonance" model, for the systems of representation depend upon feedback that allows the organism to compare behavioral outcomes with those predicted when action was initiated. Match-mismatch monitoring for dissonance allows the incorporation of new information so that the model of reality is updated. The view that critical aspects of cognitive monitoring are both conscious and continuous means that awareness is a process in time. This awareness is itself psychological time and thereby constitutes the ontological or subjective basis of phenomenal sensing. It is then a trick of linguistic construction that makes us speak of experience as if it were an objective property of information processing. Where such processing engages an issue, it is itself what is meant by "consciousness" and creates the experience of time.

We usually take the reliability of our conscious world for granted. In spite of the endless bombardment of our senses from diverse sources, and the complexity of our stored information in memory, our experience of "reality" is strangely consistent. Susan Blackmore has been impressed by the stability of our sense of the "real," particularly as a consequence of her research on unusual experiential states such as the "out-of-body" experiences (OBEs). She argues that the brain actively filters and manipulates information available to it, so that the stability of the mental condition to which "reality" is attributed is assured (Blackmore 1984). Models of reality appear to be sustained not only by filtering current inputs of information from the senses but also by controlling for stability, by drawing on information in memory to provide a structural continuum. Match-mismatch testing between fed-forward representations based on this modeling confirms the most stable model of those available to be the one most valuable as the ideational basis for action. This stable and continuously tested model is then judged to be "real," and this "reality" is projected onto the "outside" world. Should such a model be disturbed by illness, drugs, emotional distress, stress, or near-death conditions, the mind attempts to restore it, Blackmore (ibid.) argues, by drawing upon memory. Such restoration of stability is essential if the model is to continue to be a reliable basis for action. Sometimes, however, the system, denied reliable inputs, comes to depend heavily on information drawn from memory alone, so that a distorted, inadequately checked scenario becomes accepted as real because it has acquired an illusory stability. The OBE is a prime example, but statements made by acutely schizoid patients in psychiatric interviews are doubtless pointing to the same condition. Dreams and altered states of consciousness may be viewed from a similar standpoint. In considering the reality model, we can envisage three main aspects: the somatic model we have of the integrated body we appear to inhabit; the soma-situational model representing our position in topographic relationships to room, house, or landscape; and a socio-focal model representing our position in social relationships. All three combine into a complex single system, and which aspect has preeminence in experience at any one time will be a function of the ongoing situation.

What determines the focus of attention? As time passes, new or unresolved problematic *issues* are constantly arising. Some of these emerge from the diurnal rhythmicity of life, needs for food, sleep, etc. Others relate to the finding of necessities—butchers, bakers, candlestick makers, and toilets. Yet others involve uncertainties regarding social situations or personal relationships. Issues will be of varying importance, and the salience attributed to any one of them will doubtless be dependent on criteria which are socially and individually established early in life and which may be species-wide (sociobiological), culturally collective, or personally idiosyncratic. The hierarchy of criteria provides the basis for the intentionality with which an individual faces his/her world.

The notion of intentionality, which has acquired considerable importance in this field (Dennet 1986), concerns what an organism is "on-about" at any time, but it also carries the more restrictive meaning of having purposes, goals, or intentions. An issue comes into prominence as a focus of attention when its importance for an individual exceeds some sort of threshold presumably set by competing issues. The hierarchy of criteria is likely to be based upon the evolved behavior tendencies of the species but modified by criteria set by social convention and personal history. A focus of attention is selected within an intentional hierarchy structured by the strategic concerns and contemporary tactics of an individual. Awareness arises in the targeting process, and consciousness normally goes to activity at the more inclusive multi-dimensional levels of issue resolution. Familiar, lower-level problems may be resolved without awareness; even so, lower-level—say, somatic—issues can become topics in awareness if sufficient dissonance draws attention to them. For example, a backache may come into awareness before and after a focused social interaction such as a conversation, which has precluded its being experienced.

But why should some foci of attention evoke consciousness and others not? We constantly return to this question to which there is as yet no certain answer. It seems clear that a process involving high-order informational integration is an activity in which many sources of information are brought together for inspection (multilateral process). Yet, since cognition and problem resolution often occur without awareness, it seems that only those processes that are metacognitive in the sense that they review, examine, inspect, or otherwise interrelate existing representations in the context of an issue are witnessed consciously. Consciousness is the subjective aspect of such objectively conceived activities of the brain, and it may take several forms (see figure on p. 211).

Human beings are metacognitive in yet another sense, for we have a capacity for identifying our body-mind experience as both the agent of action and as the reified subject of experience. William James distinguished the *I* and the *me* as the basic experience of existing as a subject and the identification of that subject as an object respectively. Linguistically, these are the nominative and accusative forms of the personal pronoun. *I* identify *me* in a process of attribution. Humans have the ability to make explicit in language the belief in their own agency and also to describe the quality of that experience as it changes in time. The linguistic structure within which the inference of agency is embedded becomes the "identity construct" an individual builds up for himself/herself out of social relating. This construct, which is purely ideational, is then attributed reality and projected onto self as self. We relate to one another, for the most part, only indirectly, through the constructs or personal myths we have created about ourselves during a lifetime.

Theories of identity (Horrocks & Jackson 1972) tend to emphasize the defensive nature of the processes whereby the human sense of self is achieved. As an individual grows away from dependence upon mother, he/she experiences various hurtful or frightening situations. To these we adapt by establishing coping skills whereby self-esteem can be maintained. Many of us are subject to harsh treatment, inadequate loving, or experiences of childhood abandonment. Parental attitudes may be adopted as one's own. For example, when a child is repeatedly scolded and the parental stance is a blaming one, that child may come to "introject" the parent's attitude, believing "I am a bad boy/girl." Such a stance may have far-reaching and self-defeating consequences throughout life. Negative expectations come to rule social experiences by predetermining the course of what might otherwise have been novel and creative interactions. Becoming a person with self-awareness is fraught with culs-de-sac of socially induced illusion, based on learned models of social reality that often relate badly to potentials for action in the world (Sullivan 1955; Erikson 1968; Main 1981; Guntrip 1983).

The Evolution of the Capacity for Identity and Other Mental States

The cognitive processes that yield consciousness with the capacity for attributing identity appear restricted to the human species and perhaps a few advanced mammals and birds (Premack & Woodruff 1978; Griffin 1982). Although the possibility of conscious awareness in lower organisms cannot be denied, the simplicity and automaticity of relatively "hard-wired" behavior would not seem to involve the cognitive complexity to which the emergence of conscious metacognition appears to be a response. Nevertheless, a range of levels of awareness seems quite plausible and these have received some discussion in the literature (Crook 1983).

If conscious awareness is based upon the emergence of neurological mechanisms and if the imputation to self is dependent upon advanced abilities in inference and perhaps also upon language, then we may infer that natural selection for the evolution of the basic facilitating structures must have occurred. Such structures provide the hardware allowing the programming of inferences essential to metacognitive life. Nick Humphrey and I, independently of each other, have attempted to envisage the evolutionary processes involved (Humphrey 1971, 1983; Crook 1980). Already the whole subject has become the focus for intensive discussion under the heading "Machiavellian Intelligence" (Byrne & Whiten 1988), the prime notion being that self-awareness is an evolutionary response to the needs individuals have in calculating tactics of behavior in complex animal societies. Humphrey has stressed the point that an ability to understand another may depend on the emergence of empathy. An individual capable of reading another's responses as his/her own can predict that other's response on a basis of his felt knowledge of his own tendencies in comparable situations. This depends on a capacity for "feelings" in emotionality. In complex animal societies, strategies of altruistic or selfish motivation are integrated in elaborate behavior systems that are ultimately a function of the differing ecological adaptations of the individuals constituting species populations. In the performance of reciprocal interactions (Trivers 1971), empathic abilities are important because they may allow the prediction of cheating when an individual observes ambivalent attitudes in a partner. But to do this, I have argued, an ability to distinguish between self's responses and the empathic prediction of other's responses becomes vital. It would, for example, be cognitively confusing if an individual could not distinguish clearly between feelings attributed to another and those arising as a consequence of its own state. I have argued that in animals where such needs for social calculation are important for reproductive success, an evolution of metacognitive capacities involving consciousness and self-awareness will occur, perhaps rapidly. The human species is the most extreme case of this evolutionary trend, and to this evolution we owe both our extraordinary success and the complexity of our cultures.

Although the capacity for self-identification and hence action as a self-aware agent (ego) in the world is the supreme consequence of human evolution, and presumably the reason why we call ourselves *Homo sapiens,* this ability is, as it were, superimposed upon older forms of awareness implicit in the structure of the mind as we have described it. Modern education stresses the rational, pride in identity, and the critical evaluation of role performances in social life. But what of those states of consciousness wherein awareness has quite other forms? Have these also had functional significance in evolution? I believe so.

A helpful way of characterizing the range of possible personal experiences is to see them as locations on a plane defined by two dimensions. I have described this simple model elsewhere (Crook 1988) in the following way. The first dimension defines experience that ranges from being highly goal oriented (i.e. Intentional) to simply highly attentive but without a purpose other than bare attentionality itself. The second dimension ranges from experience that is focused inwardly upon oneself (Intension) to that which is outwardly focused upon the extended world (Extension). When we cross these two dimensions, we produce a circle with four quadrants defining different states of subjectivity (see figure):

Dimensions of Conscious Experience

Strong Intentionality

	Introspection. Self-referential thought.	Intellectual analysis. Discriminatory thought. Planning. Rehearsal.
Intension		Extension
	Trance states of internal awareness. Samadhi.	Here and now. Present. Centered awareness. Zen. Martial arts.

Strong Attentionality

Source: Crook 1987.

Top left: Subject-related intentional thought

Top right: Object-related intentional thought

Bottom right: Attention focused on situation

Bottom left: Attention focused on inner states

Simply put, top left is introspection; top right is objective planning, rehearsal, scheming, or thought about actions; bottom right is nonanalytical yet alert apperception of environment; bottom left consists in trance of varying depths. It so happens that in cultures other than our own, the experiences in the lower half are treated with far greater respect, veneration even, for these are often felt to be the roots of religious knowledge. Our education system emphasizes intellect and introspection at a cost to inward sensing and an open awareness of nature. In the upper half of the diagram the attribution to self as ego is pronounced and the main subject of concern, whereas in the lower half, such as attribution is weak or even barely present at all. Can these alternative states have had a value in human evolution?

The problem with the ego involvement of the upper half is that it splits the cognition of self from the direct apperception of the outer world provided by the senses and also from inner states. It creates a dualistic mode of being, an alienation from direct apprehension due to an endless self-related judgmental commentary. Bottom right permits a heightened awareness of situation without this mental split. To experience its value one has only to walk away from one's vehicle in a wilderness area full of large, wild, potentially aggressive or predatory animals. The acute alertness facilitates the detection of the slightest sound or movement. Surely this must have been the mode of awareness of primitive hunters who for many hours a day carefully worked the dangerous environment of the ancient wilderness. It will have had a high survival value in such a situation. As with the Zen-trained exponent of martial arts, for whom a misplaced thought of self-reference in combat can spell defeat, in the wilderness a split mind can yield disaster. Focused analytical thought is sometimes highly counterproductive, for it breaks the crucial focus.

The trances of bottom left include some of the least-known aspects of mind. In the absorbed inward states of this type, the shaman may become empathically intuitive and able to perceive problems of a suffering client and to evoke healing through charismatic influence. A shaman in trance may nonetheless be highly aware of subtle environmental shifts allowing him/her to predict the arrival of rain, say, with uncommon accuracy. In nontechnological societies, such intuitive wizardry based on special forms of mind training, rare today, would have had great value for the community.

I shall suggest below that the specialization of Western education in ego-based aspects of mind has dulled these ancient modes of awareness at a cost to us and distorted our philosophies through ignorance regarding half the capacity of mind.

Ecologies of a Meaningful Life

Our argument so far proposes that consciousness arises as part of a process of monitoring performance, to ensure effective adaptation to issues arising bodily, in given situations and in relation to a social world. Self-awareness is an extension of consciousness, involving the attribution of a personal self as agent to one's body-mind experience, primarily in relation to social life. Social effectiveness in our species depends largely on tactics based upon self-awareness and on the accuracy of projected inferences regarding the motivations of other selves.

Throughout history, human beings have lived in societies whose survival has been dependent on creating an effective way of life, capacities of the local ecology, and the economic predation of other humans. Success in primitive agriculture demands a set of cultural rules, for these are the means by which the society functions in its ecology. To act in accordance with culturally prescribed and tested interpretations of ecological reality is thus to live a life that is seen to have meaning. I argue here that a set of beliefs common to such a group of people is in no sense arbitrary but is given meaning through ecological adaptation and maintained by social monitoring of personal behavior for functional adequacy in a collectively defined world. To step beyond these culturally legitimated rules, or to conceive an idiosyncractic "reality" other than that prescribed, is to step outside the "sacred canopy" of the vernacular culture and to suffer the pains of an outsider. Should a deviant attitude spread, not only might it threaten ecological adaptation, it would also cause psychological confusion. To step "outside" is to threaten others with "chaos." Primitive cultures commonly fear deviance and constrict personal expression by imposing conventions that govern the values individuals hold. Ultimately, then, individual consciousness and the individual's capacity for both action and self-understanding are constrained by the social structures within which personal development occurs. Furthermore, our religious interpretation of the universe has been predominantly the expression of our social constructions derived from ecology and projected upon the unknown "chaos" beyond it (Berger 1973).

Hunter-gatherers and simple agriculturists live within mental worlds of their own construction, "ecologies of meaning," the sense of which lies in their mode of relating to the world of earth, air, and sea, from which basic subsistence is obtained. These are not imagined worlds, not fantasies, but woven fabrics of reality created in the relationship between flesh and soil, person and person, and then projected upon the world. The effect of rational civilization has been gradually to remove the awe-filled mystery of nature from its focal position; human power, potential, and capacity now assume central stage. Humanistic values replace those of religious superstition.

Primitive religion in its societal aspect accomplished two things. First, it usually provided a secure basis for the vernacular ecology of meaning by inventing one or more universal, transcendent authorities, commonly anthropomorphic in form, modeled on mother or father. Second, these authorities, functioning through their priests, legitimated the conceptual structure as a morality which provided the basis for a rational interpretation of reality as a world "out-there" (Rapaport 1979).

As civilization developed and technology was invented to solve problems of production, transportation, and security, so the ecology of people became distanced from nature by the complexity of technological means. Our world is one in which the ecological underpinning is often obscured by the economic and social structures that have grown up and covered it. Our "ecologies of meaning" have thus become based on conceptions that are no longer environmental but economic and social. Meaning is placed upon behavior and attitudes conducive to socio-economic success and no longer on the need for food, shelter, and family.

In the West, the breakdown in transcendental interpretations of the relation between God and world gradually led to a widespread rejection of Christian theodicy. Its interpretations of history simply began to make no sense; they lost meaning just as they lost the power to legitimate. Secularization has led to a worldview based on personal material success as a prime value; but such success provides little in the way of values responsive to those ultimate questions of life and death which, like nature, can be buried but which never go away. Yet secularization has forced us to confront the pretense to knowledge that orthodoxy maintained for so long. The traditional religions based on transcendence once protected us from an aching void of meaninglessness, which appears as soon as God disappears, leaving only a marketplace divorced from nature and lacking an overseer. Religion alienates by protecting us from our need to reinvent meaning as our modes of life change.

Psychology is a new science, only recently separated from philosophy. Even now, however, as in the parallel ways of thinking formerly shown by logical positivism and behaviorism, movements in the two disciplines are closely linked. The shift in our psychological understanding of consciousness and its evolution has been paralleled by changes in philosophy. It is perhaps not surprising to find that when cognitive ethologists see mind and consciousness increasingly as adaptations to emerging social complexity, so, in philosophy, it is the means of social communication, language, that has moved to center stage.

For our purpose here, the most important aspect of the contemporary philosophical movement is the rejection of the transcendent idea, the realization that this was always no more than a conceptual device to shore up those quaking thoughts that appeared to legitimate our mode of living in the world. And when the transcendent goes, we are left with nothing other than the processes of our own world-creating minds and the now-hollow-world of concrete and computers which we have created. At last we have to come face-to-face with ourselves and with the ultimate responsibility in ourselves for what we do.

The ecologies of meaning which we construct in an advanced civilization are based on philosophical texts which, in dilute form, come to constitute the prime ideas ordinary people hold about reality. Philosophy is socially powerful in exactly this way, for changes in opinion, both rooted in and created within the *zeitgeist* of a historical period, play major roles in determining how people see themselves. If we are to understand the power of ideas, it becomes important to "deconstruct" these texts in order to perceive how they influence and control our lives. The major philosophers of language, Wittgenstein and Derrida, who have engaged in their different ways in deconstruction, have shown that the entire Western tradition has been based in certain key ways of thinking originally expressed in cogent form by Plato and Aristotle (Staten 1984). The entire Western philosophical tradition can then be seen as a debate contained *within* the themes originally formulated by the Greeks.

For the Greeks, form was the essential quality of being which determined the knowability of things. Only when matter was joined with form could matter become existent, "categorizable," and able to be described. Form thus transcended the immanent properties of things. In asserting the transcendence of form, Western philosophy fought against its opposite—the flux, impermanence, "chaos," which seemed so dangerous, since of that, ultimately, nothing could be said.

The attempt to retain the transcendent against its potential dissolution has marked the entire history not only of Western theology since the Renaissance but of philosophy also. The transcendence of form implied a world behind that of appearances—a world which was potentially superior and which constituted a source for aspiration beyond this ordinary given existence. And, insofar as that aspiration remained unmet, the thinking subject found himself/herself in a condition of exile or guilt (Cupitt 1987).

But what if identity *and* values *and* cosmic interpretations are all merely attributions—cognitive devices? Then reality is reduced to the text of speech itself. The ultimate reductionism in explanation turns out not to be physics but language. And except for language, nothing is certain because everything is attributed. Wittgenstein turned classical philosophy on its head by arguing that we do not need to entertain the mysteries of form, for we are simply and directly presented with the appearances of which we speak. The record of experience is not secret, requiring an interpretation, for our knowledge of ourselves is simply the fundamental feature of our lives. There is then no problem in making the simple assumption that other humans who, like you and me, also see and feel, have minds. Meaning lies in the uses of words, not in the abstractions to which they can mistakenly lead. What we know about ourselves and others, about identity, is given in bodily behavior and in our expression of it in language (Vohra 1986). Language develops out of the interactive "games" of mother and child, out of behavior which defines the contexts and hence the meanings of words. Language emerges from ordinary life (Markova 1982; Johnson-Laird 1983). The presupposition that we have minds is then simply natural to us. And this is what we might well expect of ourselves if we have undergone the evolution outlined above.

But if everything we know about the world is constrained by language, is contained linguistically, what can we say we actually know of the world "out there"? Some writers today have taken the work of Wittgenstein and Derrida to imply that all knowledge is fiction, and should a writer wish to place science on a pillory, this is an easy argument to adopt. Today Cartesian science is often criticized in exactly this way, but science has moved beyond the Cartesian duality of mind and matter to a far more complex and holistic conception, more Hegelian in structure (Taylor 1979), and still retains the vigor of its original vision.

Science is not fiction. What it presents is models of the world in which fictional elements are always present but which nonetheless make contact with something through the strict application of method. The atom bomb, the plastics industry, the genetic code—these are not fictions merely attributed in fantasy to the world. They are rather the results of a process of interaction with it, even though what "it" ultimately is remains beyond the possibility of discourse. It seems, however, that while we can make contact with nature in this way, we have no reason for believing that nature has any interest in us. Nature is not an "other." We are ourselves pervaded by it. We *are* it and have always been so.

What do we do with a self-knowledge from which the transcendental securities have been withdrawn? It is here that Western writers are taking tentative steps outside their own constricting tradition and beginning to recognize that for over two thousand years Indian philosophy has also wrestled with similar problems and long ago proposed solutions that reach beyond those of contemporary language philosophers.

Western psychology has until recently emphasized the fact that humans perceive themselves primarily as agents in a social world. This stress on agency focuses on the separateness of people from one another and from nature. The focus is on the entity-in-identity yet without insight into the nature of this entity. In Buddhist thought the nature of this *ens* is the prime focus of interest; and as in the recent Western views we have been discussing, the result, long ago, was the realization that there is no *substance* to it as a thing. It is purely a cognitive concoction, an imputation derived from attributions of selfhood to the process of awareness itself. Furthermore, in common with all things in the universe, this cognitively constructed entity lacks permanence and is ultimately empty (*sunya*) of enduring selfhood. In the Buddhist view, it is the attachment to the falsely conceived objective reality of the self that lies at the root of human suffering. To relinquish that attachment is to discover properties of consciousness that are simply not present in a world governed by attachment (*samsara*). In the absence of attachment (*nirvana*) a free-flowing awareness simply takes the form it must for social living and then, like a wave, relaxes back into an open sea (see accounts of Buddhist philosophy in: Murti 1965; Guenther 1976; Crook 1980; Collins 1982; Rabgyas & Crook 1988). This ocean is, however, not a nothingness; for it possesses the peculiar ontology of its own nonbeing, as indeed do the ultimate particles of the physicists' 20th-century conception.

We can now see the relevance of our discussion of states of mind other than those centered upon the reference to ego. Long ago, the Buddhists in particular stressed the centrality of non-egoic frames of mind as a refuge from excessive preoccupation with the self and its conflicts both within itself and with others. The modern interest in meditation is based not only in concerns for the alleviation of stress and related psychosomatic conditions; the practice of meditation can awaken the mind to a radically fresh way of viewing itself in which the worries of the competitive ego can at last be fully understood. We may well be gradually rediscovering the functional significance of the lower half of the figure for our own times.

It looks as if these parallels between Western and Eastern thought will lead to a renewed focus on what Bailey (1986) terms "motion theory," as contrasted with "action theory." The latter is the conventional Western viewpoint analyzing identity as agency. Motion theory, by contrast, stresses the underlying processes involved in identification and assists individuals to become aware of the openness to awareness that becomes possible through appropriate dis-identification, as for example in Zen, Yoga, or martial-arts training. Any theory which reduces the focus on the entity-in-identity in favor of a focus on intersubjective processes in social communication tends to replace the dualism of self and other with a more holistic view.

Individuals, in short, are seen as having hallucinatory views of themselves as discrete agents and as being in need of restoring an awareness of the actual interconnectedness of their relations with one another and with the environment. Just as a number of physicists have noted the similarity between the physics of indeterminacy, relativism and process, and Eastern cosmological speculation (Capra 1975; Bohm 1980), so psychologists and philosophers (Parfit 1986, 1987; Crook 1988) in the Western tradition are examining the utility of motion theory. In particular, the overanxious identification with images of self that commonly underlies the worries of Westerners is responsive to the dis-identification that characterizes, for example, Yogic, Zen, or Ch'an training. Indeed, the great value of Eastern approaches to self lies in the practical manuals and psychological and phenomenological texts which go beyond theory through demonstrations which in turn are the sources of theory. By learning to let go of identity constructs often anchored in negative childhood experiences, individuals discover freer, more creative ways of being and self-expression (Kapleau 1965; Crook 1990). The pace of change in the modern world is so great that any set of closed values is likely to become painful to maintain. Only an openness to social and personal creativity and an acceptance of impermanence can allow us to create those ecologies of meaning that are relevant to our times.

Although evolution has been driven by the natural selection of devices that secured individual reproductive success, we also know that in natural ecologies of low carrying capacity, animals have often evolved complex cooperative societies with many biologically "altruistic" features (see discussion of r and k selection in MacArthur & Wilson 1967). In such societies it is in the self-interest of individuals to behave cooperatively in a range of ways. It is probably no accident that in the overexploited, overcrowded, competitive world of today, in which the carrying capacity of the planet itself is dangerously in question, the reappearance of old ideas stressing the interconnectedness of individuals with one another and with the environment is attracting increasing attention.

An old Zen story (Roshi 1973) illustrating this theme can serve as our conclusion. Once upon a time there was a bed of squashes ripening in the corner of a field. The squashes split up into factions and made a lot of noise shouting at one another. The head priest of the nearby temple, hearing the sound, rushed out to see what was wrong. He scolded the wrangling squashes, saying, "Whatever are you doing? Fighting among yourselves is useless. Everyone meditate in zazen." The priest taught them all how to sit in meditation, and gradually their anger died away. Then the priest said, "Put your hands on top of your heads." The squashes did so and discovered a peculiar thing. Each one had a stem growing from its head which connected all to one another and back to a common root. "What a mistake we had made!" they said. "We are all joined to one another and living one life only. In spite of that we quarrel. How foolish our ignorance has been."

Today our social psychology is largely the expression of a competitive urban life in which modern engineering, electronic technology, and environmental conditioning distance us from the ecologies of our evolutionary origin. Isolation in a meaningless universe that increasingly resembles the bizarre fantasy culture depicted in the film *Brazil* is the price paid for such an extreme split. To create an ecology for a meaningful life, it is essential to reexamine our understanding of the way the mind itself traps us into fearful circumstances. The coincidence of the new Western psychology of consciousness with the revival of interest in Buddhist thought offers fruitful openings, refreshed if ancient paradigms, through which we have an opportunity to reconstruct our interpretations of our place on this planet. We may come to see the universe itself in a less adversarial way, not as a resource about to let us down, but as the matrix from which we came, of which we are, and with which we must cooperate.

References

Baars, B. J. 1983. Conscious Contexts Provide the Nervous System with Coherent Global Information. In *Consciousness and Self-Regulation: Advances in Research,* vol. 3, ed. R. J. Davidson, G. E. Schwartz and D. Shapiro, 41–79. New York: Plenum.

Bailey, W. 1986. Consciousness and Action/Motion Theories of Communication. *Western Journal of Speech Communication* 59(1): 74–86.

Berger, P. 1973. *The Social Reality of Religion.* London: Penguin.

Berger, C. R., and K. A. Kellerman. 1983. To Ask or Not to Ask: Is That a Question? In *Communication Year Book,* vol. 7, ed. R. N. Bostrom, 341–68. Beverly Hills: Sage.

Blackmore, S. J. 1984. A Psychological Theory of the Out-of-Body Experience. *Journal of Parapsychology* 48:201–18.

Bohm, D. 1980. *Wholeness and the Implicate Order.* London: R.K.P.

Byrne, R. W., and A. Whiten, eds. 1988. *Machiavellian Intelligence: Social Expertise and the Evolution of Intellect.* Oxford: Oxford University Press.

Capra, F. 1975. *The Tao of Physics.* Berkeley: Shambhala.

Collins, S. 1982. *Selfless Persons.* Cambridge: Cambridge University Press.

Craik, K. J. W. 1952. *The Nature of Explanation.* Cambridge University Press.

Cranach, M. von, and R. Harre, eds. 1982. *The Analysis of Action.* Cambridge: Cambridge University Press.

Cranach, M. von, U. Kalbermatten, K. Indermuhle, and B. Gugler. 1982. *Goal-directed Action.* London: Academic.

Crook, J. H. 1980. *The Evolution of Human Consciousness.* Oxford: Oxford University Press.

_____. 1983. On Attributing Consciousness to Animals. *Nature* (London) 303:11–14.

_____. 1987. The Nature of Conscious Awareness. In *Mindwaves,* ed. C. Blakemore and S. Greenfield. Oxford: Blackwell.

_____. 1988. The Experiential Context of Intellect. In *Machiavellian Intelligence: Social Expertise and the Evolution of Intellect,* ed. R. W. Byrne and A. Whitten. Oxford: Oxford University Press.

_____. 1990. Mind in Western Zen. In *Space in Mind: East-West Psychology and Contemporary Buddhism,* ed. J. H. Crook and D. Fontana, 92–109. Shaftesbury, England: Element.

Cupitt, D. 1987. *The Long-legged Fly.* London: SCM.

Dennet, D. C. 1986. *Brainstorms: Philosophical Essays on Mind and Psychology.* Brighton, England: Harvester.

Erikson, E. 1968. *Identity, Youth, and Crisis.* London: Faber.

Griffin, D. 1976. *The Question of Animal Awareness.* New York: Rockefeller University Press.

_____, ed. 1982. *Animal Mind-Human Mind.* Dahlem Life Sciences Report 21. Berlin: Springer.

Guenther, A. V. 1976. *Philosophy and Psychology in the Abhidharma.* Berkeley: Shambhala.

Guntrip, H. 1983. *Schizoid Phenomena, Object Relations, and the Self.* London: Hogarth.

Horrocks, J. E., and D. W. Jackson. 1972. *Self and Role: A Theory of Self-Process and Role Behaviour.* Boston: Houghton Mifflin.

Humphrey, N. 1971. The Social Function of Intellect. In *Growing Points in Ethology,* ed. P. P. G. Bateson and R. Hinde. Cambridge: Cambridge University Press.

_____. 1983. *Consciousness Regained.* Oxford: Oxford University Press.

Inglis, I. 1980. Towards a Cognitive Theory of Exploratory Behaviour. In *Exploration in Animals and Humans,* ed. J. Archer and L. Birke. New York: Van Nostrand.

James, W. [1890] 1950. *Principles of Psychology.* New York: Dover.

Johnson-Laird, P. N. 1983. *Mental Models.* Cambridge: Cambridge University Press.

Kapleau, P. 1965. *The Three Pillars of Zen.* Boston: Beacon.

Langer, E. 1978. Rethinking the Role of Thought in Social Interaction. In *New Directions in Attribution Theory and Research,* vol. 1, ed. J. H. Harvey, W. Ickes, and R. Kidd, 35–58. Hillsdale, N.J.: Erlbaum.

MacArthur, R. H., and E. O. Wilson. 1967. *The Theory of Island Biography.* Princeton: Princeton University Press.

MacKay, D. 1965. A Mind's Eye View of the Brain. In *Progress In Brain Research: Cybernetics of the Nervous System,* ed. N. Wiener and J. P. Shade, 321–32. Amsterdam: Elsevier.

Main, M. 1981. Avoidance in the Service of Attachment: A Working Paper. In *Behavioural Development,* ed. K. Immelmann et al. Cambridge: Cambridge University Press.

Markova, I. 1982. *Paradigms, Thought, and Language.* Chichester, England: Wiley and Sons.

Murti, T. R. V. 1965. *The Central Philosophy of Buddhism.* London: Allen and Unwin.

Nisbett, R. E., and T. O. Wilson. 1977. Telling More Than We Know: Verbal Reports on Mental Processes. *Psychological Review* 84:231–59.

O'Keefe, J., and L. Nadel. 1978. *The Hippocampus as a Cognitive Map.* Oxford: Oxford University Press.

Parfit, D. 1986. *Reasons and Persons.* Oxford: Oxford University Press.

______. 1987. Divided Minds and the Nature of Persons. In *Mindwaves,* ed. C. Blakemore and S. Greenfield. London: Blackwell.

Premack, D., and G. Woodruff. 1978. Does the Chimpanzee Have a Theory of Mind? *Behavioural Brain Science.* 4:515–26.

Rabgyas, T., and J. H. Crook. 1988. The Essential Insight: The Central Theme in the Training of Mahayanist Monks. In *Himalayan Buddhist Villages,* ed. J. H. Crook and H. Osmaston. Warminster, England: Aris and Phillips.

Rapaport, R. 1979. *Ecology, Meaning, and Religion.* Richmond, Calif.: North Atlantic.

Roshi, Kosho U. 1973. *Approaches to Zen.* Tokyo: Japan Publications.

Sayre, K. M. 1976. *Cybernetics and the Philosophy of Mind.* London: R. K. P.

Staten, H. 1984. *Wittgenstein and Derrida.* Lincoln: University of Nebraska Press.

Sullivan, H. S. 1955. *The Interpersonal Theory of Psychiatry.* London: Tavistock.

Swenson, C. H. 1973. *Introduction to Interpersonal Relations.* Glenview, Ill.: Scott, Foresman.

Taylor, T. 1979. *Hegel and Modern Society.* Cambridge: Cambridge University Press.

Trivers, R. L. 1971. The Evolution of Reciprocal Altruism. *Quarterly Review of Biology* 46:35–57.

Uexküll, J. von. 1909. *Umwelt und Innenwelt der Tiere.* Springer: Berlin.

Vohra, A. 1986. *Wittgenstein's Philosophy of Mind.* London: Croom Helm.

Watson, J. B. 1913. Psychology as a Behaviourist Views It. *Psychological Review* 20:158–77.

The Brain as a Supercomputer

Richard M. Restak

Jonathan Swift, the 18th-century satirist, sent Gulliver to an academy which housed "projectors in speculative learning." There his hero encountered a labor-saving device with which "the most ignorant person at reasonable charge, and with little bodily labor may write books of philosophy, poetry, politics, law, mathematics and theology without the least assistance from genius or study." Swift was presenting the view that knowledge can be generated by the turning of handles in a machine. Nowadays, machines manipulate numbers instead of words, but the principle remains the same: aspects of human thinking can be duplicated, even surpassed by computers, i.e., multiplying 6384 × 271 × 38679 takes only slightly longer on a computer or a calculator than the time required to punch in the numbers, whereas only the rarest of mathematical savants can come in even a close second. Computer programs now exist that can diagnose human diseases, play superior games of chess, successfully pilot airplanes under conditions that would tax the most experienced pilots. Not surprisingly, some are suggesting that computers can perform their brainlike processes only because the human brain is itself an elaborately designed and elegantly functioning computer. Before uncritically accepting this analogy, however, consider these differences.

Each brain cell or neuron is alive and altered by its experiences and its environment. It is an "open" rather than "closed" system. As a result, neurons can cease to function or function erratically in response to tiny chemicals or electrical alterations. Brains, in contrast to computers, don't operate according to a binary code (off/on). Whether one brain cell fires depends on the influence of perhaps thousands of other cells that make contact with it. Further, these influences are both positive and negative. Subtract several hundred inhibitory influences from the neuron and it may fire. The same result can be produced adding several hundred excitatory influences. The neuron, in essence, is always in a dynamic state that can be altered within thousandths-of-a-second intervals.

Computers, unlike brains, are essentially passive. They don't reorganize themselves, radically change direction, easily give up, or carry out any operation that is not based on computation. Brains, in contrast, are not primarily computational devices. Mental states include all kinds of noncomputational items: hopes, dreams, memories, desires, regrets, fears. Furthermore, these mental states depend upon the interaction of thousands of neurons at varying distances apart. Put another way, nerve cell communication depends on the establishment of networks or cell assemblies. "Any two cells or systems of cells which are repeatedly active at the same time will tend to become 'associated' so that activity in one facilitates activity in the other," wrote neurophysiologist Donald Hebb in 1949 in perhaps the most important book on the brain written in the 20th century, *The Organization of Behavior.*

Nothing like self-assembling cell networks exists within computers, which is one of the reasons that a six-month-old infant can recognize her mother whereas a computer capable of specific facial recognition is only the stuff of science fiction. To put the matter slightly differently, the brain is a self-assembling structure whose functional capacities are distributed. In practical terms this means that if one part breaks down, another part can be recruited in its place. Any failures of performance resulting from this arrangement are distinctly human.

"That's the way the world ends, not with a whim but a banker," was one felicitous transformation of T. S. Eliot's line, "That's the way the world ends, not with a bang but a wimper," from *The Hollow Men.* While the amended quotation is not correct, it is close enough to the original to elicit in the listener Eliot's original phrase. "Graceful degradation" is the whimsical term for this loss of clarity and precision. We exhibit it (or rather our brains do), but computers do not. Either a computer comes up with the specific lines of Eliot or it does not. It does not suggest alternatives such as puns, playful variations, or wrongheaded misinterpretations. This is because only brains and not computers are good at employing alternative ways of saying the same thing. This is made possible by the interaction of the cell assemblies mentioned above.

If a sufficient number of cell assemblies are linked together, generalizations become possible that are beyond even the most sophisticated computer. For instance, we recognize a tree stump, an empty orange crate, a Chippendale chair, and a swing as things to sit on. This recognition is based on many cell assemblies involving thousands of neurons overlapping to form a meta-assembly that is responsible for the abstract concept "something to sit on."

While much is made of the computer's ability to deal with abstract concepts, no computer ever designed would be able to fathom the meaning of the proverb "The tongue is the enemy of the neck." To do so, the computer would have to have knowledge about human anatomy, people who talk too much, gossip, and the French Revolution. Furthermore, these items would have to be surveyed at a level of abstraction in which the specific elements (tongues, necks, and so on) function both metaphorically and concretely.

Most computers are designed to deal with information one bit at a time (serially). Brains, in contrast, operate via the subsystems that function in tandem (parallel processing). Parallel input and output present little difficulty for brains, but only the most recent, expensive, and sophisticated computers are capable of significant parallel processing. Even those which are endowed with such processing capabilities deal with information according to specific programs. The brain is not so restrained. It can cross-reference ideas and concepts that at first seem to have nothing in common. *Brainstorming* is an apt term for those occasions when different people get together and let their "creative juices" flow without inhibitory restraints. What's happening is that cell assemblies of several people's brains are establishing new and different approaches to a problem.

"Both brains and computers deal with symbols" it is often claimed. True enough. But symbols within a computer are not the same as symbols within the brain. We are the ones who program the computer in such a way that a series of pulses will illuminate the screen with "Flight 603 has been canceled." The computer knows nothing about flights or delays any more than a compact disc recorder knows how to differentiate a Brahms concerto from a Bach fugue.

To search for symbols within either a brain or a computer is a hopeless enterprise. There are no symbols within the brain, only statements that we can make about the brain. Nor are there symbols within a computer, only pulses and pauses that we ourselves have arranged in such a way as to conform to the symbols of our language and our thinking.

Defining the computer as an "information processor like the brain" is also not helpful. Information has a much different meaning for the human brain than it does for computers. Whatever can be coded for transmission through a channel that connects a source to a receiver—that's information in the computer sense. Now consider the following pieces of information, all of which can be encoded in a computer:

"Your plane is running two hours late."

"Russia is an evil empire."

"The Lord is my shepherd."

"$E = mc^2$"

"The best lack all conviction while the worst are filled with passionate intensity."

"Nice guys finish last."

Within a computer none of these pieces of information is any more or less meaningful than a string of letters arbitrarily chosen and converted into electrical bits and stored. Yet these pieces of information are markedly different. The first is a statement of fact; the second an opinion with implications for foreign policy; the third a religious conviction; the fourth a principle of physics; the fifth a poetic insight; the last a cynical commentary on the attitude a person must cultivate in order to come off a "winner." In each instance the meaning of the information conveyed depends upon the background, education, value systems, and state of mind of the reader. $E = mc^2$ would be entirely meaningless to a third grader, as would the lines immediately following, taken from a poem by W. B. Yeats.

The greater diversity of the brain, contrasted with a computer, also depends to a large extent on the fact that the brain is a "wet organ"; that is, it employs chemicals known as neurotransmitters and regulatory hormones in order to transmit its signals. In contrast, the computer is as dry as dust. The difference is between a hormonally driven gland (the brain) and an electrically driven device (the computer).

The brain's regulatory hormones (more than 30 are known at the moment) are thought to function like the letters of the alphabet. Every English sentence ever written has been composed using only 26 letters. The number of possible combinations of letters approaches infinity. Only some of the combinations, however, will be meaningful; the others are merely strings of letters that add up to nonsense.

The challenge for neuroscientists is to discover which combinations of neurotransmitters and regulatory hormones are functionally active. In an allied challenge, scientists must discover what they do. Some facilitate communication and neuronal firing. Others are inhibitory. Many of the hormones are locally active, while others influence nerve cells at great distances away.

In addition, and this is really the astounding part, neurons can change their chemical identity, switching from one neurotransmitter to another under different environmental influences. Neurotransmitters and regulatory hormones may also pair up. The conventional neurotransmitter will then be responsible for fast chemical signaling between neurons while the coreleased regulatory hormone will concern itself with slower, more diffuse changes in functioning.

Finally, the neurotransmitters and regulatory hormones are not restricted to the brain. They can be found in such places as the intestine, the lungs, and the sexual organs. This ubiquity has stimulated a startling question that is currently haunting neuroscientists around the world: Is it possible that our definition of the brain is too narrow? That the regulatory processes that we now localize within our heads is much more widely distributed?

As a result of their research, many neuroscientists now believe that the brain is not like a computer or a machine, at least not like any machine that anyone has ever encountered. It has no definable boundaries (neuroregulatory hormones are dispersed throughout the body). Its parts can break down through disuse or mishap and yet its functioning may not be perceptively altered. (We're losing neurons throughout our lifetimes, yet our mental capacities improve or at least hold steady until late in our lives.)

If the brain is a machine, it is a "soft machine" marked by remarkably gentle, subtle events.

5. The Man and Beast Interface: Networking with Animals

Man and Beast Interface

An Overview of Our Interrelationships

Leo K. Bustad

From earliest times there were interactions between the hominid family and other animals and their environment. Long before any domestication occurred, there was association with animals which included taming them. Early historical accounts provide valuable insights into people-pet interactions; many of our ancestors obviously formed strong enduring bonds with animals.*

In the introduction to my Wesley Spink lectures in 1979 at the University of Minnesota, I stated:

Early in our history, we identified intimately with both inanimate and animate elements of our surroundings. Some of the first drawings and paintings depicted peo-

**Human-animal bond* is a transpecies companionship involving primarily nonlinguistic engagement between two or more creatures. This engagement, or attachment, involves an emotional, enduring, and ethical commitment and a mutual but not necessarily equal (i.e., correspondingly similar) responsibility for one another. The needs of each member of the bond are fulfilled to the extent of their inherent and learned abilities. (The help of bioethicist Kathryn George, Ph.D., Washington State University, is gratefully acknowledged.)

ple with animals. There is every indication that people adopted pets or animals not only as helpers, but as companions.

Primitive people found that people-animal partnerships were important to their well-being, if not vital to their survival. Many of the earth's early inhabitants formed a strong alliance, even a symbiotic relationship, with animals (Bustad 1980).

Primitive man was quite attached to animals and, in fact, often looked up to animals as superiors. Many cave paintings were records of respect, nurture, and admiration.

People by nature are nurturers and for thousands of years had a wide array of objects to nurture—our natural environment, animals, and other people. In recent times, however, we have experienced a serious fracture in human-animal interactions, a subject admirably discussed by Katcher and Beck in this volume. Industrialization, urbanization, and mechanization have destroyed most of our objects of nurture. Our natural environment is being compromised; many people have no daily association with animals, more people are living alone, and fewer people are having children. We pay a big price for this lack of nurture; in the midst of a population explosion, one of our worst diseases is loneliness. In view of the imposing reduction in the objects for nurture and the widespread loneliness, animals have become very important to more and more people, which may explain the increase in numbers of companion animals in the recent past. There are now at least 500 million companion animals of assorted species in the United States. Although fish comprise about one-half of this number, cats and dogs receive the most attention from the public; birds and even small rodents are growing in popularity as companions. By contrast, in many countries and cultures food-producing animals serve as companion animals.

Discussing the man and beast association from a historical perspective most certainly illustrates the wide variety of human-animal interrelationships. Especially noteworthy are the implications of such attachments for the health and well-being of the "interactees."

Historical Perspective

Although historically man has associated with a wide assortment of animals, special emphasis will be given here to three species: cats, dogs, and cattle, especially water buffalo. Others and I have reviewed elsewhere the history of human-animal interactions; the reader is referred to some of these authors (Anderson 1975; Anderson et al., 1984; Arkow, 1984, 1986; Beck & Katcher 1984; Bustad 1980; Bustad & Hines 1984a, 1984b; Corson et al. 1975, 1977; Delta Society 1986; Fogle 1981, 1983a, 1983b; Katcher & Beck 1983; Katcher & Friedmann 1980; Levinson 1969, 1972; McCulloch et al. 1970; McCulloch 1981; Schwabe 1978, 1984a, 1984b; Serpell 1983a, 1986; Ten Bensel 1984).

For this historical overview cats were selected for discussion because they are well-accepted in most countries and cultures and have a remarkable history, a uniqueness which invites study. There are well over 50 million cats in the United States; for the first time their number exceeds the dog population. Indeed, cat populations now exceed the dog populations in several countries including Canada, Austria, Finland, Norway, Italy, the Netherlands, Switzerland, and West Germany (Messent & Horsfield 1983).

Dogs are given less attention than cats in this presentation because so much attention has already been given them; discussion will, therefore, emphasize how they differ from cats. Often referred to as "man's best friend," the dog is regarded as "America's sacred cow." Dogs are, however, shunned by some cultures, even though they were probably the first animals to be domesticated and have the longest association with people. Currently, dogs are receiving increased attention and recognition for their remarkable contributions as assistance animals to handicapped people as well as for their use in animal-facilitated therapy.

The water buffalo is vital to our discussion because it is such an important animal in many areas of the world, most especially in Third World countries; it has, indeed, great potential for wider use. Many cultures have developed interesting interrelationships with the water buffalo—usually regarded as a food animal rather than a companion animal—and people have formed strong bonds with individuals of this species.

Cats and Dogs

The cat and the dog are, in a way, contrasting personalities. In describing a dog, people often use the words *friendly, loyal,* and *obedient,* while a cat may be described as *independent, wild,* and *unpredictable.* They also differ greatly in the time and nature of their domestication, cleanliness, acceptance in various cultures, and behavior, as well as many other features including their present use as service animals. The comparative historical perspective which follows will stress differences (Lopez 1978; Lorenz 1952; Zeuner 1963).

Paul Leyhausen, a world authority on cats, makes a strong case for the parallel paths to diversity of man and cats. He stated (1983), "Besides man there is at least one other mammal which must be considered self-domesticated—the house-cat." This statement followed his discussion of Konrad Lorenz's (1940) description of self-domestication in man. These two alone, cat and man, unlike other domestic animals, were not victims of husbandry techniques to obtain narrowly defined production and use objectives as, for example, dogs were. Other domestic animals were subjected to very strict selection and denied free choice of mates, whereas man and the cat had a high degree of reproductive independence. Other domestic animals have also generally been restricted in their movements. It is only in more recent times that many cats have become true house cats; this confinement has also tended to promote stronger attachments with people.

Some people claim the dog was also self-domesticated. Leyhausen makes the point that among the number of animals which man chose to domesticate, the cat was not included. It chose to live with man, not so much because man wanted it, but because the cat wanted to become domestic. Leyhausen (1983) opined that the cat is domestic but not domesticated (see also Leyhausen 1979). And there is considerable evidence for this lack of domestication.

Claire Necker (1970) wrote:

> Never having fully relinquished their wild traits to domestication, cats are able to choose between a life of freedom and independence and one of relative security and human intervention. Most choose the middle path when possible, retaining a cozy berth in a human household but roaming when they get the wanderlust. Others choose to remain close to the fireside their entire lives while others consider a domestic existence stifling and leave it early never to return. . . . Then there are cats who through accident or adversity are forced to become self-sustaining. Some, in particular those who have been mistreated by humans, often elect to live the rest of their lives on their own.

In opening this discussion, Claire Necker quoted from *The Book of Sanchia Stapleton,* written by Una L. Silberrad about 1687: "At whiles it seems as if one were somewhat as the cats, which ever have appeared to me to be animals of two parts, the one of the house and the cushion and the prepared food, the other that is free of the night and runs wild with the wind in its coat and the smell of the earth in its nostrils."

Recently Schär (1983) reported on the comparative impact of people and other factors on the societal structure of cats. She observed various degrees of sociability among farm cats, with some animals preferring a solitary existence, others forming attachments to individuals, and some others forming coherent social groups. How a cat socialized seemed to depend on "natural inclination" and on the type of cat it encountered during adolescence. She suggested that human interaction seemed to accentuate the differences rather than create them. Claire Necker (1970) opined that it is impossible to state whether cats feral from birth seek habituation with people. Feral cats who seek out people appear to be of two kinds: those who crave human companionship and slowly but gradually accept it to a point or those who continue to be unapproachable and usually leave when their needs are fulfilled. The latter group may be those who are feral from birth and the former those who have experienced human interaction.

Regarding reverting to the wild state, the cat, for much of its history, has another trait uniquely shared with man. On becoming feral, each is able to develop a very complex community system (Leyhausen, 1983) which is flexible and can accommodate a wide range of ecological factors. This has not been true in dogs, although they may form packs. However, packs of domestic dogs which have become feral lack the stability and complex interrelationships observed in the truly wild canine species.

Whatever the means of domestication, it is generally accepted that cats were domesticated by 1600 B.C. in Egypt, and may have been domesticated somewhat earlier. In ancient Egypt, cats were kept to control rodents on farms and in granaries (Beaver 1980). Later, they were used to hunt and fish in some cultures and retrieve birds, especially ducks in papyrus thickets.

Bees and dogs were the first domesticated animals. Kept by neolithic peoples, dogs probably predated cats by several thousands of years (10,000 B.C.) (Caras 1982; Davis 1953; Davis & Valla 1978; Diole 1974; Ensminger 1977; Fiennes & Fiennes 1965). Farmers in the flood plain of the Nile Valley were alert for the star Sirius, which appeared in the sky each year before the flood. As soon as it appeared, the people moved their families and flocks along with their dogs to safety on higher ground. Sirius came to be regarded as a god that protected them from floods. It came to be known as the "dog star" because it was ever faithful. Later, other people who lacked appreciation for the dog came to associate it with summer heat, the so-called dog days. (The name Sirius is derived from a Greek word meaning scorching [Fiennes & Fiennes 1968].)

Religious practices involving dogs developed among the Aztecs and the Incas, who bred small dogs of high quality for both sacrificial rites and eating. Dogs were raised in temples for sacrifice (probably as scapegoats), replacing people as blood offerings to the gods (Fiennes & Fiennes 1968). There are even historical accounts of dogs who personified the devil (Caras 1982).

In Egypt, cats were incorporated into religious practices more than dogs; indeed, people worshiped them. The very important cat goddess Bastet (meaning "she rends the flesh" or "she brings back the booty") was the daughter of the sun god; she represented the fertility of plants and women and good health. When Bastet became the primary goddess, the cat, of course, became even more popular and was legally protected; killing a cat was punishable by death. When a cat died, the cat's owner would have her or his eyebrows shaved and vent grief.

The bodies of dead cats were embalmed and placed in a sarcophagus. During excavations in Beni Hasan, Egypt, in 1889, a burial site was discovered containing some 300,000 mummified cats, each buried with a mummified mouse. Cats were believed to possess miraculous powers over demons and were therefore preserved.

Two versions of the defeat of the Egyptians by the Persians in 525 B.C. illustrate the Egyptians' great fondness for their cats. In the first version, the king of Persia lay siege to the city of Pelusium. The defenses were formidable. The king, however, on learning of the Egyptians' penchant for cats, ordered his troops to collect as many cats as they could. When the Persians attacked, each soldier clutched a cat to his chest like a shield; the Egyptians gave up the city rather than chance any harm to the cats! An alternative version states that the Persian king catapulted the captured cats into the city, thereby causing the residents to capitulate in order to prevent further harm to their cats (Barloy 1974; Hall & Brown 1904). Both versions could be true.

Legends about cats and their owners abound; they cross national, religious, and cultural boundaries to include Moslems in Arab countries, Buddhists in India and Japan, and totemistic cults in Burma. In Tokyo, the Temple of the Cats is surrounded by a cemetery where Buddhists bury their cats. In times of drought, Cambodians would go house to house, dousing the animals with water in the belief that the cats' protestations would make the rains come. Similarly, Indonesians believe that dipping a cat in a pool of water will bring rain. As will be seen, these practices were certainly more humane than sacrificial rituals practiced by many keepers of water buffalo in times of drought.

Believing a cat would give strength to a structure, builders during the Middle Ages encased them in buildings during construction. In 10th-century Belgium, live cats were thrown from the top of cathedral spires, to show that cats were not supernatural and could not save themselves; this practice attempted to eliminate the worship of cat idols. Since the 15th century, the Cat Festival has been celebrated in Belgium, but now toy cats are substituted for the live cats. When cats became identified with witchcraft and as beasts of the devil, they underwent atrocious tortures, including crucifixion. Many cats were burned alive during ritual ceremonies, at one time to halt an epidemic of St. Vitus dance.

Throughout the terrible years of persecution, the cat had its admirers and protectors among the ranks of the influential and powerful. People who were obviously bonded to their cats included Richelieu and Montaigne. History relates that Pope Leo XII concealed a kitten within the folds of his robe; Charles Dickens would cease writing when his cat snuffed out the candle; Sir Walter Scott grieved deeply when his cat died (Barloy 1974).

Cat populations were very limited in distribution for an extended period because of tight export restrictions. Eventually, however, cats emigrated, often due to the efforts of merchants, monks, soldiers, and importantly, seamen. Sailors realized cats were the best means of rodent control aboard ships; in fact, that is how the cat came to America in the 1600s. Dogs and cats came to be recognized as part of the ship's crew (Thomas 1983). In the late 1600s, an official order was given that every French warship must carry two cats (Barloy 1974). Centuries earlier the first statute of Westminister, in 1275, ruled that a vessel was not technically abandoned as long as a cat and a dog were still aboard. Japanese sailors believed that tricolored cats had the power to calm a storm. In any case, the cats aboard ships probably had a calming effect on crew members and helped combat loneliness. No doubt, some seamen became closely bonded to the cats.

As the cat emigrated, its acceptance grew. As Mohammed's favorite animal, the cat was well received in Islamic countries (Necker 1970). In fact, before Islam was established, the Arabs worshiped a golden cat. In the 13th century, the city of Cairo provided food for stray cats each day. Even today, I believe, cats are permitted to enter mosques (Barloy 1974).

Although Arabs are often reported to despise dogs, the Saluki, a smooth-haired greyhound, became very popular among the Arabs and Persians. Mohammed, in fact, is reported to have owned a white Saluki, and this breed was named "the blessed one." Arabs in Africa still treat this animal as noble, and since they can attain speeds of 40–50 miles per hour, some tribes still use them for hunting (Barloy 1974).

When the cat was introduced to Europe, an apocryphal story told how the cat protected the Christ child from the devil's mouse. Yet, because the cat has remarkable eyes and an independent nature, it became associated with Diana, the moon goddess, and subsequently with witchcraft. Extermination of many cats and the people closely attached to them ensued. However, when the plague spread over Europe, cats were viewed in a positive light, since they were the most effective method of rodent control.

In 13th-century England, pet-keeping nuns were warned that such acts placed their souls in peril (Ritchie 1981), and pet-keeping nobility were accused of concupiscence, corruption, idleness, and wantonness. Later, moralists condemned "over-familiar usage of any brute creature" (Jesse 1866; Serpell 1986). In 16th- and 17th-century England, dogs were held in disrepute; they were the subject of sermons emphasizing the worst of qualities, including crudeness, disruptiveness, gluttony, lust, and promiscuity (Thomas 1983). Some excerpts from Georges L. L. Buffon in 1791, as quoted by Necker in 1970, give an opposite view of dogs and is exceedingly critical of cats.

> The cat is an unfaithful domestic. . . . Though these animals, when young, are frolicksome and beautiful, they possess, at the same time, an innate malice, and perverse disposition, which increase as they grow up, and which education learns them to conceal, but not to subdue. . . . Like thieves, they know how to conceal their steps and their designs, to watch opportunities, to catch the proper moment for laying

hold of their prey, to fly from punishment, and to remain at a distance till solicited to return. They easily assume the habits of society, but never, acquire its manners; for they have only the appearance of attachment or friendship. This disingenuity of character is betrayed by the obliquity of their movements, and the duplicity of their eyes. They never look their best benefactor in the face; but, either from distrust or falseness, they approach him by windings, in order to procure caresses, in which they have not other pleasure than what arises from flattering those who bestow them. Very different from the faithful animal the dog, whose sentiments totally centre in the person and happiness of his master, the cat appears to have no feelings which are not interested, to have no affection that is not conditional, and to carry on no intercourse with men, but with the view of turning it to his own advantage. By these dispositions, the cat has a greater relation to man than to the dog, in whom there is not the smallest mark of insincerity or injustice.

The form and temperament of the cat's body perfectly accord with his temper and dispositions. He is jolly, nimble, dextrous, cleanly, and voluptuous. He loves ease, and chooses the softest and warmest situations for repose.

In a time when dogs were not well accepted, Buffon was not the only admirer of dogs—at least some dogs, e.g., hounds. In the 1700s, when mastiffs and mongrels were considered lecherous, incestuous, filthy, sullen, and truculent, hounds were regarded as faithful, generous, intelligent, noble, and obedient. The hound lying at its master's feet became a symbol of fidelity (Thomas 1983).

Notable in cats is the unusual diversity within breeds; they, too, have very distinct personalities, perhaps more than any other domestic animal including dogs (Leyhausen 1983). Turner (1984) has commented on the great individual differences in cats, making a legitimate plea for more research on human–domestic cat relationships (see also Fox 1965, 1974; Hart 1978).

The paucity of data on the human-cat interaction comes, ironically, at a time when Americans (and many other nationalities) own more cats than dogs. Many cats, as well as dogs, are now being placed in institutions with elderly, handicapped, and sick people and with prisoners, but we lack basic data on effectiveness. To address this paucity, my associates developed a temperament profile for cats and dogs, but it has not been in use long enough for critical evaluation of its merits (Lee et al. 1987).

Many people are attracted to cats and dogs because they are forever juvenile and provoke in many people a desire to nurture them and love them.

Fondness for infants and for cuddly diminutive animals is in part due to their large eyes and foreheads. People seem to have a proclivity for neoteny, i.e., a retention of infantile or juvenile patterns both in appearance and behavior. Persian cats fulfill these requirements as do many breeds of dogs such as the poodle, pug, Pekinese, cocker spaniel, and certain other breeds. Walt Disney's Minnie and Mickey Mouse were not well accepted initially because of their adult faces. When he changed the features to appear childlike, the cartoon became famous. Hairlessness and droopy ears, too, may be contributing features to the attractiveness of animals.

However, certain breeds with juvenile physical features are less desirable because of their dispositions. Behavioral traits such as affection, docility, and playfulness may override attractive physical features (baby face) and small size. Labradors, golden retrievers, bull mastiffs, and other large dogs are appealing because of their friendly (juvenile) nature. Selective breeding has produced a new species. As the words of Alan Beck and Aaron Katcher (1984) suggest, "In a sense, man created the dog in his own image." Man has also extended this selection for juvenile traits to other domestic animals (and cartoon characters). For a more comprehensive discussion of neoteny, see the article by Aaron Katcher and Alan Beck in this volume.

People and other animals use nonverbal communication for similar reasons, since they are faced with similar biological problems and need to establish social relationships. People develop more complex social behaviors, but some animals seem more adept at understanding nonverbal communication. Both people and animals use facial expression, gestures, posture, and voice to communicate, but changes in body color are less significant with people (Argyle 1975; Bolwig 1962). The eyes, starting in infancy, are one of the very important means of communication for expressing intimacy, aggression, and dominance (Bullowa 1979; Serpell 1986). In human–companion-animal interaction, the frequency and pattern of gaze is critical. Both cats and dogs engage frequently in mutual eye contact with their owners and spend a good deal of time observing them. Owners also invite eye-to-eye contact by calling pets by name and talking to them. Serpell (1986) noted that cats have a detached kind of stare, but when stared at directly at close range, they will partially close their eyes a few times before turning away. While a cat is being petted on an owner's lap, it often looks at the owner's face wistfully. When a cat sees or smells something attractive, its eyes dilate (Hess 1983). It would be interesting to see if dilation occurs when cats are being stroked while on the owner's lap and looking into his eyes. It might serve as a quantitative indicator (see also Kendon 1967).

Dogs seem to gaze at their owners a great deal more than cats do. Extended staring at dogs, unlike cats, makes them uneasy, especially when at close range, and causes them to avert their gaze. The cat, due to anatomical limitations, does not have the remarkably expressive eyes and face of the dog, with the possible exception of manifesting alarm or anger. The common expression is one of detached contentment (Serpell 1986). Dogs can manifest expressions not unlike those of many people (and nonhuman primates), and most owners are very cognizant of this. Some dogs by breeding have a forlorn or other expression that evokes nurturing, sympathy, or humor. Animals look up to us, and most people appreciate the affirmation that implies; indeed, the affirmations, if not abused, may contribute to the health and well-being of both members of the bond (Fox 1975).

Both cats and dogs manifest behavioral signs resembling jealousy when the owner gives attention to a third party; it seems to be more pronounced with dogs than cats (Serpell 1986). Cats are thought to manifest greater independence than dogs, since they also show less separation anxiety and distress. This reaction is predictable, since the dog is a pack animal and seeks intimate contact. In this regard some observations of Turner (1984) are enlightening. He found that the time people spend interacting with dogs or cats differs. He noted that cats either allow, require, or promote less contact with their owners than dogs (or owners seek less contact or have less time for their cats). On the average, dog owners "concerned themselves" with their animals almost twice as much as cat owners did (150 minutes/day versus 86 minutes/day, respectively) but there was a remarkable variation (5 minutes/day to 400 minutes/day) with cats. Cats to some people are extremely attractive objects of nurture, and spending up to 400 minutes a day with them confirms an unusual bonding.

Historically, the cat has symbolized many virtues, among them freedom, virginity, and motherhood. Its association with freedom came from the cat's independence (some countries had flags with cats on them, e.g., the Roman legions). The cat symbolized motherhood because of its very strong maternal instinct, and virginity because of its cleanliness.

Even unusual healing powers were attributed to the cat. For instance, massaging an affected joint with cat's fur was thought to cure rheumatism, while sties were said to be cured by rubbing the affected eyelids with a cat's tail. Incredibly, it was believed that blindness could be prevented by blowing ashes from the burnt head of a black cat into the eyes three times each day, and that epilepsy and lameness could be relieved by the application of fat from a wild cat (Barloy 1974; see also Bustad 1980).

For the last few hundred years, the cat and dog seem to have gained a secure place in most societies. Dogs, however, still suffer ostracism in some places, and many rules and regulations limit their territory and their use. Too many dogs still lack proper training; the majority of owners appear to be irresponsible. Evidence for this is the 10 million dogs and cats killed in our animal control centers and veterinary hospitals in 1985; the majority of these animals were owned by someone. In the United States and most Western countries, the cat is kept chiefly as a pet, as is the dog, although a rapidly growing area is the assistance-dog programs (Hines 1983, 1985). The number of cats will increase because they adapt well to life in small apartments. There is greater variation in the temperament and other characteristics of cats, and while more is being learned about their health and behavior, further study is required. Another consideration is that people tend to maintain loyalty to a particular species they were attached to as children (Serpell 1981), and with the current increase in cat numbers, a "snowballing" effect could result.

An ambivalence should be noted regarding treatment of a given species of animal depending on its use and the owner's attachment. For example, dogs were kept as pets by native Polynesians who demonstrated deep affection for them; mothers even suckled them on their breasts (Jesse 1866). Polynesians also ate dogs, but as Serpell (1986) has noted, dogs kept as companions were seldom killed and eaten. Native Americans in many areas of the United States raised dogs for eating, although they were probably eaten only on special occasions (e.g., ceremonies) or in case of severe food shortages. In no region was dog meat a part of the regular diet. They were usually eaten in ceremonies associated with warfare or secret society performances. The prevailing attitude toward dog meat was that it was poisonous, but like other poisons it conveyed supernatural power (Driver & Massey 1957).

The Oglala Indians (popularly referred to as the Sioux) are of special interest, since eating dogs is a socially acceptable practice (Powers & Powers 1986). In fact, dog stew is considered a delicacy. For the Oglala, dogs are not members of the family. They are usually mongrels and live outdoors all year round, subsisting on what they can scavenge and on occasional table scraps. Families may own up to ten dogs and depend on them for protection and to announce the presence of visitors. They select certain dogs as pets, which are given names when quite young. Named dogs are not eaten by the Oglala. The preferred dog for eating is a puppy between 7 and 10 weeks old.

Ritual killing is performed by a medicine man and two female assistants. The medicine man first anoints the dog by drawing a line with red paint from the nose to the tail (the red road) which symbolizes in Oglala culture the straight and narrow (the good). He then articulates the virtues of his friend, the anointed dog, and what a difficult task it is for him to sacrifice a faithful and worthy creature. He then places the dog facing west, and his assistants, after taking positions on the north and south sides of the dog, each place a noose around the dog's neck and secure it. The medicine man, with a blunt instrument in hand, stands behind the dog and signals his assistants to pull the nooses tight while he strikes the dog on the head, as if struck by lightning. The dog faces west, this direction left open for the spirit to immediately depart, joining the Thunder People. These Thunder People symbolize lightning, which underscores the Oglalas' belief that storms from the west bring rains to cleanse Mother Earth. The noose prevents the dog from uttering any cry, so its spirit is still alive and carries with it the people's prayers for health and long life for all their relatives. The dog's hair is then removed. The carcass is washed, quartered, and placed in a pot to boil for several hours without any condiments added. The bones and the alimentary tract are burned. Unlike other festive meals when more than enough meat is prepared, there is never enough dog meat to go around, so only the oldest men and possibly the oldest women will receive a few morsels. The intact head is given to an important man. For the Oglalas, dog meat is a spiritual delicacy. The Powers (1986) sum up the significance of this ceremonial dog feast with these words:

> For the Oglala, the dog is man's best friend because it is man's best sacrifice. It is the animal closest to humans. Like humans, dogs are clever, sagacious, and brave, and they cling dearly to their lives. Like humans, they exist in a unpredictable, profane world and are equally *unsike,* "pitiable." Historically, their lives have been similar to those of humans; they have hunted and gathered precisely the same foods that humans have, from buffalo to table scraps.

In spite of lack of tender care being extended to dogs by some societies, one can generalize that dogs, as well as other animals that are closely bonded with people, are usually affectionately cared for and kept until the animal is very old. Euthanasia is usually not performed until the animal is moribund. In contrast, working dogs (i.e., beasts of burden) such as racing greyhounds, sled dogs in northern climes, and animals used in research are usually treated with detachment. No strong bonding occurs, and the animal is killed with little hesitation when it is no longer "useful" (Serpell 1986). As Serpell noted, "On principle that what the eye doesn't see the heart doesn't grieve over, concealment is the natural partner of detachment."

Water Buffalo (and other cattle and deer)

The domestication of cattle in many cultures was accompanied by a reverence for and worship of them. Without a doubt, they are one of the most important of the domesticated animals. Cattle, a central theme in the art, literature, and religion of many peoples, were also considered valued members of many families. This is especially true for water buffalo, a member of the Bovidae family. Some believe cattle were domesticated long before buffalo, but Randhawa (1944) claimed that people of Mohenjo-Daro, India, had buffalo and other animals contributing to the economy of Sind and Punjab as long as 5,000 years ago (Whyte & Mathur 1974).

Discussion of the interaction of people and water buffalo is based on observations by two friends, W. Ross Cockrill (1974) of the Food and Agriculture Organization of the United Nations (FAO) and Wyland S. Cripe (1985) at the University of Florida, as well as their friends and associates throughout the world. Emphasis is given to India, Indonesia, Iraq, Khmer Republic, Laos, Latin America, and Malaysia primarily because of the nature of the man-beast interface in these countries.

The estimated world population of water buffalo is currently 180 million and growing, especially in the Amazon Basin (Cripe, pers. comm. 1987). The animals are used as milk producers, work animals, sources of meat, protectors (e.g., against tigers), transportation (e.g., for hunts), and entertainment (e.g., racing and fighting); they also rank as "significant others" in families for many years, since they may live for 30 years (Cockrill 1974; MacGregor 1941; National Academy of Sciences 1981).

Most water buffalo are kept by small farmers, so that the care for the animals tends to be personal. The animals have become accustomed to the individual attention of being groomed, massaged, and fed by hand. In tropical climates, they are regularly externally drenched, sometimes several times a day, or allowed to wallow. Their hair is sometimes shaved to reduce the number of external parasites, and oil is applied to the skin to make it soft and pliant and to restore its luster. In India, the female members of the family usually care for the milking buffaloes.

Children, too, are often involved in tending the buffalo. Cockrill (1974) reported that youngsters will ride or lead these very tractable animals to wallowing places, to streams or ponds. There they clean the ears, eyes, and nostrils of the water buffalo; the buffalo appear to delight in this physical closeness. It is not unusual, in fact, to see a swamp buffalo grazing quietly while a child is lying asleep on its broad back.

The marsh Arabs, the true buffalo people in Iraq, credit water buffalo with reasoning powers. They regard them as persons and assign them names, to which they respond. The water buffalo leave when sent away, and intervene to protect the owner should conflict arise. To explain their buffaloes' intelligence and sensibility, owners cite male buffaloes which show preference for certain females and refuse to serve those they dislike. The owners' attachment to their animals results in very special care. When a buffalo becomes sick, the owners spare neither trouble nor expense to restore health to the animal. When Ross Cockrill of FAO visited a man on whose buffalo there were no brands or identification, he inquired as to how the owner recognized a buffalo as *his* property. The man responded with a question, "How do you recognize *your* friends?" Cockrill, commenting on this later, remarked that the ready recognition is mutual between the owner and his buffaloes.

Traditional rules and customs of the rural peoples of Indonesia require the presence and participation of the water buffalo in many rites. Extensive folklore and a vast range of religious ritual, as well as magic, involve the buffalo in the occupations of the agrarian population.

In Sumatra the water buffalo's influence is intrinsic to daily life. Women, in fact, wear a special headdress which copies the shape of buffalo horns. The custom has an interesting history. According to Cockrill (1974), its origin lies in a story that a queen of Sumatra and a king of Java in ancient times agreed not to go to war but rather to match two buffaloes in fight and to abide by the result. The king produced a huge, fearsome male. The queen put into the ring a small buffalo calf which had not been allowed to suck for two days. It had a sharp knife tied to its muzzle. When it was released its hunger was so desperate that it was unable to distinguish the sex of the huge animal which confronted it. It ran forward seeking the udder, got underneath the king's buffalo and neatly disembowelled it. The king honored the agreement and recognized the queen's victory.

Sumatrans believe that the spirits have great respect for buffalo, and this belief lends courage to the owners to venture alone into the forest at night. Some Sumatrans, when they undertake especially hazardous night missions into the forest, wear as a charm a carved hollow buffalo horn containing certain magical herbs. Three magical functions are assigned to the buffalo: to make rain, to carry the weight of the world, and to originate earthquakes (Kreemer 1956). As aquatic beasts, they can influence the rainfall which makes rice grow, yet if rainfall is excessive, some people will offer a white buffalo in sacrifice. How the buffalo causes earthquakes remains to be answered.

There are many occasions requiring the sacrifices of buffalo. They include:

a) major events in family life (birth, marriage, adoption, circumcision, teeth filing, death);
b) the inauguration of a new house;
c) the settlement of business matters (reconciliation, peace-making, compromise in disputes, fulfilment of promises);
d) harvest festivities;
e) after fasting;
f) when disasters are avoided (epidemics, catastrophes) (Cockrill 1974).

The manner in which people regard the white buffalo seems ambivalent. In Bali they are not used for ritual sacrifice—although it appears some groups prefer a white animal for sacrifice—but they may be prescribed for medicinal purposes. Although Muslims are allowed to kill white buffalo for food (in a rigidly prescribed fashion), many people regard albinic buffalo meat as harmful to health, a cause of skin disease—even leprosy.

In Bali, the combination of Hinduism and animalism, as well as ancestor worship, forms a way of life in which the spirits rule everything; the buffalo is, unfortunately, a victim of many ritualistic practices. Religious ritual practices and sacrificial slaughter seem to dictate buffalo production. Occasions which involve sacrificing buffalo and feasting include completion of any new constructions, weddings, and funerals. Wife-purchase with a buffalo is still practiced with the provision that if there is a divorce, the buffalo is returned. Such a practice may discourage divorce and promote longer marriages. A buffalo head is burned in the foundation of new structures, including houses, bridges, and airstrips, in order to keep evil spirits away.

Where buffalo are the exclusive sacrificial animal, a heavy burden on the people may result. More animals than can be consumed are sacrificed, so there is a great deal of waste. A whole village can become nearly bankrupt in an effort to provide the necessary animals; in fact, it may take years for the buffalo herds to regenerate. Insufficient animals may be available to till the fields, thus requiring people to be yoked to farm implements. A whole village may need to become vegetarian for an extended time. It is difficult to conjure up any redeeming consequences for such practices unless the loss of buffalo broadened the base of produce raised, which seems improbable in view of the loss of animal power. The right kind of vegetarian diet might possibly lengthen the villagers' life span if their physical activity was not too severe and debilitating. The people feel they must adhere to the ritualistic sacrifices which the ancestral spirits require of them, because if the duty is neglected, harvests will fail and disease epidemics will occur.

The Balinese have another kind of ritual that is fortunately practiced only when the economy is suffering and rain is urgently needed. The ritual involves placing a dark-colored buffalo (with a heavy boulder tied to its neck) onto a large raft on a deep lake (Danau Bratan). The raft is launched from a temple at the edge of the lake, and at the appropriate place on the lake, the buffalo is pushed overboard and sacrificially drowned (ducks may be similarly sacrificed).

Because of special desirable qualities such as color, conformation, horn type, and location of hair whorls, many buffalo are considered to bring good luck. Such animals are the first to be taken into the fields to insure a good crop; they receive very special treatment.

The Khmer Republic, predominantly Buddhist, is noted for the gentle handling of animals (Cockrill 1974). Training of the animals does not usually present any problems because the buffalo are such an integral part of the daily life for the peasant. The animals' longevity is due, in great part, to the care they receive. Cockrill (1974) reported it was not unusual to encounter buffalo over 25 years of age. Animals that are no longer fit for work are often allowed to live out their lives rather than be slaughtered. The buffalo are allowed ample time to wallow and are rested during the heat of the day. One exception to the gentle handling of the buffalo is the barbaric, crude, and cruel castration method used. The testicles are crushed with rocks, a method so painful that the ordinarily mute animal frequently emits a piercing cry.

In Laos, as in the Khmer Republic, buffalo receive gentle treatment (Cockrill 1974; his pers. comm. with C. A. Walker, 1968; and Walker's comm. with Norman Lewis). The exception is their ritual sacrifice referred to as the "buffalo spirit ceremony," which has been generally practiced throughout the country at least up to 10 years ago. The people believe their whole existence is encompassed by spirits which must be dealt with before embarking on any venture, such as occupying a new house. The buffalo is the "life force" of the people because it is so obviously important to their livelihood. A master farmer in Laos is reputed to have said, "In farming, the buffalo must be more important than the man because if the buffalo knows how to work, it is easy for us" (see also Orr 1967). An elderly Taiwanese woman succinctly remarked to Ross Cockrill, "To my family the buffalo is more important than I am. When I die, they will weep for me; but if our buffalo dies, they may starve."

In the ceremony for the new house, a well-washed buffalo is tied to a decorated sacrificial stake in front of several ceramic jars (some having held rice wine, which is attractive to spirits). The stake and the buffalo are liberally anointed with rice wine. The spirit of the house is summoned by drums, flags, gongs, chantings, and prayers, but a sacrifice is considered particularly critical. When the presiding priest determines that the spirits are present, the sacrifice begins. Since the spirits delight in fresh blood continuously flowing from the buffalo, the priest has to continue to pierce new sites with sharp lances to provide new flowing sites. After 2 or 3 hours, the priest announces the spirits are satisfied, and the signal is given to the lance men to kill the buffalo. A particular spirit attracted by the wine will enter a jar, which gives the jar great and lasting value.

The head of the buffalo is removed; the skull is cleaned, polished, and attached to a stake before sunset, when the spirit awakes and sees the skull and buffalo spirit. The latter spirit chases the former spirit, which then retires to the jar and bestows blessings. The stake and skull must remain intact for thirteen lunar months in order for the spirit to become a permanent resident in the jar. A jar containing a benevolent spirit may be worth as much as 20 buffaloes. Laotian tribes attribute the defeat of the Japanese in World War II to the fact that they broke many sacred jars, releasing spirits which in turn joined buffalo spirits to chase the Japanese out of the country.

In Malaysia, buffalo are important to the social structure of the Sarawak peoples (Cockrill 1974). Buffalo must be slaughtered for both funerals and weddings, and while the meat can be sold at the latter feast, it must be given away at funerals. The buffaloes are killed by the same method used by the Ghurkali people in Nepal. One stroke of a very sharp sword has to sever the head from the body; if it doesn't, the omen is bad and the meat is discarded. In Malaysia, people and buffalo are not so closely bonded, nor are the buffalo as gently cared for as in some other countries. The buffalo are used chiefly for plowing and harrowing during a few short weeks; then they spend much of the rest of the year in the forest.

In a recent conversation, Wyland Cripe confirmed that in many countries and cultures the water buffalo is considered a pet and a member of the family. He said that in the Balkan countries at farmers' markets, buffalo are exchanged or sold only after the seller is assured that the new master will provide proper care for the animal. Milkers in a water buffalo dairy in Romania declined the use of milking machines because their buffalo cows seemed to prefer hand milking. Cripe also noted that water buffalo are easily domesticated. After daily feeding and watering for ten days to two weeks, most of the animals become sociable, gentle, and serene (see Cripe 1985). Cripe also noted that the American Buffalo Association has been formed, with headquarters at his home institution, the University of Florida at Gainesville.

It is useful to examine how other cultures regard the livestock that are critical to human survival. The Nuer in Sudan develop remarkably close bonds with their cattle; as cherished possessions, they are vital to the economy and are the focus of social and religious life (Serpell 1986). They know their cattle very well as individuals. In the evening, the animals are petted; ticks, dirt, and other contaminants are removed from their bodies; and ashes may be rubbed on their backs. The animals are tethered within eyesight of the owner. Tassels and other decorations are attached to the animal's horns. The intimacy of the man-beast relationship restricts their slaughter; the animals are, however, bled, and their blood is consumed. This is justified, not as a source of food, but on the contention that bleeding benefits the animal. The buffalo is eaten only if it dies from natural causes or is sacrificed in a ceremony to propitiate spirits.

The water buffalo is an integral part of the economic, social, and religious practices in many countries and cultures. We must be acutely aware of these practices when we attempt to aid people, and animals, in Third World countries. The worst of the practices will die hard. The gentle handling accorded by many people is worthy of retention and emulation.

Of interest is the similar relationship of the Tungus people in Siberia to their reindeer (the only important domesticated member of the Cervidae family). Closely attached to their reindeer, they show deep affection for them, often caressing them. The reindeer have names and respond to their given names as the herders talk to them; the herdsmen believe the reindeer understand what is said (Serpell 1986). The animals, which provide milk and are used for riding, are slaughtered only to appease some supernatural power. Spilling of blood is not allowed during sacrifice.

Ingold (1980) observed that in contrast to the Tungus's regard for their animals, other Siberian people involved in more intensive reindeer farming are more detached from their animals. Their detachment is manifested by an absence of ritualistic respect and an increased level of violence directed to the animals. Instead of regarding their animals as members of their extended family, as the Tungus do, they view their animals as intractable beasts which must be forcibly subdued and restrained. In recent times, such detached husbandry measures have, in contrast to gentling and socializing food-producing animals, reduced weight gain, efficiency of feed utilization, immune competence, and reproductive performance (see Bustad 1984).

Attachment, Love, and Loneliness

The interaction of man and beast for the past thousands of years has many remarkable aspects. Admittedly, there were difficult times for animals, sometimes with heartrending cruelty and ostracism exhibited. Yet in every age there seemed to be a remnant of strong bonding between people and an assortment of beasts.

One of the expressions heard frequently in the last decade regarding the man-beast interface is "unconditional love" on the part of the beast; most often, admittedly, it was said about dogs, but it was not limited to them. Historically, people in many classes and cultures reciprocated this love. Maybe the time has come to talk about love and affection and its measurement.

In the first Smithsonian Institution symposium on man and beast, Robert Zajonc (1971) considered the subject of attachment—how long-term relationships are established between man and beast. He proposed, on the basis of studying many different creatures, that repeated exposure to a stimulus is in and of itself (without any discrete reinforcement) a sufficient condition for attachment to a given object.

In his introductory remarks to Zajonc's presentation, John Eisenberg (1971) suggested that the formation of bonds may involve something more than just preference for an object. He went on to state, "In order for bonding to take place, it would appear that the organism must be able to perform some satisfying act of a self-reinforcing nature with the bonded object." Perhaps the "payoff" is love, attachment, and nurture. Zajonc (1971) suggested as much when in his closing paragraph he remarked, "Man and other animals are endowed with a similar capacity to gain love from exposure. Familiarity does not breed contempt. Familiarity breeds!"

Invoking love usually raises hackles among scientists; they shy away from the sentimental. James Lynch (1977) reminded us that Charles Darwin (1965) stated that the emotion of love was an exception to all the general rules in that it was one of the strongest of all emotions but had no peculiar means of expression. Darwin attempted to describe love but in the end concluded that it was impossible. In his *Expression of the Emotions in Man and Animals* (Darwin 1965, originally published 1872), he stated:

> Although the emotion of love, for instance that of a mother for her infant, is one of the strongest of which the mind is capable, it can hardly be said to have any proper or peculiar means of expression; and this is intelligible, as it has not habitually led to any special line of action. . . . A strong desire to touch the beloved person is commonly felt; and love is expressed by this means more plainly than by any other. Hence, we love to clasp in our arms those whom we tenderly love. . . . We

probably owe this desire to inherited habit, in association with the nursing and tending of our children and with the mutual caresses of lovers. With the lower animals we see the same principle of pleasure derived from contact in association with love. Dogs and cats manifestly take pleasure in rubbing against their masters and mistresses, and in being rubbed or patted by them. Many kinds of monkeys . . . delight in fondling and being fondled by each other and by persons to whom they are attached (212–13).

Since Darwin's time, it seems most biomedical scientists have studiously avoided the study of love, in spite of its importance.

Walter B. Cannon, who has been required reading for all of us trained in physiology, was very concerned about the effect of emotional states on body function. In 1929 he published *Bodily Changes in Pain, Hunger, Fear, and Rage,* eliminating from the title "love"—which Darwin apparently considered the most important of his classic five emotions. Pavlov, the famous Russian physiologist, was also interested in studying the effects of emotion on physiological function. He performed feeding experiments on dogs, monitoring how the digestive juices reacted. Strongly bonded to his dogs, he chose them as subjects because they were so devoted, cooperative, and tolerant. His feeding experiments, however, seemed to go awry. Finally, Pavlov realized that just the sight of a person would stimulate secretion in the dogs' stomachs. Pavlov concluded that of all the stimuli affecting the dog, none was more powerful than human contact (Lynch 1977). To eliminate human contact, he developed an isolation chamber (Pavlovian chamber) in order to control, and hopefully eliminate, the influence of environmental stimuli, including people. Since that time, scientists have developed sophisticated environments to control or exclude human contact while studying various emotions other than love.

American physician W. Horsley Gant, after working many years with Pavlov, brought the new techniques he learned to Johns Hopkins University School of Medicine. Instead of avoiding human influence using the Pavlovian isolation chamber, he began studying the effect of human contact on the cardiovascular system of the dog. Profound changes were observed. The heart rate of the dog confined to an isolation chamber was 120–150 beats/min; when a person entered the room, the dog's heart rate decreased 20–30 beats, then fell even further when the person approached the dog. On being petted, the dog's heart rate fell 40–50 beats per minute. When a person remained with the dog and petted it at frequent intervals, the dog's heart rate sometimes fell to 20–30 beats per minute. Systolic blood pressure was 140 mm Hg when the dog was alone, but fell to 75 mm Hg when the dog was being petted. Gant also observed that human contact could have an even more remarkable effect on coronary blood flow in dogs. For some dogs, James Lynch stated that a person's presence was almost as potent an influence on coronary blood flow as violent exercise on a treadmill (Lynch 1977).

When Lynch, a psychologist, joined Gant, they performed a study of the effect of giving an unsignaled electric shock to a dog's forelimb on the heart rate. Obtaining consistent results over a period of days by this procedure, the scientists then had a person enter the room and pet the dog during electric shock. Although Lynch was quite sure the dog would bite the person when the electric shock was administered, he did not. On reading of Lynch's concern, I recalled some work from a Ph.D. dissertation by A. E. Fisher in 1955 (reported by Zajonc 1971) in which he showed that puppies formed attachments even when punished. Although Fisher punished the puppies whenever they approached their human handler, the puppies returned to their handler when the punishment ceased. It is probably not surprising, then, as Lynch observed, that petting animals during shock seemed to reduce the severity of the pain. The increase in heart rate observed when shocks were delivered to an isolated dog was, likewise, cut in half by petting the dog.

Lynch and his colleagues then repeated the experiment with what he described as

> modifications by first pairing electric shock with a tone that would warn the dog 10 seconds in advance that it was to be shocked (Lynch and McCarthy, 1967). In this situation, after a number of training trials, the dog's heart rate usually accelerated about 50–100 beats per minute when the tone was sounded. This necessarily unpleasant situation allowed us to evaluate whether a human contact could alter the dog's heart rate response to intense fear and pain. What we observed was, at first, difficult to understand or believe. If the person petted the dog during both the tone and the shock, the usual marked increase in heart rate to the tone and the shock was either eliminated or changed to a decrease in heart rate! When petted, some of these dogs did not even give the usual flexion response to the shock. And this effect was just as marked on the sixth day of the experiment as it was on the first day (Lynch 1977).

These observations on the influence of people over the cardiovascular function of an animal were an appropriate prelude to a reverse situation in a cooperative study involving Erika Friedmann, a graduate student; her advisor, psychiatrist Aaron Katcher at the University of Pennsylvania; James Lynch; and nurse Sue Thomas. In their study, coronary heart disease patients were subjects of a social inventory to which a question on pet ownership was added. The only item in the inventory that influenced 1-year survival was pet ownership; 11 out of 39 non–pet owners did not survive a year, while only 3 out of 53 pet owners died during the period. The effect was independent of the physiological severity of the illness (Friedmann et al. 1980).

This study was of great interest to many people, but no surprise to Lynch (1977, 1985) and quite a number of others. I believe, as does Lynch, that his studies with Gant and associates explain the reported positive results with animal introduction to suffering hospitalized children—e.g., those in cancer wards, head trauma units, psychiatric wards—and to elderly and handicapped people (see McCaul & Malott 1984).

There are many reasons that cats and dogs have been exceedingly popular companion animals to a great variety of people. Many of the same reasons apply to other domestic animals, such as water buffalo, which have a life expectancy greater than that of cats and dogs. Reasons for popularity include the animals' accepting nature, affection, innocence, nonjudgmental character, lack of pretense, predictability, and trustworthiness, and the relative ease of house-training. And they are attractive objects of nurture. Serpell (1986) maintains that the principal reason for the success of dogs and cats as companions is their remarkable ability at nonverbal expression.

By seeking to be near us and soliciting our caresses, by their exuberant greetings and pain on separation, by their possessiveness and their deferential looks of admiration, these animals persuade us that they love us and regard us highly, despite all our manifest deficiencies and failures. However much they may regret the fact, people need to feel liked, respected, admired; they enjoy the sensation of being valued and needed by others. These feelings are not trivial, nor are they a sign of weakness. Our confidence, our self-esteem, our ability to cope with the stresses of life, and ultimately, our physical health depend on this sense of belonging. Without it, existence would be hollow and without purpose. . . . at least their affection for us is reliable and unconditional, and it is patently absurd to argue that this kind of constant emotional support is either inconsequential or unhealthy.

The need for affection, affiliation, sense of belonging, identification, love, and nurturing is basic and has been recognized for a long time (see Anant 1967; Harlow & Mears 1979; Schachter 1959), although empirical studies are limited. It is encouraging that in this decade some research, supported principally by the Delta Society and other private sources, has shown that animal association may contribute to:

Success in psychotherapy sessions.

Assistance in helping patients work through their anxiety and despair.

Increased empathy by children for other people.

Socialization of young children with their peers.

A sense of constancy for foster children.

More appropriate social behavior in mentally impaired elderly.

Reduction in the social barriers represented by physical disabilities.

Higher 1-year survival rates following coronary heart disease.

Reduction in blood pressure, heart rate, and anxiety level in healthy subjects, as well as changes in speech pattern and facial expression.

People facing stressful situations seek affiliation or association. Schachter (1959) observed that the state of anxiety leads to the arrival of ''affiliative tendencies.'' People serve a direct, anxiety-reducing function for one another; they comfort and support; they reassure one another; and they attempt to bolster courage. In my experience as a prisoner of war in the march out of Poland, our small group's cohesiveness sustained us. I have also observed that many companion animals help sustain people. As Katcher (1981) stated, pets may, in fact, provide their owners with a special emotional support that is lacking in many human-human interrelationships.

In 1983 Serpell reported the results of a survey he performed in Cambridge, England which was designed to determine what aspects of dog behavior were most important to dog owners. The owners surveyed were requested to rate their own pet as well as a hypothetical ''ideal'' pet in terms of 22 different characteristics including affection, obedience, playfulness, and separation distress. The results showed the hypothetical dog possessed remarkable characteristics. It was exceptionally affectionate, welcoming, superbly intelligent, and obedient; it loved going for walks and was expressive and visually attentive to its owner. Serpell was most impressed with the attributes for which actual dogs closely matched their owner's ideal. Most prominent were the tendency to be affectionate, to welcome the owner intensely, to be highly expressive, and to attend closely to everything the owner said or did. In Serpell's words, "Out of 22 possible attributes, these owners unconsciously attached greatest importance to the four which were concerned with non-verbal messages of love and attachment."

What is needed, then, is a concerted effort to apply the latest techniques for measuring the effects of love, attachment, nurturing, and loneliness. It is encouraging that reports by Panksepp et al. (1980) and Vilberg et al. (1984) suggest that endogenous opioid secretion, a morphinelike compound produced in the central nervous system, may contribute to the sense of security and well-being of pups and chicks which they seem to derive from close social contact. Other reports in the recent past are encouraging.

Human-animal interaction is an exciting area of investigation with great potential for enriching the lives and conditions of both people and animals.

Acknowledgments

Grateful acknowledgment is extended to Alan Beck, Douglas Bowden, Signe Bustad, Wyland Cripe, Vicki Croft, Aaron Katcher, James Lynch, Maryann McKie, Richard Ott, Andrew Rowan, Sue Ruff, Allan Smith, and Orville Smith for their helpful suggestions and materials and to the editors, Michael Robinson and Lionel Tiger, for their interesting insights, patience, and helpfulness.

References

Anant, S. S. 1967. Belongingness and Mental Health: Some Research Findings. *Acta Psychologica* 26:391–96.

Anderson, R. K., B. L. Hart, and L. A. Hart, eds. 1984. *The Pet Connection: Its Influence on Our Health and Quality of Life.* Center to Study Human-Animal Relationships and Environments. Minneapolis: University of Minnesota.

Anderson, R. S., ed. 1975. *Pet Animals in Society.* New York: Macmillan.

Argyle, M. 1975. *Bodily Communication.* London: Methuen.

Arkow, P. S. 1986. *Pet Therapy: A Study and Resource Guide for the Use of Companion Animals in Selected Therapies.* Colorado Springs: The Humane Society of the Pikes Peak Region.

———, ed. 1984. *Dynamic Relationships in Practice: Animals in the Helping Professions.* Alameda, Calif.: Latham Foundation.

Barloy, J. J. 1974. *Man and Animals: One Hundred Centuries of Friendship.* Trans. H. Fox. New York: Gordon and Cremonesi.

Beaver, B. G. 1980. *Veterinary Aspects of Feline Behavior.* St. Louis: C. V. Mosby.

Beck, A. M., and A. H. Katcher. 1984. *Between Pets and People.* New York: Putnam.

Bolwig, N. 1962. Facial Expression in Primates with Remarks on Parallel Development in Certain Carnivores. *Behavior* 22:167–92.

Bullowa, M. 1979. Pre-linguistic Communication: A Field for Scientific Research. In *Before Speech,* ed. M. Bullowa. Cambridge: Cambridge University Press.

Bustad, L. K. 1980. *Animals, Aging, and the Aged.* Minneapolis: University Minnesota Press.

Bustad, L. K., and L. M. Hines. 1984a. Historical Perspectives of the Human-Animal Bond. In *The Pet Connection,* ed. R. K. Anderson et al. Minneapolis: CENSHARE.

———. 1984b. Our Professional Responsibilities Relative to Human-Animal Interaction. *Canadian Veterinary Journal* 25:369–376.

Caras, R. 1982. *A Celebration of Dogs.* New York: Times.

Cockrill, W. R., ed. 1974. *The Husbandry and Health of the Domestic Buffalo.* Rome: Food and Agriculture Organization of the United Nations.

Corson, S. A., E. O. Corson, and P. H. Gwynne. 1975. Pet-facilitated Psychotherapy. In *Pet Animals and Society,* ed. R. S. Anderson. Baltimore: Williams and Wilkins.

Corson, S. A., E. O. Corson, P. H. Gwynne, and L. E. Arnold. 1977. Pet Dogs as Nonverbal Communication Links in Hospital Psychiatry. *Comprehensive Psychiatry* 18:61–72.

Cripe, W. S. 1985. Water Buffalo: A Manifestation of Culture. In *First World Buffalo Congress Proceedings,* ed. World Buffalo Federation, vol. 3, pp. 622–25. Cairo, Egypt: World Buffalo Federation.

Darwin, C. 1965 (originally published in 1872). *The Expression of the Emotions in Man and Animals.* Chicago: University of Chicago Press.

Davis, H. P., ed. 1953. *The Modern Dog Encyclopedia.* Harrisburg, Penn.: Telegraph.

Davis, M., and F. R. Valla. 1978. Evidence for the Domestication of the Dog Twelve Thousand Years Ago in the Natufian of Israel. *Nature* 276:608–10.

Delta Society. 1986. *Living Together: People, Animals, and the Environment.* Ed. Linda M. Hines. Boston: Delta Society.

Diole, P. 1974. *The Errant Ark: Man's Relationship With Animals.* Trans. J. F. Bernard. New York: G. P. Putnam's Sons.

Driver, H. E., and W. C. Massey. 1957. Comparative Studies of North American Indians. *Transactions of the American Philosophical Society* 47:181–82.

Eisenberg, J. F. 1971. Introduction to Part 2. In *Man and Beast: Comparative Social Behavior,* ed. J. F. Eisenberg and W. S. Dillon, 129–41. Washington, D.C.: Smithsonian Institution Press.

Ensminger, M. E. 1977. *The Complete Book of Dogs.* New York: A. S. Barnes.

Fiennes, R., and A. Fiennes. 1965. *The Natural History of the Dog.* London: Weidenfeld and Nicolson.

Fisher, A. E. 1955. The Effects of Early Differential Treatment on the Social and Exploratory Behavior in Puppies. Ph.D. diss., Pennsylvania State University (as cited by R. B. Zajonc).

Fogle, B. 1983a. How Did We Find Our Way? In *New Perspectives on Our Lives with Companion Animals,* ed. A. H. Katcher and A. Beck, xxiii–xxv. Philadelphia: University of Pennsylvania Press.

______. 1983b. *Pets and Their People.* New York: Viking.

______, ed. 1981. *Interrelationships between People and Pets.* Springfield, Ill.: Charles C. Thomas.

Fox, M. W. 1965. New Information on Feline Behavior. *Modern Veterinary Practice* 46:50–52.

______. 1974. *Understanding Your Cat.* New York: Coward, McCann and Geoghegan.

______. 1975. *The Behavior of Wolves, Dogs, and Related Canids.* London: Jonathan Cape.

Friedmann, E., A. H. Katcher, J. J. Lynch, and S. A. Thomas. 1980. Animal Companions and One-Year Survival of Patients after Discharge from a Coronary Care Unit. *Public Health Reports* 95:307–12.

Hall, G. S., and C. E. Brown. 1904. The Cat and the Child. *Pedagogical Seminary* 11:3–29.

Harlow, H. F., and C. Means. 1979. *The Human Model: Primate Perspectives.* Washington, D.C.: V. H. Winston and Sons.

Hart, B. 1978. *Feline Behavior.* Santa Barbara: Veterinary Practice Publishing Co.

Hess, E. H. 1983. The Eye of the Cat. In *The Human-Pet Relationship*. Institut fuer Ethologie Mensch—Tier, ed. Institute for Interdisciplinary Research on the Human-Pet Relationship (IEMT). Vienna: IEMT.

Hines, L. M. 1983. Pets in Prison: A New Partnership. *California Veterinarian* 37(5): 24–25, 40.

______. 1985. Community People-Pet Programs That Work. *Veterinary Clinics of North America: Small Animal Practice* 15:319–32.

Ingold, T. 1980. *Hunters, Pastoralists, and Ranchers.* Cambridge: Cambridge University Press.

Jesse, G. R. 1866. *Researches into the History of the British Dog,* vol. 1, p. 299. London: Robert Hardwicke.

Katcher, A. H. 1981. Interactions between People and Their Pets: Form and Function. In *Interrelations Between People and Pets,* ed. B. Fogle. Springfield, Ill.: Charles C. Thomas.

Katcher, A. H., and A. Beck, eds. 1983. *New Perspectives on Our Lives with Companion Animals.* Philadelphia: University of Pennsylvania Press.

Katcher, A. H., and E. Friedmann. 1980. Potential Health Value of Pet Ownership. *Compendium of Continuing Education* 2:117–21.

Kendon, A. 1967. Some Functions of Gaze Direction in Social Interaction. *Acta Psychologica* 26:22–63.

Kreemer, J. 1956. *De Karboun.* The Hague: Van Hoeve.

Lee, R. L., M. E. Zeglen, T. Ryan, G. B. Bowing, and M. Hines. 1987. *Guidelines: Animals in Nursing Homes.* Rev. ed. Sacramento, Calif.: California Veterinary Medical Association.

Levinson, B. M. 1969. *Pet-oriented Child Psychotherapy.* Springfield, Ill.: Charles C. Thomas.

______. 1972. *Pets and Human Development.* Springfield, Ill.: Charles C. Thomas.

Leyhausen, P. 1979. *Cat Behavior: The Predatory and Social Behavior of Domestic and Wild Cats.* Trans. B. A. Tonkin. New York: Garland STPM.

______. 1983. The Image of the Cat: Mirror of People. In *The Human-Pet Relationship.* Institut fuer Ethologie Mensch—Tier, ed. Institute for Interdisciplinary Research on the Human-Pet Relationship (IEMT). Vienna: IEMT.

Lopez, B. H. 1978. *Of Wolves and Men.* New York: Charles Scribner's Sons.

Lorenz, K. Z. 1952. *King Solomon's Ring.* New York: New American Library.

Lynch, J. J. 1977. *The Broken Heart: The Medical Consequences of Loneliness.* New York: Basic.

______. 1985. *The Language of the Heart: The Body's Response to Human Dialogue.* New York: Basic.

Lynch, J. J., and J. F. McCarthy. 1967. The Effect of Petting on a Classically Conditioned Response. *Behavioral Response and Therapy* 5:55–62.

MacGregor, R. 1941. The Domestic Buffalo. Abridged by J. B. Brooksly from the original thesis. *Veterinary Record* 53:443–50.

McCaul, K. D., and J. M. Malott. 1984. Distraction and Coping with Pain. *Psychological Bulletin* 95:516–33.

McCulloch, M. J. 1981. The Pet as Prosthesis: Defining Criteria for the Adjunctive Use of Companion Animals in the Treatment of Medically Ill, Depressed Outpatients. In *Interrelations between People and Pets,* ed. B. Fogle. Springfield, Ill.: Charles C. Thomas.

McCulloch, W. F., C. R. Dorn, and D. C. Blenden. 1970. The University and the City. *Journal of the American Veterinary Medical Association* 157:1771–76.

Messent, P., and S. Horsfield. 1983. Pet Population and the Pet-Owner Bond. In *The Human-Pet Relationship.* Institut fuer Ethologie Mensch—Tier, ed. Institute for Interdisciplinary Research on the Human-Pet Relationship (IEMT). Vienna: IEMT.

National Academy of Sciences. 1981. *The Water Buffalo: New Prospects for an Underutilized Animal.* Washington, D.C.: National Academy Press.

Necker, C. 1970. *The Natural History of Cats.* New York: A. S. Barnes.

Orr, K. G. 1967. Introducing the Lao: Toward an Understanding of the Low-land Farmer in Laos. Research Paper. USAID Mission to Laos. USAID, Washington, D.C.

Panksepp, J., B. H. Herman, T. Vilberg, P. Bisop, and F. G. De Eskinazi. 1980. Endogenous Opioids and Social Behavior. *Neuroscience and Biobehavioral Reviews* 4:473–87.

Powers, W. K., and M. N. Powers. 1986. Putting on the Dog. *Natural History* 95(2): 6–16.

Randhawa, M. S. 1944. The Role of Domesticated Animals in Indian History. *Scientific Culture* 3:5–11.

Ritchie, C. I. A. 1981. *The British Dog: Its History from Earliest Times.* London: Robert Hale.

Schachter, S. 1959. *The Psychology of Affiliation.* London: Tavistock.

Schär, R. 1983. Influence of Man on Life and Social Behavior of Farm Cats. Poster, International Symposium on the Human-Pet Relationship, Vienna, 27–28 October 1983.

Schwabe, C. W. 1978. *Cattle, Priests, and Progress in Medicine.* Minneapolis: University of Minnesota Press.

______. 1984a. Drinking Cow's Milk: The Most Intense Man-Animal Bond. In *The Pet Connection,* ed. R. K. Anderson, et al. Minneapolis: CENSHARE.

______. 1984b. *Veterinary Medicine and Human Health.* 3rd ed. Baltimore: Williams and Wilkins.

Serpell, J. A. 1981. Childhood Pets and Their Influence on Adults' Attitudes. *Psychological Reports* 49:651–54.

______. 1983a. Best Friend or Worst Enemy: Cross-cultural Variation in Attitudes to the Domestic Dog. In *The Human-Pet Relationship.* Institut fuer Ethologie Mensch—Tier, ed. Institute for Interdisciplinary Research on the Human-Pet Relationship (IEMT). Vienna: IEMT.

______. 1983b. The Personality of the Dog and Its Influence on the Pet-Owner Bond. In *New Perspectives on Our Lives with Companion Animals,* ed. A. H. Katcher and A. M. Beck. Philadelphia: University of Pennsylvania Press.

______. 1986. *In the Company of Animals: A Study of Human-Animal Relationships.* New York: Basil Blackwell.

Ten Bensel, R. 1984. Historical Perspectives of Humaneness and Human Values for Animals and Vulnerable People. In *The Pet Connection,* ed. R. K. Anderson, et al., 2–14. Minneapolis: University of Minnesota.

Thomas, K. 1983. *Man and the Natural World: A History of the Modern Sensibility.* New York: Pantheon.

Turner, D. C. 1984. The Human/Cat Relationship: Methods of Analysis. In *The Human-Cat Relationship.* Institut fuer Ethologie Mensch—Tier, ed. Institute for Interdisciplinary Research on the Human-Pet Relationship (IEMT). Vienna: IEMT.

Vilberg, T. R., J. Panksepp, A. J. Kastin, and D. H. Coy. 1984. The Pharmacology of Endorphin Modulation of Chick Distress Vocalization. *Peptides* 5:823–27.

Whyte, R. O., and M. A. Mathur. 1974. The Buffalo in India. In *The Husbandry and Health of the Domestic Buffalo,* ed. W. R. Cockrill. Rome: Food and Agriculture Organization of the United Nations.

Young, P. T. 1955. Comments on Professor Rotter's Paper. In *Nebraska Symposium on Motivation,* ed. M. R. Jones. Lincoln: University of Nebraska Press.

Zajonc, R. B. 1971. Attraction, Affiliation, and Attachment. In *Man and Beast: Comparative Social Behavior,* ed. J. F. Eisenberg and W. S. Dillon. Washington, D.C.: Smithsonian Institution Press.

______, ed. 1969. *Animal Social Psychology.* New York: Wiley and Sons.

Zeuner, F. E. 1963. *A History of Domesticated Animals.* London: Hutchinson.

Animal Companions

More Companion Than Animal

Aaron Honori Katcher and Alan M. Beck

This paper will suggest that human evolution was shaped by an increasing dependence on nurturing and affectionate interchanges, initially between humans and later between humans and other animals (Tanner 1988). The incipient domestication of animals and plants was probably facilitated by the physiological and psychological rewards of nurturing as well as by economic gain. From the time that animals were first domesticated until the massive urbanization that followed the industrial revolution, most people had rewarding and clearly defined social relationships with the animals that provided essential material benefits.

Factory farming and modern pet keeping (Ritvo 1987) can be seen as two recent, and extreme, extensions of these culturally diverse and historically persistent patterns of animal care. In factory farming, the value of the animal is exclusively determined by its material utility to the farmer, and the animals neither provide nor benefit from nurturing, affectionate interchanges with human beings. In pet keeping, animals have, almost by definition, no material utility and are kept as a vehicle for display of affection, nurturance, and dominance (Tuan 1984). At both extremes the category of animal becomes, on one hand, robbed of its original significance, being reduced to the status of material object, and on the other, reduced by anthropomorphic thinking to a parody of the human.

The degree to which pets can be given social significance usually reserved for other human beings can be illustrated by the following history. Ralph Hoag is a spare, alert, carefully groomed male in his early seventies. Several years ago he retired from a successful retail business, and now he works several days a week for the new owners. In our interview, Mr. Hoag's aura of social competence passed rapidly as soon as he started to talk about his Border collie, Conner, who had died three months earlier. His face reddened and contracted into an expression of pain as he began to cry.

Mr. Hoag had been mourning the death of his dog for three months. During that time, he had given up all of his pleasurable activities that were not obligations to others. He cried constantly, feeling that an essential part of his life had been lost. He talked about his animal with an adoration that shrunk the significance of all his other relationships and accomplishments. His daily walks across a nearby college campus with his dog had been the center of his life, and the virtue of his dog was continually validated by the admiration directed at Conner by passersby. He said repeatedly, "Conner had given me the best years of my life," this despite the presence in the room of his wife of twenty years, with whom he apparently had a *loving* and successful marriage. Mr. Hoag mourned his animal as if it were unique, irreplaceable, and a close family member.

The kind of grief displayed by Mr. Hoag is not rare or classified as insane or even foolish behavior. It is recognized as excessive and, perhaps, uncommon. But most people respond with sympathy and value this kind of grief more than indifference to the death or loss of a companion animal. At a veterinary school teaching hospital, about 1 percent of the clients who lost their animals experienced grief of sufficient severity to be referred to the social worker (Quackenbush & Glickman 1983).

It is tempting to see such grief as an indication of the importance of companion animals in modern life. In contrast, Berger (1980) has argued that the tendency to treat animals as people attests to their increasing marginality and lack of utility in modern life.

> Animals came from over the horizon. They belong *there* and *here*. Likewise they were mortal and immortal. An animal's blood flowed like human blood, but its species was undying and each lion was Lion, each ox was Ox. This—maybe the first existential dualism—was reflected in the treatment of animals. They were subjected *and* worshipped, bred *and* sacrificed.
>
> Today the vestiges of this dualism remain among those who live intimately with, and depend upon, animals. A peasant becomes fond of his pig and is glad to salt away its pork. What is significant, and is so difficult for the urban stranger to understand, is that the two statements in that sentence are connected by an *and* not by a *but* [emphasis as in the original].

We have lost our economic connection with animals, and they are increasingly marginal in our society, so that urban Americans cannot love an animal and eat it. Animals no longer have discrete, unambiguous places in our social world, defined by collections of attitudes that are consistent to both their utilities and social relationships to human beings. Instead, we lack appropriate categories for animals and tend to fit them into categories used to describe relationships between humans, or we alternatively treat them as disposable objects with no residual value. An animal can be successively a family member and a valueless object. There are large variations in the character of relationships with companion animals. Millions of owners treat them like family members, spend large sums of money for their veterinary care, and mourn their deaths. Millions of others abandon adolescent dogs, once beloved puppies, to humane shelters to be killed.

Certainly urban pet owners describe their animals as "family members" with consistency. For example a large series of surveys of American owners have shown that in the United States from 48% to 80% of pet owners describe them as members of the family (Cain 1983, Katcher 1981, Katcher et al. 1983, Ganster & Voith 1983, Voith 1981, Albert & Bulcroft 1987). In our studies, 90% of bird owners and 72% of cat owners will say in response to a direct question that the animal is a member of the family (Beck & Katcher 1986). Among horse owners, 81% said that at least one of their horses was considered a member of the family (Jones 1983).

The social metaphor that pet owners are to pets as parents to children is expressed in a whole variety of sentiments and behaviors. Animals are photographed as children, and like children, they serve as social connecters. People with animals are socially more attractive (Lockwood 1983) and approached more frequently (Messent 1983); if the person is handicapped, then there are dramatic increases in approach frequency when the animal is present (Eddy et al. 1986).

This expression of sentiment is also manifest in the style of our dialogue with animals (Katcher & Beck 1983). Almost all pet owners talk to their animals as if they were human (Katcher 1981). There is also surprising consistency in the structure of the dialogue that experimental subjects create with their companion animals, which includes highly reliable changes in facial expression, voice pattern, and verbal inflection (Katcher & Beck 1986). Although the analysis of owner interaction with dogs and birds is still in its early stages, the pattern seems quite clear and appears to have the following characteristics:

1. Where possible, the head of the person is placed close to the head of the animal.
2. The volume of the voice is reduced, sometimes to a whisper.
3. The voice pitch is raised above that used for conversation with other people except when the subject is whispering.
4. The rate of speech and the length of individual utterances of sound are decreased.
5. There is considerable play with words and sounds, using combinations of words and sounds, and stress and length of syllables not found in ordinary speech.
6. Utterances are terminated with a rising inflection to indicate a question or to create a pseudodialogue with the animal. In this "dialogue" the person may either supply a response or insert a pause as if to permit a response.

This kind of talk resembles the style of dialogue used by adults with young infants—"motherese." However, the dialogue between people and pets has special characteristics. Parents tend to use exaggerated facial expressions with children, as if they were trying to teach the child appropriate emotional responses or to aid the child in the recognition of facial expressions. In interactions with animals the face is remarkably composed. The brow is usually smooth, the nasal labial fold is flat, and the eyes partially closed (Katcher & Beck 1986). This appearance of relaxation is characterized by a less-pronounced smile than the one used when talking to an infant or experimenter. The kind of smile used with an animal is similar to the one seen when a parent looks upon a sleeping child.

This relaxed style of dialogue used with animals is associated with decreases in blood pressure and heart rate. Talking to and petting a companion animal is less arousing than talking to people (Katcher 1981, Grossberg & Alf 1985). Having a companion animal in the room results in more rapid stabilization of blood pressure (Baun et al. 1984), and having an animal present in the room results in lower blood pressures both when subjects are quiet and when they read aloud (Friedmann et al. 1983). Subjects considered "Type A" and thus vulnerable to coronary artery disease also respond to pet interaction with decreased blood pressure and heart rate (Friedmann et al. 1986).

The communication with animals is clearly reciprocal. When humans kiss and nuzzle their dogs or birds, both respond as if they were interacting with a conspecific animal. Dogs exhibit appropriate submissive postures ordinarily reserved for dominant members of the pack, and birds behave as if trying to groom the person, indicating their participation by feather ruffling, neck bowing, and pecking in an inhibited manner (Beck & Katcher 1986).

We have then, on one hand, a consistency in sentiment about animals and in the style of interaction with animals, which suggests 1) that we subsume pets within the category of human being and 2) that doing so is both pleasurable and relaxing. On the other hand, many Americans seem capable of rapidly discarding unwanted pets, as if they were yet another kind of disposable object. It is estimated that 20% of the dog population passes through shelters every year, and 80% of these are killed (Beck 1973, 1974, 1984). While some people may be morally outraged at this unnecessary shortening of animal life, it is permissible, legal, and supported as a charitable activity, since humane shelters, as charitable institutions, attract very large sums of donated monies.

The pattern of animal disposal in humane shelters reflects the way that Americans deny the utilitarian value of pet animals. As a specific example, Alan Beck became aware of this conflict of values when the New York City Health Department was approached by a Korean import-export firm that wanted to buy dead dogs from the ASPCA to export as a delicacy. They were willing to pay a sizable sum for the carcasses during a time when the humane society dearly needed funds. They were even willing to pay for just the dog penises, which were highly valued for their purported effect on potency. In pleading their case, the merchants argued that it was better than sending the dead animals to a rendering plant and that the humane society could use the income to help living animals. Naturally the plan was totally unacceptable to the humane community. Perhaps the most extreme case can be seen in an event which occurred recently at the Philadelphia SPCA. There was an attempt to remove the board of directors, in part because they permitted the drawing of blood from anesthetized dogs prior to their being killed in the shelter, a procedure which had been approved because of the critical need for transfusion blood for ill dogs. In similar fashion a strong objection has been made to the use of any pound animal that was once a pet for any experimental purpose. The situation under debate was subjecting the animal to a surgery under anesthesia from which it would not recover; a procedure, from the animal's point of view, no different from the euthanasia practiced at shelters. Similarly, there are public outcries when pet carcasses are taken to rendering plants or are incorporated into pet or livestock food.

Perhaps the best expression of this loss of simultaneously held social and utilitarian values for animals is the rhetoric of the animal rights movement. An awareness of the need to protect both children and animals from cruelty arose among the same socially active people in the nineteenth century (French 1975). In the United States the legal justification for protecting children was established by equating children with animals, which were, at the time of the landmark case, already protected (Beck & Katcher 1983). Recently, authors drew similar parallels between animal rights and rights for women, blacks, and other oppressed minorities. The use of the term *speciesism* to deride the utilitarian use of animals has the explicit implication that animals should not be in separate moral or legal categories but should have the same assumed pattern of rights as human beings. Peter Singer (1975) in his book, *Animal Liberation,* makes the case that speciesism is analogous to racism and sexism. "We would be on shaky grounds if we were to demand equality for blacks, women and other groups of oppressed humans while denying equal consideration to nonhumans."

The definition of the position of animals in society inherent in the animal rights movement is the most conclusive evidence of the marginality of animals in our society because that definition almost obliterates the distinction between animals and human beings. Animals are allowed no utility, or rather, an animal's utility must not dictate our social relationships with it. The frequent coexistence of a concern for animal rights and vegetarianism suggests the need to deny *any* utility to animal relationships. The most radical statement of animal rights is to be found in the concept that no social relationships with animals are possible and that all animals should exist independently of man. Thus animals would become marginal to the point of nonexistence.

What is the gain from continuing to care for companion animals when they have lost their economic or material utility? Why do we play at treating animals like human beings and assign them a role in the family? This essay will argue that care of any animal permits the elaboration of nurturing beyond the raising of human children and that the extension of the activities of nurturing in both depth and time have had favorable health consequences which increased the fitness of human societies that kept animals. To understand what domestication of plants and animals may have done for us, it is necessary to look at that activity in an evolutionary context.

It is a reasonable hypothesis that the prolonged care of infants in primate groups was facilitated and maintained by deeply rooted physiological, psychological, and social rewards. There is evidence that the physical contact and physiological consequences of nurturing increase the fitness of both parent and offspring. The offspring benefited by more rapid growth, and both parent and offspring through greater efficiency of the immune mechanism, more resistance to disease. There is also evidence that withdrawal from nurturing roles and loss of the opportunity to exchange affection is associated with depression and greater vulnerability to disease. Thus, those not engaged in caring for others would be removed from competition for scarce resources.

There is a large literature suggesting that social isolation, loss of a spouse, and depression can result in decreased health and significantly increased vulnerability to accident, chronic disease, and death (Bowlby 1966, Harlow & Harlow 1962, Lynch 1977, Ory 1983). Depression is a complex psychobiological state in which the competence of the immune system is decreased and mortality from a broad range of pathological events is increased. One of the most important triggers for depression is loss of the opportunity to care for, nurture, and love others. Depression can be triggered by withdrawal from the company of others, and in turn, depression causes further social withdrawal. Caring and depression are both self-facilitating states, one causing us to move toward other people and health, and the other leading us to increasing social isolation and vulnerability to disease (Lynch 1977).

Perhaps the pathological effects of social isolation and loss of social relationships are a reflection of a lifelong dependence on nurturance in human populations. This dependence on social support and affection is another example of the progressive incorporation of juvenile characteristics into the adult repertoire that characterizes human evolution (and the domestication of animals as well). Gould (1981) describes the progressive retention of juvenile traits—neoteny—in human evolution:

> Flexibility is the hallmark of human evolution. If humans evolved as I believe, by neoteny, then we are, in a more than metaphorical sense, permanent children. (In neoteny, rates of development slow down and juvenile stages of ancestors become the adult features of descendants.) Many central features of our anatomy link us with fetal and juvenile stages of primates: small face, vaulted cranium and large brain in relation to body size, unrotated big toe, foramen magnum under the skull for correct orientation of the head in upright posture, primary distribution of hair on head, armpits, and pubic areas. . . . In other mammals, exploration play, and flexibility of behavior are qualities of juveniles, only rarely of adults. We retain not only the anatomical stamp of childhood, but its mental flexibility as well.

The protohuman young were nurtured for progressively longer periods of time as the size of the human brain increased. The period of dependency began, of necessity, to exceed the years in which the child was dependent upon breast-feeding for sustenance. Selection favored those infants who used behavior strategies that were effective in eliciting attention and care from adults over prolonged periods of time (Dolhinow, this volume). Because dependency of the young and the need to protect and feed them extended beyond the period of nursing, it is reasonable to assume that members of the kin network became engaged in part of this child care. The progressive neoteny of succeeding evolutionary stages in the development of man would extend the period of time and the kinds of people engaged in affectionate nurturing. It would also decrease the distinction between adult and childlike characteristics, thus blurring the distinctive traits that release affectionate care.

When human beings began to rear other animals, perhaps by bringing home the young of adults killed in the hunt, they extended their opportunities for sensual involvement in nurturing activities. Playing with, feeding, and caring for infant animals had the same pleasures and emotional and physiological rewards as tending human infants. Moreover, these rewards were available to humans who could not obtain them from the nurture of human infants.

Among the characteristics that Juliet Clutton-Brock (1981) has suggested as critical for domestication are hardiness, e.g., the ability of an infant to be removed from its mother before weaning and survive in novel environments, and a kind of sociability described as follows: "It has to be a social animal whose behavioral patterns are based on a dominance hierarchy so that it will accept man as the leader, and will remain imprinted on him in adult life."

We would amplify the argument of Clutton-Brock by suggesting that a tendency to respond positively to and seek out human nurturing would make the infant animal more attractive to humans. Moreover, hardiness and the ability to seek out nurturing are probably closely related. There is an ample literature suggesting that handling and "gentling" improve health, immunological competence, weight gain, and breeding success in domestic animals (Barnett et al. 1984, Gross & Siegel 1979, Hemsworth et al. 1981, Solomon et al. 1968). The same benefits from handling could differentially result in the better survival of genetic traits associated with an ability to elicit nurturing behavior from humans. Coppinger and Smith (1983) argue that neoteny occurs naturally in some social species as an adaptation for higher interspecific interaction, i.e., by retaining both physical and behavior attributes of the young and reducing aggression. Therefore, neotenic species were likely to be more tolerant of human settlers. They were more approachable and survived the high density of captivity without stress.

The care of animals was facilitated by both the practical value of the animals themselves and the pleasure and the physiological rewards of caring for the animals. If nurturing plants and animals had some of the same rewards as caring for other human beings, then we would also expect that the health of those groups practicing domestication would be improved both by better nutrition and by the direct beneficial effects of the increased opportunity to engage in nurturing activities. Domestication of plants and animals has also extended the opportunities for rearing human children. The limited resources available to hunting and gathering tribes requires them to space out childbearing. The increased food resources and opportunity for permanent settlement afforded by agriculture permits a greater frequency of childbirth (Fisher, this volume).

Agriculture was fully established some 10,000 years ago, providing for humankind a continual and almost universal contact with animals and engagement with nurturing plants and animals. This engagement persisted throughout the history of civilization until the last 200 years. In those 2 centuries, only 10 to 15 generations, a trivial time in the genetic history of humans beings, there has been an extraordinary disengagement of people in industrialized societies from care of animals and plants. It began well before the industrial revolution with the enclosure and expropriation of public lands and a shift in agricultural practices to support trade in grain, wool, and cattle (Williams 1973). Shifting patterns of agriculture, with the displacement of small or peasant farmers, continued into the beginning of this century in Europe and, of course, continues in South and Central America to this day. People were not attracted to labor in the cities' mills; they were driven to it.

Since the industrial revolution, there has been an enormous shift of people into cities, away from any contact with the rearing of animals or the care of gardens and orchards. In the space of 2 centuries, the United States and western Europe went from a population that was only 10% urban to one that was 90% urban. In the United States, 1910 was the first year in which there were fewer farm workers than industrial laborers, and now farm labor makes up only a small fraction of the work force. Many of those remaining laborers have tasks, like seasonal harvesting, which are divorced from the care of animals. In these relatively few years, there has been a radical transformation in the physical relationship between human beings and living things, with a very large part of the population being excluded from contact and care of living things other than their own children.

In 1800, the world population was a little less than 1 billion. By the year 2000, the population of the world's 5 largest cities will total 1 billion people. Using the Western or industrialized world as an example, never has there been a human population that has spent so little time in physical contact with animals and plants and devoted so little time to the nurturing of its own young or the care of animals. We have no idea what the cognitive, emotional, and physiological consequences of that change are.

With this progressive denaturation of humankind, pets have been thrust into a salient position as the most obtrusive vestige of our former bond with the natural world. We cling to them because nurturing them makes us feel better and contributes to our health. But in clinging to pets, we are destroying their status as animals, making them over into degraded images of human beings. Animals are therefore in a residual category; they have no utilitarian roles, and their only category is one dictated by their social relationship to human beings. Companion animals are treated in both ways—loved like a child or discarded like an old toy. Without utility, there is no way to assign value to animals, no way to have unique social relationships with them. Denial of utilitarian roles for animals does not increase their value. It only makes the position of animals in modern society more problematic and permits the enormous variation in our social responses to animals.

Despite the increasing marginality of living animals in urban life, people continue to nurture animals because such care makes people feel better and, under some circumstances, improves their health. The current interest in the behavioral, physiological, and health consequences of interaction with companion animals is part of a general cultural reassessment of the value assigned to animals and the natural world. This revaluation has energized the conservation movement, the concerns about loss of forest and species extinction, the growing public determination to control pollutants in the environment, and the increased public desire to come into closer relationships with natural environments and animals. This general cultural theme includes a rediscovery of the value of social relationships with animals. Animals and the environment are being given a new utility which is psychological and social rather than material. Perhaps the rediscovered value of an animal's society will lead to a greater appreciation of the animal's unique social behavior and the reconstruction of distinct social categories for animals. Then, to paraphrase Berger (1980), we can love our dogs and appreciate what makes them dogs, and not people.

References

Albert, A., and K. Bulcroft. 1987. Pets and Urban Life. *Anthrozoös* 1:9–25.

Barnett, J. L., G. M. Gronin, and C. G. Winfield. 1984. The Welfare of Confined Sows: Physiological, Behavioral, and Production Responses to Contrasting Housing Systems and Handler Attitudes. *Annales de Recherches Veterinaires* 15:217–26.

Baun, M., N. Bergstrom, N. Langston, and I. Thoma. 1984. Physiological Effects of Petting Dogs: Influences of Attachment. In *The Pet Connection: Its Influence on Our*

Health and Quality of Life, ed. R. Anderson, B. Hart, and A. Hart, 162–70. Minneapolis: University of Minnesota Press.

Beck, A. M. 1973. *The Ecology of Stray Dogs: A Study of Free-ranging Urban Animals.* Baltimore: York.

______. 1974. Ecology of Unwanted and Uncontrolled Pets. In *Proceedings of the National Conference on the Ecology of the Surplus Dog and Cat Problem,* 31–39. Denver, Colo.: American Humane Society.

______. 1984. Population Aspects of Animal Mortality. In *Pet Loss and Human Bereavement,* ed. W. Kay, A. H. Kutscher, R. M. Grey, and C. E. Fudin, 42–48. Ames: Iowa State University Press.

Beck A. M., and A. H. Katcher. 1983. *Between Pets and People: The Importance of Animal Companionship.* New York: G. P. Putnam's Sons.

______. 1986. Bird-Human Interaction. In *Living Together: People, Animals, and the Environment,* ed. Linda M. Hines, 76. Boston: Delta Society.

Berger, J. 1980. *About Looking.* New York: Pantheon.

Bowlby, J. 1966. *Maternal Care and Mental Health.* New York: Schocken.

Cain, A. 1983. A Study of Pets in the Family System. In *New Perspectives on Our Lives with Companion Animals,* ed. A. H. Katcher and A. M. Beck, 72–81. Philadelphia: University of Pennsylvania Press.

Clutton-Brock, J. 1981. *Domesticated Animals from Early Times.* Austin: University of Texas Press.

Coppinger R. P., and C. K. Smith. 1983. The Domestication of Evolution. *Environmental Conservation* 10(4): 283–92.

Dolhinow, P. 1986. Tactics of Primate Immaturity. Paper presented at Man and Beast Revisited, Special Smithsonian Symposium, May 6–9, 1986, Washington, D.C., Smithsonian Institution.

Eddy, J., L. Hart, and R. Boltz. 1986. Service Dogs and Social Acknowledgment of People in Wheelchairs: An Observational Study. *Living Together: People, Animals, and the Environment,* Delta Society International Conference, Abstract p. 89.

Fisher, H. 1986. The Human Divorce Pattern in Cultural Perspective. Paper presented at Man and Beast Revisited, Special Smithsonian Symposium, May 6–9, 1986, Washington, D.C., Smithsonian Institution.

French, R. D. 1975. *Antivivisection and Medical Science in Victorian Society.* Princeton: Princeton University Press.

Freidmann, E., A. H. Katcher, S. A. Thomas, J. J. Lynch, and P. R. Messent. 1983. Social Interaction and Blood Pressure: Influence of Animal Companions. *Journal Nervous and Mental Diseases* 171:461–65.

Friedmann, E., B. Z. Locker, and S. A. Thomas. 1986. Effect of a Pet on Cardiovascular Responses during Communication by Coronary-Prone Individuals. *Living Together: People, Animals, and the Environment,* Delta Society International Conference Abstract p. 137.

Ganster, D., and V. L. Voith. 1983. Attitudes of Cat Owners Towards Their Cats. *Feline Practice* 13(2): 21–29.

Gould, S. 1981. *The Mismeasure of Man.* New York: Norton.

Gross, W. B., and P. B. Siegel. 1979. Adaptation of Chickens to Their Handler, and Experimental Results. *Avian Diseases* 23(3): 708–14.

Grossberg, J., and E. Alf. 1985. Interaction with Pet Dogs: Effects on Human Cardiovascular Response. *Journal of the Delta Society* 2:20–27.

Harlow, H., and M. K. Harlow. 1962. Social Deprivation in Monkeys. *Scientific American* 207:136–44.

Hemsworth, P. H., J. L. Barnett, and C. Hansen. 1981. The Influence of Handling by Humans on the Behavior, Growth, and Corticosteroids in the Juvenile Female Pig. *Hormonal Behavior* 15:398–403.

Jones, B. 1983. Just Crazy about Horses: The Fact behind the Fiction. In *New Perspectives on Our Lives with Companion Animals,* ed. A. H. Katcher and A. M. Beck, 87–111. Philadelphia: University of Pennsylvania Press.

Katcher, A. 1981. Interactions between People and Their Pets: Form and Function. In *Interrelations between People and Pets,* ed. B. Fogle, 47–67. Springfield, Ill.: Charles C. Thomas.

Katcher, A. H., and A. M. Beck. 1983. Safety and Intimacy: Physiological and Behavioral Responses to Interaction with Companion Animals. In *The Human-Pet Relationship.* Institut fuer Ethologie Mensch—Tier, ed. Institute for Interdisciplinary Research on the Human-Pet Relationship (IEMT). Vienna: IEMT.

______. 1986. "Dialogue with Animals." *Transactions and Studies College of Physicians of Philadelphia* 8:105–12.

Katcher, A. H., E. Freidmann, M. Goodman, and L. Goodman. 1983. Men, Women, and Dogs. *California Veterinarian* 2:14–16.

Lockwood, R. 1983. The Influence of Animals on Social Perception. In *New Perspectives on Our Lives with Companion Animals,* ed. A. H. Katcher and A. M. Beck, 64–71. Philadelphia: University of Pennsylvania Press.

Lynch, J. J. 1977. *The Broken Heart: The Medical Consequences of Loneliness.* New York: Basic.

Messent, P. R. 1983. Social Facilitation of Contact with Other People by Pet Dogs. In *New Perspectives on Our Lives with Companion Animals,* ed. A. H. Katcher and A. M. Beck, 37–46. Philadelphia: University of Pennsylvania Press.

Ory, M. G., and E. L. Goldberg. 1983. Pet Possession and Life Satisfaction in

Elderly Women. In *New Perspectives on Our Lives with Companion Animals,* ed. A. H. Katcher and A. M. Beck, 303–17. Philadelphia: University of Pennsylvania Press.

Quackenbush, J., and L. Glickman. 1983. Social Work Services for Bereaved Pet Owners: A Retrospective Case Study in a Veterinary Teaching Hospital. In *New Perspectives on Our Lives with Companion Animals,* ed. A. H. Katcher and A. M. Beck, 378–89. Philadelphia: University of Pennsylvania Press.

Ritvo, H. 1987. *The Animal Estate.* Cambridge: Harvard University Press.

Singer, P. 1975. *Animal Liberation.* New York: New York Review.

Soloman, G. F., S. Levine, and J. K. Kraft. 1968. Early Experience and Immunity. *Nature* 220:821–22.

Tanner, N. M. 1988. *On Becoming Human.* New York: Cambridge University Press.

Tuan, Y. 1984. *Dominance and Affection: The Making of Pets.* New haven, Conn.: Yale University Press.

Voith, V. L. 1981. Attachment between People and Their Pets: Behavior Problems of Pets That Arise from the Relationship between Pets and People. In *Interrelations between People and Pets,* ed. B. Fogle, 271–94. Springfield, Ill.: Charles C. Thomas.

Williams, R. 1973. *The Country and the City.* New York: Oxford University Press.

The Human-Animal Interface

Chasm or Continuum?

Andrew N. Rowan

At some stage or other, anyone who campaigns for the improved welfare of animals is faced with the accusation that he or she should not waste time worrying about animals because there is so much human suffering that needs to be addressed. The implication of this is that animals are not worth the attention and that animal issues detract from more important human concerns. However, the available evidence indicates that critics of animal advocates misjudge the importance of animals and animal symbols in human culture. Anthropologists have long been aware of the importance of animals in society, but it seems there has been a tendency to categorize animals in utilitarian terms or to study animal symbols as "social metaphors." In any event, the role and place of animals in human society is generally not adequately appreciated. One relevant, notable study is Leach's (1964) remarkable analysis of animal categories and verbal abuse.

Animal Terms and Terms of Abuse

Leach's paper is rich and complex, and the arguments plumb several levels of meaning. It is thus very difficult to summarize, especially if the summarizer is a biochemist who has only a very superficial understanding of anthropological literature and concepts. Nevertheless, one does not have to be able to understand the nuances of astrophysics to be able to comprehend the broad outlines of the big bang theory. So, with Leach's paper, one does not have to be a trained anthropologist to gain insight from his arguments.

Leach notes that the language of obscenity falls into three broad categories: a) dirty words—those referring to sex or excretion, b) blasphemy and profanity, and c) animal terms, in which a human is likened to an animal. Now, one does not have to be a psychiatrist or psychologist to understand that terms dealing with sex and excretion can have linguistic potency. Similarly, even in the modern secular age, it is understandable why blasphemy and profanity should arouse or release emotions. However, animal categories of verbal abuse seem less easily accounted for. In Leach's words, "When an animal name is used . . . as an imprecation, it indicates that the name itself is credited with potency. It clearly signifies that the animal category is in some way taboo and sacred. Thus, for an anthropologist, animal abuse is part of a wide field of study which includes sacrifice and totemism." In the simplest terms, one could be provocative and state that animal symbols appear to be sufficiently important to humans to be placed on a level similar to God and sex. Thus, it can be argued that the study of human-animal interactions is of some social importance, as opposed to an academic exercise of marginal relevance.

Unfortunately, it is characteristic of academic discourse that whenever one finds a paper that agrees with one's own intuitive ideas, somebody sooner or later comes along with a contrary argument to rock the boat. Thus, anthropologist John Halverson (1976) published a stinging critique of Leach's paper 12 years later that deplored the loose and varied use of the term "taboo," that identified a host of errors in Leach's etymological scholarship, and that argued that the negative connotations associated with animal terms might simply reflect the basic "human-versus-animal" distinction rather than some deeper taboo associated with human difficulties in categorizing domestic animals as "us" or "not-us." Halverson's arguments are detailed and convincing, and yet it seems he goes too far in the other direction. He joins many others who reduce the place of animals in human life to the merely mundane and utilitarian (Harris 1985), and eliminate any role for animals or animal terms as symbols of varying degrees of potency.

Killing of Animals, Domestic and Wild

Humankind has always struggled with assigning a proper status for animals in the worldview of the moment. Hunter-gatherer societies indulge in elaborate propitiation ceremonies to appease the spirits or spirit-guardians of the animals they have killed. Modern societies appear, superficially at least, to have overcome their guilt at killing animals, and yet a closer examination suggests that we might merely be hiding a deep-seated and unexamined guilt. For example, the common use of the term *sacrifice* in animal research may be meaningful in this regard. In kosher slaughter, the actual killing is performed by a holy man, the shochet, because he has the grace and strength of character to bear the associated guilt. In Tibet, butchers are considered outcasts. Recreational hunters of the present day, especially those such as Aldo Leopold who have achieved a significant communion with nature, enjoy the hunt and the kill, and yet agonize over the paradox that their bonds with nature appear strongest only when they kill one of its denizens (Elder 1986).

On the hunting issue, Elder's (1986) article is a superb introduction to the contradictions found in a man like Leopold, who extols hunting as a *way* of life (of being wild himself) but who also asserts the personhood and the rights of other living creatures. Leopold is not blind to this conflict and, in his writings, attempts time and again to come to terms with the ethical and evolutionary challenge. Early in his life, he kills a wolf (believing that the more wolves killed, the more deer there would be), but after watching the green fire dim and die in the eyes of the mortally wounded wolf, he starts to question his approach. His quest leads him eventually to the "land" ethic, but he still hunts.

It is appropriate that Leopold's consciousness should have been stirred by a dying wolf, since wolves and bears seem to carry special meaning and symbolism for humans. For example, in Norway today the traditional wolf range carries millions of sheep, millions of people and 5 to 10 wolves. It would seem that so few wolves would not disturb people, but that is not the case. The sighting of 1 wolf in southern Norway set off a frenzied and hysterical wolf hunt and stimulated a lucrative tourist trade in wolf artifacts. The frenzy did not end until a wolf was killed and the carcass was doused with champagne and then dragged off to a school, an old people's home, and the steps of the national parliament. Even today, with modern weapons, sophisticated transport, and a well-educated population, one solitary wolf is still capable of eliciting mass hysteria.

Human Language and Human Uniqueness

The debate over ape language also reveals much about our inner insecurities over the place of animals in our anthropocentric worldview. Elizabeth Anscombe, the Cambridge philosopher, was once asked what she thought people would do if it could be shown that apes could speak (given the tremendous symbolic importance ascribed to human language). Reportedly, she responded, "Simple, they'll up the ante" (that is, *language* would be redefined so that language would still be uniquely human). The bitterness and partisan nature of the ape language debate among scholars (Fowler 1980) supports Anscombe's comments and the notion that we are unable to deal objectively with a possible breach in an important defense of our unique position—namely, language.

Eugene Linden's (1986) recent book, *Silent Partners,* describes and reveals some of the prejudices and passions underlying ape language research. So much time is spent trying to support or refute arguments and data about linguistic sophistication, he mourns, that we are ignoring the fascinating questions that the new ape-human communication systems might raise about the worldview of the Pongidae. For example, when Viki Hayes, a chimp raised in a human household, was asked to sort human and animal photographs into categories, she placed pet dogs in the pile of animal photographs but her own photograph with the human snapshots (cited in Goodall 1986).

Modern Pets/Companion Animals

If one moves a little closer to the average suburban home, there are many other examples of the ambiguous role that animals, namely, our pets, play in our lives. Most of us provide our pets with names. As anthropologists recognize, naming is not a random process. A minority of pets (22% of dogs and 10% of cats) are given common human first names (e.g., Cindy, Charlie, and Kathleen). The majority of the animals are given nonhuman names (59% of the dogs and 78% of the cats), and the remainder have names that came from foreign cultures or are human names that are out of fashion (Rowan 1987). Assigning a human name to a pet was more likely among owners who considered their pets to be important family members (Albert 1987). The significance of this point may be further elaborated by considering another culture. The Beng people of West Africa also keep dogs. However, these animals are rarely shown any affection and have to fend for themselves. Nonetheless, if the animals become sick, they are cared for and nursed back to health. Beng dogs are also given names, but the names chosen are nonsense words or are words from foreign languages that express negative or fatalistic concepts (Gottlieb 1986). The dog occupies an ambiguous place in Beng mythology, having introduced death to humanity (a variant of the Pandora's box myth, perhaps), but in another myth, the dog saves humanity while betraying his fellow animals. The ambivalent role of the dog in Beng mythology is reflected in the ambivalent place of dogs in modern Beng society.

The Place of Animals in Human Society

Given the tensions that exist over the categories that animals occupy in our modern world, it is hardly surprising that attention to the question of the moral status of animals should be controversial. However, while it is a controversial issue, it has not been considered a topic worthy of serious discussion and study until very recently. Even today, relatively few philosophers have written on the topic, although arguably more has been published in the last 2 decades than in the previous 2 millennia. This does not mean that there was no concern about animals in earlier times, however.

Among the ancient Greeks, for example, there were 4 different groups of thought about animals. The animists, epitomized by Pythagoras, held that animals and humans shared (and exchanged) souls of the same kind. The mechanists took the opposite view and held that *both* humans and animals lacked souls and were no more than machines. Both these groups placed animals, in theory at least, on a par with humans. On the other hand, the vitalists, exemplified by Aristotle, held that animals had souls but that they were not as advanced and therefore not on a par with fully entitled humans. However, by far the largest group simply believed that animals were placed on earth for human use and benefit.

The issue came up again from time to time but was not a pressing matter for most Western philosophers. St. Augustine dismissed animals from God's moral universe, but more because he was anxious to debunk the ascetic vegetarianisms of the Manichaeans (who felt that propagation through sexual intercourse contaminated animal flesh) than for any other reason. St. Thomas Aquinas also addressed the status of animals (and concluded that animals have no moral rights of any sort) in his efforts to reconcile the newly discovered Aristotelian texts with Roman Catholic doctrine. In the early 17th century, Descartes continued this tradition when he pronounced that animals had no souls and were no more than machines. By contrast, he held that a human had a soul which communicated with the human corporeal machine via the pineal gland. As a result, Descartes and other philosophers of the European rationalist tradition held that animals had no moral status per se and that humans could do what they wished with animals. The notion that animals had no feelings was an important rationalization in the development of a more mechanistic and technocratic worldview (Rosenfield 1968).

Ironically, during this period it was not uncommon for animals to be put on trial for committing such acts as murder (pigs killing infants), destruction of property (locust plagues), and sodomy. There is a case from Vanvers, France, in the 18th century in which a she-ass was caught in the act of sodomy with a local lad. The boy was burned at the stake, but the donkey was bound over under the care of the local abbot who testified that she had been, in all her ways and deeds, a most virtuous beast and that she had obviously been coerced by the human lecher (Evans 1987). So, on one hand, animals had no moral status, while on the other, they were sometimes treated as though they could and should know right from wrong.

In England, under the influence of the British empiricist school, people gradually became more sympathetic to the needs of animals (Thomas 1983). For example, animals were not seen as being equal to humans, but they were considered to be worthy of moral concern because they were capable of suffering. As the utilitarian Jeremy Bentham stated in 1789, "The question is not, can they reason? nor, can they talk? but, can they suffer?" However, accepting that animals can suffer and are therefore worthy of moral concern is a far cry from accepting that they have rights in the modern sense of the term. In fact, not even universal rights for humans were accepted at this time. In 1792, the Cambridge philosopher Thomas Taylor argued that if all humans (including women) are equal, then there is absolutely no good reason to deny equality to the "brutes" as well. The purpose of his argument was to ridicule the notion that all humans, for example, slaves or women, were equal (to the rational man of property?) and should enjoy the same rights. Today, the notion of basic inalienable rights for humans (be they men or women, black or white) is widely accepted, and certain philosophers, such as Tom Regan at North Carolina State University, are now arguing that the concept of basic rights should be extended to at least some animals (Regan 1983). For Regan, this means that mammals of above a certain age (and possibly most other vertebrates) have the right not to be used merely as a means to an end. His philosophical stand would stop most, if not at all, human uses of animals, including the raising of food animals and animal experimentation.

The philosophical debate revolves around the differences between humans and other animals. It is obvious that there are major differences, but the real issue is which of these differences are *morally relevant?* In human society over the last century, gender and skin color have come to be judged as not morally relevant. Can we say the same of other characteristics, such as the extent of hair covering, bipedalism, the length of the tail, and so on? Most people would find it absurd to judge moral standing on the basis of these characteristics.

In examining why some humans or animals are included in, or excluded from, our moral universe, we find that great weight seems to be placed on the structure of the nervous system and on relative mental capabilities.

Indeed, in the arguments over whether or not research should be permitted on human fetuses, expert committees have usually drawn the dividing line when the neural crest first appears in the developing embryo, around day fourteen. Therefore, it seems appropriate to focus attention on such properties of the nervous system as a capacity to suffer, a capacity to reason and to display purposeful behavior, and the development of self-awareness or other reflexive mental behavior.

The first criterion that might be considered in determining moral status is the notion of "sentience." The term is not usually defined, but it seems to refer to the capacity to suffer pain or distress and/or enjoy pleasure. While most of us assume that animals feel pain, the issue is not that clear-cut. For example, lobotomized humans report that while they have pain sensations, these sensations do not bother them very much (the agony has gone). The question then becomes, how much does pain bother animals, who have a much smaller frontal lobe? While no one can be certain, data indicate that most vertebrates do "feel" pain in the same way we do. However, it is not at all clear that insects or other invertebrates "feel" pain. They react to an aversive stimulus but show little evidence of a cognitive reaction to such a stimulus.

Another possible criterion that might be invoked is the extent of rationality and purposiveness shown by an animal. One can use several avenues to examine these issues in animals. First, to have thought and reason, one needs to uncouple the motor response from the sensory stimulus (in a reflex response these two are very tightly coupled; no one "thinks" about flexing the knee when a doctor taps it). One example of uncoupled mental activity is the dreaming that occurs during rapid eye movement (REM) sleep. REM sleep occurs in mammals and in birds and perhaps in some amphibians. This shared trait suggests that these animals can engage in "uncoupled" mental activity, but other lines of evidence would be required to indicate whether some of their behavior (and how much of their behavior) could be considered to be rational and imbued with purpose. A great deal of behavior, even apparently purposive human behavior, is controlled by unconscious stimuli and impulses, so one has to be very careful in determining the degree of rationality displayed by an animal.

Another characteristic that should be included is the extent of "self-awareness.'' This is a very cloudy notion and not even the experts are able to agree on a precise definition (Crook 1983), but it generally refers to some sort of ability to reflect on one's own condition. Relatively little experimental evidence is available to determine whether an animal is self-aware. Gallup (1977) showed that chimpanzees were capable of using mirrors to recognize and examine themselves and has argued from this that chimpanzees have mind. However, a broader characteristic would be intentional deception. For an animal to deceive intentionally, it must have the idea that the observer (the ''deceivee'') thinks that it (the animal) is thinking and acting in a certain way. This necessitates a self-reflexive mental capacity and, hence, self-awareness. Goodall (1986) reports various observations and studies indicating that chimpanzees are capable of deception. Most of the deceptive behavior she reports appears to be intentional.

Throughout history, human societies have questioned the role and place of animals in human society. Few if any cultures have taken the view that animals have no moral standing, but in nearly all, it has been considered that humans are justified in using animals for human ends. However, the boundaries of such an approach to animals have been very fuzzy, and the reasons given for according some attention to the interests of animals are rarely, if ever, analyzed and subjected to critical debate. The work of a few modern philosophers has challenged the standard dogma about animals, while modern ethology, neuroscience, and cognitive psychology have tended to narrow the large gap that most people have assumed exists between the mental functioning of humans and other animals.

Modern philosophers have argued that whatever characteristics (e.g., sentience, rationality, self-awareness, language, or moral agency) is chosen, one either has to exclude some humans from, or include some animals in, the orbit of moral concern. However, the problem with these challenges is that most have relied on arguments based on a *single* morally relevant characteristic. In practice, moral status is based on a complex of *several* characteristics, any one of which may be present or absent in a particular animal species and may vary qualitatively from one animal to another. Very little scholarship has been devoted to this approach, which is one of the reasons why current concepts of the moral status of animals are so blurred and ill-defined. And yet the issues are important and have bearing on controversial moral issues, including the status of fetuses. It is to be hoped that the current upsurge in the animal protection movement will spur more serious scholarship on these matters.

Ever since humans beings gradually emerged from the African savanna, other animals have been an essential part of our history and culture. It is, therefore, hardly surprising that we should have strong attitudes about our relationships with animals—as strong, perhaps, as our attitudes to such "hot" topics as sex, religion, and politics. The old but often-true cliché that politicians receive more mail from constituents on animal issues than on any other topic, including abortion and the Vietnam War, indicates the strength of our feelings about animals. When army nerve gas tests on dogs were publicized in 1974, the Pentagon received 30,000 protest letters—more than it received when General MacArthur was fired (Holden 1974).

Our attitudes toward our use of animal symbols, and the roles such symbols play (e.g., the Exxon tiger in the tank, the eagle of the United States Postal Service), have been subjected to relatively little careful review and study. Animal symbols are usually taken for granted, and there is a tendency to dismiss phenomena relating to animals as peripheral and unimportant. The growing momentum of scholarship in this field must be nurtured and encouraged. A greater understanding of the similarities and differences between humans and animals, and of the nuances of human-animal interactions, will not only lead to better treatment of animals but will enrich human culture and society.

References

Albert, A. 1987. The Significance of Names. *Anthrozoos* 1:134.

Crook, J. H. 1983. On Attributing Consciousness to Animals. *Nature* 303:11–14.

Elder, J. 1986. Hunting in Sand County. *Orion Nature Quarterly* 5(4): 46–53.

Evans, E. P. 1987. *The Criminal Prosecution and Capital Punishment of Animals.* London: Faber.

Fowler, S. 1980. The Clever Hans Phenomenon Conference. *International Journal for the Study of Animal Problems* 1:355–359.

Gallup, G. G. 1977. Self-Recognition in Primates: A Comparative Approach to the Bidirectional Properties of Consciousness. *American Psychologist* 32:329–38.

Goodall, J. 1986. *The Chimpanzees of Gombe: Patterns of Behavior.* Cambridge: Harvard University Press.

Gottlieb, A. 1986. Dog: Ally or Traitor? *American Ethnologist* 13:477–88.

Halverson, J. 1976. Animal Categories and Terms of Abuse. *Man* 11:505–16.

Harris, M. 1985. *Good to Eat: Riddles of Food and Culture.* New York: Simon and Shuster.

Holden, C. 1974. Beagles: Army under Attack for Research at Edgewood. *Science* 185:130–31.

Leach, E. R. 1964. Anthropological Aspects of Language: Animal Categories and Verbal Abuse. In *New Directions in the Study of Language,* ed. E. Lennenberg, 23–64. Cambridge: MIT Press.

Linden, E. 1986. *Silent Partners.* New York: Times.

Regan, T. 1983. *The Case for Animal Rights.* Berkeley and Los Angeles: University of California Press.

Rosenfield, L. C. 1968. *From Beast-Machine to Man-Machine.* New York: Octagon.

Rowan, A.N. 1987. Editorial. *Anthrozoos* 1:63–64.

Thomas, K. 1983. *Man and the Natural World.* New York: Pantheon.

One Man and the Beasts

An Autobiographical Approach

Michael H. Robinson

The relationship between man and beast has many manifestations. Originally it was almost certainly a predator-to-prey, hunter-to-hunted, interaction. In certain areas this interaction could have fluctuated from man's being the hunter to his being the hunted, so that animals engendered fear and respect as well as hunger. During this long hunting and gathering period, man certainly developed a sense of fascination and wonder that attached to animals, and this led to the first graphic art. The cave paintings of early man have been subject to a wide range of functional interpretations, but whatever their purpose, they are undoubtedly a reflection of the central place of animals in the life of primitive man. Animals figured in the first attempts at written language and undoubtedly featured in the first spoken language. Egyptian hieroglyphics feature a wide range of mammals, birds, and insects and speak powerfully of early civilization's closeness to the natural world. They have a marvelous sense of the quiddity of the animals and foreshadow the 20th-century phenomenon of the logo. Art, literature, music, magic, and religion have reflected the central role of the man-beast relationship in human life, and the beasts are always present in all these cultural elements. Biology is an intellectualization of man's fascination with the living world, and the history of how one person became a biologist can shed light on the wider phenomenon of the man-beast relationship. That is what this essay is about; it is about what E. O. Wilson called biophilia in a powerfully poetic and passionate book of that title. In this case it is also an explanation of apparent egocentrism.

A history of biology has been attempted several times but has not yet been written. Clearly the subdisciplines of zoology and botany are not equivalent, either in their origins or rate of development. Interestingly enough, the first recorded collections of nondomestic animals and plants probably occurred around the same time. The pharaonic collection of wild animals at Saqqara is said to have contained 1,134 gazelles, 1,305 oryxes, and 1,244 other antelopes. It dates to around 2500 B.P. and its function is not entirely clear. Royal menageries were, in general, prestige collections, but the size of this one suggests that it could have been a breeding farm as well. If so, history repeats itself, because the Arabian oryx has been rescued from extinction by a zoo breeding program. A very early botanic garden was the Shen Ming gardens in China. Collections of plants were from the start associated with medicine, and botanic gardens have a continuing firm association with science. There are clearly whole series of confluent trends in the origins of biology, or more loosely in the study of plants and animals. Like astronomy, which had practical application in predicting seasonal phenomena, animal and plant studies were, at the start, almost surely utilitarian in intent. Studying animal behavior would aid the hunter both directly, to predict the movement of prey animals, and indirectly, in providing the raw materials of sympathetic magic. Even today many dances of hunting tribes accurately portray aspects of the behavior of the hunted. It is interesting to speculate whether these dances served some intrinsic function or, like millennial movements, simply lived on despite their failure to produce results. Perhaps they were closer to the "vacuum activities" of animals denied the "normal" outlet for a powerful drive.

It is easy to see how accurate "biological" observations, clearly reflected in the detailed precision of Stone Age art, could lead eventually to domestication attempts that were guided by real insights into animal nature. The shaman may have been a good intuitive ecologist as well as an experienced astronomer and meteorologist. Clearly the next step in the evolution of biology involved domestication and selective breeding. These revolutionary biological experiments involved plants and animals. The wild sources of all major crops have very low yields, and they must have been improved quite rapidly as civilization developed and villages grew to be cities. Along the way a rudimentary science of anatomy grew out of butchering food. Medieval butchers recognized many anatomical structures even if they did not call "tubes" arteries or "windpipes" tracheas. The steps from Aristotle to Harvey, Malpighi, Leeuwenhoek, Linnaeus, Pasteur, and Darwin are ones of degree and not of revolution. There is no doubt that all along the line the sense of wonder played a part. Animals and plants were not merely useful as food, or drugs, or medicines, or laborers, or companions, or scapegoats, or sacrifices to the gods; they were also marvels and often seemed to be signposts to a Creator.

So why did I become a biologist? Looking back more than 50 years, I have absolutely no doubt that the origins of my interests in the living world are affectional as opposed to rational. Some memories stand out from the dim crepuscular gloom of childhood and early puberty. They flash like shooting stars on the retina of the mind, and their light comes from something that is past and gone forever. A substantial part of these memories comes from ego-gratifying events, but many are of experiences connected with the living world and, in particular, with animals. I can trace some of these recollections much further back than I thought possible. One, in particular, must go back to the age of 3 or 4. My mother wheeled me to a nearby public park in a stroller, and there, on the grass, I encountered the red furry bee. This was the early 1930s in Preston, Lancashire, England, Europe, the World, the Universe, and so on (as I later inscribed in my school notebooks). The bee was a glorious velvety red and crawled into small holes in the soil, beneath the grass. Inside the hole it buzzed in an exciting way.

The reappearance of this insect in my life, 20 years later, was one of those strange coincidences that would have impressed Shakespeare with his belief in "the star-crossed" hand of fate. After miserable days of military service as a conscript in the Royal Air Force, itself a life in succession to 5 arduous and soul-shattering years as an apprentice bricklayer, I escaped to Teacher's Training College. This is a peculiarly British institution that trains teachers in a 2-year course. I intended to get back to my adolescent passion for biology after the years of bleeding fingers on the building sites and the ego-destroying sarcasm of the drill corporals. It turned out to be a blessed 2 years of intellectual challenge, regained self-respect, and glorious freedom. It was at college that I reencountered the red furry bee. By a ridiculous quirk of fate, I had chosen the only college in the country where the biology lecturer was an enthusiastic field entomologist. More improbably still, the man was one of the fewer than 10 entomologists in Europe who knew anything about solitary bees. Despite being a poor teacher, he conveyed his enthusiasm for this group to me when I was ripe to acquire an outlet for my chaotically unfocused interest in animals! The solitary bees are a widespread group of hymenopterans that live alone, in contradistinction to the honeybees and bumblebees that live in colonies and are true social insects. They have extraordinarily diverse habits, are relatively unstudied, and are quite common despite their unfashionableness among amateur entomologists. With the dedication of a neophyte, I started spending my abundant spare time pursuing these insects with entomological net and insect-killing bottle. This sparked the improbable conjunction: the red furry bee of my early childhood was the commonest bee in Cheshire, on the college doorstep! I learned that it was really *Andrena armata,* a burrowing insect that is really as remarkable as my long-lasting memory of it would warrant. Actually it is only the female that is clothed in lustrous red hair, the texture of rich velvet and as impressive as the royal robes of the queen. The male is much less hairy and much less magnificent.

The passion for collecting can become an end in itself, but somehow I escaped the full course of the disease. I had the fever but never reached the syncope. Instead I became obsessed by the process of species determination, embroiled in the inexorable logic of using a dichotomous identification key. This process, which is a stepwise process of elimination, has much of the same satisfaction as crossword puzzling. It also embroiled me in a return to the despised and rejected Latin of my ancient grammar school. The entomological language of the keys was unfindable in the dictionary, unfathomable, and inexplicable. Later in life when I heard nothing but Spanish for days on end, my mind would buzz with a babble of half-understood words whenever it was unoccupied. Similarly, at an earlier stage, in the midst of key mania it would buzz with the Latin- or Greek-derived in-language of entomology. Glabrous, hirsute, cinereous, fulvous, fuscous, griseous, testaceous, pictous, tomentose, punctate, pubescent, and a host of other adjectives attached themselves to the laterofrontal margins, declivities, and distal portions of bees' bodies and legs. Wow! True education really sets in when you are driven to solve a problem because you desperately want to know the answer. Not only was this a language to show off with, but it was an intellectual puzzle for a mind freshly released from the groves of bricks and mortar. Even better was the fact that, in pursuing the bees to kill and then pin them in ordered squads, I was forced to find them. This led me to study the flowers that they visited for pollen and nectar. I thus became an enthusiastic amateur botanist—the "sublime consequence of a meaner motive." Not only did I need to identify the flowers to record the collection data, but I needed to "know their seasons," to know when they would bloom, and also to know their ecological distribution. All this challenged the computing power of the brain as well as the sharpness of the eye and the swiftness of the net-wielding arm. Finally I made the final transition to inductive science. What I accumulated in my head gave rise to questions and hypotheses.

Through all this I reveled in the beauty of the beasts. The wonderful pantaloon pollen baskets of *Dasypoda hirtipes* and the startling green eyes, actually jade green eyes, of *Coelioxys canoidea.* From form came function. I started asking how? One bee that I loved was a fine long-tongued bee belonging to the genus *Osmia.* These bees build their cells, to raise their young, in holes in wood. Some species like *Osmia rufa* will use any suitable hole that they can find and have been known to enter old-fashioned keyholes and glue up locks with their building material. My osmia, the golden osmia, *Osmia aurantia,* builds its cells inside empty snail shells in sand-dune areas. In such places snails perish and their shells linger on to become homes for the nurseries of golden-haired bees. Here followeth my first scientific question. The bee builds the first cell inside the inner whorl of the shell, provisions it with pollen, lays an egg, seals the cell, and then repeats the process. Eventually, after 5 or 6 cells are built, the bee reaches the outside and closes the door. The end result is a succession of cells occupying a spiral corridor with the oldest inside. I hope the question is obvious. The inside cell should contain the oldest pupa, which should hatch first. If it does, what stops it from blundering out and wreaking havoc on all the younger pupae that block its runway to freedom? Lots of lovely hypotheses are possible. Since the inner cell is in a narrow part of the shell, the pupa could be constricted into prolonged development; or it could be smaller and therefore unable to fight its way out; or the bees, being related, could adjust their emergence patterns to an orderly procession by buzzing little messages to each other; or the food supply could be adjusted so that the outer bee pupated first; and so on and so on.

What a nice puzzle. I never solved it because I was never around in early spring when the bees hatched, and I was too unsophisticated to experiment. But I could solve it now. And I would like to try, but those sand dunes of my youth have disappeared under the ticky-tacky boxes of the burgeoning bourgeoisie. The red furry bee has disappeared from that park in Preston because the park has become a remote island in an ocean of concrete, brick, and asphalt. Are there bees in St. Anne's or Newhaven or at the town dump at Launceston, or have their food plants been blasted by the herbicides in the name of tidiness? Dylan Thomas fantasized about when he was young and "there were wolves in Wales." They were only in his imagination, but when I was young, there were masterpieces in the meadows, bees the like of which we may never see again.

Another one of those momentous moments occurred when I was 12 or 13. By that time I had joined the local Scientific Society, a not-yet-moribund relic of the intense Victorian zeal for learning. It met 5 nights a week. Monday night was biology and natural history, Tuesday night was photography, Wednesday night astronomy, and so on. I attended the lectures on Monday and rambles on the weekend. It was after a pond-dipping ramble that we were admitted to the laboratory room, where in padlocked cabinets there were gleaming brass microscopes. These museum pieces were a forbidden joy, an addict's delight, released like drugs from their sealed and secured fastnesses on very rare occasions. It was there, at 10 Red Lion Chambers, that I saw my first *Stentor,* my first *Volvox,* and my first *Vorticella*—all in the same afternoon. *Stentor* is trumpet shaped, hence the wonderful word *stentorian* that so describes a particular kind of trumpeting upper-class English type. The animal is a ciliate, one of the microscopic hairy ones, which attaches itself to a substrate and then uses a specialized crown of hairs to create a vacuum-cleaner current into its gullet. That sweeps up masses of the bacteria upon which it feeds. One species is as blue as a sapphire.

Either one is profoundly moved by the experience of descending a microscope tube into a tiny bright world of water, or one simply yawns. For me it was a concentrated magical experience. Only recently I recaptured that innocent delight in the National Zoo's new Invertebrate Exhibit, where we have set up a MicroTheatre. This is a microscope connected to a huge television screen through a videocamera. Our keepers take water out of our long-established seawater tanks, put a drop under the microscope, and do a Jules Verne voyage of "Twenty Thousand Microns under the Lens." This particular Saturday morning our operator had found a radiolarian, a tiny protist related to *Amoeba.* There it was, with immensely long narrow pseudopodia radiating out from a complex geometric minishell, its so-called test. I could see granules streaming inside the extraordinary pseudopods. Each pseudopod looked like an aerial view of a freeway with diminutive cars speeding along it. It dawned on me that I had never seen a live radiolarian, and I was awed by the utter complexity of this tiny, organless, unicellular, and supposedly simple life-form. Without an organized and delimited nervous system, it was under more complex internal control than a macrocomputer. Even a jaded administrator can marvel.

Life in water has a quality that can be totally absorbing. Sir Alistair Hardy, an engagingly eccentric former professor of zoology at Oxford, has proposed that man first arose as a recognizable human on the seashore and not in the forest. This would certainly explain a lot. For me a memory akin to that of the red furry bee concerns my first aquarium. It was an out-of-the-blue present from my father, who managed a corn, feed, and pet shop. He knew all sorts of odd people, which accounts for the almost anachronistic gift, in the mid 1930s, of a tank of tropical fishes. I was led into the best room of the house, reserved for the vicar's infrequent visits, Saturday night bridge games, and damned piano practice. There in the dark was a glowing jewel, a lambent startling surprise, a small aquarium illuminated from below and packed with brightly colored fishes. There was a black molly, a small angel, and a swordtail of sorts. How can I possibly remember that? It was at least 50 years ago, and I was certainly no more than 6 years old. By the time I was 14 I was the youngest ever secretary of the Preston Aquarists' Society, fanatical about fishes and breeding cichlids, nandids, and anabantids. The first fishes that I ever bred were paradise fish, from tropical Asia. I can still remember the strikingly iridescent nuptial colors of the male, flashing like a neon sign. He was transmogrified by sex from a plain, pale, totally unremarkable beast into a glowing and resplendent gem. Later I watched his parental patience as he caught the young dropping out of his surface nest of bubbles and repeatedly spat them back to its protection. I still remember a holiday in Devon, 2 years before the start of World War II, when I first peered into a rock pool and was so excited by the colorful microcosm of blennies, gobies, starfish, and sea anemones that I dipped my face into the water in my enthusiasm for getting closer. The same holiday I had a painful tooth abscess that the doctor said would "have to be lanced." What a verb to use in front of a kid who was steeped in Ivanhoe! Somebody left the tap running in our room and the subsequent flood brought down a large area of the ornate ceiling of the hotel restaurant. Was I the guilty party? I don't remember, but I do remember the sea anemones and the gigantic school of sand eels that I saw on a boat trip! Years later I now have a 130-gallon aquarium in my office and have spent many years in the tropics with many of the species from the aquarists' bible, Innes's *Exotic Aquarium Fishes* almost on my doorstep.

Later, as a schoolteacher, I built a saltwater aquarium for the classroom and kept a wide range of littoral species in it. That was in Cornwall, where I taught biology in a girls' grammar school. I was hired as biology teacher without a degree because, I think, the headmistress knew I was a better teacher than the applicant with a degree. This was another long shot in life's improbable lottery. The position of biology teacher in a school that prepared girls for university education allowed me to catch up the lost years of blue-collar work and prepare myself for university. As I taught, so I also learned, and secretly passed the examinations that I was preparing my pupils to take. At last, with courses passed in zoology, botany, and geology, I was eligible for university entrance and was admitted at the age of 31.

It was a nerve-wracking experience competing with kids straight from school with "the light of science in their eyes" and a youthful facility for learning. Could I keep up with them? I had chosen the University College of Swansea, in Wales, because it had a spanking new natural sciences center, was on the beautiful Gower coast, and had a faculty known and respected by the only professional biologist that I knew. It was a good choice. The Welsh have a great feeling for education and, paradoxically, for the majesty of the English language. I was sublimely happy and spent 3 wonderful years lapping up excitement. The head of the Zoology Department, "The Prof," as he was known, was an impossibly discursive lecturer. Students threw up their hands in despair at sorting out any thread from his courses, but if you really listened, he was scattering pearls at every breath. Provocative, challenging, rambling, hopelessly disorganized, he was a true scholar of incredible breadth. He did me a world of good. I realized how much there was to think about, not merely how much there was to learn. Not only that, but he inspired in me a lifelong affection for marine polychaete worms as well as a detailed knowledge of the classification of the reptiles. The final examinations were a nightmare of stress, but it came out right in the end and I obtained the standard of degree necessary to be accepted for graduate studies at Oxford.

By this stage I had decided that I wanted to become an ethologist and study under Niko Tinbergen. I had read *The Study of Instinct,* which gave me the same blinding sense of revelation that I had found in the theory of evolution. Reading Konrad Lorenz's *King Solomon's Ring* and *Man Meets Dog* confirmed my resolution. Before my final examinations, I went up to Oxford to be interviewed. Students from red-brick universities do not enter easily through the "needle's eye" gate to Oxford. Meeting Niko was an experience that he himself would have called "crazy," meaning remarkable. He was a white-haired, chain-smoking ball of energy with a marked Dutch accent. His eyes twinkled like a bird's, and he talked enthusiastically about research topics while miming the subjects. As he hand-rolled crazily crumpled cigarettes, he talked with a kind of electrostatic enthusiasm. While talking, he flitted about his office, popping up as a black-headed gull in one corner, imitating its head-flagging display, while being totally embroiled in a stickleback story in another corner. It was a charismatic *tour de force;* I would have followed him to the gates of hell!

Oxford turned out to be upper-class, snooty, condescending, and saved only by the remarkable collection of characters in the Animal Behaviour Research Group. This, in 1963–66 was a breccia of eccentric, egotistic, friendly, helpful, tolerant, and downright brilliant people. The improbable band of biologists included Cullen, Dawkins, MacFarland, Delius, Impekhoven, Kruuk, Henty, Hansell, and Mash. Amazing grace. They filled me with a deep sense of inferiority and helped me mightily. Those were great years; lunchtime conversations turned into profound seminars, and the whole thing hinged on a dialectical exchange of ideas that is certainly the lost great attribute of medieval learning. We surely shall not see its like again. My research subject dealt with the behavior of tropical insects, and my research room/office had to be maintained at a stifling heat. This foreshadowed my future, which turned again in one of those rotation points of chance, which, if one were not rational, could only be attributed to fate. Niko decided that I should really spend some time in the tropics studying the wild life of my tropical insects and their predators. Almost on cue, his former student Martin Moynihan came through Oxford on a trip. Moynihan is one of the great names in gull studies and was a legend among Niko's crew. He was then director of the Canal Zone Biological Area, a research bureau of the Smithsonian Institution, centered on Barro Colorado Island in Panama. Here was a tropical connection at last, and he happened to be carrying in his pocket, so to speak, the Smithsonian's first-ever fellowships in tropical biology. I was offered and accepted one of these munificent (by British standards) grants.

I spent 9 months as a student on Barro Colorado Island, was stupefied by the biological richness of the tropical rainforest, and wanted nothing better than to stay there for the rest of my life. Before I returned to Oxford, an unexpected job opportunity came up at Barro Colorado and, miracle of miracles, it was offered to me. I seized it like a terrier grabs a rat. At that stage I would have taken a job as a boatman or a carpenter just to stay there. From red furry bees I had finally progressed to my goal. I had become a professional biologist in a biologist's paradise. I was being paid for doing what I would have given my right ear for the chance to do.

In time the Canal Zone Biological Area became the Smithsonian Tropical Research Institute, and I traveled to do research in Africa; Asia; Papua, New Guinea; Australia; and South America. The dull moments were very few and the frustrations many, but the constant input of things to wonder at and wonder about never ceased. If I had not been at Oxford at that particular time, it is unlikely that I would have spent half my life in the tropics. I would never have shared my life, for nearly 2 years, with an otter; would never have lived with a kinkajou, a crab-eating raccoon, and a jaguarundi or become fascinated by spiders. The otter I raised from a pup that I found dying in Panama's Mercado Central. He had been caught by fishermen when they trapped his mother in a seine net. Though unweaned, he was being offered raw fish by his captors. Fearing that this appealing animal might die, I bought him for $5. Because the animal was interesting and exciting, I called him Niko. He prospered on a diet of egg-fortified cows milk and eventually grew to over 25 pounds, utterly imprinted and absurdly tame. Niko was unsurpassed among the wild species with which I have shared my life. He also inadvertently provided me with a new insight into arthropod defensive systems and triggered a research project. We walked together daily along the trails of Barro Colorado Island, and Niko particularly enjoyed flopping and splashing along the streambeds. One day on Lutz Creek we scared up one of the highly specialized terrestrial crab species. Because the crab moved, he attacked it, and in the melee of snapping, rolling over, and head-tossing, something happened so quickly that I missed it. But the end result soon became obvious: Niko returned to me yelping with pain with a crab's detached claw firmly attached to his soft upper lip. I pulled it off as painlessly as possible and was about to throw it away when the uniqueness of it all dawned on me. This cheliped had broken off at its basal joint. Was this autotomy, the deliberate shedding of an appendage? If so, it was a new kind of autotomy, not comparable to the shedding of a lizard's tail or an insect's leg. In this case the shed appendage "bit" into the predator. It was actively attacking after it had been jettisoned. All this led to an extensive cooperative research project designed to test the reactions of a series of crab species to attacks by mammalian predators. Since we could not use Niko as our attack dog on the beaches of Panama, we simply mounted a teddy bear on a long pole and used its furriness as a substitute for a live mammal. The crowds on some of the beaches must have thought that this was some kind of bizarre and exotic perversion that was peculiar to crazy gringos. However, we did prove our point. This *was* a previously undescribed form of defense. We called it attack autotomy. The subsequent description of this study, in *Science,* should have included Niko as a contributor; he did at least appear on the cover of that issue, looking characteristically smug. At one point during the study, I allowed a crab to autotomize its claw on my first finger, to determine how long it would continue to exert enough force to cause pain. In the written description of this incident, I referred to being sufficiently "anesthetized by consuming a bottle of Mateus Rose to sustain the pain for over five minutes"; the editor was either a purist or a moralist and cut out that entire section.

Living with a female jaguarundi provided another insight, this time about learning processes. These are the delight of experimental psychologists. The cat in question was being studied by Griff Ewer, a remarkable mammalian ethologist who died tragically, soon after her sabbatical in Panama. She was studying the behavior of the little-known cats and mustelids of Central America and had a large collection of hand-raised animals living *en famille* with her. There is a limit to the number of margays, tayras, grisons, and jaguarundis with whom one can share a house and still remain sane. Griff's threshold for destructivity and chaos was conspicuously higher than that of most other people, but she still had a limit. Jackie, the jaguarundi, was beyond that limit and was consequently boarded out with me. During the months that I shared a bed with Jackie, I learned, among other things, that jaguarundis urinate in water. This revelation came about the hard way. Jackie refused the normal cat box and, by day, simply urinated on the tiled house floor. This was perfectly acceptable, since it could be easily mopped up and left no permanent effect. However, at night she slept in a warm hollow at the small of my back and would not spoil her relaxation by getting up to urinate on the floor. I woke frequently to a warm glow. The discovery of the water-box solution came by chance. One day she stood in the raccoon's water manipulation tray and used that; afterward we provided a water-filled cat box.

The important insight came when my wife reported that Jackie started vocalizing at the precise moment when I turned into the driveway of the house, just before I arrived home. Jaguarundis whistle a high-pitched, birdlike contact call. This may be a vocal deception device to fool potential prey when the cats are hunting. The Robinson house was in a district 20 miles north of Panama City right off the main Interamerican Highway, an extremely busy and noisy road. The driveway was at least 200 feet long, and yet this cat could pick up the sound of my car, a Renault 16, amid all the other traffic. It had learned this during its relatively short stay. What was the reward in this extraordinary learning paradigm? Play! Every night when I returned home, I had a long period of rough-and-tumble play with Jackie. We chased, wrestled, pounced, and play-fought. The cat must have anticipated this play as the highlight of the day. There is no other explanation I can think of for such a finely tuned behavior. And, no, my arrival times were too irregular for her to be consulting a biological clock.

Becoming obsessed by the biology of spiders was another piece of happenstance. At Swansea that innovative ecologist, Amyan Macfadyen, had taught our undergraduate course on arachnids. This turned me on to a previously unknown subject. I became fascinated by the complexity of the airs and variations that arachnids play on the themes of their anatomy and life-style. They are a class of arthropods fundamentally more variable than the insects. Their superbly sculptured bodies excited me; they were marvelous material for an exercise in evolutionary speculation. Despite this, I would have remained an arachnological dilettante if I had stayed in England. The spider fauna of that "blessed Isle" is depauperate and relatively inconspicuous. The climate militates against spiders being present for long periods or their attaining much diversity or complexity. Despite these inauspicious conditions, there has been a plethora of prominent British arachnologists. It started with Dr. Muffet: "Little Miss Muffet, sat on a tuffet eating her curds and whey, when along come a spider" and so on. The good doctor, whose daughter is immortalized in that verse, started a tradition of studying British spiders and was followed by prominent twentieth-century spider men such as Theodore Savory and W. S. Bristowe. Along with British ornithologists, herpetologists, and mammalogists, they were moved not by natural wealth but by intimacy with the small-scale wonders of a very limited palette. The tropics, on the contrary, teem with arachnids, from amblipygids to scorpions. Being in Panama literally surrounded me with conspicuous and stupefyingly beautiful spiders. In the clearing on Barro Colorado Island (hereafter BCI) were dozens of silver argiopes (*Argiope argentata*). This species is singularly attractive. The females have more than half of the upper surfaces of their bodies apparently silver-plated, and build large, conspicuous webs. The males are minuscule. Days end early close to the equator and should be marked by a sundowner. That was how I started studying spiders, the sublime consequence of an alcoholic moment. Sitting on the veranda of BCI's dormitory building, watching the vista of the Panama Canal and its shipping, one could revel in that late afternoon setting for serendipity. A cold beer and conversation provided a preprandial winding down for residents. One day while at this pleasant task I started throwing insects into the nearby webs. The spider's attack behavior was startlingly efficient. It rushed down to the struggling grasshopper and enswathed it in scintillating sheets of silvery silk. The insect was entombed in seconds. This was a predatory prowess more remarkable than a tiger's muscular attack. I might have left it at that, mere admiration, if I had not chanced to throw the spider a moth. Then there was an instant change in the spider's behavior. Instead of the swaths of silk, the spider simply sank its jaws into the insect; it bit deep and long. Why did I notice? I don't know, but that one observation sparked years of spider studies. The first question was: Did the spider really have a taxonomic sense? Did it really distinguish between lepidopterans and other insects? By the time that I was sure that it did, a whole slew (a colloquial word, derived from the Irish *slaugh*) of exciting fields had opened up; the entire behavioral repertoire of the spider lay before me: courtship, mating, web-building, thermoregulation, egg-laying, antipredator responses, and so on. Eventually the questions raised as a result of the BCI "happy hour" led to broad comparative studies of the predatory behavior of many species of orb weavers. These eventually made it possible to piece together a coherent and consistent picture of how complexity could have evolved from simple beginnings. Very few things are more satisfying. Watching predatory behavior in webs that contained males soon forced spider courtship to my attention. It became obvious that the great classical studies of spider courtship, based on research on nontropical species, were seriously flawed, incomplete, and inaccurate. This realization provoked a massive comparative study of the courtship and mating behavior. When finally completed, this involved more than 50 species of web-building spiders in a great geographical spread of study sites. Apart from another evolutionary synthesis, it led to the uncovering of some bizarre details of prurient interest.

One of these is worth describing. Male spiders, when courting, approach a female that is a fierce predator. She is resident in a large trap, and the males are in some danger of being the subject of her predatory drives. In many cases they identify themselves from outside her web by attaching a silk line to it and strumming on this so-called mating thread. It has been suggested that these bouts of vibratory courtship are species recognition signals. Of course, they may also stimulate the female sexually. However, since potential prey organisms also cause vibrations, there is an ever-present prospect of confusion. In South Africa I observed a species (with no common name, but of the genus *Isoxya*) in which the male constructed his mating thread in the normal way and then did something very peculiar. Once it was in position, attached to a radius so that it connected straight to the nerve center of the web, he cut it in two and attached one cut end to his silk supply. The end that he attached was that facing the female. He bridged the gap with his body and presumably held the other cut end with one or more feet. This created a situation in which he could continuously add to the thread on the female's side by releasing silk from his spinnerets. Of course, this degree of complexity was not really obvious until the female ran out toward him as he strummed his courtship "melody." Then, if she ran too fast or too vigorously, he simply paid out more silk and there she was running hard and getting nowhere. Once she had exhausted her predatory drive, he stopped the silk production and sex predominated. I called this the "treadmill effect," but I suppose that is a sexist interpretation.

Out of all this, what are the outstanding moments of discovery and wonder? Some of them will never reach scientific publication because they are isolated and unverified. Some have been published. Some are trivial and only beautiful to *me* in the same sense that a finely detailed model ship is beautiful. I admire perfection in fineness, in the highly detailed small scale, as in a Breughel. Other discoveries are of broader significance and may even have transient importance in the progress of science. It is not egotism, I hope, to tell about some of the more memorable research occasions. It would be presumptuous to think they might help to stimulate others to look inquiringly at what they see. I am firmly convinced that the notion of a closed "guild of science," together with the witch-doctor mystique surrounding professional scientists, deters many amateurs from pursuing scientific questions. To use Tinbergen's wonderful book title, we are all "curious naturalists," and a degree does not guarantee that its owner's eyes will be perceptive. Thus some anecdotes of discovery and ratiocination.

An early moment of startlement came when I was studying stick insects (walking sticks: phasmids) at Oxford. I had huge cages of several leaf-eating species in my room and was able to watch them constantly. One species, the Javanese stick insect, *Orxines macklotti,* was particularly fine. It is very sexually dimorphic. Females are large, lichenose, and have vestigial wings. Males are smaller, attenuated, thin, and have functional wings. Many stick insects have small males, and some are entirely parthenogenetic and have thus abolished males altogether. Anyway, I was attracted to the beautiful orange and black underwings of *Orxines* and kept a bigger culture than my research merited. Because of this, I saw a pair actually start their prolonged copulation. It was easy to see pairs *in copula* because they stayed together for hours, but to be watching at that brief moment when they coupled was a very lucky chance. Luck, in this case, was enhanced because of the number of chances I had. These chances resulted from the large number of adults that I was keeping in conditions of propinquity. The mating process was bizarre, and they really did couple in the sense that a pair of railroad cars can couple. The male approached the female until he was standing on her back facing to her front. He then curled his abdomen down past her left-hand side. His next move is almost impossible to describe in words. He curled the terminal part of his abdomen into a serpentine reversed S shape. This, in fact, is the only way he can bend it so that he can easily bring the lower (ventral) surface of his abdominal apex in contact with her ventral abdomen. In this position, somehow, after much sliding and probing, the two abdomens locked together. Then the male descended to the ground on the left of the female and walked through a full circle to climb up on her right-hand side. Throughout the process they were coupled, or locked, by their abdomens. It is amazing that something that looked so bizarre can be made to sound so simple. The drawings (fig. 1) show what actually happened. It looked crazy, the S-shaped kink at the beginning of the walkabout was replaced by a comfortable looking curve at the end. I did not understand how it could happen, and sketching it out convinced me that it was geometrically impossible. However, I built a paper model of the male and female and found that it did indeed "work" the way I saw it. Anatomical studies later provided the clue to the mechanism. In essence it was simple. The male had a stiff hook close to the apex of his abdomen, on its lower surface. The complex reversed S position allowed him to insert this hook into a complementary groove on the underside of the female's abdomen, close to its apex. When hooked together he was left with what was clearly an unsustainable posture. But by circling the female he removed the kink in his tubular abdomen and brought his intromittant organs in apposition to the female's genitalia. Thus coupled (or hooked!), he could remain copulating for hours on end and also block the access of other males to the female. This was a trivial discovery, but it is a really nice mechanism, and I found it incredibly satisfying to be able to explain the apparently impossible.

That tiny piece of research, the first I ever published, established an appetite for puzzles in adaptation. Later, in Panama, when I found a large golden silk orb-web spider, *Nephila clavipes,* with 15 tiny Drosophila-like flies sitting on its back, I knew that this was another trivial but provocative

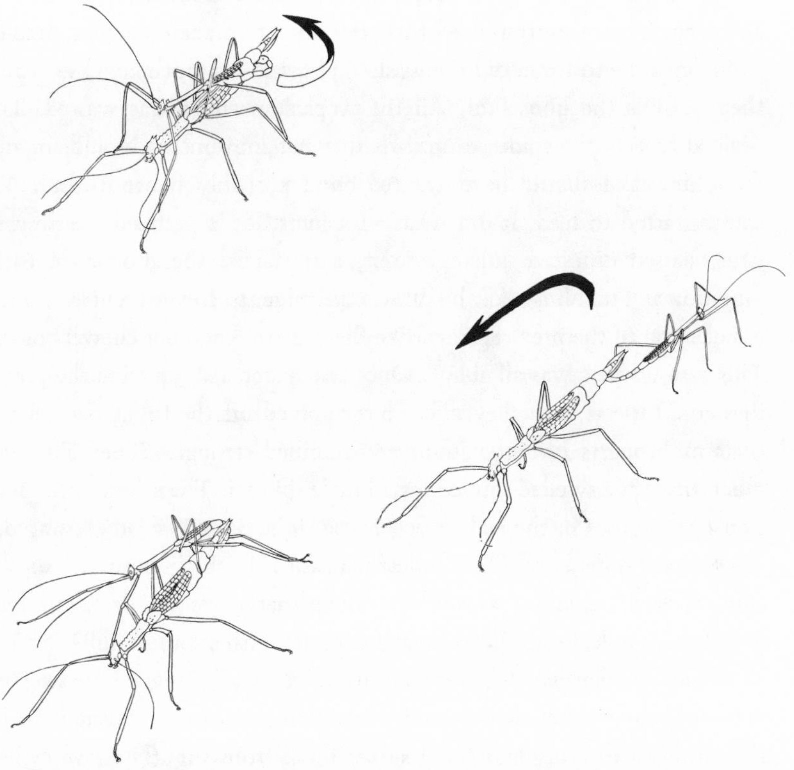

Fig. 1. Stick insect *Orxines macklotti* circling into copulatory position (see text). *Top left:* Start, male mounts left hand side of female, circles; *Center:* Pair are facing away from each other; *Lower left:* Final position—male abdomen to right of female.

puzzle. The flies were packed together like airplanes on the flight deck of an aircraft carrier. What were they doing there? Flies don't belong on spiders. To solve this problem meant being able to produce a magnified view of these tiny beasts to see whether they were feeding on the spider. Flies are all suckers; their mouthparts can't cope with solid food. So I had to first invent and then make some equipment. This is always fun and also an ego-boosting chance to show off ingenuity. I finished up by mounting a stereoscopic binocular microscope on a focusing rail attached to a camera tripod. This I could set up so that I could view the vertically oriented spider through the horizontal microscope, and focus on the flies on its cephalothorax (front end). All this ingenuity was actually in vain because the flies were not doing anything. They simply moved their feet, fluttered their wings sporadically, and from time to time, did the wash- and brush-up movements so typical of their cousins the houseflies. All the workshop effort was wasted. Then I decided to feed the spider to see whether her movements would stir up the flies. Eureka! I should have shouted but I probably swore instead. As the spider started to feed, it did what all spiders do; it grabbed the prey in its jaws, passed digestive juices into it, and started the process of external digestion and nibbling. All this allows the spider to create a *bouillon d'insecte,* a liquefaction of the prey. Spiders, like flies, are suckers, not chewers of solids. This was what it was all about. Once the spider had liquefied the prey, the flies could use it, and they did. They zoomed off the flight deck, lowered their mouthparts into the soup, and imbibed strongly. They absorbed so much that they swelled into distorted little spheres. The whole crazy association put the flies in the right place at the right time to steal a strong drink. There was no name for this kind of parasitism in the literature. I suggested *dipsoparasitism* or *bibiocommensalism.* These marvelous words, alas, seem to have fallen on deaf ears. Lives there a scientist with a soul so dull?

A more expansive discovery occurred in Wau, New Guinea. There I worked frequently at night using a headlight, a battery-powered flashlight that attaches to a headband and shines forth from slightly above eye level. With it, one can see at night without having one's hands full. It is a great aid to field research, and if Darwin had possessed one during the voyage of HMS *Beagle,* he might well have discovered a nocturnal fauna as broad and seminal as the diurnal fauna that he described so accurately and lovingly. It is disturbing to think that a whole biosphere remained unexplored until the dry cell was invented and the flashlight replaced the oil lantern and candle power. Wallace would, perhaps, have been even more productive than Darwin if some genie had provided him with a headlight! He lived in the tropics and was not just a passerby. Anyway, at night in Wau I came across a very strange orb web that raised a whole series of why and how questions and eventually filled in a space or two in the incomplete jigsaw puzzle of evolution. Conventional orbs are essentially wheel-like structures with sticky silk laid in a spiral on top of the spokes. The dry-silk frame of the web, containing the spokes and spiral, is attached to suitable anchors and holds the whole thing aloft, usually in the flight paths of insects. The viscid spiral is the only sticky part, and it transforms the dry-silk frame into a trap that is operated by the spider with commendable speed and efficiency. Some insects nevertheless escape the tigerish web owner. Among the insects that have a high escape potential are the butterflies and moths. They have large wings covered in loose wing scales, and when they strike a web, the wing scales slip off onto the glue. This inactivates the trap because the glue is fouled up. Some spiders have escalated the arms race by devising new versions of the original trap (in an evolutionary sense, that is). Thereby hangs this tale, to anticipate.

The strange Wau web was triangular in shape and strung horizontally between the branches of a bush. It was clearly derived from an orb because it was a sector of a circle, like a slice of pie out of a circular dish. It had 3 spokes, and between them were the derivatives of the sticky spiral, but here there was a striking departure from "normal." This was *not* the usual section of viscid spiral. Rather, instead of the sticky strands being taut and under tension, they hung in deep loops between the horizontal supports. In the light of the headlamp the drops of glue glistened like diamonds, and the illusion of jewelry was heightened because they hung down in deep loops. For all the world they looked like strings of beads hanging from some sort of silken display stand. The spider sat at the apex of the triangle, touching the three spokes, waiting. Why? How? What on earth? The questions were obvious. The answer was not. The first clue came when a moth came flying toward my headlight, fluttering across my field of vision. Serendipity again? It struck the hanging beads and stuck. At that instant the outer end of the sticky thread detached from the web frame, this left it attached only on the center thread. The moth was then stuck to a hanging line. The whole structure was transformed, the moth flew round and round the axis of the thread's attachment like a model airplane on a string. At this stage the spider rushed along the central radius and hauled up the moth "hand over hand" to bite it. The whole thing was reminiscent of an angler playing and landing a fish. This sectorial and specialized derivative of an orb web was a three-dimensional trap. Further experimentation proved that the outer ends of the viscid loops were attached to the frame by low shear joints. Since these broke under light loads, an insect's impact immediately severed them. The whole thing, when sprung, shock-absorbed the initial tearing impact that often allows an insect to escape from a fixed web. It was clearly a specialized moth trap.

Not only was the new-style web intrinsically interesting but it also provided a link with the evolution of such specialized "webs" as that of the bolas spider. This device, a single line with a single blob of glue, was described later by my friend Bill Eberhard. In the process of puzzling out the link, I found an interesting description of an unusual web that is built by an Australian orb weaver. This web is a complete horizontal orb, circular and, as such, not unusual. But the description emphasizes its *most unusual* hanging sticky threads, clearly like those of my Wau web. Since it was a full orb, not a segment, it qualified as the precursor from which the Wau web could have been derived, by reduction. I eventually saw one of these webs and was able to confirm my suspicions that its discoveror, Australian film-maker and naturalist Densey Clyne, had missed the low shear joints that are crucial to its operation. Bill Eberhard's story of the bolas spider is an exciting one. His spider, closely related to the Wau species, builds a single thread terminating in one drop of glue, which it holds dangling from one leg. It is called a bola spider because the thread is periodically whirled around. Unlike the gaucho's bolas, the thread is never released and thrown, so the name is something of a misnomer. In fact, the spider itself actually attracts moths by producing a bodily secretion that mimics a female moth's sex-attractant pheromone. If that were not enough, the glue on the bolas is a superglue.

These are a few snatches from moments of elation, wonder, and dawning discovery. There were also moments of sensual delight, like seeing my first saki monkey in Amazonian Colombia. This monkey is known in Spanish as a *volador,* since, with outstretched plumed tail, it seems to fly as it leaps from tree to tree. On this same list I must include waking in Panama to find the footprints of an ocelot in the sand of the riverbank next to my al fresco sleeping bag; finding the porcelainlike azure blue eggs of a tinamou; spotting that improbable bird, the lesser potoo, which almost exactly mimics a broken branch by day; hearing my first electric fish buzzing in the earphones of the electronically transduced electric-fish detector; watching free-living black palm cockatoos flying over the coastal forests of New Guinea; and a host of other joys. Inevitably this all left me with a fundamental concern for the future of tropical habitats and, in particular, for the fate of the rain forests and coral reefs. These habitats are the treasuries, the Fort Knoxes, of life on earth. They contain the richest and most diverse assemblages of animals that have ever occurred in the history of our planet. They are irreplaceable galleries of evolutionary masterworks. All this is pointed out by Norman Myers in a later essay herein.

Living in the tropics also put me face-to-face with the human dilemma facing all the Third World tropical peoples. There is no doubt that the international class division into rich and poor nations must be abolished. Unfortunately, the present and most expeditious way to do this involves destroying the treasure houses of evolution to advance the condition of man. Conservationists often argue that all we need to do to solve the problem is to increase environmental education. This is the height of enlightenment folly. No amount of education can divert us from this disastrous scenario. We destroy the tropics not out of ignorance but because of urgent human needs, political pressures, and economic expediency. Is there any hope? I think so. After a lifetime of involvement in science, I now believe even more strongly than ever that there are no problems that are beyond the capacity of the human intellect. We only need to provide the resources for a massive program in tropical biology, in the broad sense (and of course I include anthropology, sociology, agronomy, forestry, animal husbandry, and medicine as subdisciplines of biology), to find a solution to our fundamental problem: how to develop the tropics without destroying their biological heritage. Niko Tinbergen once neatly reversed the World War II slogan "Give us the tools and we'll finish the job" to read "Give us the jobs and we'll produce the tools." We could produce the tools to save the tropics if somebody, somewhere, assigned the job to the legion of bright youngsters with the "light of science in their eyes," and idealism in their hearts.

At this point I should have moved the cursor down the file menu to "quit," clicked the mouse, and left the word-processing program. Enough is enough. But I suddenly had that feeling in the abdominal plexus that comes with the cold realization of mistakes. After the final zoology practical examination, flushed with euphoria, you hear someone say, "Did you recognize the transverse section of *Amphioxus?*" and you realize that you identified it as a section of the larva of a lamprey. It was a lamprey and all the class were wrong, but that is another story. The cold feeling over this spate of recollections came when it dawned on me that I had completely ignored the influence of man (actually men) on my attitudes to the beasts. In an adrenalin-inspired reaction to getting ready to quit, I knew that there were some other important influences to describe. Apart from my mother's role in tolerating the smelly tadpoles and space-consuming fish tanks, I have been moved to an interest in animals by a surprisingly disparate group of humans. Up to the point of becoming a professional biologist, these were, in roughly chronological order: Thornton W. Burgess, David Seth Smith, Frank Buck, Arthur Conan Doyle, H. G. Wells, Bernard Stevenson, Julian Huxley, W. H. Hudson, Rear Admiral C. M. Beadle, J. B. S. Haldane, Niko Tinbergen, and Konrad Lorenz.

My father read Thornton W. Burgess to me when I was very young, and from the two of them I learned of such exotic beasts as beavers and muskrats (Sammy the Beaver and Jerry the Muskrat). I see no harm in anthropomorphizing animals for kids. I also had a book, by an unrecollected author, about animals in a pet shop that told their life stories after hours. When the shop was shut, the animals talked about their lives. This was an excellent plot device and I still remember "The Prairie Dog's tale."

Who was David Seth Smith? He was from the London Zoo and broadcast a regular feature on the BBC's "Children's Hour." He was known as the "Zoo Man" and from his broadcasts I learned about the discovery of the Okapi in the then Belgian Congo. Frank Buck's films, *Bring 'em Back Alive!,*" were part of my regular moviegoing diet and really excited me. Were they faked? I have not seen them as an adult, but even if they *were* faked, they profoundly influenced me. In one of them there is a sequence in which he traps a Malayan tapir, and I saw one shortly after at Dudley Zoo. Great stuff! On Barro Colorado I was to see Baird's tapirs regularly, begging for sliced loaves when life was tough in the jungle. People who think that life in the wild is innocent splendor, à la Rousseau (Jean-Jacques and the artist), should think again. For a wild tapir to brave the clearing on BCI, with all its alien stink and din, it must be driven by extreme hunger.

Arthur Conan Doyle wrote not only mystery stories, to which I have been addicted all my life, but a series of adventures in which the hero is a zoologist, Professor Challenger. In the stories Challenger is constantly at odds with a wimpish botanist, Professor Summerlee, and that situation fit all my youthful prejudices. By far the best of the Challenger stories is the exquisitely plotted *The Lost World.* This was broadcast as a serial on the BBC Children's Hour. It is a gripping story of the discovery of a plateau in South America on which prehistoric monsters survived the ice ages. The BBC produced some remarkable sound effects, and as a result, I believed for years that iguanodons hopped like kangaroos.

H. G. Wells crept into my life through my father, who had all his novels. I started with *The War of the Worlds* and finished up with *The Science of Life.* In between came *Kipps,* and some early sex education in *The Bulpington of Blup.* Wells was a biologist and it permeated all his work. *Science of Life* is a literally monumental work that he wrote with his son G. P. Wells and Sir Julian Huxley. In the mid-1930s it was a remarkable adventure in popular biology and years ahead of its time in its holism and excellent illustrations. I bought a copy recently and it is still worth reading.

Bernard Stevenson was my high school biology teacher and by far the best teacher in the entire school. I can still remember his lessons on osmosis, digestion, and suction pressure in plants. When I eventually taught the same syllabus myself, I even used his jokes: elodea (the scientific name of Canadian pond weed)—that's what telephone operators say. Pretty weak, I suppose, but memorable. Steve let me use the biology lab during the lunch hour, an unheard-of privilege.

Julian Huxley became one of my first hero figures. I guess that we all need hero figures, and the world is now pitifully short of anybody worth admiring. Huxley appeared on a BBC radio show called *The Brains Trust* where he regularly slew the philistines of nonscience; he demolished the bishops just as Thomas Henry, his uncle, flattened Wilberforce. I read his superbly crafted essays and was particularly taken by one on the size of animals. This expounded the structural limits on maximum and minimum sizes. The drawings showed the smallest and largest mammals, birds, arthropods, and so on.

W. H. Hudson stirred and focused the incipient naturalist in me. I came to his magical novel, *Green Mansions,* late in life, but read his natural history books in my teens. His book about Argentine natural history, his youth, and the development of his doubts about religion and his subsequent conversion to an evolutionary viewpoint is prose of a high order. It is called *Far Away and Long Ago,* and it took me to Strauss's *Life of Jesus* and books on evolution. Surprisingly, one of the books on evolution that I found in the local library was *A Picture Book of Evolution,* written by a nonbiologist, Rear Admiral C. M. Beadle. It armed me with all the right responses to deal with the local curate, who was teaching creationism in my confirmation classes. When did animals acquire souls? I asked indignantly.

What can one say about Haldane except that he was probably the best popularizer of science in this century. His essays were gems and they are worth reading and rereading. Niko and Konrad were both heroes before I met them, and they lived up to my picture of outstanding commanding and charismatic figures after the event. Konrad even looked like the picture of God in the illustrated family Bible. I was in New Guinea when Niko, Konrad, and Karl von Frisch were awarded the Nobel Prize. I can remember being livid with rage when a visiting New York professor of biology dismissed the award as being unwarranted. This representative of some extreme liberal (or was it lumpen Marxist?) opinion said that Niko's work was outdated, that Lorenz was a Nazi in World War II, and that all von Frisch's work had been disproved. How shortsighted can scientists become when their opinions are influenced by ideology? This is my short list of nonbeastly influences. There have been more since I joined the ranks. I have found other hero figures. I remember sitting with Theodosius Dobzhansky in the jungles of Darien . . .

In retrospect, I now know that my early absorption with wonder for the world of beasts has determined all the major features of my life. I am virtually certain that the man and beast relationship is more fundamental to human relationships than would be the case if it were simply a cultural acquisition. The enormous volume of the pet trade; the popularity of natural history programs on TV; the legion of bird watchers; the attendance at zoos that exceeds the attendance at field sports; the growth of the animal liberation movement—all these bespeak a fundamental affectional response to animals. It would not surprise me if we had, deep within us all, an innate predisposition to react to animals with curiosity, interest, and involvement. Our symbiosis with the rest of the animal kingdom is irrevocable; it may also be ancient and fundamental. What of the future? Conservation is a major issue, but there are others. For instance, I believe, at a strictly intellectual level, that biology is now as essential for a civilized and cultured system of education as theology and classical languages were once considered to be. As a zoo director I would like to transform the zoo of today into a new kind of bioexhibit: the zoo that is not, the biopark. This new entity would combine the exhibit functions of zoos, botanical gardens, arboretums, aquariums, natural history museums, and museums of man. This would be the ultimate holistic view of the living world. I would hope that it could enshrine, in the original sense of the word, a sense of wonder for the living world.

References

Hardy, A. 1960. Was Man More Aquatic in the Past? *New Scientist* 7:642–45.

Lorenz, K. 1952. *King Solomon's Ring*. London: Methuen.

______. 1954. *Man Meets Dog*. London: Methuen.

Tinbergen, N. 1951. *The Study of Instinct*. Oxford: Oxford University Press.

______. 1953. *The Herring Gull's World*. London: Collins.

______. 1958. *Curious Naturalists*. London: Country Life.

6. Have Man and the Beasts a Future?

Man's Future Needs the Beasts

Norman Myers

We share this planet with at least 5 million animal species. Of these, about 4,100 are mammals, 9,000 are birds, 6,300 are reptiles, 3,000 are amphibians, and 23,000 are fishes. These, being the vertebrates, are by far the best known of animals. Yet they make up only a small minority of all animals. The great bulk are insects and related arthropods. As the British biologist J. B. S. Haldane once remarked, God must have had "an inordinate fondness for beetles," for he made several millions of them, more than any other category of animals.

So we share the one-earth habitat with a remarkable array of other animals (also 300,000 plant species). But the estimate of 5 million species altogether could be a gross underestimate. According to some recent research by Terry Erwin and his colleagues at the Smithsonian Institution (Erwin 1987), there could well be 30 million, and conceivably 50 million, insects in tropical-forest canopies alone. It is surely a scandal of modern science that we do not know, to within an order of magnitude, how many species exist on earth—this being the sole planet in the universe, so far as we know, to support life. We now know about many other natural phenomena with extreme precision.

We can measure the distance from a given point on the earth's surface to a given point on the moon's surface, at a given point in time, to within less than half a centimeter. But when it comes to a vastly more interesting and vital topic, the plethora of life-forms that await our wonder in the world outside the window, we are absurdly ignorant.

Extinctions

Nor shall we ever know, beyond a rough idea, how many species currently exist. Without a finding-and-naming effort of exceptional scale, we shall not identify new species nearly fast enough: they are becoming extinct in huge numbers, right now. According to a strong consensus of scientific opinion, we are witnessing the demise of several species per day (Myers 1987; Raven 1987; Western & Pearl 1987; Wilson 1987). Worse, by the end of this century we may well lose at least 1 million species in tropical forests alone. Within just the next 50 years, we shall witness the demise of probably one quarter of all species and possibly one third, and conceivably one half, of all species. In terms of sheer numbers and the telescoped time scale of the phenomenon, this will be as big an extinction spasm as any since the sudden passing of the dinosaurs and their kin, plus whole assemblies of associated species, 65 million years ago.

Many people may murmur that this is all very regrettable, but we do not lose much sleep over the dodo, so why should we really worry? After all, saving species cannot rank as a "true priority" like feeding people and overcoming mass diseases. Yet wild animals, through their genetic resources and other materials, contribute to modern agriculture and medicine in all manner of unsuspected ways. Were our children to grow up into a world that has become depleted of much of its animal life, they might find themselves impoverished, not only in terms of the aesthetic beauty of the natural world, but in terms of their material welfare as well.

Contributions of Animals to Modern Agriculture

A good number of wild animal species offer potential as sources of new foods. Several dozen wild antelopes and other herbivores of African savannas are prime examples (Myers 1972), as are certain species of Amazona (Wetterberg et al. 1976). The kouprey is a secretive cowlike creature that inhabits the forests of the Thailand-Kampuchea border. The animal is believed to have been one of the wild ancestors of the humped zebu cattle of southern Asia, suggesting that fresh crossbreeding between the two bovids could boost cattle raising throughout the entire region. Regrettably, the kouprey's survival is doubtful, due to military activities within its habitats during the past 20 years. Other wild bovids of Southeast Asia's forests, such as the selatang, the tamarau, and the anoa, could help cattle husbandry. Like the kouprey, their numbers have been severely reduced through human disruption of their life-support systems.

Cattle breeds elsewhere can likewise be improved through hybridization with related species from the wild. In California, a crossbreeding of domestic cattle with bison has led to an animal that reputedly produces meat costing less than beef because of the creature's capacity to thrive on grass, without the $750 worth of feedstuffs that conventional cattle consume before slaughter. In addition, the "beefalo" can reach a weight of 450 kgs. in half the time that cattle usually take (Mason 1975). Similarly, the domestic goose could be improved by an infusion of genes from Arctic-breeding species of wild geese that feature short incubation periods and ultrarapid growth rates (Short 1976). Temperate-zone breeds could also be helped through tropical species of geese, which have a capacity to produce eggs throughout the year. And let us remember that our domestic chicken, the world's most important bird to humans, is derived from the jungle fowl, a common pheasant of Southeast Asia, where there are many other rain forest birds that offer further potential.

In similar style, cattle raising in Africa can be assisted through a highly localized breed of cattle that lives around Lake Chad. This Kuri breed of cattle is able to swim, and it feeds on lake-bottom vegetation. The breed is threatened with "genetic swamping" through excessive and haphazard crossbreeding with local zebu cattle. Also in West Africa is a dwarf shorthorn breed of cattle, the N'dama, with tolerance for trypanosomiasis disease, which limits cattle raising in some 10 million sq. kms. of Africa, or one third of the continent. Yet the N'dama is in danger of disappearing.

Finally, let us consider a form of agriculture that may prove to be one of the fastest-growing sectors of all agriculture in the foreseeable future. It may also turn out to represent the most promising means for us to grow large amounts of that critical form of food, animal protein. It is technically known as aquaculture, a term that refers to, among other things, the raising of fish in ponds. More than 90% of the fish we consume is obtained through "hunting" of wild species. Yet fish have been reared in enclosed structures, usually ponds, in Asia for at least 4,000 years. Of global fish consumption today, amounting to some 70 million metric tons (60 million from the oceans and 10 million from fresh waters), only a little over 6 million metric tons are derived from aquaculture, including 4 million of finfish and more than 1 million of mollusks such as oysters, mussels, clams, and other high-priced gourmet items. So great is the scope for increasing aquaculture that the Food and Agriculture Organization believes this practice could contribute, by the year 2000, at least 3 times more animal protein than at present, possibly 6 times more.

Specially suitable candidates for aquaculture are a number of species of the *Tilapia* genus of finfish. Originally raised by the ancient Egyptians, tilapias are now grown widely in eastern Asia. Their production doubled between 1970 and 1975 and is continuing to grow fast. So proliferate are tilapias that a hybrid species raised in garbage-enriched ponds can generate 3 metric tons per hectare in 180 days (Legner 1978). True, these figures are for well-managed ponds in the United States, using the computerized efficiency of modern agribusiness. In Cameroon, small-scale farmers' ponds regularly yield 1 to 2 metric tons of tilapias per hectare per year. But experimental farms in Africa, with year-round warmth, produce at least 20 metric tons per hectare using intensive cultivation methods, and pilot projects under optimal conditions reach 50 metric tons per hectare. All this contrasts with production of wild fish species in seas or lakes, a mere 35–60 kgs. per hectare.

A wide range of possibilities lie ahead of us when we consider the large numbers of tilapia species that we can use for selective breeding. Lake Tanganyika contains 126 endemic tilapia species, Lake Victoria 164, and Lake Malawi 196 (Lowe-McConnell 1977). These tilapia species differ from one another in their diets and breeding patterns, which suggests that a systematic approach to aquaculture could utilize combinations of tilapia species in order to expand the protein yield. Different species could divide up the food supplies of a pond much as they divide up the food supplies in each of the three great African lakes, efficiently exploiting many food types that would not be consumed by a single species. But just as we are becoming aware of the immense potential of tilapias as a source of that prized food form, animal protein, the wild stocks are running into trouble. In Lake Victoria, introduced predators, among other problems, are likely to reduce the flock of endemics by 80%–90% within another decade at most (Barel et al. 1985). An even greater tragedy could be in the making at Lake Malawi, with almost 500 endemic fish species (the lake is only one eighth the size of North America's Great Lakes, which feature a mere 173 species, fewer than 10% of them endemic). Lake Malawi is threatened not only through proposed introduction of alien species but through pollution from industrial installations.

Contribution of Animals to Modern Medicine

Animals contribute to modern medicine in a broad variety of ways. Blowfly larvae secrete a substance, alantoin, that promotes healing of deep wounds, decaying tissues, and osteomyelitis. The European blister beetle provides cantharidin, used in the treatment of disorders in the urogenital system. The bloodsucking leech contains hirudin, a material that serves as a valuable anticoagulant of human blood. Even the venom of several creatures helps modern medicine. Bee venom is used to counter arthritis. The venom of several snake species can be utilized as a nonaddictive painkiller, and offers promise for treatment of thrombotic disorders (Neill 1974). A snake of Brazil, the jaceracea (about 2 meters long), harbors material in its venom for the drug captopril, which helps many of the 25 million Americans who suffer from high blood pressure and other hypertension problems; captopril is especially helpful for those people who fail to respond to conventional treatments. The venom of a Malaysian pit viper related to the rattlesnake is commonly used as an anticoagulant, an agent that prevents the formation of blood clots that may cause heart attacks. Even toads may assist us. All toads secrete skin substances with toxic chemicals that could one day yield important drugs. An unusually good source could be the Houston toad—one of the most endangered vertebrates in the United States.

Not only can animals yield drugs, they can help the medical cause in indirect fashion. Malaria ranks among the most widespread diseases on earth. Reduced to low levels by insecticides during the 1950s, it has bounced back as mosquitoes have become resistant to toxic chemical sprays. So an answer may lie with a larvivorous fish, known scientifically as *Gambusia* and popularly as "the mosquito fish." It gobbles up insect larvae in its native habitats (Legner & Fisher 1980). A similar function is performed in California by certain flatworms of the genus *Mesotoma,* which paralyze mosquito larvae in rice fields (Case & Washino 1979). These species could be considered for introduction into malarial zones in many parts of the world, provided that they do not conflict with creatures other than mosquitoes in their new environments.

So much for a selection of animals' contributions to medicine in the form of their biodynamic compounds and life-styles. Numerous and diverse as these are, they are far surpassed by the medical insights that animals give us through their role as models for research.

The physiology of many creatures affords clues to the origins and nature of many human ailments. Butterflies, wasps, mice, salamanders, toads, sea urchins, and fruit flies have helped us with our basic understanding of genetics and embryology in humans. They have thereby supplied us with clues on how to tackle genetic defects such as Down's syndrome and sickle-cell anemia. For example, the African mocker swallowtail butterfly features unusual genetic processes that govern the production of its different color forms, and these genetic characteristics have enabled scientists to fathom the mysteries of human genetic blood disease that leads to "rhesus babies." Still more important in the long run, the insights afforded by these creatures into our understanding of human genetics and embryology may eventually assist our research on cancer, which in essence amounts to a breakdown in the genetic control of cells.

Similarly, understanding the physiology of the cheetah could eventually provide benefits for human health. The animal can accelerate from a standing start to 70 kms. per hour in a few strides, and it can then maintain a 100-km.-per-hour chase for several hundred meters. The creature obviously possesses an efficient heart, together with finely tuned respiratory and circulatory systems, that allows it to sustain a sudden and severe oxygen debt. Hence the cheetah could provide clues for treatment of heart disease, blood pressure, and circulatory disorders in humans.

One of the longest-standing scourges of humankind, and still one of the most persistent, is Hansen's disease, or leprosy, which afflicts at least 15 million people in developing countries. Despite decades of research efforts, scientists have not properly unraveled the mechanism of the disease. There have been plenty of human sufferers to observe, but that is not the same as saying there are plenty of groups on which to experiment with drugs. Nor, until very recently, have scientists been able to track down an animal species that contracts leprosy. So far as the scientists could discern, the disease was confined to humans, making it much harder to devise a treatment. Fortunately, scientists have now come across two animal species that oblige by contracting leprosy. One is the armadillo. This discovery has greatly promoted research in recent years (Convit & Pinardi 1974; Maugh 1982). The armadillo's body temperature is 2°–5°C lower than that of most other mammals, and because of this feature, or possibly because of its weak immune system, the armadillo serves as a suitable incubator for the bacilli that cause the disease. When a typical armadillo is injected with diseased cells, it can supply sufficient spleen and liver tissue to provide as many as 10^{12} bacilli for each of the 150–250 grams of tissue, an ample quantity for use in production of an antileprosy vaccine.

The second animal to assist is the mangabey monkey, which also contracts leprosy. As a primate and thus a close relative of humans, the monkey serves as a first-rate research model and is greatly increasing our hopes of coming up with a cure for the dreaded disease (Meyers et al. 1981).

There is even prospect that the green monkey of central Africa may assist with research into AIDS. The monkey, though frequently infected by a virus similar to the one that causes AIDS in humans, remains largely unaffected by it. This means, by virtue of its capacity to serve as a unique research model, it could well provide scientists with important clues to controlling AIDS, perhaps through an effective vaccine (Kanki et al. 1986).

It is because of their close relatedness to humans that primates are especially valuable for medical research, contributing to the development of many drugs and vaccines. For example, the chimpanzee—of which only 50,000 are left in the wild—is the sole creature other than humans on which the safety of antihepatitis vaccines can be tested. The cotton-topped marmoset, a species of monkey susceptible to cancer of the lymphatic system, is used to help produce a potent anticancer vaccine; tests with the monkey show that we can possibly prevent lymphatic cancer by immunization (Laufs & Steinke 1975). Related work with the marmoset reveals that a virus thought to be implicated in at least some human cancers can occur in that animal; the same virus also can occur in the owl monkey. The African green monkey serves as a research model for a virus that causes diarrhea in human infants—with an appalling death rate among babies in developing nations (Wyatt et al. 1980). The baboon assists in resolving urinary incontinence in humans. Various primates at the Penrose Research Laboratory at the Philadelphia Zoo have served in the development of a standard tuberculosis skin test for humans.

We are even learning important secrets from the black bear. The bear hibernates for 5 months during the winter, relying on hormonal adaptations that are assisting scientists in developing a low-protein and low-fluid diet for humans suffering from kidney failure (Nelson 1977). Also contributing to kidney research is the springbok, a gazelle of southern Africa. As many as one American in 500 suffers from polycystic disease of the kidneys. It is an ailment that has not been encountered in any domestic or laboratory animal, making research difficult—until Professors David Senior and Elliott Jacobson of the University of Florida came across it in the springbok.

Other illustrations are legion, too numerous to list here. Let us conclude with the Florida manatee, a species so endangered that only 850 survive in the wild. The manatee possesses blood with poor clotting capabilities, a trait that helps research on hemophilia.

So much, then, for major forms of animal life. We should not overlook those lowly forms of life that are neither plant nor animal, and that are too small for us to see with the naked eye and hence too small for our passing attention. These are the microcreatures, including viruses. We might think that we can do without viruses. The sooner they are made extinct, the better for us and for our children in perpetuity. An obvious example is the smallpox virus, which has been backed into a corner by modern medicine to the extent that no human being suffers from the disease: the organism now exists only in a few flasks in the laboratory. Should we, by conscious and rational decision, obliterate this manifestation of life's diversity? Or should we keep it alive on the grounds that it does not cost us much to preserve, and that it may one day, one remote day, serve our needs?

In response to the second question, many people might feel that the cornered virus cannot conceivably assist our welfare, either now or in the indefinite future. But wait a moment. Let us bear in mind that viruses, including many pathogenic species, have been the sources of many of the momentous discoveries in biology during the recent past. If we were to lose, let alone despatch, a single such species, we could eventually find that we have deprived ourselves of an important asset in our research on comparative biochemistry and genetics, even for basic investigations on the nature and origin of life.

Too vague, some might say. Curiously enough, however, the smallpox virus could offer direct utilitarian benefits for us. Scientists are pretty sure that it will assist our studies on the antigenic relationships among a number of similar viruses, including the monkey pox and other viruses that have emerged into growing prominence as the smallpox virus has given way before our eradication campaigns. If ever these smallpox-related viruses were to threaten our health, the smallpox virus itself could, as a research model, prove exceptionally important to us. In addition to supporting analytic research, the smallpox virus could help us in a still more critical endeavour, to develop a recombinant virus as a basis for an improved vaccine. A strategy along these lines has recently been applied in developing vaccines against influenza, and scientists believe that a parallel approach could be utilized with respect to the smallpox virus (Dixon 1976).

All forms of animal life, in short, can serve the needs of modern medicine. As in the case of medical research involving the plant kingdom, scientists have made only a bare start on the challenge of tapping our fellow animal species for the many ways in which they can support human health. If researchers could undertake a systematic investigation of all that the animal world has to offer to modern medicine, they could accomplish much more than we can realistically envisage now.

Abundant and diverse as are the ways in which wild animals already contribute to our daily welfare, they represent only a tiny fraction of what could lie ahead if scientists were to investigate the animal kingdom for its full utilitarian value to us—and were the species to remain available for scientific investigation. Of the millions of animal species on earth, scientists have conducted intensive research into only a few thousand, at most, to assess their material worth to us. Were all species to remain in existence, there would surely be whole cornucopias of new foods awaiting us, and entire pharmacopoeias of new medicines and drugs. By saving wild creatures' lives, we could be saving our own.

A great case could be made for the potential of the dodo for domestication were it not extinct. Flightless, a giant pigeon with the capacity to eat seeds and fruits unprocessable by human teeth! Wow! The dodo could be a great tropical "turkey."

References

Barel, C. D. N., et al. 1985. Destruction of Fisheries in Africa's Lakes. *Nature* 315:19–20.

Case, T. J., and R. K. Washino. 1979. Flatworm Control of Mosquito Larvae in Rice Fields. *Science* 206:1412–14.

Convit, J., and M. E. Pinardi. 1974. Leprosy: Confirmation in the Armadillo. *Science* 184:1191–92.

Dixon, B. 1976. Smallpox: An Unresolved Dilemma. *New Scientist* 69(989): 430–32.

Erwin, T. L. 1988. *The Tropical Forest Canopy: The Heart of Biodiversity.* In *Biodiversity,* ed. E. O. Wilson, 123–29. Washington, D.C.: National Academy Press.

Kanki, P. J., et al. 1986. New Human T-Lymphotropic Retrovirus Related to Simian T-Lymphotrophic Virus Type III. *Science* 232:238–43.

Laufs, R., and H. Steinke. 1975. Vaccination of Non-Primates Against Malignant Lymphoma. *Nature* 253:71–72.

Legner, E. F. 1978. Mass Culture of *Tilapia zillii* (Cichlidae) in Pond Ecosystems. *Entomophaga* 23(1): 51–55.

Legner, E. F., and T. W. Fisher. 1980. Impact of *Tilapia zillii* on *Potamogeton pectinatus, Myriophyllum spicatum var. exalbescens,* and Mosquito Reproduction in Lower Colorado Desert (USA) Irrigation Canals. *Acta Oecologia-Oecologia Applicata* 1(1): 3–14.

Lowe-McConnell, R. H. 1977. Ecology of Fishes in Tropical Waters. *Studies in Biology,* no. 76. London: Edward Arnold.

Mason, I. L. 1975. Beefalo: Much Ado About Nothing? *World Review of Animal Production* 11(4): 19–23.

Maugh, T. H. 1982. Leprosy Vaccine Trials to Begin Soon. *Science* 215:1083–86.

Meyers, W. M., et al. 1981. Naturally Acquired Leprosy in a Mangabey Monkey. *Laboratory Investigation* (Annual Meeting Abstracts) 44:A44.

Myers, N. 1972. *The Long African Day.* New York: Macmillan.

______. 1987. *Tackling Mass Extinction of Species: A Great Creative Challenge.* The Horace M. Albright Lecture in Conservation. University of California, Berkeley, College of Natural Resources.

Neill, W. T. 1974. *Reptiles and Amphibians in the Service of Man.* London: Pegasus.

Nelson, R. A. 1977. *Urea Metabolism in the Hibernating Black Bear.* Rochester, Minn.: Mayo Clinic.

Raven, P. H. 1987. *We're Killing Our World.* In *The Global Ecosystem in Crisis.* Chicago: MacArthur Foundation.

Short, R. V. 1976. The Introduction of New Species of Animals for the Purpose of Domestication. *Symposium of Zoological Society of London* 40:1–13.

Western, D., and M. Pearl, eds. 1987. *Conservation for the Twenty-First Century.* Oxford, England: Oxford University Press.

Wetterberg, G. B., et al. 1976. *An Analysis of Nature Conservation Priorities in the Amazon.* Technical Series No. 8. Brasilia, Brazil: Brazilian Institute for Forestry Development.

Wilson, E. O. 1988. *Biodiversity.* Washington, D.C.: National Academy Press.

Wyatt, R. G., et al. 1980. Human Rotavirus Type 2: Cultivation in Vitro. *Science* 207: 189–191.

Human Nature and the Psycho-Industrial Complex

Lionel Tiger

There seems little question that a basic impulse behind the effort to explore human biology is directly connected with the question, if we can determine what is natural to human experience and behavior, cannot we then make informed judgments about which kind of social arrangement is better for people, and which is worse? This question has its roots in the history of English utilitarianism—the first use of the *ethology* was evidently by John Stuart Mill—and is also, of course, at the heart of the heat of the controversy about the role of biology in the human social sciences. The fact that the first Man and Beast symposium in 1969 appears to have caught the beginning of an important wave of acrimony and assertion, to say nothing of good science as well, makes it timely and interesting to assess where the matter stands a generation later.

Some words of background first, which are personal and yet rather formally illustrate the larger issues under review here. In 1965 Robin Fox and I wrote a brief and impudent article called "The Zoological Perspective in Social Science," which appeared in 1966 in Vol. 1:2, (n.s.) of *Man: The*

Journal of the Royal Anthropological Society. Some people thought Fox wrote it and I cosigned it to draw the blame away from him, whereas others thought I wrote it and asked Robin to cosign it because he knew the editor of the journal and could induce its publication. A few people thought it was interesting in its own right. But there was no overwhelming outcry over it, which I attribute now to the fact that it made no comments specific enough to attract the attention of people concerned with the policy implication of scientific statements. We were left alone.

Three years later and 2 weeks after the first Man and Beast symposium, my book *Men in Groups* (1969) was published. Among other things, it suggested that some human sex differences were possibly linked to human biology, as sex differences in other animals seemed to be. I suggested that what I called "male bonding" was a form of human association perhaps as fundamental to the human evolutionary process as male-female relations were—though for productive, not reproductive, purposes and therefore potentially pertinent to the contemporary lives of people.

In all innocence, I produced the book in part because I thought the overwhelming bias in social science was to study male behavior and equate it with human behavior. Thus political behavior, which was basically the behavior of males, or managerial behavior, or military, or police, were nonetheless uncritically deemed to encompass both males and females, even though empirically they did not. It seemed to be time to emphasize sex differences, first, to get the facts right and, then, perhaps to understand the sources and meaning of these differences. Indeed, I had been told by a teacher at the University of London that there had not been a formal study of male association since a publication in *Annees Sociologique* in 1904.

But now the response was hot. Policy issues were thought to be at stake. The feminist movement, which was emerging into prominence, seemed to define my assertions as advocacy for the Upper Paleolithic rather than as an analysis of an existing situation—an analysis which was in many ways similar to feminists' and from which in fact they drew factual materials. It became almost physically dangerous to discuss sex differences in public. I was offered bomb threats before lectures in Montreal and Vancouver, and at the New School for Social Research in New York a student spy reported to an administrator that during—or better, before—my forthcoming lecture on biology and gender, I was to have my legs broken. Against this possibility, during my night out at the New School I was never allowed to walk or talk more than 6 yards from two enormous uniformed experts in securing academic freedom.

When in 1971 Fox and I published *The Imperial Animal,* there was Sturm und Drang again, which was reflected in one splendid comic moment during a rump caucus of self-styled radical anthropologists at a regular meeting of the American Anthropological Association when the Ruth Benedict Collective offered the dual proposal that a) there be no Stalinism in the radical anthropology movement and b) that Fox and I be forbidden to speak at any American campus. There was an important issue at stake. Were men and women the same? Or were there genotypically linked characteristics to which a thoughtful and fair-minded community should respond with realistic providence?

Which brings me to my main subject of concern. This is that the effort to introduce biology into the array of analytical instruments of human behavior represents to some critics—and in a way inescapably so—the effective introduction also of the factor of the primordial into human conduct. After all, the essential point of evolutionary analysis is to estimate the impact of a species' genetic history on its behavioral present. If this also applies to people, then we are perforce in some sense constrained, goaded, or at least affected by the accumulated impact of selective decisions made over thousands of generations.

This is not the modern style. It is particular anathema to protagonists of an industrial way of life, which appears to reject the intrusions of nature on behavior as much as on physical process. The great history of technology has been one revelation after another that the seeming inevitability of nature can be overcome by technologic—by aircraft, reactors, vaccines, polymer chemistry, rockets, and the like. The resistance to biology as a form of human social science can be seen as a reflection of the successful experience of our species in overcoming precisely the grip of physical nature. Of course there are other reasons, too, which have been well accounted for and formidably rebutted, such as the impact of social Darwinism, of Nazi racism, of the effort to account for racial inequality by genetic inheritance.

However, the resistance which interests me most here is that which emerges almost ineluctably from the industrial system itself, with its dramatic conquest of physical nature, which I will suggest has stimulated enthusiasm for an equivalent control over social nature. It is the effort to locate the point of contact between our ancient species and an industrial system barely 10 generations old which may mark a new phase of the survey of man and beast—of industrial man and Upper Paleolithic hunter-gatherer beast.

The Psycho-Industrial Complex

In greater detail elsewhere (Tiger 1987) I have described the characteristics of the industrial system as essentially involving a pattern of socioeconomic life rooted in technology, to be sure, but also in a structure of psychological and social life linked to the growth of "possessive individualism." This probably first emerged in the late 17th century in England and may well be the formal prerequisite for the form of society we are discussing here (see Macpherson 1962). Broadly, possessive individualism involves a shift of emphasis from the kin group and community as the basic unit of acquiring and sharing resources, to the individual. The individual becomes his own property, able to improve and market himself and essentially conducting a long-term contract with the system overall—that system which from another point of view Adam Smith saw as generally profiting from the specific accomplishments of individuals. In a rather surprisingly and hauntingly prescient letter to Charles James Fox in 1801, the poet of pastoralism William Wordsworth wrote, "It appears to me the most calamitous effect, which has followed the measures which have lately been pursued in this country, is a rapid decay of the domestic affections among the lower orders of society. This effect the present Rulers of this Country are not conscious of, or they disregard it" (quoted in Jennings 1985). This "decay of the domestic affections" has in a real sense continued, reflected, for example, in the increase in family dissolution represented by divorce statistics and the decrease of interactive familial complexity represented by the decline in family size and increase in the number of persons living alone. For example, 50% of people in rental accommodation in Manhattan in 1984 lived alone.

While the individual adult is no longer able to make enduring claims for support on the kin group, at the same time the family is not entitled to firm claims on the individual contractor's time and resources. Employers are not responsible for the domestic or affectional circumstances of employees. In some communities, such as the United States, it is in fact against the law to inquire about or take into formal account the marital, sexual, or reproductive status of a prospective or actual employee. First, antinepotism rules and, more recently, stern civil-rights enactments have determined that the only characteristic relevant to the employer of the individual contractor must be that person's willingness and ability to accomplish work.

This socioeconomic change did not occur in a social-scientific vacuum. The emergence of psychology and sociology as significant endeavors coincide with the maturation of the industrial way of life. At the turn of the century Pavlov and his successors, and Spencer, Weber, and particularly Durkheim and their successors, all succeeded in establishing important academic disciplines which can be seen as involved in the furtherance and consolidation of the industrial form.

A characteristic of sociology for many years was precisely its emphasis on the study of industrial—as opposed to so-called primitive, or pretechnological—society. An animating stimulus to psychology was its function in assessing and often seeking to facilitate the relationship between individual and employer, both in the workplace itself, in the form of industrial or personnel psychology, and more broadly, in the community at large, for which psychologists prepared a plethora of tests claimed to be objective. In effect, these were quality-control measures which evaluated the marketability of the individual contractor as he or she moved through the life and work cycles. Of course these were and are defined not only as objective but also as essential for the fair-minded provision of equality of opportunity. This they may be, which I personally doubt, but there seems little question that the vast industry of testing is a central and generic feature of the industrial system itself. And if we regard these tests from the perspective of students of evolved behavior, we can wonder about how broadly or narrowly such testing instruments evaluate the capacities for gregarious sociality, sexuality, and resource accrual which were central to human evolution. That is to say, if industrialization is the epitome of the process of marrying specialization and precision to energy, then it is striking indeed that in its North American version it depends so heavily on a series of tests which are claimed to be, and boasted to be, culture-free. Which is odd, given the significance human culture is considered to have in distinguishing human society from that of other animals.

And there is another paradox, too, in this effort to create culture-free tests, which is that if the tests do not select for cultural experience, then they must reveal the inherent functional essence of the test taker—his or her basic quality and capacity as a human being. And since this is not culture dependent, then it must be biology dependent, which is a genuine oddity in a culture which severely rejects any significant role for biology in the operation of communities.

One other point about the intersection of the individual contractor and the testing system for individual quality control. Overwhelmingly, the tests in question are taken by individuals and graded by machine, and the results are distributed along a bell-curve distribution. The individual is thus marketable according to an impersonal comparison between 1 individual and the wider group. However, this individual is a member of a highly gregarious species. But his or her gregarious capacities are not measurable by the solitary test which is the basis for SAT scores, GREs, and the like. At the college level, it seems to be mainly in sports that an individual's ability both to perform tasks and engage in gregarious behavior is evaluated and rewarded. It is also notorious that college athletes, for example, are frequently held to a different, usually lower standard of testing competence than other students, and their graduation rates are strikingly lower than normal. However, to an evolution-minded observer, it may seem odd that the remarkable combination of cooperative social accomplishment with individual skill and strategic assessment involved in a good basketball team is rarely fully rewarded by collegiate institutions claiming as their mandate the transmission of the culture's cherished social and intellectual values. In a crude but perhaps accurate way, perhaps we can assert that college athletics represent the primordial in the university. This may begin to account for the moral confusion and procedural squalor which often accompany successful athletic programs in academic institutions.

The confusion of assumptions and of ends and means which surrounds the testing industry represents more broadly the nature of the relationship between human nature and the psycho-industrial complex. In the metaphor I am drawing here, the athlete engaged in a process of disciplined, thoughtfully planned, cooperative, and usually aggressive play is representing fairly directly those evolved enthusiasms and capacities which were centrally pertinent to human evolution under the varying conditions and pressures which we endured. Perhaps this is why athletes are so celebrated in this and other societies and why sports loom so large in the time budgets of televiewers and other spectators. It is also of more than incidental interest that in other areas of the industrial economy as well, there is greater emphasis placed on individual competence and accomplishment and less-than-sufficient emphasis on abilities for social interaction. For example, it has become clear that airplane accidents frequently result from human error—error which may result from the poor or insensitive interaction of the members of the cockpit crew. In general, flight crews are assigned to planes and flights on an individual basis and do not form permanent working groups presumably able to develop a culture of competence and collective understanding which could prepare for the management of airborne crisis. It is fascinating that athletic coaches will spend full days drilling high school halfbacks about cooperative play, inducing morale, stimulating field leadership and the like, while the managers of airplanes pay little heed to equivalent forms of social interaction of the most critical work teams in their organizations. The independent contractor flies alone.

There is acknowledged to be general communal difficulty in inducing people to read and write effectively and with enthusiasm, and to pursue higher education with avidity for its own sake. This may reflect the fact that the system of quality control and testing which the educational community enshrines is anathema to, or of little interest to, persons who have not made an explicit decision to become successful individual contractors with relatively good rewards of status and resources. This may be related to the fact that literacy is the preeminent operating mode of economic communication in industrial systems. But it is a modality evidently difficult for humans to learn; compare the ease with which children learn to watch television—often they must be restrained from doing so—with the energetic and time-consuming efforts necessary to teach them to read. Recall that the notion of universal literacy did not emerge until the industrial system was well-established. Prior to that, literacy was a specialized skill, associated with government and religion but hardly at all with the general work of society in which ordinary people had an active role. So the industrial system has adopted a method of communication which is ethologically rather exotic and certainly difficult to acquire and this may be an additional and highly significant reason for the awkwardness of the "fit" between the system and those who must try to inhabit and master it. It is also suggestive to consider the contrast between the apparently efficient and successful underground economies of South America and Eastern Europe, which operate principally on verbal communication, and the centrally organized literacy-dependent economies now widely acknowledged to be stagnant and uninteresting to participants.

The Revenge of the Cradle

In general, organisms convert resources into offspring. It is therefore fascinating that the wealthiest of human organisms, those of the industrial world, have the fewest offspring and are in fact in a number of important cases now reproducing at below rates of replacement. I am of course aware that there is general sentiment that this is a good thing in terms of the planet's ecology and its limited capacity to regenerate resources. Nevertheless, it is also a canon of zookeepers that animals reproduce better in zoos which suit their natures than in those which do not. The obvious question is, are humans in the zoos we have created for ourselves in a comparable situation? I raise the issue solely to identify another facet of the human nature-industrial system interaction and not to enter a dialogue about policy. Nevertheless, insofar as reproduction is the process at the absolute core of a species' formation and persistence, then it becomes exceedingly interesting when members of a species in considerable control of their circumstances elect to reproduce at a historically low level. Invoking the law of parsimony on this issue asserts the possibility that a fundamental process is most likely to be affected by another fundamental process. Therefore the explanation of what is going on may well involve significant elements of contemporary life.

In *The Manufacture of Evil* I outlined what may be some plausible reasons for this reproductive austerity, and there is no reason to detail them here. Suffice it perhaps to say that the impact of medical intervention is plainly formidable, involving as it does the industrialization of the body either with contraceptive drugs, IUDs, or sterilization. It is also striking how significant sterilization is, as a contraceptive; on the West Coast of the United States it is the most widely used method of contraception of all. When one considers that there is at the same time a high divorce and remarriage rate there, and that 1 sterilized partner means that 2 effectively are, then the impact of this technique is clear. Perhaps one is allowed to wonder about the medical ethics involved in choosing the drastic contraceptive of sterilization when less drastic but still effective ones are available. Certainly it seems that medical practitioners may lack a generous sense of the meaning of reproductive option to healthy people and underestimate the social and possibly symbolic impact of this operation. Nevertheless, it is perhaps characteristic of the industrial mode to assume the appropriateness of solving human problems by such stern surgical intervention.

As a general matter, there is good theoretical reason to consider very thoroughly and seriously the significance and implication of the low birth rate of the industrial communities. This may in fact constitute one of the central scientific challenges to scholars concerned with the relationship between biology and human social behavior. And there are major political and economic issues which pertain here, ranging from the forms of support for parents (it is extraordinary that to receive maternity benefits in the United States, women must claim "disability" benefits when what they have, of course, is an ability) to taxation patterns affecting family businesses to consideration of the desirable levels of participation of men and women in institutions ranging from day care to the armed forces to legislatures.

Modernizing the Primordial

My intent has not been to claim that whatever primordial social propensities are, they are "better" than those stimulated and supported by the industrial system. However to the extent that evolved biology finds some rendition in the life cycles of contemporary individuals, then such primordial factors must be taken into account in considering scientific programs and confronting political realities. The relative conquest of physical nature does not necessarily imply a commensurate control over biosocial nature. The issue is of course first to identify what such biosocial nature may be, and there are considerable accomplishments in hand in that area, and then to move to an effort to relate our social organization to these in some responsive manner.

Shortly after the first Man and Beast symposium, I wrote a brief essay advocating "biological Fabianism" (Tiger 1970). This was to be an adaptation of the role of the Fabian society in the early 20th century in England, when a number of social reformers such as Bernard Shaw, the Beveridges, Wells, and others determined that the first step in dealing with the depredations of the industrial world as it affected people was in systematically finding out what was happening. In practice that led to Keynesian economics, major welfare, social-service initiatives, and other adjustments of economic practice to perceived reality. Perhaps biology can do at the end of the century what economics did at the beginning, which is determine what is really happening and why, so that those who have to plan for the future can do so intelligently, using real information about a real species. There is little point in creating a zoo, however elegant, for a mystery species.

References

Jennings, H. 1985. *Pandemonium: The Coming of the Machine as Seen by Contemporary Observers, 1660–1886.* New York: Free.

Macpherson, C. B. 1962. *The Political Theory of Possessive Individualism: Hobbes to Locke.* London: Oxford University Press.

Tiger, L. 1970. Biological Fabianism. *Forum* (Canada)(December) 50:1.

______. 1987. *The Manufacture of Evil: Ethics, Evolution, and the Industrial System.* New York: Harper & Row, Bessie Books.

Tiger, L., and R. Fox. 1971. *The Imperial Animal.* New York: Holt, Rinehart & Winston.

Climate Change

Causes and Effects

Stephen H. Schneider

To predict the result of some event in nature, it is common to build and perform an experiment. But what if the issues are very complex or the scale of the experiment unmanageably large? To forecast the effect of human pollution on climate poses just such a dilemma, for this uncontrolled experiment is now being performed on Laboratory Earth. How then can we be anticipatory, if no meaningful physical experiment can be performed? While nothing can provide certain answers, we can turn to a surrogate lab, not a room with test tubes and Bunsen burners, but a small box with transistors and microchips. We can build mathematical models of the earth and perform our ''experiments'' in computers.

Mathematical models translate conceptual ideas into quantitative statements. Models usually are not faithful simulations of the full complexity of reality, of course, but they can tell us the logical consequences of explicit sets of plausible assumptions. To me, that certainly is a big step beyond pure conception—or to put it more crudely, modeling is a major advance over ''hand waving.''

Let me first point out that not all knowledgeable scientists are in agreement as to the probability that such changes will occur. In fact, if one has followed the very noisy, often polemical debate in the media recently, one might get the (I believe false) impression that there are but 2 radically opposed schools of thought about global warming: (1) that climate changes will be so severe, so sudden, and so certain that major species extinction events will intensify, sea-level rise will create tens of millions of environmental refugees, millions to perhaps billions of people will starve, and devastated ecosystems are a virtual certainty; or alternatively, (2) there is nothing but uncertainty about global warming, there is no evidence that the 20th century has done what the modelers have predicted, and the people arguing for change are just "environmental extremists"; thus there is no need for any management response to an event that is improbable, and in no case should any such responses interfere with the "free market" and bankrupt nations (for example, see Brookes 1989). Unfortunately, while such a highly charged and polarized debate makes entertaining opinion-page reading or viewing of the ratings-dominated media, it provides a very poor description of the reality of the actual scientific debate or the broad consensus on basic issues within the scientific community. In my opinion, the "end of the world" or "nothing to worry about" are the two *least likely* cases, with almost any scenario in between having a higher probability of occurrence.

Figure 1 shows a projection of global warming possibilities into the 21st century drawn by a consensus group of scientists that was convened by the well-established International Council of Scientific Unions. It shows warming from a very moderate half-degree C (.9°F) up to a catastrophic 5°C (9°F), or greater warming before the end of the next century. I do not hesitate to call the latter extreme catastrophic because that is the magnitude of the global warming that occurred between about 15,000 years ago and 5,000 years ago, from the end of the last ice age to our present interglacial epoch. It took nature some 5 to 10 thousand years to accomplish that warming, and it was accompanied by a 100-meter (330-foot) or so rise in sea level, thousands of kilometers' migration of forest species, radically altered habitats, species extinctions, species evolution, and other major environmental changes.

Critics of immediate policy responses to global warming are quick to point out the many uncertainties that could reduce the average projections made by

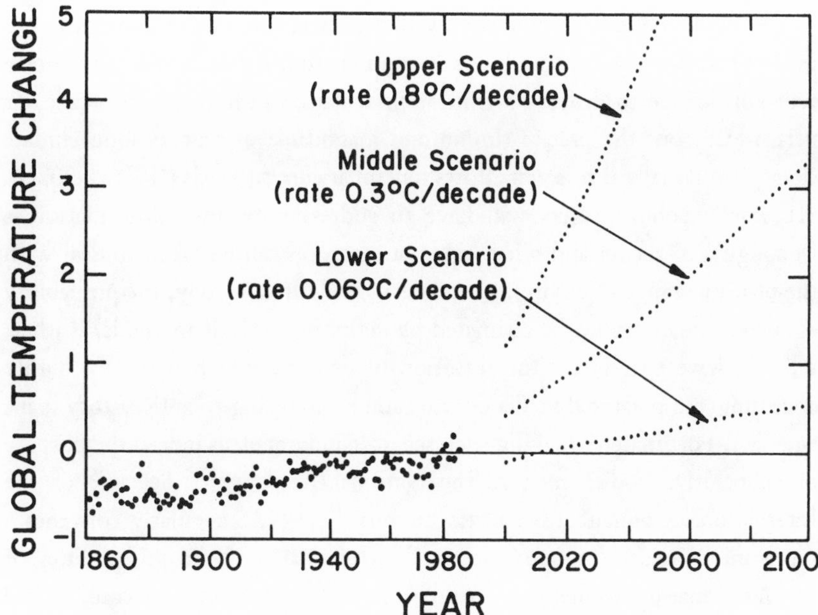

Fig. 1. Three scenarios for global temperature change to the year 2100 derived from combining uncertainties in future trace greenhouse gas projections with uncertainties of modeling the climatic response to those projections. Sustained global temperature changes beyond 2°C (3.6°F) would be unprecedented during the era of human civilization. The middle to upper range represents climatic change at a pace 10 to 100 times faster than typical long-term natural average rates of change. (Source: J. Jager, 1988. *Developing Policies for Responding to Climatic Change.* Geneva, Switzerland: World Meteorological Organization.)

climate models (such as the middle line on figure 1). Indeed, most climate modelers include similar caveats in their papers, and many of us do resent somewhat the implications of some critics that they are the ones who are responsibly pointing out these uncertainties to the public, whereas the modelers are somehow deliberately suppressing uncertainties in order to overstate the issue (e.g., see *Detroit News* 1989 and Schneider 1989a). Many critiques (e.g., see George C. Marshall Institute Report 1989) somehow forget to stress that the sword of uncertainty has 2 blades; that is, uncertainties in physical or biological processes which make it possible for the present generation of models to have overestimated future warming effects are just as likely to have caused the models to have underestimated change.

The public policy dilemma is how to act, even though we will not know in detail what will happen. It is my opinion that the scientific community will not be able to provide definitive information over the next decade, or perhaps 2 about the precise timing and magnitude of century-long climate changes, especially if research efforts remain at current levels (IPCC 1990, ch. 11). Public policy makers will have to address how much information is "enough" to act on and what kinds of measures can be taken to deal with the plausible range of environmental changes. Unfortunately, the probability of such changes cannot be estimated by definitive analytic methods. Rather, we will have to rely on the intuition of experts, which is why a highly confusing and polarized media debate can be paralyzing to anticipatory management. Fortunately, making such scientifc judgments is indeed the purpose of deliberative bodies such as the National Academy of Sciences or the International Council of Scientific Unions. The NAS regularly convenes a spectrum of experts to provide the best estimates of the probabilities of various scenarios of change. These people can deliberate to a considerable extent away from the confusion of the noisy media debates in which extreme opposites are typically pitted. Half a dozen such assessments over the past 10 years have all reaffirmed the plausibility of unprecedented climate change building into the next 50–100 years. The most recent, the U.N.-sponsored Intergovernmental Panel on Climate Change (IPCC 1990), also came to similar conclusions as past NAS and ICSU assessments.

Let me briefly summarize the arguments of critics, some of whom challenge these assessments. Many critics contend that the warming trend of the past century of about 0.5°C (e.g., Jones & Wigley 1990) is suspect because the thermometer record is not very reliable (e.g., Ellsaesser 1984). Of course, the scientists who produce such records say the same thing (e.g., Karl & Jones 1989), but many aren't certain whether the needed corrections will necessarily reduce the trend as opposed to increasing it. Moreover, some critics cite the neglect of ocean temperature data collected from buckets dropped over the sides of schooners in the Victorian or pre-Victorian times, since some of those records suggest that the 1850s may have seen ocean temperatures nearly as warm as the present (e.g., Bottomley 1990; Lindzen 1990). The reason that those kinds of pre-1900 ocean temperature data are typically discounted in most assessments is that they were collected over only a few percent or so of the earth's surface (see fig. 2). In addition, the measurements simply aren't very reliable. The most reliable statement that seems reasonable to infer from the available temperature records is that a warming of some 0.5°C (0.9°F) has occurred globally over the past 100 years (IPCC 1990, ch. 17). If greenhouse gas pollution were the only cause of that warming trend, then this is broadly consistent with the middle of the lower half of the projected range of warming made by climate models as seen in figure 1. Does this mean that nature has already told us that future global warming will be half of what most models typically project? Unfortuantely, we have only been accruately measuring the energy output of the sun from space over the past 10 years or so and have very little knowledge of the precise quantitative nature of this or other factors that could have influenced the temperature trends this century. Without such factors being accounted for precisely, even accurate temperature data over the past century couldn't tell us very much about how the earth has responded to the pollution injected since preindustrial times. Furthermore, although some critics have suggested that a century-long heating up of the sun of a few tenths of a percent could account for the 20th-century warming of the earth (e.g, Marshall Institute Report 1989), these critics often forget to mention that it is equally likely, since it was essentially unmeasured, that the sun could have cooled down by that amount. A cooler sun would thereby have damped any greenhouse effect that otherwise would have been in the record, thus fooling us into thinking that the global warming from pollution to date is half of that which we actually had. Quite simply, the critics can't have it both ways. What we don't know could increase or decrease our estimates.

Finally, the principal reason that advocates of concern over the prospects of global warming—and I am unabashedly one of them (e.g., Schneider 1989b)—stand before groups such as congressional committees and take up their time with that concern is not based solely on speculative theory. Rather, the concern is based on the fact that the models which we use to foreshadow the future have already been validated to a considerable degree, although not the the full satisfaction of any responsible scientist. For example, we know from observations of nature, a point often neglected by the critics of global warming, that the last ice age, which was about 5°C (9°F) colder than the present era, also had carbon dioxide levels about 25% less than the preindustrial values. Methane, another very potent greenhouse gas, also was reduced by nearly a factor of 2 relative to preindustrial values. Ice cores in Antarctica have shown us, since these cores contain gas bubbles that are records of the atmospheric composition going back over 150,000 years,

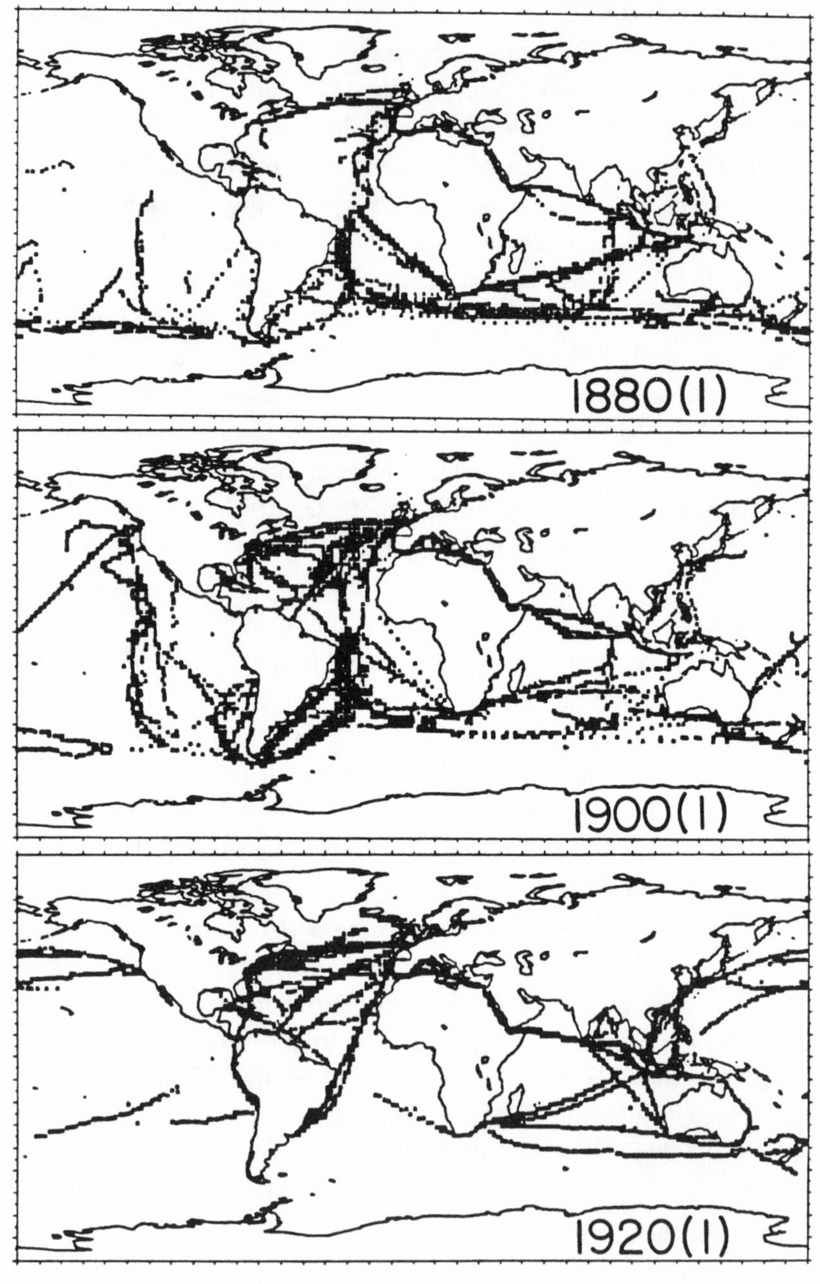
COADS SST COVERAGE – 1 or more observations
1880(1)
1900(1)
1920(1)

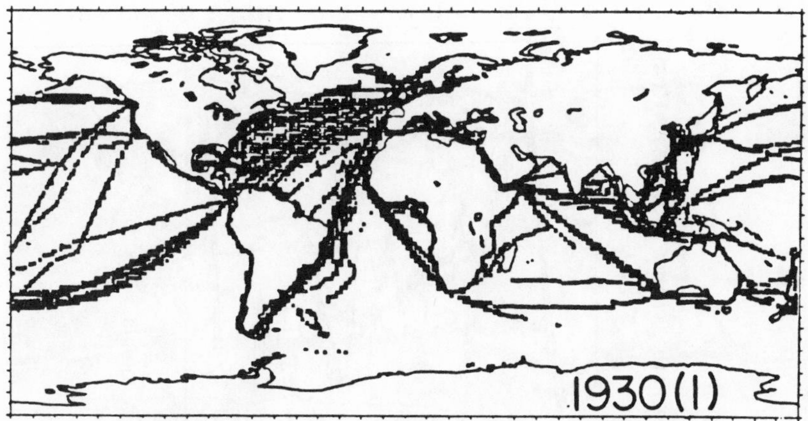

Fig. 2. Ship tracks in the oceans from which temperature measurements have been made for the decades shown for the month of January. Note that coverage before 1900 is on the order of 10% of the surface area, and thus very little reliable inferences can be made for temperature events before then. (Source: D. Shea and K. Trenberth, National Center for Atmospheric Research, pers. comm., 1990.)

that the previous interglacial age some 125,000–130,000 years ago had CO_2 and methane levels comparable to those in the present interglacial. The nearly simultaneous change in these greenhouse gases and in planetary temperature over geological epochs (see fig. 3) is roughly what one would expect, based on projects from today's generation of computer models. However, we still cannot assert that this greenhouse gas–temperature coincidence is proof that our models are quantitatively correct, since other factors were operating during the ice age–interglacial cycles. The best we can say is that the evidence is strong, but circumstantial.

One final comment about the scientific discussions that is often not well represented in the more visible public debate is that it is not at all true that the bulk of the scientific community is in constant controversy and disarray about the basic science of the greenhouse effect. The greenhouse effect, the heat-trapping properties of the atmosphere and its gases and particles, is well understood and well validated. Indeed, it is as good a theory as there is in the atmospheric sciences. It explains, for example, the very hot conditions under the thick atmosphere of Venus and the very cold conditions under the thin, weak "greenhouse" of Mars. It explains the thousands of laboratory

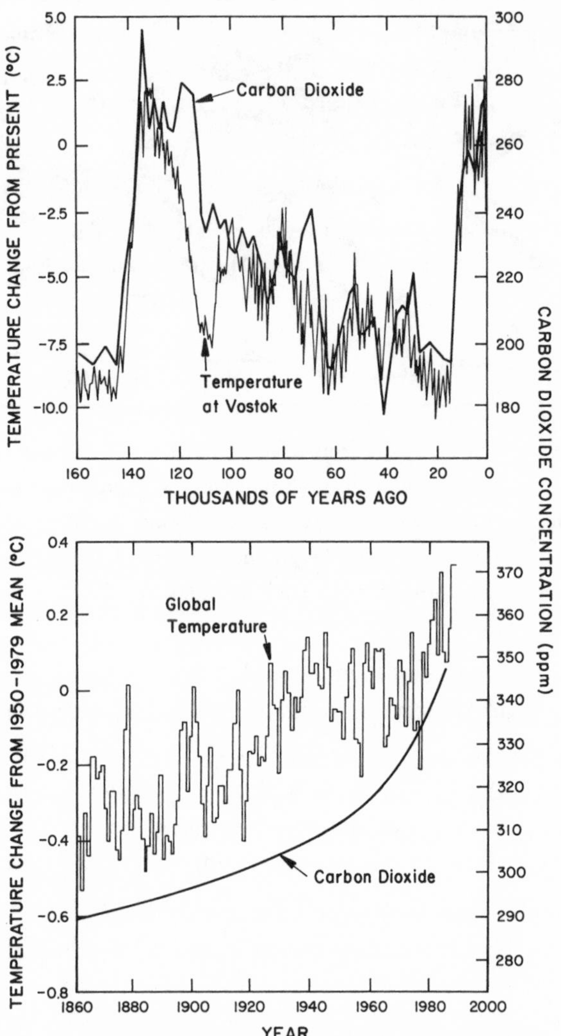

Fig. 3. Carbon dioxide and temperature are very closely correlated over the past 160,000 years (*top*) and, to a lesser extent, over the past 100 years (*bottom*). The long-term record, based on evidence from Antarctica and interpreted by the glaciology group at Grenoble, France, shows how the local temperature and atmospheric carbon dioxide rose nearly in step as an ice age ended about 130,000 years ago, fell again at the onset of a new glacial period, and rose again as the ice retreated about 10,000 years ago. The recent temperature record shows a slight global warming, as traced by workers at the Climatic Research Unit at the University of East Anglia. Whether the accompanying buildup of carbon dioxide in the atmosphere caused the half-degree warming is hotly debated. (Source: S. H. Schneider. 1989. The Changing Climate. *Scientific American* 261 3: 70–79.)

observations of the transfer of radiant energy through various gases, the millions of aircraft and balloon observations of the earth's temperature structure and its radiative fluxes, and the literally billions and billions of satellite observations of the same quantities. Moreover, very recently A. Raval and V. Ramanathan of the University of Chicago used satellite observations to study the very important water vapor–greenhouse feedback mechanism, a process that is central to most models' estimates of some 3° plus or minus 1.5°C equilibrium warming from doubling CO_2. They conclude that "the greenhouse effect is found to increase significantly with sea surface temperature. The rate of increase gives compelling evidence for the positive feedback between surface temperature, water vapour and the greenhouse effect; the magnitude of the feedback is consistent with that predicted by climate models" (Raval & Ramanathan 1989). In other words, the heat-trapping capacity of the atmosphere is well understood and well measured on earth, and much of the sometimes polemical debate in the media over the scientific basis of the greenhouse effect has little reality. This empirical confirmation of the natural greenhouse effect, which is consistent with the greenhouse effect calculation of climate models, stands in stark contrast to the theoretical postulates of Lindzen (1990) that negative (i.e., stabilizing) temperature–water vapor feedback processes in parts of the tropics will reduce present estimates of global warming by a factor of 4 to 8 (Schneider 1990a).

It is well known that the 25% increase in carbon dioxide that is documented since the industrial revolution, the 100% increase in methane since the industrial revolution, and the introduction of man-made chemicals such as chlorofluorocarbons (also responsible for stratospheric ozone depletion) since the 1930s should have trapped some 2 extra watts of radiant energy over every square meter of earth. That part is well accepted by most climatological specialists. However, what is less well accepted is how to translate that 2 watts of heating into *x* degrees of temperature change, since this involves assumptions about how that heating will be distributed among surface temperature rises, evaporation increases, cloudiness changes, ice changes, and so forth. The factor of 2 to 3 uncertainty in global temperature rise projections as cited in typical National Academy of Sciences or the IPCC reports reflects a legitimate estimate of uncertainty held by most in the scientific community. Indeed, recent modifications of the British Meterological Office climate model to attempt to mimic the effects of cloud droplets halved their model's sensitivity to doubled CO_2—but was still well within the often cited 1.5–4.5°C range. However, the authors of the study, Mitchell, Senior, and Ingram (1989) wisely pointed out that "although the revised cloud scheme is more detailed, it is not necessarily more accurate than the less sophisticated scheme." I have never seen this forthright and important caveat quoted by any of the global warming critics who cite the British work as a reason to lower our concern. Finally, as stated earlier, prediction of the detailed regional distribution of climatic anomalies—that is, where and when it will be wetter and drier, how many floods might occur in the spring in California or forest fires in Siberia in August—is simply highly speculative, although some plausible scenarios can be given. Some such scenarios are given in Table 1, from the National Academy of Sciences 1987 assessment.

Projecting Regional Climatic Response

In order to make useful estimates of the effects of climatic changes, we need to determine the regional distribution of climatic change. Will it be drier in Iowa in 2010, too hot in India, wetter in Africa, or more humid in New York; will California be prone to more forest fires or will Venice flood? Unfortunately, reliable prediction of the time sequence of local and regional responses to variables such as temperature and rainfall requires climatic models of greater complexity and expense than are currently available. Even though the models have been used to estimate the responses of these variables, the regional predictions from state-of-the-art models are not yet reliable.

Although climatic models are far from fully verified for future simulations, the seasonal and paleoclimatic simulations are strong evidence that state-of-the-art climatic models already have considerable skills. An awareness of just what models are and what they can and can't do is probably the best we can ask of the public and its representatives. Then, the tough policy problem is how to apply the society's values in choosing to face the future, given the possible outcomes that climatic models foretell.

Although there is considerable experience in examining regional changes (e.g., fig. 4), considerable uncertainty remains over the probability that these

Table 1. Possible Climate Changes from Doubling of CO_2

Large Stratospheric Cooling (virtually certain). Reduced ozone concentrations in the upper stratosphere will lead to reduced absorption of solar ultraviolet radiation and therefore less heating. Increases in the stratospheric concentration of carbon dioxide and other radiatively active trace gases will increase the radiation of heat from the stratosphere. The combination of decreased heating and increased cooling will lead to a major lowering of temperatures in the upper stratosphere.

Global-Mean Surface Warming (very probable). For a doubling of atmospheric carbon dioxide (or its radiative equivalent from all the greenhouse gases), the *long-term* global-mean surface warming is expected to be in the range of 1.5 to 4.5°C. The most significant uncertainty arises from the effects of clouds. Of course, the *actual* rate of warming over the next century will be governed by the growth rate of greenhouse gases, natural fluctuations in the climate system, and the detailed response of the slowly responding parts of the climate system, i.e., oceans and glacial ice.

Global-Mean Precipitation Increase (very probable). Increased heating of the surface will lead to increased evaporation and, therefore, to greater global mean precipitation. Despite this increase in global average precipitation, some individual regions might well experience decreases in rainfall.

Reduction of Sea Ice (very probable). As the climate warms, total sea ice is expected to be reduced.

Polar Winter Surface Warming (very probable). As the sea ice boundary is shifted poleward, the models predict a dramatically enhanced surface warming in winter polar regions. The greater fraction of open water and thinner sea ice will probably lead to warming of the polar surface air by as much as 3 times the global mean warming.

Summer Continental Dryness/Warming (likely in the long term). Several studies have predicted a marked long-term drying of the soil moisture over some mid-latitude interior continental regions during summer. This dryness is mainly caused by an earlier termination of snowmelt and rainy periods and an earlier onset of the spring-to-summer reduction of soil wetness. Of course, these simulations of long-term equilibrium conditions may not offer a reliable guide to trends over the next few decades of changing atmospheric composition and changing climate.

High-Latitude Precipitation Increase (probable). As the climate warms, the increased poleward penetration of warm, moist air should increase the average annual precipitation in high latitudes.

Rise in Global-Mean Sea Level (probable). A rise in mean sea level is generally expected due to thermal expansion of sea water in the warmer future climate. Far less certain is the contribution due to melting or calving of land ice.

Source: National Research Council, 1987. *Current Issues in Atmospheric Changes.* Washington, D.C.: National Academy Press.

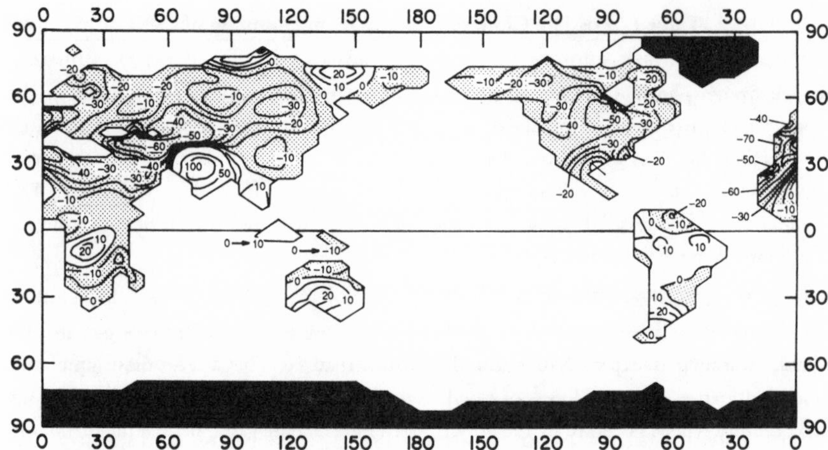

Fig. 4. CO_2–induced change in July soil moisture expressed as a percentage of soil moisture obtained from a computer model with doubled CO_2 compared to a control run with normal CO_2 amounts. Note the nonuniform response of this ecologically important variable to the uniform change in CO_2. (Modified from S. Manabe & R. Wetherald. 1986. Reduction in Summer Soil Wetness Induced by Increase in Atmospheric Carbon Dioxide. *Science* 232: 626–28.)

predicted regional features will occur. The principal reasons for the uncertainty are twofold: the crude treatment in climatic models of biological and hydrological processes and the usual neglect of the effects of the deep oceans. The deep oceans would respond slowly—over many decades to centuries—to climatic warming at the surface and would also act differentially (that is, nonuniformly in space and through time). Therefore, the oceans, like the forests, would be out of equilibrium with the atmosphere if greenhouse gases increased as rapidly as typically is projected and if climatic warming were to occur as fast as, say, 2° to 5°C during the next century. This typical projection, recall, is 10 to 50 times as fast as the natural average rate of temperature change that occurred from the end of the last Ice Age to the present warm period (that is, 2° to 5°C warming in a century from human activities, compared to an average natural global warming of 1° to 2°C per millennium from the waning of the Ice Age to the establishment of the present interglacial epoch). If the oceans are out of equilibrium with the atmosphere, then specific regional forecasts like that of figure 4 will not have much credibility until fully coupled atmosphere-ocean models are tested and applied. The development of such models is a formidable scientific and computational task and is still not very advanced. However, preliminary results with coupled atmospheric-oceanic circulation models (e.g., Washington & Meehl 1989; Stouffer, Manabe & Bryan 1989) do confirm that regional surprises in transient runs are quite likely.

Most recent climatic models predict that a warming of at least 1°C should have occurred during the past century. The precise "forecast" of the past 100 years also depends upon how the model accounts for such factors as changes in the solar constant, volcanic dust, trace greenhouse gases, and CO_2. Indeed, the typical prediction of a 1°C warming is broadly consistent but somewhat larger than that observed (see fig. 3). Possible explanations for the discrepancy include: (1) most state-of-the-art models are too sensitive to increases in trace greenhouse gases by a rough factor of 2; (2) modelers have not properly accounted for such competitive external forcings as volcanic dust or changes in solar energy output; (3) modelers have not accounted for other external forcings such as regional tropospheric aerosols from agricultural, biological, and industrial activity; (4) modelers have not properly accounted for internal processes that could lead to stochastic or chaotic behavior; (5) modelers have not properly accounted for the large heat capacity of the oceans taking up some of the heating of the greenhouse effect and delaying, but not ultimately reducing, warming of the lower atmosphere; (6) both present models and observed climatic trends could be correct, but models are typically run for equivalent doubling of carbon dioxide, whereas the world has only experienced a third of this increase and nonlinear processes have been properly modeled and have produced a sensitivity appropriate for doubling but not for a 30% increase; and (7) the incomplete and inhomogeneous network of thermometers has underestimated actual global warming this century (Schneider 1989c).

Despite this array of excuses why observed global temperature trends in the past century and those anticipated by most climate models disagree somewhat, the twofold discrepancy between predicted and measured temperature changes is not large but is still of concern. This rough validation is reinforced by the good simulation by most climatic models of the seasonal cycle, diverse ancient paleoclimates, hot conditions on Venus, cold conditions on Mars (both well simulated), the water vapor–greenhouse effect over the oceans, and the present distribution of climates on Earth. When taken together, these verifications provide *strong circumstantial evidence that the current modeling of the sensitivity of global surface temperature to given increases in greenhouse gases over the next 50 years or so is probably valid within a rough factor of 2.* Most climatologists do not yet proclaim that the observed temperature changes this century were caused beyond doubt by the greenhouse effect. The correlation between the observed century-long trend and the predicted warming could still be due to chance occurrences; or other factors, such as solar constant variations or volcanic dust, may not have been adequately accounted for correctly during the past 100 years, except during the past decade, when accurate measurements began to be made. However, very recent analyses of CO_2-induced and natural temperature trends since 1900 support a significant connection between the data sets (Wigley & Raper 1990).

Another decade or 2 of observations of trends in Earth's climate, of course, should produce signal-to-noise ratios sufficiently high that we will be able to determine conclusively the validity of present estimates of climatic sensitivity to increasing trace greenhouse gases. That, however, is not a cost-free enterprise because a greater amount of change could occur then than if actions were undertaken now to slow down the buildup rate of greenhouse gases.

Scenarios of the Environmental Impact of CO_2

Given a set of scenarios for regional climatic change, we must next estimate the impacts on the environment and society. Most greenhouse studies have focused on the direct effects of CO_2 increases or have used model-predicted maps of temperature and rainfall patterns to estimate impacts on crop yields or water supplies (e.g. Smith & Tirpak 1988). Also of concern is the potential that temperature increases will alter the range or numbers of pests that affect plants, or diseases that threaten animal or human health. Also of interest are the effects on unmanaged ecosystems, principally forests. For example, ecologists are concerned that the destruction rate of tropical forests attributed to human expansion is eroding the genetic diversity of the planet. That is, because the tropical forests are in a sense major banks for the bulk of living genetic materials on Earth, the world is losing some of its irreplaceable biological resources through rapid development (e.g., Wilson 1989). Tropical rainfall changes from CO_2 doubling have been suggested on the basis of climatic models. Thus, reserves (or refugia) that are currently set aside as minimal solutions for the preservation of some genetic resources into the future may not be as effective as currently planned (e.g., Peters 1990).

Climate changes resulting from greenhouse gas increases could also significantly affect water supply and demand. For example, a local increase in temperature of several degrees Celsius could decrease runoff in the Colorado River Basin by tens of percent (e.g., Waggoner 1990). A study of the vulnerability to climate change of various water resource regions in the United States showed that some regions are quite sensitive to climatic changes (see table 2).

Water quality will be diminished if the same volume of wastes are discharged through decreased stream flow. In addition, irrigation demand (and thus pressure on groundwater supplies) may substantially increase if temperatures increase without concomitant offsetting increases in precipitation. A number of climate models suggest that temperatures could increase and precipitation could decrease simultaneously in several areas, including the central plains of the United States. Peterson and Keller (in Waggoner 1990) estimated the effects of a 3°C warming and a 10% precipitation change on United States crop production based on crop water needs. The greatest impact would be in the western states and the Great Plains, the least in the northwest. The warm, dry combination would increase depletion of streams and reduce viable acreage by nearly a third in the arid regions. New supplies of water would be needed, threatening groundwater and the viability of agriculture in these regions. On the other hand, farmers in the east, and particularly in the southeast, might profit if the depletion of eastern rivers were relatively less severe than that in the west or the plains. However, increases in the efficiency of irrigation management and technological improvements remain achievable and would help substantially to mitigate potential negative effects. Drying in the west could also markedly increase the incidence of wildfires, which in turn could act as major agents of ecological change.

Some workers project that an increase in global temperature of several degrees Celsius will cause sea level to rise by about 0.3 m $\pm$ 0.4 m generally

Table 2. The Vulnerability to Climate Change of the Water-Resource Regions of the U.S. Shown by Ratios Defined in the Test

		Vulnerability Category				
		Consumption	Storage	Variability	Hydro-electric	Ground-water
Basin	**Lamps on**	**D/Q**	**Q/S**	**Q05/Q95**	**H/E**	**GO/GW**
Great Basin	5	*	*	*	*	*
Missouri	4	*		*	*	*
California	4	*	*	*	*	
Arkansas—White—Red	3		*	*		*
Texas—Gulf	3	*		*		*
Rio Grande	3	*		*		*
Lower Colorado	3	*			*	*
Tennessee	2		*		*	
Lower Mississippi	2		*	*		
Upper Colorado	2	*		*		
Pacific Northwest	2		*		*	
Alaska	2		*		*	
Caribbean	2		*	*		
New England	1		*			
Mid-Atlantic	1		*			
South Atlantic—Gulf	1		*			
Great Lakes	1		*			
Ohio	1		*			
Upper Mississippi	1		*			
Souris—Red—Rainy	1			*		
Hawaii	1		*			

Note: Ratios: *D/Q* for high consumption, *Q/S* for little storage, *Q05/Q95* for high variability, *H/E* for dependent on hydroelectricity, and *GO/GW* for groundwater overdraft. If the ratio exceeds a threshold, the warning lamp is on as indicated by an * in the table. The column labeled *Lamps on* shows the number of thresholds exceeded in a region, and the regions with most on are at the top of the table. The table suggests which American basins would be most jeopardized by increases in temperature that decreases runoff by increasing evaporation, or which could benefit most should the climate change increase precipitation sufficiently to overcome any increases in evaporation caused by temperature increase.
Source: P. H. Gleick, 1990. Vulnerability of Water Systems, in Waggoner, P. E. (Ed.) *Climate Change and U.S. Water Resources,* New York; John Wiley and Sons.

in the next 50 to 100 years (Meier 1990); the upper range of such a rise would endanger coastal settlements, estuarine ecosystems, and the quality of coastal freshwater resources. However, the mean estimate includes a dubious assumption that the Greenland ice sheet will grow with climatic warming (Schneider 1990b). It probably underestimates sea level rise potential.

Economic, Social, and Political Impacts

The estimation of the distribution of economic "winners and losers," given a scenario of climatic change, involves more than simply looking at the total dollars lost and gained—were it possible somehow to make such a calculation credibly! It also requires looking at these important equity questions: who wins and who loses? and how might the losers be compensated and the winners charged? For example, if the corn belt in the United States were to "move" north and east by several hundred kilometers from a warming, then a billion dollars a year lost in Iowa farms could eventually become Minnesota's billion-dollar gain. Although some macroeconomists viewing this hypothetical problem from the perspective of the United States as a whole might see no net losses here, considerable social consternation could be generated by such a shift in climatic resources, particularly since the cause was economic activities (i.e., CO_2-producing) that directed differential costs and benefits to various groups. Moreover, even the perception that the economic activities of one nation could create climatic changes that would be detrimental to another has the potential for disrupting international relations—as is already occurring in the case of acid rain. In essence, what greenhouse gas-induced environmental changes create is an issue of "redistributive justice."

If July soil moisture decreases, such as that projected for the United States in figure 4, were to occur, then it would have disturbing implications for agriculture in the United States and Canadian plains. Clearly, present farming practices and cropping patterns would have to change. The more rapidly the climate changed and the less accurately the changes were predicted (which go together), the more likely that the net changes would be detrimental. It has been suggested that a future with soil moisture change like that shown in figure 4 could translate to a loss of comparative advantage of United States agricultural products on the world market (Easterling et al. 1988). Such a scenario could have substantial economic and security implications. Taken together, projected climate changes into the next century could have major impacts on water resources, sea level, agriculture, forests, biological diversity, air quality, human health, urban infrastructure, and electricity demand.

Policy Responses

The last stage in diagnosing the greenhouse effect concerns the question of appropriate policy responses. Three classes of actions could be considered. First, engineering countermeasures: purposeful interventions in the environment to minimize the potential effects (e.g., deliberately spreading dust in the stratosphere to reflect some extra sunlight to cool the climate as a countermeasure to the inadvertent CO_2 warming). These countermeasures suffer from an immediate and obvious flaw: if there is admitted uncertainty associated with predicting the unintentional consequences of human activities, then likewise substantial uncertainty surrounds any deliberate climatic modification. Thus, it is quite possible that the unintentional change might be overestimated by computer models and the intentional change underestimated, in which case human intervention would be a "cure worse than the disease" (Kellogg & Schneider 1974). Furthermore, the prospect for international tensions resulting from any deliberate environmental modifications is staggering, and our legal instruments to deal with these tensions is immature. Thus, political acceptance of any substantial climate countermeasure strategies for the foreseeable future is hard to imagine, particularly because there are other more viable alternatives.

The second class of policy action, one that tends to be favored by many economists, is adaptation (e.g., Schelling 1983). Adaptive strategists propose to let society adjust to environmental changes. In extreme form, some believe in adaptation without attempting to mitigate or prevent the changes in advance. Such a strategy is based partly on the argument that society will be able to replace much of its infrastructure before major climatic changes materialize, and that because of the large uncertainties, we are better off waiting to see what will happen before making potentially unnecessary investments. However, it appears quite likely that we are already committed to some climatic change based on emissions to date; and therefore, in my value system, some anticipatory steps to make adaptation easier certainly seems prudent. We could adapt to climate change, for example, by accelerating development of nonfossil fuel alternative energy supply systems or by planting alternative crop strains that would be more widely adapted to a whole range of plausible climatic futures. Of course, if we don't know what is coming or we haven't developed or tested the seeds yet, we may well suffer substantial losses during the transition to the new climate. But such adaptations are often recommended because of the uncertain nature of the specific redistributive character of future climatic change and because of high discount rates.

In the case of water supply management, an American Association for the Advancement of Science (Waggoner 1990) panel made a strong, potentially controversial, but, I believe, rather obvious adaptive suggestion: governments at all levels should reevaluate the legal, technical, and economic components of water supply management to account for the likelihood of climate change, stressing efficient techniques for water use and new management practices to increase the flexibility of water systems, recognizing the need to reconsider existing compacts, ownership, and other legal baggage associated with the present water system. In light of rapid climate change, we need to reexamine the balance between private rights and the public good, because water is intimately connected with both. Regional transfers from water-abundant regions to water-deficient regions are often prohibited by legal or economic impediments that need to be examined as part of a hedging strategy to adapt more effectively to the prospect of climatic change, even though regional details cannot now be reliably forecast.

Finally, the most active policy category is prevention, which could take the form of sulfur scrubbers in the case of acid rain, abandonment of the use of chlorofluorocarbons and other potential ozone-reducing gases (particularly those that also enhance global warming), reduction in the amount of fossil fuel used around the world, or fossil fuel switching from more CO_2- and SO_2-producing coal to cleaner, less polluting methane fuels. Prevention policies, often advocated by environmentalists, are controversial because they involve, in some cases, substantial immediate investments as "insurance" against the possibility of very large future environmental change—change whose details cannot be precisely predicted. The sorts of preventive policies that could be considered are: increasing the efficiency of energy production and end use, the development of alternative energy systems that are not fossil fuel based, or in a far-reaching proposal, a "law of the air," proposed in 1975 by William Kellogg and Margaret Mead (1976). They suggested that various nations would be assigned polluting rights to keep CO_2 emissions below some agreed global standard. A "law of the atmosphere" was recently endorsed in the report of a major international meeting (statement from the conference, "The Changing Atmosphere: Implications for Global Security," Toronto, Ontario, Canada, June 27–30, 1988).

A Scientific Consensus?

In summary, a substantial warming of the climate through the augmentation of the greenhouse effect is very likely if current technological, economic and demographic trends continue. There already are validations of the overall sensitivity of climate models to large-scale radiation changes (e.g., see fig. 5) which support this conclusion. Rapid climatic changes will cause both ecological and physical systems to go out of equilibrium—a transient condition that makes detailed predictions tenuous. The faster the changes take place, the less societies or natural ecosystems will be able to adapt to them without potentially serious disruptions. Both the rate and magnitude of typical projections up to the year 2050 suggest climatic changes beyond that experienced by civilization could occur. Quite simply, the faster the climate is forced to change, the more likely there will be unexpected surprises lurking (e.g., Broecker 1987). The consensus about future global change begins to weaken over detailed assessments of the precise timing and geographic distribution of potential effects, and begins to crumble over the value question of whether present information is sufficient to generate a societal response stronger than more scientific research on the problems—appropriate (but self-serving) advice which we scientists, myself included, somehow always manage to recommend.

High Leverage Actions to Cope with Global Warming

Clearly, society does not have the resources to hedge against all possible negative future outcomes. Is there, then, some simple principle that can help us choose which actions to spend our resources on? One guideline is called the "tie-in strategy." Quite simply, society should pursue those actions

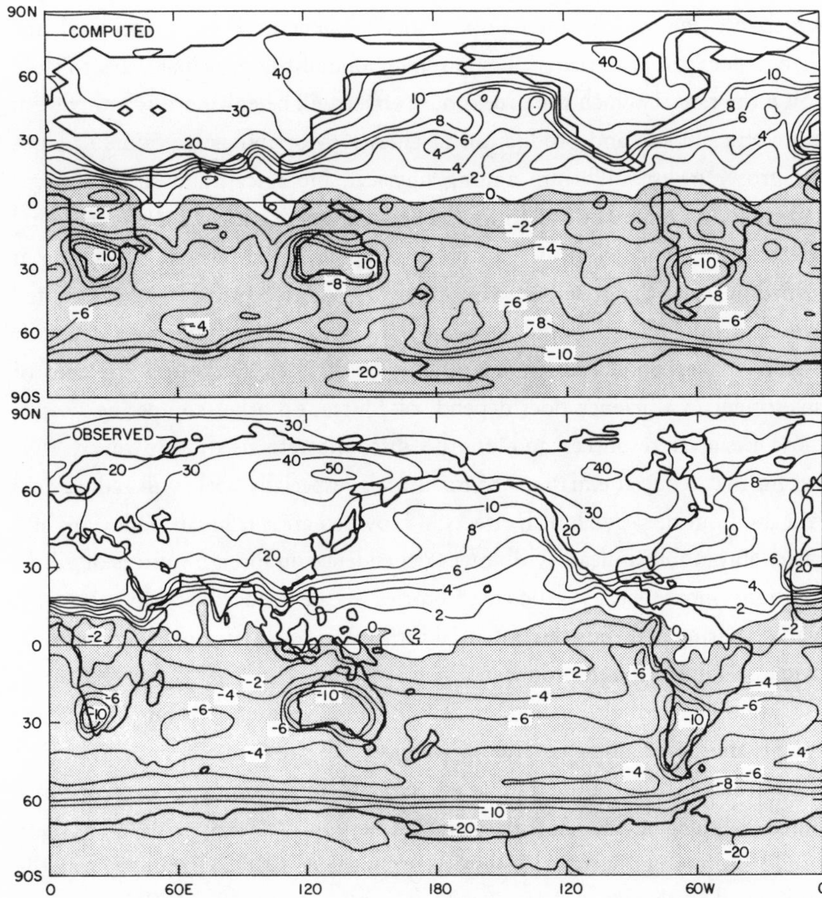

Fig. 5. A 3-dimensional climate model has been used to compute the winter-to-summer temperature extremes all over the globe. The model's performance can be verified against the observed data. This verification exercise shows that the model quite impressively reproduces many of the features of the seasonal cycle. These seasonal temperature differences are mostly larger than those occurring between ice ages and interglacials or for any plausible future carbon dioxide change. While this cannot validate models for processes occurring on medium-to-long time scales (greater than 1 year), it is very encouraging for validating to a rough factor of 2 to 3 such ''fast physics'' paramaterizations as clouds. (Source: S. Manabe & R. J. Stouffer. 1980 Sensitivity of a Global Climate Model to an Increase in CO_2 Concentration in the Atmosphere. *Journal of Geophysical Research* 85:x 5529–54.)

which provide widely agreed-upon societal benefits even if the predicted change does not materialize. For instance, one of the principal ways to slow down the rate at which the greenhouse effect will be enhanced is to invest in more efficient use and production of energy. More efficiency would reduce the growing disequilibrium among physical, biological, and social systems and could buy time both to study the detailed implications of the greenhouse effect further and to ensure an easier adaptation. However, supposing it turned out that the greenhouse effects now projected prove to be substantial overestimates. What would be wasted by an energy-efficient strategy? It usually makes good economic sense to be efficient (although the rate of investment in efficiency does depend, of course, on other competing uses of those financial resources and on the discount rate used). However, it is certain that reduced emissions of fossil fuels, especially coal, will reduce acid rain and limit negative health effects in crowded areas from air pollution; and better automobile mileage will lower dependence on foreign sources of oil. In addition, more energy efficient factories mean reduced energy costs for manufacturing and thus the potential for greater long-term product competitiveness against foreign producers.

Development of alternative, environmentally safer energy supply technologies is another example of a tie-in strategy, as is the development and testing of alternative crop strains, trading agreements with nations for food or other climatically dependent strategic commodities, and so forth. However, there would be in some circles ideological opposition to such strategies on the grounds that these activities should be pursued by individual investment decisions through a market economy, not by collective action using tax revenues or regulatory incentives. Indeed, that was the position of the Bush administration in 1989 and 1990. In rebuttal, a market which does not include the potential costs of environmental disruptions can hardly be considered a truly free market. Furthermore, strategic investments are made routinely on noneconomic criteria (that is, cost-benefit analyses are secondary), even by the most politically conservative people—to purchase military security, for example. A strategic consciousness, not an economic calculus, dictates investments in defense. Similarly, people purchase insurance as a hedge against plausible, but uncertain, future problems. The judgment here is whether strategic consciousness—widely accepted across the political spectrum—needs to be extended to other potential threats to security, including a substantially altered environment occurring on a global scale at unprecedented rates. Then, the next problem is to determine how many resources to allocate.

If we choose to wait for more scientific cerrtainty over details before preventive actions are initiated, then this is done at the risk of our having to adapt to a larger, faster occurring dose of greenhouse gases than if actions were initiated today. In my value system, high-leverage, tie-in actions are long overdue. Of course, I repeat that whether to act is not a scientific judgment but a value-laden political choice that cannot be resolved by scientific methods.

It must be recognized that incentives for investments to improve energy efficiency, to develop less-polluting alternatives, control methane emissions, or phase out CFCs may require policies that charge user fees on activities in proportion to the amount of pollution each generates. Some might argue that this would differentially impact poor people, less developed nations, or selected segments such as coal miners. Indeed, an equity problem is raised through such strategies. However, is it more appropriate to subsidize poverty, for example, through artificially lower prices of energy, which distort the market and discourage efficient energy end use or alternate production; or is it better to fight poverty by direct economic aid? Perhaps targeting some fraction of an energy tax to help those immediately disadvantaged would improve the political tractability of any attempt to internalize the external costs of pollution not currently charged to energy production or end use. In any case, consideration of these political issues will be essential if global-scale agreements are to be negotiated, and without global-scale agreements, no nation acting alone can reduce global warming by more than 10% or so.

The "bottom line" of the implications of atmospheric change is that we perturb the enviroment at a faster rate than we can understand or predict the consequences. In 1957, Roger Revelle and Hans Suess (1957) pointed out that we were undergoing a "great geophysical experiment." In the 30 years since that prophetic remark, carbon dioxide has risen more than 10% in the atmosphere, and there have been even more dramatic increases in methane and CFCs. The 1980s have seen the warmest temperatures in the instrumental record, and 1988 saw a combination of dramatic circumstances that gained much media attention: extended heat waves across most of the United States, intense drought, forest fires in the west, an extremely intense hurricane, and flooding in Bangladesh. Indeed, many people interpreted (prematurely, I believe) these events in 1988 as "proof" that human augmentation of the greenhouse effect had finally arrived. Should the rapid warming in the instrumental record of the past 10 years be maintained into the 1990s—a good bet in my view—then a vast majority of atmospheric scientists will undoubtedly agree that the greenhouse signal has been felt. Unfortunately, if society chooses to wait another decade or more for 99% certain proof, then this behavior raises the risk that we will have to adapt to a larger amount of climate change than if actions to slow down the buildup of greenhouse gases were pursued more vigorously today. At a minimum, we can enhance our interdisciplinary research efforts to reduce uncertainties in physical, biological, and social scientific areas. But I believe enough is known already to go beyond research and begin to implement policies to enhance adaptation and to slow down the rapid buildup of greenhouse gases—a buildup that poses a considerable probability of unprecedented global-scale climatic change well within the lifetime of most of us.

References

Bottomley, M., C. K. Folland, J. Hsiung, R. E. Newell, D. E. Parker. 1990. Global Ocean Surface Temperature Atlas, Bracknell, United Kindgom Meteorological Office.

Broecker, W. S. 1987. Unpleasant Surprises in the Greenhouse?, *Nature* 328:123–126.

Brookes, W. T. 1989. The Global Warming Panic. *Forbes,* 25 Dec., 96–102.

Loads of Media Coverage. 1989. *Detroit News,* 22 Nov.

Ellsaesser, H. W. 1984. The Climatic Effect of CO_2: A Different View. *Atmospheric Environment* 18:431–34.

Easterling, W. E., M. L. Parry, P. R. Crosson. 1989. Adapting Future Agriculture to Changes in Climate. In *Greenhouse Warming: Abatement and Adaptation,* ed. N. J. Rosenberg, W. E. Easterling, P. R. Crossan, and J. Darmstadter. Washington, D.C.: Resources for the Future.

Intergovernmental Panel on Climate Change. June, 1990. Scientific Assessment of Climate Change, Report Prepared for IPCC by Working Group I, Geneva: World Meteorological Organization: Jones, P. D., and Wigley, T. M. L. 1990. Global Warming Trends, *Sci. Amer.,* 263, No. 2, August:84–91.

Karl, T. R., and P. D. Jones. 1989. Urban Bias in Area-Averaged Surface Air Temperature Trends. *Bulletin of the American Meteorological Society* 70:265–70.

Kellogg, W. W., and M. Mead, eds. 1976. *The Atmosphere: Endangered and Endangering.* Fogarty International Center Proceedings No. 39. Washington, D.C.: Government Printing Office.

Kellogg, W. W., and S. H. Schneider. 1974. Climate Stabilization: For Better or Worse? *Science* 186:1163–72.

Lindzen, R. S. 1990. Some Coolness Concerning Global Warmings. *Bull. Amer. Met. Soc.* 71:288–299.

George C. Marshall Institute. 1989. *Scientific Perspectives on the Greenhouse Problem.* Washington, D.C.: George C. Marshall Institute.

Meier, M. F. 1990. Reduced Rise in Sea Level. *Nature* 343:115–16.

Mitchell, J. F. B., C. A. Senior, and W. J. Ingram. 1989. CO_2 and Climate: A Missing Feedback? *Nature* 341: 132–34.

Peters, R., ed. In press. *Proceedings of the Conference on the Consequences of the Greenhouse Effect for Biological Diversity.*

Raval, A., and V. Ramanathan. 1989. Observational Determination of the Greenhouse Effect. *Nature* 342:758.

Revelle, R., and H. E. Suess. 1957. Carbon Dioxide Exchange between Atmosphere and Ocean and the Question of an Increase of Atmospheric CO_2 during Past and Present Decades. *Tellus* 9:18–27.

Schelling, T. C. 1983. Climatic Change: Implications for Welfare and Policy, in *Changing Climate,* Report of the Carbon Dioxide Assessment Committee. Washington, D.C.: National Academy Press.

Schneider, S. H. 1989a. News Plays Fast and Loose With the Facts. *Detroit News,* 5 Dec.

______. 1989b. *Global Warming: Are We Entering the Greenhouse Century?* San Francisco: Sierra Club Books.

______. 1989c. The Greenhouse Effect: Science and Policy. *Science* 243:171–81.

______. 1990a. The Global Warming Debate Heats Up: An Analysis and Perspective. *Bull. Amer. Met. Soc.* 71:1292–1304.

______. 1990b. Is the Downward Revision of Global Sea Level Rise Projections Premature? Submitted to *Nature.*

Smith, J. B., and D. Tirpak, eds. 1988. *The Potential Effects of Global Climate Change on the United States: Draft Report to Congress.* 2 vols. U.S. Environmental Protection Agency, Office of Policy, Planning, and Evaluation, Office of Research and Development. Washington, D.C.: Government Printing Office.

Stouffer, R. J., S. Manabe, and K. Bryan. 1989. Interhemispheric Asymmetry in Climate Response to a Gradual Increase of Atmospheric CO_2. *Nature* 342:660–62.

Waggoner, P. E. ed. 1990. *Climate Change and U.S. Water Resources.* New York: John Wiley and Sons.

Washington, W. M., and G. A. Meehl. 1989: Climate Sensitivity Due to Increased CO_2: Experiments with a Coupled Atmosphere and Ocean General Circulation Model. *Climate Dynamics* 4:1–38.

Wigley, T. M. L., and S. C. B. Raper. 1990. Nature Variability of the Climate System and Detection of the Greenhouse Effect. *Nature* 344:324–27.

Wilson, E. O. 1989. Threats to Biodiversity. *Scientific American* 261 3: 108–16.

Notes on the Contributors

ALAN M. BECK received his baccalaureate from Brooklyn College and his master's degree from California State University at Los Angeles. He received his doctorate in animal ecology from The Johns Hopkins University School of Hygiene and Public Health. He has directed the Center for the Interaction of Animals and Society at the University of Pennsylvania's School of Veterinary Medicine and is presently with the Department of Patho-Biology in the School of Veterinary Medicine, Purdue University. With Aaron Katcher, he coedited *New Perspectives on Our Lives with Companion Animals* and co-wrote *Between Pets and People: The Importance of Animal Companionship.*

LEO K. BUSTAD, M.S., D.V.M., and Ph.D., is professor and dean emeritus of the College of Veterinary Medicine at Washington State University. From 1949 to 1965 he was a biomedical scientist and component manager with General Electric; from 1965 to 1973 he was a professor at University of California at Davis's Schools of Medicine and Veterinary Medicine and directed two laboratories. Bustad is the author of *Animals, Aging, and the Aged* and coauthor of *Learning and Living Together:*

Building the Human-Animal Bond. He is a pioneer on the health benefits of human-animal interaction and was cofounder and first president of the Delta Society. He is a member of the National Academies of Practice and the Institute of Medicine of the National Academy of Sciences.

JOHN HURRELL CROOK completed his doctorate at Cambridge, England, in 1958 following degree work at Southampton University and military service as a radar officer in Hong Kong during the Korean War. At Bristol University (Psychology Department) he led an internationally known group of research ethologists throughout the 1970s, focusing on the evolution of bird and primate social organization. Since 1980 Crook has increasingly developed an interest in the social anthropology of Buddhist villagers in the Himalayas and has completed a study of the sociobiology of polyandry among Tibetans, work on the social psychology of Ladakhi families, and theoretical work on the evolution of consciousness. With Henry Osmaston he has co-written *Himalayan Buddhist Villages,* and with David Fontana he has co-written *Wordless Views: East-West Contributions to the Understanding of Mind*—both in press.

RICHARD DAWKINS did undergraduate work at Oxford University and doctoral work with the Nobel-prize-winning ethologist Niko Tinbergen. He was assistant professor of zoology at the University of California at Berkeley from 1967 to 1969, and he has been a fellow of New College, Oxford, since 1970. Dawkins is author of *Selfish Gene* (1976), *The Extended Phenotype* (1982), and *The Blind Watchmaker* (1986), and he was presenter of two BBC television programs in the *Horizon* series: *Nice Guys Finish First* (1985) and *The Blind Watchmaker* (1986).

PHYLLIS DOLHINOW is professor of anthropology at the University of California at Berkeley, where she teaches and undertakes research within the general fields of human and nonhuman primate behavior and evolution. Her field work has been on a number of Old World nonhuman primates in Asia and Africa, with particular emphasis on the Colobine langur monkey of India. Field observations have been combined with a detailed long-term study of the life stories of 3 generations of langur monkeys in a colony setting.

JOHN F. EISENBERG received his B.S. degree in zoology from Washington State University and then completed his master's and doctoral research at the University of

California at Berkeley. For some 18 years he was associated with the University of Maryland and the National Zoological Park, Smithsonian Institution. During his tenure at the Smithsonian, he conducted field research in Panama, Venezuela, Madagascar, and Sri Lanka. Since 1982 Eisenberg has been the Katharine Ordway Professor of Ecosystem Conservation at the University of Florida. He is the author of numerous scientific publications and editor of several books. His most well-known book is *The Mammalian Radiations* (1981).

HELEN FISHER is research associate in the Department of Anthropology at the American Museum of Natural History. Among her publications are "Evolution of Human Serial Pairbonding," *American Journal of Physical Anthropology* (1989), "The Four Year Itch," *Natural History Magazine* (1987), *The Sex Contract: The Evolution of Human Behavior* (1982), and *The Evolution and Future of Marriage, Sex, and Love* (in press).

ROBIN FOX is professor of social theory at Rutgers University and was previously professor of anthropology. He received his bachelor's and doctor's degrees from London University and also studied at Harvard University and at Stanford Medical School. He taught full-time at Exeter University and the London School of Economics, and has lectured at the Universities of Cambridge, Paris, Oxford, California, and Los Andes in Bogotá. Fox has done fieldwork among the Pueblo Indians in New Mexico and the Donegal Islanders in Ireland. His work has been mainly on evolutionary interpretations of systems of kinship and marriage. The books he has written are *The Keresan Bridge, Kinship and Marriage, The Imperial Animal* (with Lionel Tiger), *Encounter with Anthropology, Biosocial Anthropology, The Tory Islanders, The Red Lamp of Incest, Neonate Cognition* (with Jacques Mehler), and *The Violent Imagination.*

AARON HONORI KATCHER is associate professor of psychiatry at the University of Pennsylvania and associate director of the Center for Interaction of Animals and Society at the School of Veterinary Medicine. He is a graduate of Williams College and of the University of Pennsylvania School of Medicine. His research has included studies of the physiology of emotions and of the influence of social and environmental conditions on patterns of disease. Recently he has published studies of the physiological and behavioral correlates of interaction with companion animals.

MARTIN H. MOYNIHAN was educated in Switzerland, France, the United States, and England. His research has been conducted under the auspices of Cornell and Harvard universities and in connection with the Smithsonian Tropical Research Institute. He specializes in animal behavior and the evolution of social and signal systems, with particular reference to birds (passerines, coraciiformes), New World primates, and coleoid cephalopods (octopuses, cuttlefishes, and squids).

NORMAN MYERS is a consultant in environment and development. He has worked since 1970 on the general subject area of environment and natural resources, with emphasis on species, gene reservoirs, and tropical forests. He has undertaken this consultancy work for the Rockefeller Brothers Fund, the National Academy of Sciences, the World Bank, the Smithsonian Institution, United Nations agencies, the World Resources Institute, National Research Council, and International Union for the Conservation of Nature, among other organizations. His main professional interest lies with resource relationships between the developed and developing worlds. Among his publications are *The Sinking Ark* (1979), *Conversion of Tropical Moist Forests Wild Species* (1980), *A Wealth of Wild Species* (1983), *The Primary Source* (1984), and *The Gaia Atlas of Planet Management* (1985).

RICHARD POTTS is associate curator of anthropology, National Museum of Natural History, Smithsonian Institution, Washington, D.C. After receiving a B.A. in anthropology from Temple University and a Ph.D. in biological anthropology from Harvard, he taught at Yale University from 1981 to 1985. As head of the Smithsonian's Human Origins Program, he conducts excavations at Early and Middle Pleistocene sites in East Africa, and is currently directing fieldwork at the famous handaxe site of Olorgesailie in Kenya. His research focuses on the behavioral and ecological history of early human ancestors.

RICHARD M. RESTAK is assistant professor of neurology, Georgetown University Medical School and is author of *The Brain* and *The Mind.* His writing has appeared in textbooks of psychiatry, and he has written the entry on the brain in the 1990 *Compton's Encyclopedia* and the 1990 *World Book Encyclopedia*. Restak's interests are the neurosciences and the brain/mind relationship. He is presently writing a series of essays on the relationship of brain and mind to be published in 1991.

MICHAEL H. ROBINSON, director of the Smithsonian Institution's National Zoological Park, is an animal behaviorist and a tropical biologist. Immediately prior to his appointment to the National Zoo, he served as deputy director of the Smithsonian Tropical Research Institute in Panama, which institution he joined in 1966 as a tropical biologist. He received his doctor of philosophy from Oxford University after being awarded his bachelor of science, summa cum laude, from the University of Wales. His scientific interests include predator-prey interactions, evolution of adaptations, tropical biology, courtship and mating behavior, phenology of arthropods, and freshwater biology.

ANDREW N. ROWAN is director, Center for Animals and Public Policy, and assistant dean for New Programs, Tufts University School of Veterinary Medicine. He received a B.S.c. from Cape Town University and an M.A. and D. Phil. (biochemistry) from Oxford University. He worked for 6 months for Pergamon Press, Oxford, before taking a job with FRAME (Fund for the Replacement of Animals in Medical Experiments) in London, promoting the concept of alternatives for a scientific audience. He moved to Washington, D.C., in 1978 to take up a position as laboratory animal specialist with the Humane Society of the United States. In 1983 he moved to Tufts School of Veterinary Medicine and is responsible for biochemistry teaching, the school's programs on animals and society, and various administrative functions. He is author of *Of Mice, Models, and Men* (1984), editor of *Animals and People Sharing the World* (1988), and author of numerous articles in scientific journals. He is the recipient of a Rhodes Scholarship (1968) and an AFS International Exchange Scholarship (1964) and is founding editor of *Anthrozoös,* a multidisciplinary journal of human-animal interactions.

STEPHEN H. SCHNEIDER received his Ph.D. in mechanical engineering and plasma physics from Columbia University and is currently head of the Interdisciplinary Climate Systems Section at the National Center for Atmospheric Research. He is author of *The Genesis Strategy: Climate and Global Survival,* with L. Mesirow (1976), *The Coevolution of Climate and Life,* with R. Londer (1984), *Global Warming: Are We Entering the Greenhouse Century?* and is author and coauthor of over 170 scientific papers, proceedings, edited books, and book chapters. He is editor of the scientific journal *Climatic Change* and a frequent witness at congressional hearings. He has been a member of the Defense Science Board Task Force on Atmospheric Obscuration, and was a consultant to the Carter and Nixon administrations. Schneider is a frequent contributor to commercial and noncommercial print and broadcast media on climate and environmental issues, and is a fellow of the American Association for the Advancement of Science. His current research interests include climatic change;

food/climate and other environmental/science public policy issues; and climatic modeling of paleoclimates and of human impacts on climate. He is also interested in advancing the public understanding of science.

THOMAS A. SEBEOK was Smithsonian Institution regents fellow in 1983–84 and research associate in 1984–87. He has been on the faculty of Indiana University since 1943, where he holds the titles of distinguished professor of linguistics and semiotics, and professor of anthropology and of folklore. Among his books, including collaborative anthologies, are *Perspectives in Zoosemiotics, Animal Communication, Approaches to Animal Communication, Speaking of Apes, The Clever Hans Phenomenon, How Animals Communicate,* and two forthcoming: *Animal "Language": Fact or Illusion* and *Prefigurements of Art.*

IRWIN I. SHAPIRO is the director of the Harvard-Smithsonian Center for Astrophysics in Cambridge, Massachusetts. His personal research is concerned primarily with the application of radar and radio techniques, as appropriate, to taking the measure of the earth, the solar system, and the universe, and to testing theories of gravitation.

LIONEL TIGER studied at McGill University and the University of London, and has taught at universities in Ghana and British Columbia, and at McGill and Rutgers, where he is Charles Darwin Professor of Anthropology. He was research director of the H. F. Guggenheim Foundation from 1972 to 1984 and is treasurer and executive board member of the PEN American Center. His books are *Men in Groups, The Imperial Animal* (with Robin Fox), *Women in the Kibbutz* (with Joseph Shepher), *Female Hierarchies* (edited with Heather Fowler), *Optimism: The Biology of Hope, China's Food* (with photographs by Reinhart Wolf), and most recently, *The Manufacture of Evil: Ethics, Evolution, and the Industrial System.*

ROBERT TRIVERS studied mathematics and history as an undergraduate at Harvard. A job writing children's books exposed him to the delights of animal behavior and evolutionary theory. Under the guidance of William Drury and Irven DeVore, he concentrated on social theory based on natural selection. In 1972, he received a Ph.D. in biology from Harvard. Trivers taught at Harvard until 1978, when he moved to the University of California at Santa Cruz. Retaining a strong interest in sexual selection, sex ratio, reciprocal altruism, and deceit and self-deception, he has added an interest in evolutionary genetics, especially the evolution of the sex chromosomes.

SHERWOOD L. WASHBURN is university professor of anthropology emeritus at the University of California at Berkeley. In teaching, his principal interest was and is human evolution. In research, he developed experimental methods suitable for the analysis of the problems of human evolution. His fieldwork on monkey behavior helped him to relate structure and function through the study of the evolution of behavioral systems. Washburn received his Ph.D. from Harvard in 1940. He taught in the Department of Anatomy at Columbia University Medical School and in the Department of Anthropology at the University of Chicago before coming to the University of California at Berkeley in 1958.

MARY JANE WEST-EBERHARD received her B.A., M.S. and Ph.D. degrees in zoology from the University of Michigan, and was a post-doctoral fellow at the Museum of Comparative Zoology, Harvard University (1967–69). She then spent 10 years (1969–79) in Cali, Colombia, followed by 10 years (1979–present) in Costa Rica, conducting field studies of tropical social wasps and writing on the evolution of social behavior (including sexual selection and effects on speciation).

EDWARD O. WILSON is Frank B. Baird Jr. Professor of Science and curator in entomology at Harvard University. He received a master's degree in biology at the University of Alabama and, in 1955, a Ph.D. in biology at Harvard University. He has been at Harvard ever since. Wilson's research has been, and continues to be, concentrated on the social insects, biogeography, systematics, and sociobiology.

Author Index

Ackerman, C., 99, 123
Ahlquist, J. E., 62, 69, 72
Albert, A., 267, 275, 283, 288
Alf, E., 269, 277
Altmann, J., 141, 142, 151, 153, 154
Altmann, S., 154
Anant, S. S., 257, 259
Anderson, D. C., 155
Anderson, R. K., 235, 259
Anderson, R. S., 235, 259
Andrews, P., 58
Ardrey, R., 52, 55, 57
Arensburg, B., 47, 58
Argyle, M., 242, 259
Arkow, P. S., 235, 259
Armstrong, E. A., 161, 172
Arnold, L. E., 259
August, P. V., 137

Baars, B. J., 205, 220
Baerends van Roon, J. M., 200, 201
Bailey, W., 218, 220
Barel, C. D. N., 323, 328
Barends, G. P., 201
Barloy, J. J., 238, 239, 240, 244, 259
Barnes, J., 99, 123
Barnett, J. L., 275, 277
Bateson, P., 141, 151, 153
Baun, M., 269, 275
Beaver, B. G., 237, 259
Beck, A. M., 235, 242, 259, 261, 267, 268, 269, 270, 276, 277
Behrensmeyer, A. K., 53, 57
Berge, C., 116, 123
Berger, C. R., 205, 220
Berger, J., 266, 275, 276
Berger, P., 214, 220
Bergstrom, N., 275
Bernstein, I. S., 150, 153
Bertalanffy, L. von, 141, 153
Beynon, A. D., 48, 57
Binford, L. R., 52, 57

Birdsell, J. B., 115, 123
Bishop, N. H., 141, 153
Bisop, P., 262
Blackmore, S. J., 206, 207, 220
Blenden, D. C., 262
Boggess, J. E., 141, 153
Bohm, D., 218, 220
Boltz, R., 276
Bolwig, N., 145, 153, 242, 259
Bottomley, M., 344, 364
Bowing, G. B., 261
Bowlby, J., 147, 153, 271, 276
Bowler, P. J., 61, 68
Bramblett, C. A., 141, 151, 157
Brauer, G., 57
Briggs, J. L., 115, 123
Broecker, W. S., 360, 364
Bromage, T. G., 48, 57, 117, 123
Brookes, W. T., 342, 364
Brown, C. E., 238, 261
Bryan, K., 365
Bulcroft, K., 267, 275
Bullowa, M., 242, 259
Bunn, H. T., 52, 57
Bustad, L. K., 235, 244, 252, 259
Byrne, R. W., 210, 220

Cain, A., 267, 276
Campbell, B., 159, 172
Cann, R. L., 57
Capra, F., 218, 220
Caras, R., 237, 238, 259
Carpenter, C. C., 199, 201
Carpenter, C. R., 131–132, 137
Case, T. J., 324, 328
Chagnon, N., 111, 123
Chalmers, R. M., 70
Chapple, E. D., 127, 137
Chase, P. G., 54, 57
Cheney, D. L., 187, 191
Cherlin, A. J., 96, 107, 118, 123
Cherry, C., 195, 201
Chism, J., 141, 142, 153
Clark-Wheatley, C. B., 156
Clutton-Brock, J., 273, 276
Cockrill, W. R., 246, 247, 248, 250, 251, 259
Cohen, R., 113, 119, 124
Colinvaux, P., 137
Conkey, M. W., 54, 57
Collins, S., 218, 220
Conroy, G. C., 48, 57, 117, 124
Convit, J., 325, 328
Coppinger, R. P., 273, 276
Corson, E. O., 259
Corson, S. A., 235, 259
Cott, H. B., 177, 191
Coy, D. H., 263
Craik, K. J. W., 206, 220
Cranach, M. von, 203, 205, 221
Crane, J., 200, 201
Crick, F. H. C., 34, 39
Cripe, W. S., 246, 251, 260
Crockett, C. M., 133, 134, 136, 137
Crook, J. H., 129, 137, 203, 206, 209, 210, 211, 218, 219, 221, 287, 288
Crosson, P. R., 364
Cupitt, D., 216, 221
Curtin, R. A., 153
Curtis, G. H., 64, 68

Daly, M., 97, 98, 120, 124, 140, 153
Darwin, C., 57, 159, 160, 164, 165, 172, 253, 260
Davis, H. P., 237, 260
Davis, M., 237, 260
Dawkins, R., 24, 29, 35, 39
Dean, M. C., 48, 57, 117, 123
de Benedictis, T., 151, 153
Deegener, P., 129, 137
De Eskinazi, F. G., 262
Delta Society, 235, 260
DeMay, M., 144, 154
Dennet, D. C., 207, 221
DeVitt, M., 195, 201
DeVore, I., 52, 55, 58
Dibble, H. L., 54, 57
Dickemann, M., 148, 153
Dillon, W. S., 65–66, 128, 137
Diole, P., 237, 260
Dixon, B., 327, 328
Dolhinow, P., 142, 143, 144, 151, 154, 276

Dorn, C. R., 262
Driver, H. E., 244, 260
Dupaquier, J., 118, 124

Easterling, W. E., 344, 357, 364
Eberhard, W. G., 163, 169, 172
Eckerman, C. D., 145, 157
Eco, U., 195, 201
Eddy, J., 268, 277
Edmunds, M., 177, 191
Eisenberg, J. F., 114, 125, 128, 129, 132, 133, 134, 135, 136, 137, 138, 253, 260
Elder, J., 281, 288
Ellsaesser, H. W., 364
Emde, R. N., 144, 154
Ensminger, M. E., 237, 260
Erikson, E., 209, 221
Erwin, T. L., 319, 328
Evans, E. P., 284, 288

Fedigan, L., 151, 154
Fernando, D. F. S., 118, 124
Fiennes, A., 237, 238, 260
Fiennes, R., 237, 238, 260
Fisher, B., 260
Fisher, H. E., 96, 98, 99, 106, 112, 113–114, 116, 119, 121, 124, 276
Fisher, R. A., 27, 31, 39, 162, 172
Fisher, T. W., 328
Fogle, B., 235, 260
Folland, C. K., 364
Fossey, D., 98, 124
Fowler, S., 282, 288
Fox, M. W., 241, 243, 260
Fox, R., 331, 333, 340
French, R. D., 276
Friedl, E., 99, 111, 113, 124
Friedmann, E., 235, 256, 260, 261, 269, 276, 277

Gage, R. L., 114, 124
Ganster, D., 267, 277
Gallup, G. G., 287, 289
Gartlan, J. S., 129, 137
Gebhard, P. H., 124
Gilbert, M. D., 154
Glickman, L., 266, 278
Goldberg, E. L., 277
Goodall, J., 67, 68, 141, 149, 154, 282, 287, 289
Goodman, L., 277
Goodman, M., 62, 68, 72, 277
Gordon, T. P., 155
Gorer, G., 115, 124
Gottlieb, A., 283, 289
Gould, K. G., 155
Gould, S., 272, 277
Gould, S. J., 116, 124
Gouzoules, H., 151, 154
Gowlett, J., 50, 57
Greenberg, B., 199, 201
Gregory, W. K., 62, 63, 68, 72
Griffin, D., 203, 204, 209, 221
Gronin, G. M., 275
Gross, W. B., 273, 277
Grossberg, J., 269, 277
Guenther, A. V., 218, 221
Guntrip, H., 209, 221
Gur, C. R., 177–178, 191
Gwynne, P. H., 259

Hall, G. S., 238, 261
Halverson, J., 280, 289
Hamilton, W. D., 130, 138, 140, 154
Hamilton, W. J. III, 128, 138
Hankins, R. J., 151, 157
Hansen, C., 277
Hardy, A., 297, 315
Harlow, H., 271, 277
Harlow, H. F., 257, 261
Harlow, M. K., 271, 277
Harmon, R. J., 144, 154
Harre, R., 203, 221
Harris, M., 281, 289
Hart, B., 241, 259, 261
Hart, L., 259, 276
Hausfater, G., 133, 138, 142, 154
Hawkes, T., 196, 201
Hawthorn, G., 96, 124
Hebb, D., 226
Helin, E., 124
Hemsworth, P. H., 273, 277

Herdt, G. H., 154
Herman, B. H., 262
Hess, E. H., 242, 261
Hill, A., 57
Hinde, R. A., 141, 154
Hines, L. M., 235, 244, 259, 261
Hines, M., 261
Holden, C., 288, 289
Hölldobler, B., 79, 80
Horrocks, J. E., 209, 221
Horsfield, S., 235, 262
Howell, N., 113, 115, 124
Howells, W., 62, 66, 68
Hrdy, S. B., 120, 124, 133, 138, 141, 142, 154
Hsiung, J., 364
Humphrey, N., 203, 210, 221
Hunt, M., 121, 124

Iersel, J. J. van, 200, 201
Inglis, I., 206, 221
Ingold, T., 252, 261
Ingram, W. J., 365
Intergovernmental Panel on Climate Change, 344, 364
Isaac, G. L., 54, 57

Jackson, D. W., 209, 221
James, W., 203, 221
Jennings, H., 334, 340
Jesse, G. R., 240, 244, 261
Johanson, D. C., 47, 58
Johnson, C. K., 142, 154
Johnson-Laird, P. N., 216, 221
Jones, B., 267, 277
Jones, P. D., 344, 365

Kanki, P. J., 325, 328
Kaplan, S., 189, 191
Kapleau, P., 219, 222
Karl, T. R., 344, 365
Kastin, A. J., 263
Katcher, A. H., 235, 242, 256, 257, 259, 260, 261, 267, 268, 269, 270, 276, 277
Kaufman, I. C., 145, 155
Kaufmann, J. H., 145, 155
Kawai, M., 142, 155
Kawamura, S., 142, 155
Keith, A., 62, 63, 68
Kellerman, K. A., 205, 220
Kellogg, W. W., 358, 359, 365
Kendon, A., 243, 261
Kimura, M., 33, 34, 39
King, F. A., 155
Kinsey, A. C., 121, 124
Kinzey, W. G., 97, 119, 125
Kleiman, D. G., 97, 98, 114, 115, 116, 117, 125
Klein, R. G., 52, 58
Kraft, J. K., 278
Kreemer, J., 248, 261
Krishnan, P., 107, 125
Kroll, E. M., 52, 57
Krusko, N., 142, 154
Kuzel, P., 107, 125

Lack, D., 97, 125
Lampe, P. E., 98, 121, 125
Lampl, M., 58
Lancaster, C. S., 51, 59, 115, 116, 125
Lancaster, J. B., 115, 116, 125, 142, 155
Landau, M., 67, 68
Langer, E., 205, 222
Langston, N., 275
Laslett, P., 124
Laufs, R., 325, 328
Leach, E. R., 279, 289
Leakey, L. S. B., 58
Leakey, M. D., 49, 58
Lee, M. D., 55, 58
Lee, P. C., 142, 155
Lee, R. L., 241, 261
Legner, E. F., 322, 328
Levine, S., 142, 155, 278
Levinson, B. M., 235, 261
Lévi-Strauss, C., 96, 125
Lewin, R., 116, 117, 125
Lewis, M., 142, 155
Leyhausen, P., 236, 237, 241, 261
Liebowitz, M. R., 121, 122, 125
Lindburg, D. G., 115, 116, 125
Linden, E., 282, 289

Lindzen, R. S., 344, 349, 365
Livi-Bacci, M., 124
Locker, B. Z., 276
Lockwood, R., 268, 277
Lopez, B. H., 236, 261
Lorenz, K. Z., 196, 201, 236, 262, 299, 315
Lovejoy, C. O., 48, 58
Lowe-McConnell, R. H., 322, 328
Lynch, J. J., 253, 254, 255, 260, 262, 271, 276, 277

MacArthur, R. H., 219, 222
McCarthy, J. F., 255, 262
McCaul, K. D., 256, 262
McCulloch, M. J., 235, 262
McCulloch, W. F., 235, 262
McGregor, O. R., 107, 125
MacGregor, R., 247, 262
Mack, D., 138
MacKay, D., 206, 222
McKenna, J. J., 141, 142, 155
McKinney, W. T., 143, 144, 155
Macpherson, C. B., 334, 340
Main, M., 209, 222
Malott, J. M., 256, 262
Manabe, S., 365
Mann, A., 48, 58 117, 125
Maple, T. L., 150, 156
Markova, I., 216, 222
Marler, P. R., 128, 138, 194, 198, 201
Marshall, E. R., 198, 201
George C. Marshall Institute, 343, 345, 365
Marshall, J. T., Jr., 198, 201
Martin, C. E., 124
Mason, I. L., 321, 328
Massey, W. C., 244, 260
Mathur, M. A., 246, 263
Maugh, T. H., 325, 328
Maynard-Smith, J., 196, 201
Mayr, E., 25, 34, 39, 171, 172
Mead, M., 359, 365
Means, C., 257, 261
Meehl, G. A., 353, 366
Meier, M. F., 356, 365
Messent, P., 235, 262, 268, 276, 277
Meyers, N., 320, 321, 328
Meyers, W. M., 325, 328
Midgely, M., xviii
Milton, K., 131, 138
Missakian, E., 142, 155
Mitchell, G. D., 150, 151, 155
Mitchell, J. F. B., 365
Mitchell, R. W., 177, 191
Mohnot, S. M., 141, 156
Money, J., 122, 125
Monge, J., 58
Montagu, A., 116, 125
Morris, C. W., 197, 200, 201
Morris, D., 201
Morton, E. S., 195, 198, 201
Moynihan, M., 196, 198, 201
Muckenhirn, N., 137
Murdock, G. P., 96, 97, 99, 111, 120, 125
Murphy, G., 142, 143, 144, 151, 154
Murti, T. R. V., 218, 222

Nadel, L., 206, 222
Napier, J., 58, 66, 68
Nash, L. T., 141, 142, 151, 156
National Academy of Sciences, 247, 262
Necker, C., 236, 237, 240, 262
Neill, W. T., 323, 329
Nelson, R. A., 326, 329u
Newell, R. E., 364
Nicolson, N. A., 142, 156
Nisbett, R. E., 205, 222
Noble, G. K., 199, 201

O'Connell, M. A., 137
Ohala, J. J., 186, 191
O'Keefe, J., 206, 222
Oliver, J. I., 142, 155
Orban-Segebarth, R., 123
Orr, K. G., 250, 262
Ory, M. G., 271, 277
Oyama, S., 141, 147, 156

Packard, A., 199, 202
Panksepp, J., 258, 262, 263
Parfit, D., 218, 222

Parker, D. E., 364
Parry, M. L., 364
Paul, A., 142, 156
Pearl, M., 320, 329
Penfield, W., 66, 69
Peters, R., 355, 365
Pinardi, M. E., 325, 328
Poirier, F. C., 141, 156
Pomeroy, W. B., 124
Pope, T., 134
Potts, R., 49, 51, 52, 53, 58
Powers, M. N., 244, 245, 262
Powers, W. K., 244, 245, 262
Premack, D., 209, 222

Quackenbush, J., 266, 278
Quiatt, D. D., 142, 156

Rabgyas, T., 218, 222
Rak, Y., 47, 58
Ramanathan, V., 349, 365
Rand, A. S., 194, 199, 202
Randhawa, M. S., 246, 262
Ransom, T. W., 141, 156
Rapaport, R., 214, 222
Raper, S. C. B., 354, 366
Rasmussen, T., 66, 69
Raval, A., 349, 365
Raven, P. H., 320, 329
Regan, T., xviii, 285, 289
Revelle, R., 363, 365
Rheingold, H. L., 145, 156
Rightmire, G. P., 58
Ritchie, C. I. A., 240, 262
Ritvo, H., 265, 278
Robinson, J. G., 198, 202
Rodaniche, A. F., 196, 202
Rodman, P. S., 156
Rosenblum, L. A., 142, 145, 155
Rosenfield, L. C., 284, 289
Roshi, Kosho U., 219, 222
Rossi, A., 147, 151, 156
Rowan, A. N., 283, 289
Rowell, T., 150, 151, 156
Rowell, T. E., 141, 156
Rudran, R., 132, 133, 134, 137, 138
Rue, L. L., 114, 125
Ruiz, J. C., 138
Ryan, T., 261

Saavedra, C. J., 134, 136, 138
Sackeim, H. A., 177, 191
Sade, D. S., 142, 156
Samuels, A., 156
Sarich, V. M., 62, 65, 69, 72
Saussure, F. de, 195, 202
Sayre, K. M., 204, 222
Schachter, S., 257, 262
Schär, R., 237, 262
Schelling, T. C., 358, 365
Schmid, P., 123
Schneider, S. H., 343, 345, 349, 353, 356, 358, 365
Schwabe, C., 235, 263
Scrimshaw, S., 148, 156
Sekulic, R., 131, 134, 137, 138
Senior, C. A., 365
Serpell, J. A., 235, 242, 243, 244, 246, 251, 252, 256, 257, 258, 263
Seyfarth, R. M., 128, 138, 187, 191
Shannon, C. E., 37, 39
Shipman, P., 52, 58
Short, R. V., 321, 329
Shostak, M., 121, 125
Sibley, C., 62, 69, 72
Siegel, P. B., 273, 277
Silk, J. B., 142, 156
Singer, P., xviii, 270, 278
Smith, B. H., 48, 58
Smith, C. K., 273, 276
Smith, J. B., 354, 365
Smith, W. J., 128, 138, 194, 202
Smuts, B. B., 147, 156
Soloman, G. F., 278
Sogner, S., 124
Staten, H., 215, 222
Statistical Office of the United Nations, 97, 99, 106, 113–114, 126
Steinke, H., 325, 328
Sterelny, K., 201
Stern, J., 47, 58
Stoneking, M., 57

Stouffer, R. J., 353, 365
Straus, W. L., 62–63, 66, 71–72
Stringer, C. B., 58
Strum, S., 147, 157
Suess, H. E., 363, 365
Sullivan, H. S., 209, 222
Suomi, S. J., 141, 145, 151, 157
Susman, R., 47, 58
Swenson, C. H., 222
Swindler, D. R., 66, 69

Tague, R. G., 48, 58
Tanner, J. M., 66, 69
Tanner, N. M., 265, 278
Taylor, T., 217, 222
Tembrock, G., 198, 202
Tenaza, R. R., 198, 202
Ten Bensel, R., 235, 263
Tennov, D., 122, 126
Terrace, H. S., 198, 202
Textor, R. B., 99, 126
Thoma, I., 275
Thomas, K., 239, 240, 241, 263, 285, 289
Thomas, S. A., 260, 276
Thommen, D., 142, 156
Thompson, N. S., 177, 191
Thorington, R. W., Jr., 131, 138
Tiger, L., 331, 332, 333, 334, 338, 340
Tilson, R. L., 97, 114, 126
Tinbergen, N., 299, 315
Tirpak, D., 354, 365
Tobias, P., 58
Tooby, J., 52, 58
Toth, N., 49, 58
Trevathan, W. R. N. D., 115, 126
Trinkaus, E., 47, 59
Trivers, R. L., 162, 172, 176, 177, 183, 187, 191, 210, 223
Tuan, Y., 266, 278
Turner, D. C., 241, 243, 263

Uexküll, J. von, 128, 138, 204, 223

Valla, F. R., 237, 260
Van den Berghe, P. L., 96, 97, 126
Vannier, M. W., 57, 117, 118, 124
Vilberg, T. R., 258, 262, 263
Vogel, C., 141, 157
Vohra, A., 216, 223
Voith, V. L., 267, 277, 278

Waggoner, P. E., 355, 359, 366
Washburn, S. L., 51, 59, 72, 126, 150, 157
Washington, W. M., 353, 366
Washino, R. K., 324, 328
Watson, J. B., 203, 223
Weaver, W., 37, 39
Weghorst, S. J., 124
West-Eberhard, M. J., 169, 171, 172
Western, D., 320, 329
Wetterberg, G. B., 321, 329
White, R., 54, 59
Whiten, A., 210, 220
Whyte, R. O., 246, 263
Wickler, W., 177, 191
Wigley, T. M. L., 354, 366
Williams, E. E., 199, 202
Williams, G. C., 26, 39, 162, 172
Williams, K., 200, 202
Williams, R., 278
Wilson, A. C., 57, 62, 69
Wilson, E. O., 79, 80, 95, 129, 130 138, 141, 151, 219, 222, 320, 329, 355, 366
Wilson, M., 97, 98, 120, 124, 140, 153
Wilson, T. O., 205, 222
Winfield, C. G., 275
Wittenberger, J. F., 97, 114, 126
Wolf, A. P., 118, 126
Wolfe, L., 98, 126
Wolfheim, J. H., 141, 157
Wood, B. A., 48, 57
Wood, C. R., 66, 69
Woodruff, G., 209, 222
Wyatt, R. G., 326, 329
Wynne-Edwards, V. C., 162, 172

Yarbrough, C. J., 155
Young, G. H., 141, 151, 157
Young, P. T., 263

Zajonc, R. B., 253, 255, 263
Zeglen, M. E., 261
Zeuner, F. E., 236, 263
Zipf, G. K., 195, 202

Subject Index

Acid rain, 357
Adaptation, to climate change, 358–359
Adultery, human and animal, 98, 120–123
Aggregations v. social organizations, 128–129
Aggression, xviii-xix, 81–93
  innate v. external cause, 82–90
  ritualization of, 83, 84, 87
  and social organization, 129
  and view of history, 90–93
Agriculture
  animal contributions to, 320–323
  and climate change, 355–357
Altruism, 95, 128, 187–188, 219
Animal rights, 270–271, 285
Anscombe, Elizabeth, 282
Anthropomorphism, 95, 194, 198, 266
Aquaculture, 322–323
Arachnids, 303–305, 306–310
Arbitrariness, of human language units, 196
Ardrey, Robert, xviii-xix, 83, 87
Athletes, 336–337
Attachment, 122, 144–145, 252–258

Bartlett, M. S., 33
Beadle, C. M., Rear Admiral, 312, 313
Behavior (see also Aggression; Social organization)
  adultery, 96, 98–99, 120–123
  desertation/divorce, 99–114
  male bonding, 332
  monogamy, 114–118
  sexual selection and social, 159–172
  tactics of immaturity in primates, 139–157
Bell, Daniel, 78
"Big bang," 4
Biogeography, 78, 79
Biology, history of, 292–293
Birds, communication experiments, 182–183, 185–188
Birth rates in industrial communities, 338–339
Bonding, human/animal, 252–258

Brain-computer analogy, 225–230
Bristowe, W. S., 303
Buddhism, 217–220
Burgess, Thornton W., 312

Carbon dioxide, 349–364
Cattle
  interactions with humans, 246–252
  wild species as food sources, 320–321
Cats
  behavior, 243
  domestication, 235–237
  in history, 238–241
Central nervous system, and consciousness, 188–190
Clark, J. Desmond, 53
Climate change, 341–365
  mathematical models and, 341, 345, 347, 349, 350
Communication (see also Language)
  animal-human, 182–188, 242–243
  companion animals and, 256–258, 268–269
  structuralist approach to animal, 193–200
  syntax in animal, 184–185
  verbal behavior and consciousness, 181–182
Competition
  nonsexual social selection, 167–168
  sexual selection for mates, 161–167
Consciousness, 203–221
  and deception, 177–180
  evolution of, 209–213
  and meaning, 213–220
  and self-awareness, 203–209
  and verbal behavior, 181–182
Culture
  and attachment relationships, 148
  individual consciousness and social structures, 213–214

Dart, Raymond, 83
Darwinism, 23–39 (see also Human evolution)
  adaptation, 26–27, 34
  directed variation, 34
  mutation, 26–27, 34
  segmentation, 32–33
Deception, 95, 176–182, 190, 287
Dillon, Wilton S., 61
Dinosaurs, 14–20
Display
  sexually selected interactions, 161–168
Divorce and sexual strategy, 99–114
Dobzhansky, Theodosius, 314
Dogs, 237–238, 243, 244–246
Doyle, Arthur Conan, 312

Eisley, Loren, 95
Entropy, 29–30
Eiver, Griff, 302
Evolution (see also Human evolution)
  of universe, 3–20
Extinction, 320

Fabianism, 86, 340
Freud, Sigmund, 23–24, 87, 91

Galaxies, 5–7
Gene-culture coevolution, 79
Gibbs, Willard, 30
Global warming, 342–364
Greenhouse effect, 347–364

Haldane, J. B. S., 312, 313, 319
History, and environment of evolutionary adaptedness, 90–92
Howler monkey (*Alouatta*) social organization, 130–137
Hudson, W. H., 312, 313
Human/animal interactions (see also Killing animals)
  attachment, 252–258
  companion animals, 265–277, 283
  historical overview, 234–252
Human evolution, 41–59
  bipedalism, 46–48
  brain size, 49–50
  culture and language, 53–54
  and domestication of animals, 271–273
  home bases, 50–52
  hunting and eating meat, 52–53
  maturation rates, 48–49

molecular biology and technology advances, 61–73
of self-awareness, 210–212
and sexual and social selection, 161–168
tool manufacture, 49–50
Human sex differences, 332–333
Hunting, 52–53, 281–282
Huxley, Julian, 312, 313
Huxley, T. H., 26

Impact theory of dinosaur extinction, 15–20
Industrial system, and biology, 332–338
Infancy, nonhuman primates, 139–146
Infanticide, 133–134
Intentionality, 207

James, William, 203, 205, 208

Killing of animals
disposal in humane shelters, 269–270
euthanasia, 246
hunting, 52–53, 281–282
ritual, 244–245, 249, 250–251, 281
!Kung San, 115, 120–121

Lamarck, Jean Baptiste, 34–36
Language, 148, 149, 168
and aggression, 88
animal, used by humans, 182–188
animal terms in obscenity, 280–281
anthropocentrism and ape language, 282
complexity of form, 195–196
deconstruction, 215–217
and self-awareness, 208–209
verbal behavior and consciousness, 181–182
Levins, Richard, 77
Lewontin, Richard, 77
Literacy, 337–338
Lorenz, Konrad, xviii, 83, 87, 312, 313–314
Lumsden, Charles, 79

MacArthur, Robert, 77
Macfadyen, Amyan, 302–303
Marx, Karl, and Marxism, 23–24, 78, 82, 90
Medicine, animal contributions to, 323–327
Mill, John Stuart, 331
Monogamy
adultery, 98, 120–123
in animals, 97–98, 114–115
divorce, 99–114
evolution of human, 115–118, 121
Montagu, Ashley, xix
Moral status of animals, 283–288
Morris, Desmond, xx
Motion theory, 218–219
Moynihan, Martin, 300

Natural selection, 83–84, 128
Neoteny, 241, 242, 272, 273

Oglala Indians, 244–245

Pain, 189, 255, 286
Pair bonding, 107–108, 114–116, 118, 120
Preventive policies, climate change, 359–360, 362–364
Primates
anthropocentrism and ape language, 282
first aggression in, 88–89
human/nonhuman comparison, 147–149
and medical research, 325–326
sexual strategies of, 116, 118–119, 120
social organization of *Alouatta*, 130–137
successful social skills of, 149–152
tactics of immaturity, 139–157
Psycho-industrial complex, 334–338

Religion and secularization, 214–215
Reproductive strategy
adultery, 98, 120–123
desertation/divorce, 99–114
monogamy, 97–98, 114–118
Robinson, Michael H., 293–315

Savory, Theodore, 303
Self-awareness
of animals, 286–287
and consciousness, 205–209
Self-deception, 176–182, 190

Sexual selection, 159–172
experimentation on sea anemones, 189–190
kinds of interactions, 161–167
and social selection, 167–168
Shaw, George Bernard, 86–87, 340
Smith, David Seth, 312
Smithsonian Tropical Research Institute, 300
Social organization
classification of, 129–130
communication analysis, 128
evolution of, 130
howler monkey, 130–137
insects, 130
population density and behavior, 133–134, 136
Sociobiology, 77–80
Speciation, 169–172
Stars, 8
Stevenson, Bernard, 312, 313
Stick insects, 305–306
Storr, Anthony, xviii
Structuralism, 195
Supernovas, 9–10

Tabula rasa, 87
Testing and culture, 335–336
Third World tropics, 311
Tinbergen, Niko, 299, 312, 313–314
Tropical forests, 311, 320, 354–355

Unconscious/conscious, 177–182 (see also Consciousness)

Viruses, 326–327
Volcanic theory of dinosaur extinction, 17–20
Von Frisch, Karl, 314

Water buffalo, 246–252
Water resources and climate change, 356, 357, 359
Wells, H. G., 312, 313
Wittgenstein, Ludwig, 215–217

1909